OXFORD MEDIEVAL TEXTS

General Editors
J. W. BINNS   D. D'AVRAY
M. S. KEMPSHALL   R. C. LOVE

CONTINUATIO EULOGII

CONTINUATIO EULOGII

The Continuation of the *Eulogium Historiarum*, 1364–1413

EDITED AND TRANSLATED BY
CHRIS GIVEN-WILSON

CLARENDON PRESS · OXFORD

OXFORD
UNIVERSITY PRESS

Great Clarendon Street, Oxford, OX2 6DP,
United Kingdom

Oxford University Press is a department of the University of Oxford.
It furthers the University's objective of excellence in research, scholarship,
and education by publishing worldwide. Oxford is a registered trade mark of
Oxford University Press in the UK and in certain other countries

© Chris Given-Wilson 2019

The moral rights of the author have been asserted

First Edition published in 2019

Impression: 3

All rights reserved. No part of this publication may be reproduced, stored in
a retrieval system, or transmitted, in any form or by any means, without the
prior permission in writing of Oxford University Press, or as expressly permitted
by law, by licence or under terms agreed with the appropriate reprographics
rights organization. Enquiries concerning reproduction outside the scope of the
above should be sent to the Rights Department, Oxford University Press, at the
address above

You must not circulate this work in any other form
and you must impose this same condition on any acquirer

Published in the United States of America by Oxford University Press
198 Madison Avenue, New York, NY 10016, United States of America

British Library Cataloguing in Publication Data

Data available

Library of Congress Control Number: 2019939542

ISBN 978–0–19–882337–7

Printed and bound by
CPI Group (UK) Ltd, Croydon, CR0 4YY

PREFACE

I AM GRATEFUL to the following, who have helped me in various ways to bring this edition to completion: to Peter Maxwell-Stuart and Rob Bartlett for advice on occasional passages of Latin; to Cressida Williams, head of Canterbury Cathedral Archives and Library, for providing me with access to both printed works and manuscripts; to Brother Kevin, OFM, for showing me round the delightful site of the original Franciscan house at Canterbury; to the staff of the British Library manuscript and reading rooms for their help and courtesy; to the editors of Oxford Medieval Texts for their useful and encouraging comments on the first draft of this edition; and to Bonnie Blackburn for her expert copy-editing of the typescript.

Chris Given-Wilson

St Andrews, August 2018

CONTENTS

ABBREVIATIONS	ix
INTRODUCTION	xi
The Manuscript: Cotton MS Galba E VII	xii
The Authorship and Provenance of the *Continuatio*	xiv
The Canterbury Grey Friars and the English Franciscan Province	xxi
The Structure, Composition, and Sources of the *Continuatio*	xxvii
The Value of the *Continuatio*	xxxvii
Texts Related to the *Continuatio*	xlvi
Editorial Conventions and Orthography	li
CONTINUATIO EULOGII	1
BIBLIOGRAPHY	163
INDEX	169

ABBREVIATIONS

BIHR	*Bulletin of the Institute of Historical Research*
BRUO	A. B. Emden, *A Biographical Register of the University of Oxford to A. D. 1500* (3 vols., Oxford, 1957–9)
CCR	*Calendar of Close Rolls in the Public Record Office* (London, 1892–1963)
CP	*Complete Peerage by G. E. Cokayne*, ed. V. H. Gibbs (13 vols., London, 1910–59)
CPL	*Calendar of Papal Registers relating to Great Britain and Ireland: Letters*, ed. W. H. Bliss (London, 1893–1998)
CPP	*Calendar of Papal Registers relating to Great Britain and Ireland: Petitions*, ed. W. H. Bliss (London, 1893–1998)
CPR	*Calendar of the Patent Rolls in the Public Record Office* (London, 1901–)
CR	*Chronicles of the Revolution, 1397–1400*, ed. C. Given-Wilson (Manchester, 1993)
EHR	*English Historical Review*
Eulogium	*Eulogium Historiarum sive Temporis*, ed. F. S. Haydon (3 vols., RS; London, 1858–63)
Flete	John Flete, *History of Westminster Abbey*, ed. J. A. Robinson (Cambridge, 1909)
Foedera	*Foedera, Conventiones, Litterae, etc.*, ed. T. Rymer (20 vols., London, 1727–35)
HBC	*Handbook of British Chronology* (3rd edn., London, 1986)
NLW	National Library of Wales, Aberystwyth
ODNB	*Oxford Dictionary of National Biography*, ed. H. C. Matthew and B. Harrison (60 vols., Oxford, 2004)
OMT	Oxford Medieval Texts
PROME	*Parliament Rolls of Medieval England, 1275–1504*, ed. P. Brand, A. Curry, C. Given-Wilson, R. Horrox, G. Martin, M. Ormrod, S. Phillips (16 vols., Woodbridge, 2005)
RS	Rolls Series
SAC I	*St Albans Chronicle: The Chronica Maiora of Thomas Walsingham*, ed. J. Taylor, W. Childs, and L. Watkiss, i: *1376–1394* (OMT, 2003)

ABBREVIATIONS

SAC II   *St Albans Chronicle: The Chronica Maiora of Thomas Walsingham*, ed. J. Taylor, W. Childs, and L. Watkiss, ii: *1394–1422* (OMT, 2011)

SHF   Société de l'Histoire de France

TNA   The National Archives, Kew, London

Usk   *The Chronicle of Adam Usk 1377–1421*, ed. C. Given-Wilson (OMT, 1997)

VCH   Victoria County History

INTRODUCTION

AROUND 1350 an anonymous monk of Malmesbury abbey in Wiltshire, wearying of 'the tedium of the readings and the monotony of the prayers' and hoping to dispel the 'most evil thoughts' that disrupted his claustral meditations, began compiling a history of the world. Dividing it into five books and covering (by his reckoning) some 6,500 years, he finished his chronicle in 1362, although either he or one of his fellow monks subsequently added further entries up to 1366. He called his 'little work' the *Eulogium*; it is more commonly referred to as the *Eulogium Historiarum*, or *Eulogium Temporis*. F. S. Haydon, whose three-volume edition of it for the Rolls Series was published between 1858 and 1863, entitled it *Eulogium Historiarum sive Temporis*.[1]

World, or universal, chronicles were in vogue at the time. The most famous of them was the *Polychronicon* of Ranulf Higden, a monk of Chester, which was completed around 1340. The author of the *Eulogium* was fully acquainted with the *Polychronicon*, and copied extensive passages from it in his own work, although this did not stop him criticizing 'that new compiler from Chester... that befuddled monk' for his temerity in questioning the reliability of historians such as Bede, Jerome, Isidore, or William of Malmesbury.[2] There was doubtless a touch of jealousy here. The *Polychronicon* was immensely popular: it survives in more than 130 manuscripts and became, in effect, the text from which later medieval English men and women learned their world history, and to which later medieval chroniclers most commonly appended the continuations which carried the story forward to their own times. The *Eulogium*, in contrast, seems to have circulated little beyond Malmesbury. The complete text survives in only four medieval manuscripts, now held in libraries in London (two), Cambridge, and Dublin, while a

---

[1] *Eulogium*, i. 1–5 ('hoc libellum conglobatum Eulogium volo nominari... Terminatum est hoc opusculum in anno Domini mccclxii'). Haydon assigns Archbishop Ussher's later widely accepted date of 4004 BC to the chronicler's account of the Creation, but there was considerable disagreement about this at the time, and the chronicler's own calculations suggest that he believed around 5,100 years to have elapsed between the Creation and the birth of Christ (iii. 246; cf. C. Given-Wilson, *Chronicles: The Writing of History in Medieval England* (London, 2004), pp. 122–3).

[2] *Eulogium*, ii. 130–1 ('ille novus compilator Cestriae... ille madidus monachus'); A. Gransden, *Historical Writing in England II: c. 1307 to the Early Sixteenth Century* (London, 1982), p. 104; J. Taylor, *English Historical Literature in the Fourteenth Century* (Oxford, 1987), p. 106.

further two manuscripts contain extracts from the fifth book.[3] However, one fifteenth-century chronicler does appear to have considered it worth extending, for a manuscript of the *Eulogium* in the British Library (Cotton MS Galba E VII) has appended to it a continuation beginning *sub anno* 1364 and ending in 1413. It is this 'Continuation of the *Eulogium*' (*Continuatio Eulogii*) which is the subject of this edition, referred to henceforth as the *Continuatio*.

THE MANUSCRIPT: COTTON MS GALBA E VII

British Library Cotton MS Galba E VII is a leather-bound volume with gold tooling containing 208 vellum folios,[4] each approximately 365 × 240 mm, the first and last few of which show evidence of fire damage (presumably from the Ashburnham House fire of 1731), although the legibility of the text is not greatly affected. There are fifty-one complete gatherings of eight folios each, with collections of stubs between fos. 57 and 58, 89 and 90, 121 and 122, and 185 and 186. Folio 1^v has a heading in a post-medieval hand, 'Elenchus contentorum in hoc codice' ('Review of the contents in this book'), which describes it as a chronicle from the Creation to the accession of Henry V—that is, to the end of the *Continuatio*. Also manifestly post-medieval is the note near the top of fo. 3^r, dated 25 September 1574, that the manuscript was owned by Dr John Dee, the well-known Elizabethan mathematician and philosopher; this records, apparently in his own hand, that he received it 'of the gift of Mr Dyckenson at Popular [Poplar], by London'. The name of 'Mr John Stow, the chronicler' also appears here, indicating that he probably borrowed it from Dee.[5] The remainder of fo. 3^r and the next thirteen folios (to 16^r) are given over to a *Chronicon Brevius* from the birth of Christ to the year 1364. This 'Shorter Chronicle' is presented in tabular form, with the annual dates on the left side of the folio and corresponding events on the right; the last event noted is the death of King John of France in London in 1364.

---

[3] Trinity College, Cambridge, MS R. 7. 2; British Library, London, Cotton MS Galba E VII; Trinity College, Dublin, MS E. 2. 26; Lincoln's Inn, London, MS Hospit. Lincoln. Hale No. 73; (*Eulogium*, i, pp. iv–xii). Another late 14th-c. manuscript of book 5 of the *Eulogium* (to 1240 only) was held in the library of Bristol Baptist College (MS Z. c. 20) from 1784 to 2014, when it was sold at Sotheby's for £32,500 (N. Ker, *Medieval Manuscripts in British Libraries* (Oxford, 1977), ii. 188–9; Sotheby's sale catalogue, 2 December 2014). London, British Library, Cotton MS Cleopatra D II, an early 15th-c. manuscript, includes the text of book 5 of the *Eulogium* to 1346.

[4] Renumbered in pencil from 207 folios in 1863. N. Ker, *Medieval Libraries of Great Britain* (London, 1964), p. 357, rejected Leland's attribution of this MS to Malmesbury abbey.

[5] Cf. *Eulogium*, i, p. xxxiv.

Haydon printed the *Chronicon Brevius* in his edition of the *Eulogium*, taking his text from the Cambridge manuscript (Trinity College Cambridge MS R. 7. 2), which he believed to be the monk of Malmesbury's autograph.[6]

The text of the *Eulogium* begins on fo. 18^r. It is written in double columns throughout, a uniform forty-six lines per page, with ample margins, apparently in one hand of the early fifteenth century. There are red and blue coloured initials on almost every page, with occasional gilding and a few perfunctory attempts at foliage illumination and grotesque faces added to capital letters. Brief marginal notes in both medieval and later hands abound. Book I of the text ends on fo. 41^r, Book II on fo. 60^v, Book III on fo. 84^v, Book IV on fo. 117^r, and Book V on fo. 191^r.[7] The final entry of the *Eulogium* (line 11 of column A of fo. 191^r) records the proposed translation of John Barnet, bishop of Bath, to Ely, in 1366, as it does in the Cambridge autograph.[8] The introductions to the three volumes of Haydon's edition analyse the text and manuscripts of the *Eulogium* in great detail, but since it is not the *Eulogium* which is the subject of this edition, they will not be discussed further here except inasmuch as they affect elucidation of the *Continuatio*. Suffice it to say that Haydon was an excellent palaeographer and Latinist, and his meticulous work on the *Eulogium* has been of great value in preparing this edition.

The *Continuatio* begins at line 12 of column A of fo. 191^r with an entry recording the visit of the king of Cyprus to England in 1364 (*recte* 1363), thus running straight on from the last entry of the *Eulogium* without even a line-break. Next to this entry, a later hand has written in the margin: 'Hucusque codex archiepiscopi Ardmachani' ('To this point, the book of the archbishop of Armagh'). This archbishop of Armagh was the well-known bibliophile and scholar James Ussher, archbishop of Armagh and primate of all Ireland from 1625 to 1656, to whom the equally well-known bibliophile and scholar Sir Robert

---

[6] This and what follows is based on Cotton Galba E VII and Haydon's discussion of 'Manuscripts and Text' in *Eulogium*, i, pp. iv–xxvi; see also S. Clifford, 'An Edition of the Continuation of the *Eulogium Historiarum*, 1361–1413' (M.Phil. thesis, University of Leeds, 1975), pp. 66–8. The *Chronicon Brevius*, collated with Cotton Galba MS E VII, is in *Eulogium*, iii. 245–313.

[7] Beginning on fo. 111^r and continuing intermittently for more than sixty folios, three different hands have added supplementary texts recounting the history of the kings of the Anglo-Saxon Heptarchy and the story of Britain from its Trojan origins under Brutus until the time of Henry III in the 13th c., taken mainly from Bede and William of Malmesbury (Haydon discusses and transcribes these in *Eulogium*, ii, pp. v–viii, lxxxi, and 158 ff., ending at iii. 139).

[8] Cf. *Eulogium*, iii. 242.

Cotton (d. 1631), founder of the Cottonian Library, presented a copy of the *Eulogium*.[9] This is now Trinity College Dublin MS E. 2. 26. Whoever inserted the marginal 'Hucusque codex archiepiscopi Ardmachani' must thus have compared the Cotton Galba and Dublin manuscripts—and, according to Haydon, there is 'a remarkable agreement' between them, although he thought it unlikely that one was copied from the other, concluding instead that they were copied from 'some common original', now lost.

Beginning in a different hand on fo. 191[r], the *Continuatio* occupies the last eighteen folios of Cotton Galba E VII, ending close to the bottom of column A of fo. 208[v]. The fact that it is transcribed into this manuscript, thus appearing to build upon what precedes it, does not prove beyond question that it was originally composed as a continuation of the *Eulogium*. The text of the *Continuatio* is extraordinarily free from erasures, interlineations, and other signs of progressive composition; given that it is also written in one hand (later, obviously, though not much later, than that of the *Eulogium* itself), it is virtually certain that the scribe of the last eighteen folios of the Cotton Galba manuscript was copying from a pre-existing text.[10] There is nothing to suggest that this text was composed at Malmesbury, nor does its author at any point refer back to the *Eulogium* or give any indication that it was a world history that he was continuing. It is possible, therefore, that the *Continuatio* was originally written as a continuation of a different chronicle, or even as a free-standing text, and subsequently recycled by a scribe into Cotton Galba E VII. It is an independent composition, by a different author, almost certainly composed elsewhere. Nevertheless, the likelihood must be that it was written as a continuation of the *Eulogium*, and since it is universally referred to as the *Continuatio Eulogii*, changing the name would only cause confusion.

THE AUTHORSHIP AND PROVENANCE OF THE *CONTINUATIO*

The *Continuatio* is a Latin chronicle of some 22,200 words, written, like the *Eulogium*, in double columns, with minimal adornment. The top and bottom corners of the folios are slightly damaged, especially the last few, but hardly ever to the point of illegibility. Some initials are

---

[9] Cotton had in turn been given the manuscript by William Camden in 1609 (*Eulogium*, i, pp. x–xi).

[10] There is the occasional error indicative of copying, for example 'per notam' for 'priuatam' *sub anno* 1400.

coloured red or (occasionally) blue, but none is illuminated. There are forty-six lines per column throughout, with occasional incomplete lines to indicate 'paragraph' breaks, but no full line-breaks. It is written in one hand of the first half of the fifteenth century, rather untidy, with extensive use of suspensions and contractions. Changes of nib can be detected on fos. 198^v and 201^v. Marginals occur throughout, some in a contemporary or near-contemporary hand, some in hands of the sixteenth or seventeenth century; all are in Latin. Occasional words or phrases are underlined, and twice a hand is drawn in the margin pointing to an entry. The entire text includes no more than thirteen interlineations and one detectable erasure. There are very few manifest grammatical errors or apparent omissions of words. All these features of the text are noted in the *apparatus criticus*. As already noted, the accumulated evidence points overwhelmingly to the likelihood of the *Continuatio* having been copied into Cotton Galba E VII from an existing text, although no other copy is known to survive.[11]

Although the author of the *Continuatio* does not at any point reveal personal information identifying his name, location, or qualifications, there is no mistaking his interest in and knowledge of, first, events at Canterbury, and secondly, the affairs of the Franciscans. His local knowledge, for example, included events such as the dispute over the location of Canterbury's fairs and markets in 1378; Archbishop Sudbury's plans to create a 'most beautiful and powerful city' there in the same year, and to use his archiepiscopal revenues to fund the work; the crimes committed in the city by the 1381 rebels; the measures taken for the safeguard of Becket's shrine in 1386; the lavish preparations for the visits to Canterbury of Roger Walden in 1398 and Richard II in 1399; and the unsuccessful attempt by Walden to remove his jewels from the archiepiscopal palace in 1399.[12] That a chronicler of national affairs should have occasion to make reference to the doings of successive archbishops of

---

[11] However, it may be that John Leland (1503–52) saw a different copy. He certainly saw, and transcribed sections from, the *Continuatio*, as well as from the *Eulogium*, and apparently thought that they were written by the same scribe, even though the two hands in the Cotton Galba MS are different (*Johannis Lelandi Antiquarii de Rebus Britannicis Collectanea*, ed. T. Hearne (6 vols., Oxford, 1715), i (ii), pp. 302–14; see also the comments of Haydon in *Eulogium*, iii, p. li and n. 2).

[12] Cross-references to the text and translation below can be found via the annual signifiers for each year. Note the comment that the 1381 rebels 'came back' (*redierunt*) to Canterbury. His interest in the building works at Queenborough and the collapse of Rochester bridge, and his description of the inhabitants of Thanet as 'the islanders', also suggest local attachment. Clifford, 'An Edition', pp. 226–8, treated the supposed Canterbury provenance of the chronicle with caution, but Gransden is surely correct to note the 'obvious Canterbury connection' (*Historical Writing*, p. 158, n. 5).

Canterbury is hardly surprising, but in this case the author's interest in their activities is both disproportionate and repeatedly augmented by what is evidently personal knowledge. For example, he noted Langham's distribution of money to each of the monks at the cathedral in 1373; Sudbury's alleged indifference to the controversy over Wyclif's views, and his dying words as he was beheaded by the rebels in 1381; and Walden's conversation with the 'northern hermit' in early 1399.

It was Thomas Arundel, however, who really caught the author's eye. The fact that it was the cathedral chapter that proposed his candidacy for the office in 1396; his reluctance to bring his brother, the earl, into the king's presence, and the king's shameful treatment of both brothers in 1397; his valedictory invective to Richard before he went into exile, and the king's fear of his 'wisdom and counsel', even when abroad; Arundel's interview with the pope while in exile; his second tirade against Richard at Flint castle in August 1399; his request to Henry IV that the intruder Walden's life be spared; his narrow escape from the rebel earls during the Epiphany rising of 1400, the account of which appears to be based on information from a member of the archbishop's household; his employment of a notary to record the king's duplicity in response to his pleas for the life of his fellow archbishop of York, Richard Scrope, in 1405; all these are indicative of special knowledge of Arundel on the author's part.[13] Antonia Gransden speculated that one of the sources used by the author of the *Continuatio* might have been a lost biography of Arundel.[14] This is not impossible—it is not just his words and deeds that are recounted, but even at times his feelings—but it is more likely to be based simply on local interest in and tales about Canterbury's formidable archbishop. What is certain is

---

[13] Further 'special knowledge' of Arundel may be revealed in the assertion that 'in the year of the Lord 1390, Boniface promoted the archbishop of York to the office of cardinal'. Arundel was archbishop of York from 1388 to 1396. Whether the chronicler is correct or not is another matter. This information is not recorded in any other source or in Aston's biography of Arundel to 1397 (M. Aston, *Thomas Arundel* (Oxford, 1967)). However, in a chronicle which exhibits uncommon knowledge of the archbishop, it should not be dismissed out of hand. It may be worth noting that in the introduction to his 'Epistle' to Arundel, John Gower described him as 'Cantuariensi Archiepiscopo, tocius Anglie Primati et apostolice sedis legato'; a papal legate was not the same as a cardinal, but the two offices were often combined. (I am grateful to R. F. Yeager for this information; he cites All Souls, Oxford, MS 98.) It is possible, but improbable, that the *Continuatio* author meant to refer to the recently exiled archbishop of York, Alexander Nevill, who visited Rome briefly in 1390 before spending the last two years of his life serving as a parish priest at Louvain, dying in 1392 (R. B. Dobson, 'Neville, Alexander', *ODNB*, xl. 482). What seems clear is that if Arundel was indeed offered a red hat in 1390, he declined it, as did his contemporaries William Courtenay, Philip Repingdon, Robert Hallum, and Thomas Langley.

[14] *Historical Writing*, p. 141, n. 166.

AUTHORSHIP AND PROVENANCE xvii

that, in a chronicle the tone of which is generally quite factual and the pace of which often gives the impression of wanting to move hastily to the next topic, the archbishop was one of the few subjects on which the chronicler chose to linger.

The fact that Arundel showed himself in 1401–2 to be a friend to the friars must also have enhanced his standing in the eyes of the author,[15] whose interest in Franciscan affairs is even more noticeable than his familiarity with Canterbury and its archbishops. This is especially evident in his account of the dispute within the order in 1404–5 and his detailed and sympathetic narration of the 1402 trials and executions of the grey friars accused of spreading the rumour that Richard II was still alive.[16] However, it extended well beyond these episodes. He noted royal visits or acts of generosity to Franciscan houses in 1392 and 1401, and prominent individuals who became friars minor, such as Chief Justice Shareshull in 1370 and the 'brother of the king of Spain' in 1379;[17] the fortunes of minorite houses or individual Franciscans during the 1381 revolt, the Welsh rebellion, the northern risings of 1405 and the floods of 1408; meetings of provincial councils in 1401–2 and 1405, and the visits to England of the minister-general of the order in 1407 and 1412; and the important part played by Franciscan theologians in the controversies over clerical taxation in 1373 and the determinations of John Wyclif at Oxford around 1380, when, according to the author, it was the regent of the friars minor who was foremost in refuting Wyclif's views on transubstantiation at the university. Predictably, the author was delighted by the election of a Franciscan as Pope Alexander V in 1409, describing him (in marked contrast to his distinctly ambivalent attitude to other popes of his age) as well educated, wise, agreeable, and likely to have brought unity to the Church had he not died after just ten months in office. He also preserved what appear to be Franciscan in-jokes, such as the story of the master of theology and the fool at the Bristol convent in 1402. The author's interest in the Franciscans also extended, with less obvious signs of approval, to the other fraternal orders—for

---

[15] C. Cotton, *The Grey Friars of Canterbury, 1224 to 1538* (Manchester, 1924), p. 47, says that both he and Courtenay gave bequests to the convent.

[16] Other chroniclers talked of Henry IV's hanging of the friars in 1402 as 'cruel' or 'inhumane', while Roger Frisby was widely seen as a martyr (D. W. Whitfield, 'Conflicts of personality and principle: The political and religious crisis in the English Franciscan Province, 1400–1409', *Franciscan Studies*, 17 (1957), 321–62, at 331. E. F. Jacob, *The Fifteenth Century* (Oxford, 1961), p. 28, suggested that the chronicler might have used the *coram rege* roll for his account of the trial of Frisby and his fellows, but there is actually very little verbal similarity between the two accounts.

[17] The chronicler also notes both the Londoners' and Glyn Dwr's 'love for the friars'.

example, he noted dispensations to the Dominicans and Carmelites to eat meat in 1376–7, the notorious case of the Carmelite who accused John of Gaunt of treason at the Salisbury parliament of 1384, and the Dominican whose (unspecified) behaviour placed Richard II in danger during his campaign to Ireland in 1394–5—but it fell well short of the attention he paid to the affairs of the grey friars.

There is much to indicate that the chronicler also had some legal knowledge: for example, the significance he attached to notarial instruments, the use of seals in validating (or forging) documents, and the swearing of oaths.[18] It was a wise royal justice who, in 1397, handed the duke of Gloucester's confession to the king only 'on condition that he kept a copy for himself authenticated with the king's seal'; a prudent archbishop who had a notary draw up an instrument recording the king's response to his plea for mercy for his fellow archbishop in 1405, 'to be presented to the pope should it prove necessary'. His account of the debate in the parliament of 1378 on rights of sanctuary is succinct but subtle; little wonder that he regarded with such distaste the exclusion of those who were 'learned in the law' from the parliaments of 1397 and 1404. The proceedings in 1397, he wrote, 'were not conducted according to the law of England but according to civil law'. Knowledge of the law is especially detectable in his pithy and well-informed reportage of disputes, be they between popes and cardinals, kings and their enemies, or English and French diplomats. Time and again, he exhibits a desire not just to record the outcomes of such encounters, but also the legal basis of the arguments deployed. At the outbreak of the Schism in 1378, for example, he reported the advice of

learned men... citing canonical privilege, that it was not necessary in every case for an election to be completely free, and that the Romans were perfectly entitled to put pressure on the cardinals in such cases if the cause was lawful, just as every community can put pressure on its lord for the common good and public utility; and that after the acceptance of the election by the whole of Christendom, even if there was something irregular with the form of election, it was nevertheless not permissible for the cardinals to go against ecclesiastical liberty because of that.

In good lawyerly fashion, the chronicler often cites the authorities— the Scriptures, civil law precepts, statutes, ancient privileges, letters testimonial—upon which legal arguments were based.

---

[18] See also his comment that the duke of Norfolk spoke to the duke of Hereford under 'seal of confession' in 1398.

His legal knowledge is also apparent in his treatment of the relationship between Church and State (frequently personified as pope and king), one of the pre-eminent concerns of the chronicle as a whole. Excluding the momentous enactments of 1397 and 1399, the majority of the acts of parliament or convocation which he noted involved secular regulation of ecclesiastical affairs, especially the Statutes of Provisors and the regulation of preaching (always a fraternal concern). Conversely, it was papal dominion that lay at the heart of the disputes which attracted his attention during the 1370s, such as the Westminster council of 1373, the interdict on Florentine merchants in 1376, the feud over the abbacy of Bury St Edmunds in 1379, and the imprisonment of Wyclif in 1377–8. It also surfaces on a number of other occasions, such as Bishop Despenser's leadership of the 'Flemish Crusade' of 1383, Henry IV's condemnation of Archbishop Scrope in 1405, and the role of king and pope in attempting to settle the internal Franciscan dispute of 1404–5. All these involved conflict over the demarcation of secular and ecclesiastical jurisdiction, a formal distinction which the chronicler believed it was important to uphold: in 1373, for example, he noted that it was up to the prelates to decide on the scriptural authority for the pope's claim to universal dominion, but up to the lords to rule on the validity of King John's 'charter' to Innocent III. He also indicated approval, in 1396 and again in 1404, of the fact that apprehended clerics were handed over to their officials for correction, rather than to the secular authorities. However, the 1408–9 councils that preceded the English decision to abandon Pope Gregory XII and attend the Council of Pisa are presented as a fruitful example of Church and State working together.

The upholding of ancient privileges was also a matter close to the chronicler's heart, be they those of the English Church as a whole, of individual religious houses or orders, of the university of Oxford, the citizens of London, or the townsmen of Ghent. Especially instructive in this context is the chronicler's attitude towards John Wyclif, whom he called 'the flower of Oxford' and whose subtle logic he undoubtedly admired but whose influence he ultimately believed to be pernicious. The four passages in which he addressed Wyclif's determinations at Oxford, although chronologically confused, all date from the period 1377–82. For the most part, the author's tone is one of intellectual curiosity rather than the entrenched hostility characteristic of other chroniclers of the time. In 1377–8, when the first papal bulls ordering Wyclif's arrest reached the university, he was nevertheless permitted to argue his case before the authorities, following which all the masters of theology

'declared publicly in the schools that [Wyclif's conclusions] were true, but that they sounded offensive to the ears of listeners'; and thus, stated the chronicler, 'the said Wyclif proved in the presence of the archbishop of Canterbury and the bishop of London that [his] conclusions are true, but they asked him not to speak of such matters any further'. Within another two years, however, by which time Wyclif had moved on to the question of transubstantiation, 'all the masters in theology lecturing at Oxford determined against [his] teaching, and the regent of the friars minor in particular, whose determination is still preserved in the university's archives, strongly refuted this doctrine and showed these people to be Lollards'. Resentment of papal and royal threats to the university's privileges undoubtedly contributed to the chronicler's initial, more favourable, attitude to Wyclif, but once he began to question the Eucharistic miracle and to attack the friars (especially the Franciscans), and once his followers began to disseminate and 'pervert' his opinions, 'not merely among many common and illiterate people but also among the well-born and the literate', the chronicler's attitude changed. When Wyclif died in 1384, there was not a word of praise for him, simply a note that later, 'by universal decree of the Church, [his body] was exhumed and his bones were burned'. However, for the outright Eucharistic heresy of Lollards such as William Sawtre in 1401 and John Badby in 1410, the chronicler had no sympathy whatever.

The chronicler's interest in Wyclif's opinions also allowed him to display his theological learning. His discussion of the Eucharist, although terse, cites the authority of St Paul, the Book of Revelation, Berengar of Tours, and Hugh of St Victor, and provides an informed summary of Wyclif's argument as well as his conclusion:

that bread [the communion host] is the body of Christ, just as the rock was Christ. However, the body is there in a different way from where it is a sign, because it is there by sanctifying grace worthily assumed, nor can an accident be there without a subject.... The accident is not the sacrament of the altar, but the substance, since otherwise the bread of rats would be more perfect than the sacrament of the altar, because every substance is more perfect than any accident. To speak briefly, the contrary is not found, as can be established from the scriptures.

Taken together with the chronicler's knowledge of and concern for Oxford, such passages indicate that he probably studied theology at the university, possibly around the time of Wyclif's controversial determinations.[19] He was certainly sensitive to academic distinctions and

---

[19] Note his comment that it was 'some people' at the university who requested the papal bull of 1377. Note also his account of the university procession that greeted the severed head

achievements, noting whether scholars were bachelors, masters, or doctors (Pope Alexander V, who had studied at both Norwich and Oxford, was even 'a renowned doctor of theology') and well acquainted with the university's structure of governance and teaching (he mentions the chancellor, vice-chancellor, council, regents, non-regents, even its archives).[20]

The internal evidence thus suggests that the author of the *Continuatio* was almost certainly a Franciscan, and probably based at the grey friars' convent at Canterbury; that he had studied theology, probably at Oxford, during which time he had also acquired some knowledge of canon law. The mendicant orders were better known for theology and philosophy in the British Isles than for their historical output, which was in no way comparable to that of the monastic orders. For monks, especially Benedictines, history had something of the aspect of a communal undertaking, and in some houses, such as St Albans and Westminster, it was virtually an institutional obligation. For friars, it was an individual enterprise, a personal choice, for which institutional support was uncertain and an itinerant lifestyle somewhat inhibiting.[21] Nevertheless, the author must have spent time in his home convent, and it is reasonable to assume that at least parts of the chronicle were written there.

THE CANTERBURY GREY FRIARS AND THE ENGLISH FRANCISCAN PROVINCE

Founded in 1224, the Canterbury convent was the first Franciscan house in England and enjoyed something of a reputation for learning.[22]

---

of Roger Frisby at Oxford in June 1402, which seems to be based on either local knowledge or an eyewitness report.

[20] Rank and the rituals of deference, such as the doffing of cardinals' hats (1373, 1408) or the wearing of episcopal vestments (1379), clearly mattered to him.

[21] Taylor, *English Historical Literature in the Fourteenth Century*, pp. 20–4.

[22] The remains of the two-storied convent, straddling the River Stour, still stand, located in a secluded spot known as Binnewith Island close to the heart of the modern city. For an account of the friars' arrival there and the hardships they initially endured, see the chronicle of Thomas de Eccleston in *Monumenta Franciscana*, ed. J. S. Brewer (2 vols., RS; London 1858), i. 5–9. Originally located in the garden of the poor priests' hospital, the site was bought by a local citizen, John Digge, and given to the friars in 1267, the church being consecrated in 1325. An impression of the house's seal dated 1294 is preserved among the archives of Canterbury cathedral: it is elliptical, of brown wax, 1 × 1½ inches, showing Thomas Becket's martyrdom surmounted by tabernacle work, and the legend S[*igillum*] *Fratrum Minorum Cantuarie*. The convent of Canterbury was one of eight houses within the *custodia* of the London convent (the English Franciscan province was divided into seven *custodiae*). It was transferred to the Franciscan Observants in 1498 on the orders of Henry VII, and dissolved in 1538. In July 1539 it was sold to Thomas Spilman for £100; five years later, when he sold it to Thomas Rolf for £200, it was described as having two messuages, two

Remarkably, despite the fact that neighbouring Christ Church possessed a library of no fewer than 1,850 books in the late thirteenth century, Prior Henry Eastry was obliged between 1285 and 1314 to employ successive Canterbury Franciscans to act as lectors in theology, apparently because 'England's premier cathedral library lacked monks capable of providing competent lectures in theology within the cloister'.[23] Whether or not the Canterbury Franciscans enjoyed access to the cathedral library, they did in any case have a small library of their own. Around 1300, this included glossed copies of the New Testament and the book of Isaiah, the gospels of SS Matthew and Mark, the epistles of St Paul, a Life of St Francis, and philosophical and theological works by Philip the Chancellor of Paris, Peter Lombard, Albertus Magnus, William Ockham, and St Anselm. Historical works included a volume, now in the British Library, containing the *Historia Regum Britanniae* of Geoffrey of Monmouth, the *Historia Hierosolimitana* of Jacques de Vitry, a *Gesta Alexandri* continued with a *Historia Romanorum*, and the *Chronicle of Popes and Emperors* of Martin of Troppau (Martinus Polonus),[24] as well as a volume containing the *Historia Ecclesiastica Tripartita* with extracts from William of Malmesbury's ecclesiastical history.[25] In 1289 there were apparently some sixty grey friars at the

---

orchards, two gardens, three acres of arable, ten acres of meadow and four acres of pasture, with pertinences in neighbouring parishes (Cotton, *Grey Friars of Canterbury*, pp. 12–16, 26, 31, 42, 59–63; Canterbury Cathedral Archives CC/Supp. MS 11, fos. 117ʳ, 131ʳ; DCC Ch Cant C1031 (seal); C. Cotton, 'Notes on the documents in the Cathedral library at Canterbury relating to the Grey Friars', *Collectanea Franciscana*, 2, ed. C. L. Kingsford (Manchester, 1922), pp. 1–9; 'Friaries: The Franciscan friars of Canterbury', in *A History of the County of Kent*, ii, ed. W. Page (VCH; London, 1926), pp. 190–4).

[23] The named Franciscan lectors were Ralph de Wydheye and Robert Fuham; there may have been a third (R. B. Dobson, 'The monks of Canterbury in the later Middle Ages', in P. Collinson, N. Ramsay, and M. Sparks, eds., *A History of Canterbury Cathedral* (Oxford, 1995), pp. 69–153, at 100 (quote), 109–10; N. Ramsay, 'The Cathedral archives and library', ibid. pp. 341–407, at 354).

[24] This is British Library Cotton MS Galba E XI, a leather-bound volume of 155 parchment folios. Folio 1ʳ has an inscription, partly cropped, stating that 'Iste liber est de communitate fratrum minorum Cantuarie de procuracionem [et con]firmacionem Fratris Hugonis de Hertepol tunc ministri Anglie. Historie'. Hugh of Hartlepool, regent master of the Franciscan school at Oxford in the late 13th c. and provincial minister of the order from 1299, died in 1302 (J. Catto, 'Hartlepool, Hugh of', *ODNB*, xxv. 603–4). The manuscript is thus presumably late 13th c., although a letter from Thomas Palmer, prior provincial of the English Dominicans, which has been used as a flyleaf, is dated at Canterbury on 15 Aug. 1395, suggesting that the manuscript was still in Canterbury at that time.

[25] This is entitled *Notabilia super Ecclesiasticam Historiam et Tripartitam cum Extractionibus Willelmi Malmesburiensis*, a book said to be *in conventu fratrum minorum Cantuarie* (Cotton, 'Notes on the documents', p. 9). Cassiodorus–Epiphanius' work, often known as the *Historia Tripartita*, was a 6th-c. narrative composed at the request of Cassiodorus at Vivarium, partly based on Rufinus's translation from Greek into Latin of Eusebius's 4th-c. *Historia Ecclesiastica*, a history of the early Christian Church.

Canterbury convent, although normally the number was around thirty-five to forty, and following the Black Death it dropped further.[26] Nevertheless, a library continued to be maintained and indeed augmented. During the fourteenth century, manuscripts of the books of Genesis and Exodus, of Isaiah, Jeremiah, and Daniel, and another copy of the Epistles of St Paul were all acquired; so too, perhaps, was a copy of the *Eulogium Historiarum*.[27] Thus what is known of the grey friars' house at Canterbury indicates that the author of the *Continuatio* would have enjoyed an environment conducive to study, even if the convent never achieved the prominence that might have been expected from its location.

The early fifteenth century was, however, a turbulent time for the Franciscan order. To what extent the Canterbury convent was embroiled in the quarrel that broke out within the English order in 1404 is not clear. The author of the *Continuatio* is discreet, doubtless a touch defensive, about what he calls this 'great and truly shameful dispute'. Nevertheless, he is one of our most important sources for it. According to his account, it erupted when the provincial minister (John de la Zouche, elected in 1400) revoked the privileges of a number of English convents, especially the London house, intending to reissue them 'according to his own liking'. Not surprisingly, this did not go unchallenged: appealing to the pope, the king, and the mayor of the city, the London Franciscans and Zouche's opponents within the order managed to secure a papal commission to investigate his conduct, although he refused to appear before it. Eventually a provincial chapter was summoned to meet at Oxford on 3 May 1405; although Zouche attempted to obstruct it, the king overruled him. And there, unfortunately, the chronicler leaves the story, with Zouche having fled abroad and the provincial chapter about to meet. In fact, Zouche was on his way to put his case to the newly elected minister-general, Antonio de Pereto, who reinstated him. Yet it was not for another two years, in June 1407, when Pereto was obliged to visit England 'in order to put a stop to the disorders arisen in the said order', and Henry IV expediently agreed to promote Zouche to the bishopric of Llandaff, that the conflict subsided. Yet Zouche continued to attract controversy: in 1408, contrary to the decision of the English ecclesiastical and secular

---

[26] Around 1300, there were about 1,500 Franciscans in sixty convents in England; by the late 14th c., about 750: J. Moorman, *The Franciscans in England* (London, 1974), pp. 14, 75, 87.

[27] In 1498 Richard Martin, suffragan of the archbishop and a former warden of the house, bequeathed another ten (unidentified) books to the Canterbury convent: Cotton, *Grey Friars of Canterbury*, pp. 32–4, 96 (but this is not the Richard Martin who became bishop of St David's in 1482–3); Ker, *Medieval Libraries*, p. 48; 'Friaries: The Franciscan friars of Canterbury', p. 192.

hierarchy and the General Chapter of the Franciscan order, he refused to abandon Pope Gregory XII or support the Council of Pisa.[28]

What lay behind this dispute was the growing rift between the Franciscan Observants—the late fourteenth-century heirs to the Spirituals, whose desire to return to the strict poverty imposed upon his followers by St Francis had been rebuffed by Pope John XXII in 1323, but whose ideals were gaining increasing support in Europe—and the Conventuals, who advocated strict obedience to the papacy and a less rigorous lifestyle. Until 1400, the English Franciscan province remained immune from this controversy, but John de la Zouche, it seems, was a reformer— a 'pseudo-Observant', as he has been described; his reforms were not so much to reorder the privileges of the English Franciscans 'to his own liking', but to bring them into line with what he believed to be the true mission of the friars. His principal opponent within the English province, and the man who succeeded him as provincial minister in 1407, was William Butler, against whose laxity, deceitful conduct, and general character, 'tending rather to avarice than to poverty', Zouche would fulminate two years later in a stream of letters addressed to the English proctor at the Curia.[29] How many of his fellow English

---

[28] Whitfield, 'Conflicts of personality', pp. 344–6. The king approved a licence for Pereto to come to England on 22 June 1407, ordering him on his arrival to 'hasten straight to our presence, wherever we may be'; the licence was issued a month later: *CCR 1405–9*, 217; *Royal and Historical Letters of Henry IV*, ed. F. C. Hingeston (2 vols., RS; London, 1965 reprint), ii. 179–80); *Calendar of Signet Letters of Henry IV and Henry V, 1399–1422*, ed. J. L. Kirby (London, 1978), no. 946, and for evidence of the ongoing dispute in the order, no. 648. See also *CPR 1405–8*, 238; *CCR 1405–9*, 63.

[29] These letters are printed in Whitfield, 'Conflicts of personality', pp. 346–60. Zouche also accused Butler of heterodox views about the Eucharist and almost never celebrating mass, claiming that he suffered from headaches; a close ally of Butler's was Robert Harding, whom Zouche described as the 'root and instigator of the dispute in our province' (*radix et origo brige in provincia nostra*) with a history of crimes and deceptions, who became Butler's 'personal counsellor'. Butler was an Oxford theologian of considerable note, described in the 'Catalogue of Illustrious Franciscans' as 'the flower of the university during his times' (*flos universitatis temporibus suis*). In 1401, as regent master of the Franciscans at Oxford, he determined unequivocally against the translation of the Bible into English, claiming that the vernacular was inadequate to the task and the lay intellect incapable of understanding the mysteries of the faith without the guidance of an instructed priesthood. His conservative viewpoint also comes through in his opposition to Zouche's attempted reforms. According to the latter, the two men met on 18 Dec. 1406, when Butler requested permission to leave the Franciscan Order and join the Benedictine monastery at Abingdon, claiming that he could not adhere to the strict poverty of the Order. The truth of Zouche's account is naturally open to question; in any case, Butler did not leave the Order, acting as provincial minister from 1407 to 1413/14, in which capacity he preached at the English church council of July 1408 which discussed the Schism, and was chosen to attend the Council of Pisa. He also seems to have gone to the Council of Constance. He probably died around 1416–17. His determination is printed in M. Deanesly, *The Lollard Bible* (Cambridge, 1920), pp. 399–418; see also

Franciscans supported Zouche's proposed reforms is difficult to say: a minority, almost certainly, but perhaps quite a substantial minority. The *Continuatio* hints at quite widespread disaffection within the province during these early years of the fifteenth century: it was not outsiders, anti-fraternal agitators, who betrayed the friars from Aylesbury, Leicester, and elsewhere condemned to death in 1402 for sympathizing with Richard II, but their fellow friars. Henry IV's comment to Zouche, when he approached the king to beg mercy for them ('They refuse to be disciplined by you, so they will have to be disciplined by me') did not lack wider significance; while the riposte of the London friars to Zouche's accusations—that it was not they who were the troublemakers, but that 'all the scandals were caused by incomers from abroad and others such as those who were hanged there'—implies that the Franciscans hanged in 1402 were supporters of Zouche, of the Observant persuasion.

Nevertheless, Zouche's attempt at reform was a failure, and following his promotion to Llandaff in 1407 (which was undoubtedly supported by the minister-general) the influence of the Observant movement seems rapidly to have subsided in England; not until the last quarter of the fifteenth century, with strong royal support, did it begin to make real headway there.[30] Despite the discretion exercised by the author of the *Continuatio* in his account of the 1404–7 dispute (he names no names, fails to mention that it was still unresolved in 1407 when Pereto visited England, and implies that Pereto's mission was for a different purpose), it is not difficult to see where his sympathies lay. Zouche, he stated, 'acting on the advice of some troublesome friars and encouraged by a number of their inexperienced supporters', behaved in a high-handed manner throughout, refused to submit to papal or royal authority, and fled the country rather than face his opponents. This is not to say that the author of the *Continuatio* was irredeemably partisan: for example, he described the messenger sent by Zouche's opponents to the minister-general as 'a crafty (*callidus*) friar'. Yet it was not just Zouche's intransigence that irritated the author: there can be little doubt that he was a conservative, a Conventual, at heart. His discretion, as well as his knowledge, suggest that he might have held a position of some responsibility in the Franciscan order.

A. G. Little, *The Grey Friars in Oxford* (Oxford, 1892), pp. 254–5; A. G. Little, *Franciscan Papers, Lists and Documents* (Manchester, 1943), pp. 198–9; *Monumenta Franciscana*, i. 561; A. Hudson, 'Butler, William', *ODNB*, ix. 235.

[30] Moorman, *Franciscans in England*, pp. 79–82.

As to the chronicler's identity, there are unfortunately no lists and few other records available between the years 1328 and 1455 from which to discover the names of the friars at the Canterbury convent, and there were over a hundred Franciscans at Oxford in the late 1370s.[31] There are, however, two names of more than passing interest: John Bruyl and Robert Wicheford. Bruyl, who was attached to the convent at Newcastle before moving to Canterbury, became a papal chaplain in 1396 and warden of the London Franciscan convent in 1397 (in which capacity he entered into an indenture with Richard ('Dick') Whittington, the philanthropist and mayor of the city, for the extension of the London convent; Whittington later contributed most of the cost of the new library there). Although he is not recorded as having studied at Oxford, Bruyl also possessed a fourteenth-century collection of treatises by Aristotle, Albertus Magnus, and others relating to natural science and astronomy, which are now in the Bodleian Library there (MS BL Digby 153). In 1402 he was promoted to the episcopal see of Annaghdown (Enachdun) in Ireland, although he never seems to have gone there, instead acting successively between 1402 and 1420 as suffragan bishop of Winchester, Lincoln, and York. After 1420 he disappears from the records, presumably having died.[32]

Robert Wicheford was attached to the Canterbury convent at the time of his ordination as subdeacon and deacon in 1378 and studied for many years at the university of Oxford, where he became at least a master and possibly a doctor of theology; it may be that as a result he became attached to the Oxford rather than the Canterbury convent. Little is known about him apart from the fact that he was involved in the 1404–5 dispute as a supporter of William Butler, but was apparently still considered sufficiently impartial for Zouche to recommend him to the Curia as one of fifteen commissioners who might be appointed to re-examine his grievances against Butler. This was in March 1409, and appears to be the last time Wicheford is mentioned in the records.[33] If it is correct to think that the *Continuatio* was written by a

---

[31] Cotton, *Grey Friars of Canterbury*, pp. 80–3. Moorman, *Franciscans in England*, pp. 75–6.

[32] He is also sometimes called Bryll or Brytt: C. L. Kingsford, *The Grey Friars of London* (London, 1915), pp. 20, 56–7, 65, 174; *HBC*, p. 331; *Monumenta Franciscana*, i. 523; *The Friars' Libraries*, ed. K. W. Humphreys (Corpus of British Medieval Library Catalogues; London, 1990), p. 216; Ker, *Medieval Libraries*, p. 246. He is not mentioned in Emden, *BRUO*.

[33] Emden (*BRUO*, iii. 2044–5) calls him 'doctor', but Zouche's letter of 1409 refers to him as *magister de cathedra Oxonie* (Whitfield, 'Conflicts of personality', p. 352). Wicheford may have come from Wichenford (Worcestershire); a Hugh Wicheford, also a Franciscan, possibly a relative, was ordained deacon by Simon Sudbury, bishop of London, in 1362 (*Sudbury's Register 1362–75*, ed. R. Fowler and C. Jenkins (2 vols., Canterbury and York Society; Oxford,

STRUCTURE, COMPOSITION, AND SOURCES xxvii

Canterbury grey friar who had studied at Oxford in the 1370s, probably held a position of responsibility within the order, was well acquainted with Franciscan internal affairs in the early fifteenth century, and was still active enough in 1409 to suggest that he probably lived a few years longer, then Robert Wicheford would appear to be a plausible candidate; but that is as far as speculation can go.

THE STRUCTURE, COMPOSITION, AND SOURCES
OF THE *CONTINUATIO*

Scholars who have studied the *Continuatio* have disagreed radically over the question of its composition, principally for two reasons: the eclectic nature of its subject matter, and its numerous chronological errors. Writing in 1915, Charles Kingsford argued that it was largely derivative, a composite work compiled around 1430 which integrated up to five pre-existing narrative sources, none of which covered the whole period from the early 1360s to 1413; one of the problems with this theory, although it is not insuperable, is that these sources do not survive. E. J. Jones, writing in 1937, suggested that most of the chronicle was written by John Trevor, bishop of St Asaph, but his argument is weak and has found no support. Stephen Clifford's unpublished thesis, written in 1975, proposed that the *Continuatio* was 'the work of one man, whose chronicle is a contemporary and independent account of the period which he describes'.[34] The manifest errors of dating in the chronicle could to some extent be explained, he suggested, by surmising that the chronicle was written in three stages: the early 1390s, c.1400, and shortly after 1413 (with the most egregious errors being confined to the early years of each stage, namely, the 1360s and 1370s, the early 1390s, and the first half a dozen years of the fifteenth century). Elements of Clifford's argument have received some support,[35] but the process of composition of the *Continuatio* is still fundamentally an unresolved question and bears re-examination.

As in so many medieval chronicles, the framework upon which the *Continuatio* was constructed was chronological—or, to be more precise,

---

1938), ii. 5). Wicheford should not be confused with his more distinguished contemporary, Robert Wikeford, archbishop of Dublin (d. 1390).

[34] C. L. Kingsford, *English Historical Literature in the Fifteenth Century* (Oxford, 1913), pp. 28–31; E. J. Jones, 'The authorship of the Continuation of the *Eulogium Historiarum*: A suggestion', *Speculum* xii (1937), 196–202 (remarkably, Jones only identified two chronological errors before 1390); Clifford, 'An Edition', p. 23.

[35] Gransden, *Historical Writing*, p. 158, n. 5; Taylor, *English Historical Literature in the Fourteenth Century*, p. 21.

annalistic. The first year of the chronicle is the only one not to begin with the word 'Anno'; it begins 'Rex Cipri anno Domini [1364]...' ('The king of Cyprus, in the year of the Lord 1364'...). The years 1365–70 omit 'Domini' and begin simply 'Anno [1365, etc.]', but from 1371 to 1413, the events recorded under each year begin with the words 'Anno Domini', with the initial 'A' almost invariably set at the opening of a new line and highlighted in red or blue; in 1373, and from 1377 onwards, most of these *sub anno* openings are reinforced with a contemporary marginal in Arabic numerals.[36] Beginning in 1397 and continuing until 1413, AD dates are supplemented with a note of the regnal year, for example, 'Anno Domini [1397] et anno regni regis Ricardi uicesimo' ('In the year of the Lord 1397 and the twentieth year of the reign of King Richard').[37] Subsequent events, until the next annual opening, often begin with 'eodem anno', 'quo anno', 'hoc etiam anno', or similar constructions. The chronicler's (or copyist's) intention is clear: to create the impression of chronological precision, to locate each event within its temporal context. However, this impression is deceptive, for numerous events are misdated, often by several years, as demonstrated in Table 1.[38]

As this table shows, although the majority of events recorded in the *Continuatio* are assigned either to the correct year or within a year or two either side of it, there are a significant number of events misdated by between four and eight years. The years 1364–76 and 1390–6 are the least accurate in this respect (thereby lending some support to Clifford's proposed process of composition in three stages). What is at any rate clear is that, despite its formal annalistic structure, it is impossible to believe that the *Continuatio* was composed on an annual basis. Parts of it at least must have been composed several years later, and this is not a fact that the chronicler tried to conceal. Thus he noted *sub anno* 1386 that 'not long afterwards, this earl [of March] was killed in Ireland'; March did not die in Ireland until 1398. In 1405, he declared that, following the execution of Archbishop Scrope, Henry IV was afflicted by leprosy, 'and it was from this illness that he later died' (in 1413); the Council of Pisa,

---

[36] These are included as annual headings in the text and translation. The years between 1377 and 1413 which lack annual signifiers in the margin are 1385, 1391–6, and 1401. The 'Anno Domini' openings for 1371, 1397, and 1404 are the only ones that do not begin a new line.

[37] Note also his comment at the end of his account of the year 1399: 'Hec omnia facta sunt anno primo regis huius [Henry IV] et anno uicesimosecundo Ricardi, et anno Domini millesimo trecentisimo nonagesimo nono.' The regnal year is not included in 1401, presumably an oversight. It should also be noted that the chronicler errs in describing both 1402 and 1403 as the 'third year of the reign of King Henry IV', following which his regnal years for Henry IV's reign are always one year out.

[38] The great majority of events noted in the chronicle can be accurately dated with reference to other sources, but there are a few for which evidence has not been discovered.

STRUCTURE, COMPOSITION, AND SOURCES   xxix

TABLE 1. *Chronological Structure of the Continuatio*

Dates AD as given in the text	Correct dates of events in the order recorded (by modern reckoning)
1364	1363–5, 1361–3, 1363
1365	1365–6
1366	1366, 1368
1367	1367, 1372, 1369
1368	1369, 1369–70
1369	1368–9, 1370, 1368–9, 1367–70
1370	1369–73, 1370, 1375–7, 1377
1371	1373, 1373
1372	1375
1373	1369
1374	1371–3, 1373, 1372, 1378, 1375
1375	1374–5, 1370
1376	1376, 1370
1377	1377, 1377, 1377–80, 1377
1378	1378, 1378, 1378, 1378, 1377, 1378, 1378–81, 1378
1379	1379–82, 1379, 1377–8, 1380
1380	1384, 1380, 1379–80, 1380, 1381, 1381, 1380
1381	1381, 1381
1382	1381, 1382, 1382, 1379–82, 1381–2, 1382, 1382
1383	1382–3, 1385–6, 1382
1384	1385, 1385
1385	1386, 1386, 1386–7
1386	1386, 1385, 1377–90, 1385–6, 1387
1387	1387, 1387, 1388, 1384, 1388–9
1388	?1391, 1387–9
1389	1388–92, 1389
1390	1388–9, ?1393, 1390
1391	no events recorded
1392	1393
1393	no events recorded
1394	no events recorded
1395	1392
1396	1394, ?1394, ?1390, 1394–5, 1394–5, 1394, 1396, 1396
1397	1396, 1397, 1397, 1398, 1398, 1398
1398	1398, 1398, 1398
1399	1399, 1399, 1399, 1399, 1399, 1400, 1400, 1401
1400	1400, 1401, 1400, 1401
1401	1400, 1402, 1402, 1402
1402	1402, 1402, 1402, 1402, 1403, 1402, 1402, 1402
1403	1403, 1403, 1403, 1402, 1403, ?1406–7, 1403, 1404
1404	1404, 1405, 1405, 1403–4, 1404, 1404, 1405, 1405, 1404, 1400, 1403, 1402, 1404, 1404–5
1405	1405, 1405, 1406, 1406
1406	1406, 1406, 1406, 1407
1407	1407, 1407, 1407–8, 1407, 1407, 1407, 1408
1408	1408, 1408, 1408, 1408, 1408, 1408, 1409
1409	1409, 1409, 1409, 1409–10, 1410
1410	1410, 1410, 1410, 1409, 1410, 1410
1411	1411, 1411, 1411, 1411, 1411
1412	1412, 1412, 1411–12, 1412, 1412–15
1413	1412–13, 1413, ?1411, 1413, 1413, 1413, 1413

he stated *sub anno* 1409, was 'later transferred to Constance' (in 1414); while the reference *sub anno* 1413 to Thomas Beaufort as duke of Exeter cannot have been written before 1416, when he was created a duke. Especially notable is his account of the death of John Wyclif *sub anno* 1387, to which he added that later, 'by universal decree of the Church, [his body] was exhumed and his bones were burned'; this was not done until 1428, and it is now generally assumed that this must be a copyist's interpolation, although it is possible that the chronicler (or copyist) was reacting to the *order* to exhume Wyclif's body, first issued on 4 May 1415, rather than to the fulfilment of that order thirteen years later.[39] It is also tempting to speculate as to whether his assertion that the 'brother of the king of Spain', a friar minor, prophesied that it would be a Franciscan pope who brought the Schism to an end, which is noted *sub anno* 1379, was written in the knowledge of Alexander V's election at the Council of Pisa thirty years later. It is in any event apparent that the version of the *Continuatio* inserted into Cotton MS Galba E VII was not written before 1416 and may not have been completed for another twelve years or more.[40] On the other hand, sections of it must originally have been written earlier: of Richard II's failure to marry the daughter of the count of Flanders, for example, the chronicler commented *sub anno* 1382 that 'the duke of Burgundy who now holds the county married her', seemingly a reference to Philip the Bold of Burgundy, who died in 1404.[41]

Also worth considering is the configuration of the chronicle. More than two hundred separate items of information are recorded in the *Continuatio*.[42] Most of the entries are quite brief, but major political or ecclesiastical events are treated at greater length. The most noteworthy of these are the outbreak of the Schism (1378); the great revolt of 1381; the Flemish Crusade of 1383; the political crisis of 1386–8; the arrest

---

[39] In fact Wyclif died on 31 Dec. 1384. The first order to exhume Wyclif's body was issued in 1415 by the Council of Constance—hence, perhaps, the chronicler's 'universal decree of the Church'. Philip Repingdon, bishop of Lincoln and a former follower of Wyclif, declined to act on this, so on 9 Dec. 1427 Pope Martin V wrote to the royal council and Archbishop Chichele ordering them to carry out the sentence, which they did in the spring of 1428. His ashes were cast in the River Swift (H. Workman, *John Wyclif: A Study of the Medieval English Church* (2 vols., Oxford, 1926), ii. 319–20).

[40] Note also a number of less precise comments, such as (*sub anno* 1380) that Rochester bridge was 'broken for a long time'; that the lords exiled in 1388 'never came back'; and (*sub anno* 1405) that Archbishop Scrope was a miracle-worker 'to this day'.

[41] This passage shows much confusion. It was in fact Richard's uncle, Edmund of Langley, who had come close to marrying Margaret of Flanders in the mid-1360s, not Richard himself.

[42] What constitutes an 'item of information' is obviously debatable; in a general sense, it is used here in the sense of moving on to a different topic rather than providing additional detail on an existing topic, but no such definition can be watertight.

of the Appellants and the parliament of 1397–8; the revolution, deposition, and murder of Richard II (1399–1400); the Percy rebellion and the battle of Shrewsbury (1403); Archbishop Scrope's rising (1405); the negotiations to end the Schism (1408–9); and the French civil war, beginning in 1411–12. Events of this magnitude were reported by almost all chroniclers of the time, and no one purporting to compile a credible record of English events could afford to ignore them.

The dating of these great events is consistently accurate.[43] It is the lesser events—those which the chronicler reckoned less important or about which he knew less—that are regularly misdated. In other words, it was great events, the dates of which were easily remembered or discovered, that provided the skeleton of his chronicle, around which lesser events were tucked in or simply tacked on to the record of each year in what the chronicler hoped, or had been informed, was their correct place and/or sequence. Most of these consist only of a sentence or two, although others stretch to half a dozen sentences or more. A lot of them repeat news or rumours that were widely known, and to identify the sources from which they were taken would be an almost impossible (and rather pointless) task, although verbal resonances do occasionally reveal the likely provenance of individual items.

The two shortest annals in the *Continuatio* are also the most eccentric. For the year 1391, the chronicler wrote: 'nothing is recorded here, because the kingdom of England was in a poor state (*in malo statu*)'; then, following a brief annal for 1392 (*recte* 1393), he continued: 'What was done in the realm in the years 1393 and 1394 is not recorded here, on account of the vicissitudes (*uarietatem*) of the kingdom of England.' Indeed, the chronicler's reportage of the years 1390–5 as a whole is feeble, which might reflect the fact that this interlude between the great crises of 1386–9 and 1397–9 failed to catch his imagination. Yet when it came to events which were not widely reported but in which he had a special interest, he provided detailed and vivid accounts: for example, the two disputes relating to papal dominion over England in the 1370s (the interdict against the Florentines, and the Westminster Council of 1373); four passages relating to John Wyclif at Oxford between 1377 and 1381; the trials of the Franciscan friars in 1402; and the dispute within the Franciscan order in 1404–5. Even so—and perhaps surprisingly—the only one of these which can unhesitatingly be said to be

---

[43] As was customary at the time, the chronicler reckoned that the new year began on 25 Mar.; thus he recorded the parliaments of Feb. 1388, Jan. 1404, and Jan. 1410 under 1387, 1403, and 1409 respectively.

correctly dated is the last. The dispute over the Florentines occurred in 1375–7 but is placed *sub anno* 1370; the Westminster council of 1373 is placed *sub anno* 1374. The papal bulls concerning Wyclif were received and debated at Oxford during the winter of 1377–8 but are placed in 1379, while Wyclif's determination there on the universal Christian religion is placed in 1382, by which time he had left the university for Lutterworth. Even the trials of the friars and their associates, for which the chronicler had access to a colourful source, are initially placed *sub anno* 1401 before being enlarged upon *sub anno* 1402, the correct year.

This is one of several examples of information being repeated. The promotion of the dukes of York and Gloucester, for example, is noted first *sub anno* 1384 and then again *sub anno* 1386 (the correct date was 1385); Gaunt's expedition to Spain of 1386–9 was first noted in 1385, then again in 1388, when items of news such as Philippa of Lancaster's Portuguese marriage and Gaunt's financial settlement with Enrique of Castile are needlessly, or just heedlessly, reiterated; and the earl of March's death in Ireland is anticipated *sub anno* 1385, then repeated under its correct year, 1398. Sometimes the chronicler added 'as noted above', obviously realizing that he was repeating information, but more often he seems to have been oblivious of the fact: thus he noted *sub anno* 1402 that Henry IV married Joan of Navarre, and two years later that her daughters and several of her Breton servants were expelled from England as part of the anti-alien purge in the parliament of January 1404; shortly after this, however, he was once again writing, as if *de novo*, that 'Lady Joan, duchess of Brittany, also arrived in England, and King Henry solemnly married her in St Swithun's abbey at Winchester'. The correct date was 7 February 1403 (old style 1402).

Repetition of material, errors of dating, and an inherent sense of unevenness in both the quality and the quantity of the information presented all tend to the same conclusion: the *Continuatio* is, in some sense at least, a composite work, a concoction of material from a number of different sources—written, oral, or eyewitness—cobbled together to form a disjointed and at times clumsy whole. That does not mean, however (as Kingsford appeared to suggest) that the chronicler was simply a plagiarist. The only source which he copied (almost) verbatim was the legendary account of the foundation of Westminster abbey, inserted *sub anno* 1378. For major political events, he often used official or semi-official records, but invariably abridged them. The closest he came to reproducing a government document in full was the Questions to the Judges of 1387—the *mirabiles questiones*, as he termed them—for

which he followed his text closely for the most part but either compressed or paraphrased what he evidently regarded as superfluous verbiage. Usually he pruned much more radically. His accounts of the parliaments of 1378 (the dispute over clerical immunity), 1382 (the statute on ravishers of women), 1386 (the charges against de la Pole and the establishment of the Commission), 1388 (the trials of the royal favourites), 1394 (the Anglo-French peace negotiations), 1397–8 (the trial of the earl of Arundel, Richard II's statutes, and the Hereford–Norfolk quarrel), 1399 (Henry IV's revocation of Richard's acts) and January 1404 (the negotiations over taxation) owe something, although not always a great deal and not necessarily directly, to the rolls of parliament.[44] Sometimes he just inserted into his narrative a sentence or two from a document, such as the papal bull authorizing the Flemish crusade of 1383, Richard II's blank charters of 1398, the 'prophecy of the eagle' in 1399, a verse about the battle of Shrewsbury in 1403, or the manifestos of the cardinals justifying their abandonment of Urban VI in 1378 and Gregory XII in 1408. The reports of the Westminster council of 1373, the discovery of the Epiphany rising, the death of the duke of Orléans in 1407, Cardinal Ugguccione's speech to the English church council of October 1408, and the trial of Badby in 1410 seem ultimately to be based on, or at least to glean some details from, eyewitness accounts, perhaps via newsletters. This might also be the case with the murder of John Hauley in 1378, the discussions in the Tower prior to the battle of Radcot Bridge, the interview between Richard II and the Londoners at Nottingham, the negotiations preceding the battle of Shrewsbury, and the papal conclave of 1409 (for which the chronicler's source could have been Bishop Hallum or William Butler, both of whom went to Pisa). Reports of Wyclif's examinations and determinations at Oxford place some stress on his and his followers' relationship with the friars and may well be based on accounts circulating within the Franciscan order—which was surely also the case with the accounts of the trials of the friars in 1402 and the dispute within the order in 1404–5. Like many other chroniclers, the author of the *Continuatio* felt no compunction about interweaving passages from written sources into his narrative without acknowledgement. One result of this was to blur the distinction between his own opinions, the opinions of those he had spoken to, and the documents which he had

---

[44] For some of his accounts of events in parliament, he may well have used parliamentary tracts of the kind that were now quite frequently being produced (Given-Wilson, *Chronicles*, pp. 176–7).

consulted. Yet there are signs that he selected his sources with care. For example, his use of 'The Manner of King Richard's Renunciation' for the deposition of Richard II and his detailed summary of the articles of complaint circulated by Archbishop Scrope in 1405 present a much more equivocal picture of Henry IV's actions than the blatantly partisan (and widely circulated) 'Record and Process' or the parliamentary record of the trials of those accused of rebellion in 1405.[45]

The most plausible solution to the riddle of the *Continuatio*'s composition is that the author, realizing that he was living through momentous events, began writing at some point in 1399–1400. As can be seen from Table 1, although dating errors occur throughout the fifty years covered by the chronicle, there are far fewer of them after 1397—surely a sign of more contemporaneous composition.[46] Yet his account of the 1397 parliament cannot have been written before October 1399, for that is when the details of the duke of Gloucester's murder were made public. Nevertheless, it was from 1397 onwards that he endeavoured to maintain a consecutive record of events. What came before 1397—the annals from 1364 to 1396—was presumably compiled to provide an impression of continuity, to fill in the three decades between the moment when the *Eulogium* came to an end and the chronicler's real story began. Much of this backstory is notable only for its brevity and was presumably taken from whatever materials came to hand. (It also includes some egregious errors, such as the belief that the earl of Hereford was hanged secretly on the orders of Edward III in 1373.) For the most part, it is of little value to the historian, although embedded in the dross are a number of high-quality nuggets which the author must have got hold of through his knowledge of or contacts within the university of Oxford, the Franciscan order, or other ecclesiastical sources. It is hard to believe that he could not have discovered more about the years 1391–5 had he wished to (that is, in fact, the impression he

---

[45] For 'The Manner of King Richard's Renunciation', see *CR*, pp. 162–7.

[46] A number of other passages also suggest contemporaneous composition. For example, his description *sub anno* 1404 of the bishops involved in various royal marriages over the previous few years: William Wykeham, he declared, 'was still alive' at the time of Blanche of Lancaster's wedding, and thus still bishop of Winchester, while Henry Beaufort, who replaced Wykeham in 1404, was 'then bishop of Lincoln'; Richard Clifford, however, he described without qualification as bishop of Worcester. Since Clifford was translated to London in October 1407, this entry was probably written between 1404 and 1407. (The author of the *English Chronicle* (*An English Chronicle 1377–1461*, ed. W. Marx (Woodbridge, 2003), p. 34), writing later, incorrectly called him 'then bishop of London'). Similarly, in his account of the 1406 parliament, the *Continuatio* states that the commons refused to grant taxation to the king ('and thus matters remained undecided that year'), but a little later (presumably following the third session of the parliament) notes that a fifteenth was granted.

conveys) but perhaps laziness or impatience got the better of him, or perhaps he felt that, following the first great crisis of Richard II's reign, that of 1386–9, it would make more sense to move directly on to the second. Once he began writing, however, the great events that shook England between 1397 and 1405 (and then Europe for the next few years) clearly fired his imagination. It is above all for its well-informed and original narrative of English events on either side of the revolution of 1399 that the *Continuatio* has been most valued.[47] There are still, undoubtedly, too many errors of dating in the annals from 1397 to 1413 to indicate that it was written on an annual basis,[48] but it is well within the bounds of possibility that the majority of it was composed within a year or two of the events described, with a few additions being interpolated shortly after 1413—such as the alleged fact, *sub anno* 1405, that it was leprosy that later killed Henry IV (in 1413), or that the 1409 Council of Pisa was later continued at Constance (in 1414). Moreover, as more information about the earlier years (either written or oral) became apparent, the chronicler occasionally added notes to what he had already written (such as the burning of Wyclif's remains) or inserted items that now revealed themselves as being of greater significance (for example, perhaps, the prophecy of the king of Spain's brother about the ending of the Schism). When it was copied into Cotton MS Galba E VII, these interlineations or marginalia would simply have been incorporated in the text. It is, at any rate, not easy to find an alternative explanation for the process by which this rather puzzling chronicle was concocted.

Yet, puzzling as it is, the *Continuatio* is not simply a patchwork. There is a unifying style and tone, a consistent authorial voice strongly suggestive of a single guiding hand behind the assemblage of information it presents—the voice, presumably, of the Canterbury grey friar. Brisk, chatty, and impatient, he was a man who preferred allusion to explanation and seldom used three words when one would suffice. Homilies, exempla, and addresses to the reader are entirely absent. Prophecies are mentioned, but only in passing, and a number of portents and prodigies are recorded, but the only one to which he seemed to attach much significance was the 'extraordinary portent' that

---

[47] These were the annals that chroniclers later in the 15th c. chose to copy into their narratives, while Leland copied hardly anything before 1397 and nothing after 1405 (below, pp. xlix–li; *Johannis Lelandi Collectanea*, i (ii), pp. 308–14).

[48] Especially odd is the repetition, *sub anno* 1404, of the visit to England of the Byzantine emperor, which had already been noted under its correct year, 1401 (as the chronicler himself was aware). But even in 1411–12, the dispatch of the duke of Clarence to France is repeated under two consecutive years, 1412 (the correct date) and 1413.

accompanied the birth of Edmund Mortimer. Apart from this, the closest he came to trying to explain the meaning of portents was to say that the comet seen above the decapitated head of Hotspur after the battle of Shrewsbury 'foreshadowed grim events', or that the 'large fish of unknown species' caught in the Thames in 1411 'seemed to foretell something new'. He makes no pretence at having inside knowledge, no attempt to gild his prose, and wears his learning lightly (although quoting not infrequently from the Scriptures, he does not advertise the fact). His dry sense of humour surfaces regularly: for example, when the spokesman for the bishop of London remarked sarcastically to a mystified crowd at St Paul's Cross that 'It is extraordinary that you, who hear so many sermons here, are incapable of understanding what is being said'; or when the crowd of rebels at Smithfield believed that the king was knighting Wat Tyler, when in reality he was being struck down; or when the bishop of Norwich's army was afflicted with dysentery in Flanders in 1383, at which the chronicler exulted that 'God smote them in the posterior'. Although he certainly had an eye for human foible, the chronicler was not usually openly judgemental, but in the case of the Flemish Crusade he was unable to restrain himself: 'Blessed be God who confounds the presumptuous!', he expostulated, as the bishop's army limped home, 'flowing with blood and infecting the country.' Another who aroused unconcealed ire in him was Duke Louis of Orléans, 'an exceedingly arrogant and evil man', who 'was greatly hated in France' (and, he might have added, in England). Yet even his obituary for Richard II, whom he evidently regarded as his own worst enemy, reads more like a cry of exasperation than an outpouring of the sort of hatred he felt for Orléans, and although he did not have a very high opinion of the popes of his age (Alexander V excepted), he does not openly criticize them. His hostility towards the 1381 rebels and the Lollards is also a good deal less virulent than that of most of the other chroniclers of the time.[49] The abiding impression of the author is of a sceptical, practical, no-nonsense man, a man who simply wanted to get on with the story he had to tell.

Yet if gilded prose is eschewed, much of the *Continuatio* is written in a colourful and anecdotal style. Even the most momentous of events are sometimes introduced as if the author was about to tell a bar-stool tale. His account of the great revolt of 1381, for example, begins, 'In this year two esquires sitting in a certain tavern in London said...',

---

[49] Taylor, surveying the sources for the great revolt of 1381, described the *Continuatio*'s account as 'clear and interesting' (*English Historical Literature in the Fourteenth Century*, p. 322).

while his version of the unmasking of the Epiphany rising in 1400 opens: 'Meanwhile, a member of the king's household lay one night with a London prostitute.' Was this the habitual technique of a friar accustomed to preaching as a way of life? He certainly knew how to enliven his narrative with touches of melodrama, such as Henry IV drawing a dagger on Hotspur shortly before the battle of Shrewsbury (to which Hotspur responded, 'Not here, but on the battlefield'), or the 'revolting spider' that crawled across John Badby's lips as he denied the Eucharistic miracle, or the Black Prince's contemptuous 'You ass' to Archbishop Whittlesey, who (not by coincidence) had just delivered himself of a jibe against the fraternal orders. He also makes extensive use of direct or reported speech, indeed his ability to convey the essentials of a debate through quick-fire verbal exchanges is at times masterly. The most striking example is to be found in his account of Henry IV's interrogation of the rebellious friars in 1402, but it was also his habitual way of characterizing debates in parliament. 'Kings are not accustomed to giving account', retorted Henry curtly when the commons asked him in the parliament of 1406 to keep his promise to make available for audit the accounts of the taxes granted in the previous assembly. The one-liners the author ascribes to the commons in 1401 and 1404—that 'they cared naught for barefooted buffoons' (the Welsh), or that the wars the king was obliged to fight on all fronts 'do not trouble England greatly'—encapsulate admirably the myopically Anglocentric stance of the knights and burgesses in the early fifteenth century, while Henry's blunt 'You have money. I want money. Where is it?' to the wool merchants in 1407 provides a fitting epitaph to the king's ceaseless financial woes. From the earl of Kent threatening to 'shave off' Henry IV's crown in 1400, to the councillors who enriched themselves by 'sucking out of him the goods ordained for the common profit' in 1405, the *Continuatio* abounds with picturesque and quotable turns of phrase and, regardless of whether or not these really were the *ipsissima verba* of those into whose mouths the chronicler put them, it has, not surprisingly, been much quoted in histories of the period.

THE VALUE OF THE *CONTINUATIO*

The *Continuatio* is one of a dozen or so major narrative sources for the reigns of Richard II and Henry IV. The scope of its coverage clearly does not match that of the monastic-based chronicles of Thomas Walsingham for the period as a whole, or of the monk of Westminster and Henry Knighton for the reign of Richard II, but its independent

viewpoint and range of unfamiliar sources place it squarely in the second rank, comparable in the originality of its material to the chronicle of a secular clerk such as Adam Usk. Its importance lies primarily in four areas: first and most importantly, the fact that it includes much that is not found in any other primary source; secondly, the original and often colourful detail that it adds to information noted elsewhere; thirdly, its distinctive slant on the rule of Richard II and Henry IV; and fourthly, its integration of common themes in political and ecclesiastical history. These will be discussed in turn.

The passages which are wholly original to the *Continuatio* are the following: (1) the Westminster council of 1373; (2) the proclamation of the earl of March as Richard II's heir in 1385/6; (3) John of Gaunt's request to the parliament of (probably) 1394 that his son rather than March be recognized as Richard's heir, and the subsequent debate; (4) Archbishop Arundel's two harangues against Richard II in 1397 and 1399; (5) the description of the enthroned Richard in his chamber obliging his courtiers to kneel to him; (6) the story of the prostitute who helped to reveal the Epiphany rising in January 1400; (7) most of the details surrounding the trials and executions of the Franciscans who opposed Henry in 1402; (8) the dispute within the Franciscan order in 1404–5; (9) the request for Thomas of Clarence to go to Rome to lead the papal army in 1412; and (10) the natural disasters which struck a number of churches in 1413.

In addition to this unique information, there are numerous places where the chronicler adds significant detail, some of it seemingly derived from eyewitnesses, to known accounts of events described in other sources. The most notable of these (in the order given by the chronicler) are: the dispute concerning the papal interdict on the Florentines; Cardinal Langham's doffing of his hat to Edward III; the death of Robert Hauley in Westminster abbey; the 1381 revolt, especially the events leading up to the death of Wat Tyler, which is presented as more planned than accidental; preparations to resist the proposed Franco-Scottish invasion of 1386; the battle of Radcot Bridge; the decision by Gloucester, Arundel, and Warwick in 1388 never to enter Richard II's presence together in the future; the interview between Richard II and the Londoners in 1392; John of Gaunt's peace proposals in the parliament of 1394; the arrest of the earl of Arundel in 1397, especially the part played by his brother; Justice Rickhill's precautions when presenting Gloucester's confession to the king; the earl of Arundel's trial; the intrusion of Roger Walden to the see of Canterbury; the dispute between the dukes of Hereford and

THE VALUE OF THE *CONTINUATIO* xxxix

Norfolk (he is the only English chronicler to note, almost certainly correctly, that Hereford publicly accused Norfolk of Gloucester's murder); the words of the 'northern hermit' to Archbishop Walden; the fates suffered by the conspirators following the failure of the Epiphany rising; the bishop of St Asaph's (alleged) warning to the parliament of 1401 concerning the Welsh rebellion, and parliament's response; Henry IV's treatment of the friars of Llanfaes in 1401; the debates on taxation in the parliaments of 1402, January 1404, and 1406; the conversations between the king and the Percys preceding the battle of Shrewsbury; the portent accompanying the birth of Edmund Mortimer; Glyndwr's treatment of the friars at Cardiff; William Serle's theft of Richard II's signet; the arrest, condemnation, and death of Scrope and Mowbray in 1405 (which also appears to have made use of one of the hagiographical accounts of Scrope's death); the capture of Berwick in the same year; the mutiny of the Calais garrison in 1407; Cardinal Ugguccione's doffing of his hat to the king at the council held in October 1408; the floods of 1408; the holding of processions in England to celebrate the election of Pope Alexander V in 1409; the new pope's retort to a friar who sought an Irish bishopric; the trial of John Badby; and the destruction of the duke of Burgundy's 'very large castle of wood' in the spring of 1410.

Turning now to the chronicler's attitude towards the kings who bestride his history, it is clear that the hinge upon which the *Continuatio* as a whole turns is the change of regime in 1399. More than 40 per cent of a chronicle covering fifty years is devoted to the eight years either side of the revolution (1397–1405). Edward III is a shadowy figure, and although one or two lively incidents are recorded from the latter part of his reign, it is his family or ministers rather than the king himself who act on his behalf. Of Edward himself, little is heard and almost nothing discerned, although there are revealing insights into the masterfulness of the Black Prince and plenty of evidence for the power of kingship, albeit mediated.

With Richard II and Henry IV, the unmediated power of kings takes centre stage. The fact that the chronicler only began writing after 1399 naturally colours his portrayal of Richard, and if, as seems likely, his chief source of information about the king was Thomas Arundel, that too must have influenced his impressions. He is at any rate unlikely to have had much personal knowledge of the king, although he may well have seen Richard when he visited Canterbury. Nevertheless, he presents a coherent portrait of the king. That Richard strove to exercise his powers to the full, the chronicler had no doubt, but it was above all his

vainglory that he stressed. This is most memorably demonstrated in the much-quoted passage from 1398 describing the king, bedecked in his regalia, sitting on his throne in his chamber on feast days, 'talking to no one but watching everyone; and when his eye fell on anyone, regardless of their rank, that person had to kneel'. It has been suggested that this is a later interpolation,[50] but it is in keeping with the view presented throughout by the chronicler. 'Richard', he concluded, following his account of the king's deposition,

strove to outdo all his predecessors in riches and to rival the glory of Solomon.... In treasure and jewels, in kingly robes and adornments, which he accumulated inordinately, in the splendour of his table, in the palaces that he built, no one in [the Books of] Kings was more glorious in his time than he.

The denunciations of Richard's behaviour which the chronicler put into the mouth of Archbishop Arundel, and with which he clearly sympathized, endorsed this view: about to go into exile in the autumn of 1397, Arundel 'delivered a lengthy sermon concerning the extravagance which reigned among those about [Richard], and the rapacity and arrogance of the court, through which they corrupted the whole realm'.[51] Two years later, addressing the captive king in North Wales, Arundel was equally forthright:

You did not rule your kingdom but despoiled it, imposing great tolls, extorting taxes annually, not for the benefit of the kingdom, which you never cared about, but to satisfy your own greed and flaunt your vainglory.... You lived a life of debauchery, and by your foul example you besmirched your court and the kingdom.

Richard's penchant for extravagant display is also apparent in a number of other passages: for example, when he wore his crown and regalia while dining with the Franciscans at Salisbury in 1393; when he reentered London 'like an angel of God' following his quarrel with the city in the same year; the 'pomp and glory... much solemnity and great expense' involved in the welcome extended to his new queen, the 7-year-old Isabella, in 1396; his 'fearsome' ride through the heart of London with (allegedly) 100,000 armed men in September 1397; and

---

[50] G. Stow, 'The continuation of the *Eulogium Historiarum*: Some revisionist perspectives', *EHR* cxix (2004), 667–81, at 681.

[51] A similar account of Richard's duplicity towards the archbishop and Arundel's plainspeaking to him can be found in the thirty-third and final deposition charge brought against the king in the 'Record and Process'; this might indicate that the chronicler had seen the latter, but if so, he evidently decided to use 'The Manner' instead (*CR*, pp. 183–4).

the lavish reception laid on by Archbishop Walden when the king and his 'great multitude of Cheshiremen' visited Canterbury early in 1399.

Like most of the contemporary chroniclers, the author of the *Continuatio* saw the poisoning of relations between the king and a powerful coterie of magnates as the central issue in the politics of Richard's reign, and he highlights two facets of the king's character which contributed to this: his duplicity and his susceptibility to flattery. This is a king who cannot be trusted to keep his word. He gives undertakings to his enemies which he has no intention of keeping, lays ambushes to ensnare them, and revokes his own pardons. Especially devious is his treatment of the Arundel brothers. Having promised on the host not to arrest the earl, he promptly does so; having promised the archbishop that he could go in peace, he proceeds to banish him— then, to compound his duplicity, he promises not to replace him but once again breaks his word. With respect to the crisis of 1386–9, the chronicler seems willing to ascribe much of Richard's perfidy to those who surrounded him, the 'toadies' and 'sycophants' upon whose advice he relied and whom the king's opponents identified as 'the enemies within'. By the late 1390s, however, it is becoming clear that it is Richard's own inclinations—his wilfulness, his insecurity, his vindictiveness, his vainglory—that underlie England's descent into tyranny.

This is not to say that the chronicler exculpates the king's opponents. Those whom the Appellants coerced parliament into condemning to a barbarous death in 1388 were, he says, accused of many things of which they were not guilty; the Appellants too acted above the law, introducing unheard-of procedures, denying their victims the means to defend themselves, condemning Simon Burley (that 'worthy knight of the Garter') to death, and exacting unprecedented oaths from the populace to endorse their ascendancy. This came back to haunt them: more than any other chronicler, the author of the *Continuatio* stresses the degree to which the Appellants' actions in 1388 were mimicked by Richard ten years later. Like them, he overrode the common law, exacted novel oaths, and manipulated a servile commons; as Gaunt pointed out to the earl of Arundel during his trial, it was 'according to your own law' that he was denied any right of reply, and it was upon Tower Hill, 'where Simon Burley was beheaded', that he too was condemned to lose his head.[52] Nevertheless, although the author was keenly aware of the fact that the Appellants had in many ways reaped their own whirlwind, there is no doubt that fundamentally he believed Richard to be a foolish and

---

[52] L. Duls, *Richard II in the Early Chronicles* (Paris, 1975), pp. 86–7.

dangerous king, a man largely responsible for his own downfall; and when, confronted by the final and greatest crisis of his reign, he cast around desperately for support, it simply evaporated.

Yet by 1402, less than three years into Henry IV's reign, the people of England once again 'yearned for King Richard'. Although the chronicler gives no real indication of personal hostility to Henry, he certainly did not succumb, as some of his contemporaries did, to the propaganda circulated by the new king and his supporters in the aftermath of the revolution.[53] Like Richard, Henry is also duplicitous: for example, he went back on his promise to the parliament of 1404 to allow his financial accounts to be audited. Especially revealing is his reaction to Archbishop Scrope's rising in 1405: both the arrest of Scrope and Mowbray by royal agents and the king's condemnation of them while Arundel and his familiars were dining are portrayed as deeply deceitful, as well as ruthless. That Henry had little option but to be ruthless at the outset of his reign is something that the chronicler seems to accept,[54] but following the execution of the Franciscan friars in 1402 he became less forgiving. Nevertheless, he saw a clear distinction between Henry's and Richard's kingship. Despite his draconian treatment of rebels, Henry is not shown as a tyrant. His dealings with the commons reveal, rather, a king backed into a corner by the circumstances of his accession—and it is the commons who now play the most prominent role in the chronicler's reports of parliamentary debates, rather than the magnates as in Richard's reign. Yet Henry does not react as Richard had, with threats and intimidation; however distasteful he finds the commons' responses, he continues to talk to them, and they speak frankly to him.

The *Continuatio*'s attitude towards the first Lancastrian king was in fact deeply ambivalent. At the heart of Henry's problems was, of course, the question of legitimacy, a subject which the king and his supporters went out of their way to ignore but which the chronicler does not; indeed, no other contemporary chronicler raises as many questions about Henry's claim to the throne as he does, and although the evidence is, as usual, presented without judgment, its accumulation is telling. No other chronicler reported that Richard publicly proclaimed in 1385–6 that the earl of March should succeed him, or that the rival claims of Mortimer and Lancaster were subsequently debated in parliament. His use of the 'Manner of King Richard's Renunciation'— with its emphasis on Richard's initial refusal to resign, his forced

---

[53] Cf. C. Given-Wilson, *Henry IV* (New Haven and London), pp. 401–4.
[54] For example, the executions of Richard's supporters at Bristol in 1399, or following the Epiphany rising in 1400.

abdication, and Henry's claim as the male heir rather than the heir general—presents a more ambiguous view of the usurpation than the well-oiled and much-publicized fabrications of the 'Record and Process', the official Lancastrian account of the revolution. What follows is even more damning. The dramatic account of the king's interrogation of Roger Frisby, the leader of the friars on trial for claiming that Richard II was still alive in 1402—in effect a debate on the claims made in the 'Record and Process', stripped to its essentials and driven by inescapable logic—is one of the most compelling passages in the chronicle and makes no effort to spare the king's blushes: *Henry*: 'Do you say that Richard II is alive?' *Frisby*: 'I do not say that he is alive, but I say that if he is alive he is the rightful king of England.' *Henry*: 'He resigned.' *Frisby*: 'He resigned, but unwillingly and under coercion in prison, so his resignation has no validity in law.' *Henry*: 'He resigned of his own free will.' *Frisby*: 'He would not have resigned if he had been at liberty, and a resignation made in prison is not free.' *Henry*: 'He was also deposed.' *Frisby*: 'While he was king, he was captured by force of arms, imprisoned, and deprived of his kingdom, and you usurped the throne.' *Henry*: 'I did not usurp the throne, I was properly elected.' *Frisby*: 'An election is invalid if the rightful holder is still alive. And if he is dead, he was killed by you. And if you killed him, you lose your claim and any right that you might have to the kingdom.' *Henry*: 'By this head of mine, you shall lose your head.'

If the practical outcome of this was that the king 'won'—for Frisby did indeed lose his head—the moral victory lay with the friar, a man who, along with several of his fellows, was courageous enough to speak truth to power, while Henry, confronted with the undeniable truth, could only respond by summarily ordering his dispatch.[55] Later in the *Continuatio* the point is repeated. 'You are not the heir to the kingdom', says Hotspur before the battle of Shrewsbury, to which Henry replies once again that 'he had been elected as king by the kingdom'. Yet the 'true heirs', declared the chronicler in 1405, were generally believed to be the sons of the earl of March, since they were descended from 'the nearest line of descent', Lionel of Clarence; and, much as he disliked the duke of Orléans, he does not hesitate to repeat the latter's scornful retort to Henry in 1402: 'I do not acknowledge in you that [royal] status

---

[55] The author of *Mum and the Sothsegger* (c.1405), the underpinning theme of which was the poet's search for a truth-teller (*sothsegger*) bold enough to speak candidly to Henry, since all about him were in thrall to weak-willed sycophancy (*Mum*), took Frisby and his fellows as one of his points of reference: Given-Wilson, *Henry IV*, pp. 402–3; more generally, see J. Nuttall, *The Creation of Lancastrian Kingship* (Cambridge, 2007).

which you unjustly usurped, so it is perfectly appropriate for you to fight with me, just as you murdered the king, your cousin.'

Henry's insistence on election as the cornerstone of his claim to legitimacy (that, at least, is how his justification is presented in the *Continuatio*) is refracted through the chronicler's integration of political and ecclesiastical disputes involving questions of electoral legitimacy, especially his various references to the Great Schism. Urban VI, claimed the contumacious cardinals in 1378, 'had not been freely elected', since they had been pressurized by the Roman mob; they had only elected him 'in the hope that, once the opportunity arose, they would quash that election'. 'Learned men', however (with whom the chronicler appears to agree), said that it was a perfectly legitimate tactic to exert pressure on electors, and that once the result of an election had been declared and accepted, it could not be overturned. Thirty years later, however, it is with the cardinals who abandoned the 'perjurer' Gregory XII that the chronicler appears to sympathize (not least, perhaps, because it resulted in a Franciscan being elected pope, an election which he presents almost as a model of its kind). Debate on the rights and wrongs of overthrowing a legitimate ruler was a longstanding topic, but the Schism, allied to the deposition of both a Holy Roman Emperor (Wenzel) and an English king within a year of each other, made it one with particular relevance in the late fourteenth and early fifteenth centuries, and it is not surprising that it is one of the leitmotifs of the *Continuatio*, providing a touchstone for the strife that continued to swirl around the 1399 revolution. For Henry IV, to be sure, it was a dilemma from which there was no escape, and the fact that he himself was—according to Archbishop Scrope's 1405 manifesto—no respecter of parliamentary elections did nothing to enhance his moral authority.

It is through this exploration of similar themes, rather than any attempt at direct comparisons, that the chronicler reconciles the lessons of political and ecclesiastical history. His juxtaposition of material is abrupt, discontinuous; he does not so much meld as simply weld his topics together. Yet what is brought to bear throughout the chronicle, and what helps to assimilate the variegated strands of this disjointed text, is the legally informed viewpoint that no power below God, however great, was above the law. The law was scrupulous, an ineradicable point of reference. This constitutionalist mindset is manifested in his constant reference to deliberative assemblies of all kinds: conclaves, chapters, convocations, church councils, great councils, privy councils, university councils, and above all parliaments. Between 1378 and 1388, and then again after 1394, every parliament held in England except one

(1407) finds a place in the *Continuatio*, the rhythm of the almost annual meetings punctuating the narrative with much the same predictability as the *anno Domini* openings to each year. For this chronicler, as for some others, parliament has become the place where the great business of the realm is transacted,[56] and attacks on its constitutional integrity, such as the Questions to the Judges of 1387 or Richard II's establishment of a parliamentary committee ten years later—to say nothing of his intimidation of lords and commons in both the 1397–8 sessions—are seen as attacks on fundamental liberties. After 1399 the focus in parliaments shifts to the commons rather than the lords, yet the adversarial tone of these assemblies is evidently seen by the chronicler as a sign that parliament is doing its job. On the other hand, Henry is certainly not blameless: he manipulates elections, excludes lawyers, and is shifty about financial affairs, although this pales into insignificance compared to his greatest crime, the execution of Archbishop Scrope. There was no doubt in the chronicler's mind that rulers who abused their prerogatives in such fashion would not escape their fate. For Richard II, this took the form of popular retribution. For Henry, it was divine justice, in the form of leprosy, that struck him down; or so, at any rate, our chronicler believed. Appropriately, it is with a demonstration of Scrope's miraculous power, rather than the death of the king, that the *Continuatio* ends.

The *Continuatio* is also of some value for European history, although it added nothing to what was already well known from fuller narratives of the time. Events such as the Castilian civil war of the 1360s, the Flemish civic rebellions of the early 1380s, Gaunt's Iberian campaigns of 1386–8, and the intermittent negotiations and hostilities with France are seen from an exclusively English point of view. The death of Urban V in 1370 is made the subject of an amusing anti-papal anecdote, seen in retrospect almost as a prelude to the outbreak of the Schism eight years later. After 1407, however, the chronicler's interest in Continental affairs deepened. The assassination of Louis of Orléans, an event which shocked all of Europe, is given the prominence it deserved, primarily because it proved—again in retrospect—to be the catalyst for renewed English intervention in France, in the form of Arundel's and Clarence's expeditions of 1411–13. Generally speaking, the chronicler's coverage of the years 1408–13 alternates between domestic affairs, the French civil war, and the efforts of kings and cardinals to resolve the Schism, which entailed both conciliar pressure and military offensives in the

---

[56] Given-Wilson, *Chronicles*, pp. 174–9; Taylor, *English Historical Literature in the Fourteenth Century*, pp. 195–216.

Italian peninsula. In this respect, the *Continuatio* mirrors closely the subject matter of the St Albans chronicle, providing further evidence of renewed English interest, after a decade of introspection, in the deepening tremors that now threatened to shake western Europe apart.[57]

TEXTS RELATED TO THE *CONTINUATIO*

Although it is only Cotton MS Galba E VII that contains the full text of the *Continuatio*, two further fifteenth-century manuscripts are closely related to it: British Library Additional MS 11714, and National Library of Wales, Aberystwyth, MS 21608. The former is often referred to as the *Southern Chronicle*.[58] It is a very brief universal chronicle, neatly presented in double columns of forty-six lines separated by a red strip. Genealogical roundels and blue initials with delicate red edging mark the beginnings of reigns. The hand is of the first half of the fifteenth century. It is a manuscript of fifteen folios, four of which (10^v to 13^v) cover the reigns of Edward III, Richard II, Henry IV, and Henry V; they are entirely free of interlineations and erasures. It is a clean and attractive manuscript.[59]

Between the mid-1360s and 1402, the *Southern Chronicle* is manifestly based either upon the *Continuatio* directly or upon a common original.[60] Although it is much shorter than the *Continuatio* and omits a great deal that is mentioned by the latter, and although the process of abridgement inevitably led the author to use different phraseology at times, in those passages where the same topics are covered the consistent agreement between the language used in each is unmistakable. However, if most of the *Southern Chronicle* up to 1402 reads like an abridgement of the longer chronicle, some passages reveal independent knowledge or opinions. The most noteworthy of these are the fact that the English and the men of Ghent destroyed a dyke in Flanders in order to divert the attentions of the French invasion force in 1385; the characterization of Anne of Bohemia as 'the best' of queens; and some

---

[57] *SAC* II, pp. 536–618.

[58] Kingsford printed the text for the years 1399–1422 (Kingsford, *English Historical Literature in the Fifteenth Century*, pp. 275–8). Clifford, 'An Edition', pp. 158–73, referred to it as the *Epitome* and printed the text from 1363 to 1413.

[59] Although one word has been left unfinished ('propon...' for 'proponens' on fo. 11^r) and on another occasion two words are repeated ('anno undecimo' on the top line of fo. 11^v). Fos. 14–15 provide an index.

[60] The correspondence between the *Continuatio* and the *Southern Chronicle* begins four lines from the bottom of column A of fo. 10^v, with the words 'Princeps transiuit in Aquitanniam', referring to the Black Prince's crossing in 1363.

TEXTS RELATED TO THE *CONTINUATIO*   xlvii

additional details relating to the ringleaders of the Epiphany rising in 1400.[61] From 1402 onwards, apparently wearying of his task, the author simply wrote a few sentences summarizing the rebellions of the years 1403–8 before concluding with a strikingly favourable, and apparently original, obituary for Henry IV.[62] His account of Henry V's reign is also favourable but very brief, occupying less than one folio.[63] This is unusual, for chronicles generally become fuller as they approach the time of writing, and it points to the likelihood of a later rather than an earlier time of writing—that is, several years after Henry V's death rather than shortly after it, when great events were still remembered but lesser ones had slipped beyond memory.

The *Southern Chronicle* is austerely political and military in its subject matter, indicating that the author made a deliberate decision to omit almost all the material relating to ecclesiastical affairs which is such a prominent feature of the *Continuatio*. Church councils, the controversies over Wyclif, and the Schism (both its beginning and its ending) are entirely absent; the word 'friar' does not appear. One brief paragraph, employing the same language as the *Continuatio*, relates the accession of Boniface IX and the Provisors legislation in 1389–90,[64]

---

[61] 'Interim Gandauenses et Anglici litus artificiale Flandrie fregerunt, totam patriam submergere intentes, ad quod malum repellendum unus exercitus Gallie occupatus, in Angliam non uenit, et sic tercius exercitus etiam remansit' (fo. 11ʳ). 'Mortua Anna optima regina' (fo. 12ʳ). For the Epiphany rising, the *Southern Chronicle* notes that the earl of Huntingdon took money with him when he fled to Essex, hoping to escape abroad, but the countess of Hereford (Henry IV's mother-in-law) ensured that he was beheaded; that the number of conspirators executed at Oxford was twenty-six; and that William Ferriby, dean of York, and a chaplain of King Richard (Richard Maudeleyn, though his name is not given here) were two of the ecclesiastics executed in London (fo. 13ʳ).

[62] 'Iste Henricus quartus, non obstante quod taxas et tallagia omni tempore regni sui exegit a communitate, tamen semper amantissi[m]us communitati fuit. Fuit etiam multum liberalis erga extraneos, in se uero multum probus, et in iuuentute sua rebus militaribus multum exercitatus; in ecclesiasticos in principio regni sui multum austerus, tandem in fine penitens satis fuit eis beniuolens. In fine quoque uite sue infirmitate lepre grauissime percussus, grauissima morte uitam finiuit quartodecimo anno regni sui, et Cantuarie in ecclesia Sancte Trinitatis sepelitur' (fo. 13ʳ).

[63] It begins five lines from the bottom of fo. 13ʳ and ends with fourteen lines of fo. 13ᵛ to spare. It emphasizes his reformed character once he became king, but then simply rehearses the major military events of his reign (Harfleur, Agincourt, the visit of Emperor Sigismund, the conquest of Normandy, the Treaty of Troyes, Clarence's death at Baugé), ending with his reformation of the coinage and the arrangements he made for the governance of England and Normandy during the minority of his baby son. A roundel then announces the beginning of the reign of 'Henricus VI rex Anglie', but no further text follows.

[64] It is, however, worth noting that the *Southern Chronicle* adds the words 'alioquin illud reassument' to the injunction that ecclesiastics should confer benefices according to the wishes of lay patrons, thereby strengthening the extent of lay resolve behind the statute ('otherwise they would take it back'—that is, the right to present) (fo. 11ᵛ).

but the accounts of the Flemish crusade and the burning of William Sawtre are seen in a political rather than a religious context, while Archbishop Scrope's power as a miracle-worker is only noted as being 'according to popular opinion' ('secundum famam uulgi'). Although the author apparently approved of Henry IV's generosity towards churchmen in his later years,[65] the chronicle as a whole displays little interest in or sympathy with ecclesiastical concerns.

Kingsford believed that the *Southern Chronicle* was written 'perhaps not later than 1426', since its concluding sentence mentions the duke of Exeter (Thomas Beaufort) and the bishop of Winchester (Henry Beaufort), but does not note either the death of the former or the latter's creation as a cardinal, both of which occurred in 1426.[66] This argument is hard to sustain: there is no good reason, in the context of the passage (the arrangements made by Henry V for his son's minority), why the chronicler should have mentioned these facts; nevertheless, Kingsford's argument has helped to confuse discussion of the relationship between the *Southern Chronicle* and the *Continuatio*,[67] the salient points of which are really as follows. That the *Southern Chronicle* was written after 1422 is self-evident, but it could have been written ten or twenty years later. That it is closely related to the *Continuatio* is also self-evident, but its inclusion of material not found in the latter makes it unlikely that it was based directly on the *Continuatio*. The fact that the *Southern Chronicle* continues to 1422, whereas the *Continuatio* does not, makes it equally unlikely that the longer text was an expansion of the former—that is, that the *Southern Chronicle* (or the lost original from which it was derived) was used by the author of the *Continuatio* as his base text, or framework, to which he added (a great deal of) additional material.[68] It is surely unlikely that, had the *Continuatio* been based on the *Southern Chronicle*, it would have omitted any mention of the morale-boosting events of Henry V's reign, from which English chroniclers derived so much satisfaction. In summary, the most plausible explanation of the relationship between the two chronicles is that they both made some use of a common original, the precise content of which is impossible to determine, although it must have provided at the very least an outline of English political history from the 1360s to the death of Henry IV, and it probably included much more than this.

[65] As mentioned in his obituary for Henry (above, n. 62).
[66] Kingsford, *English Historical Literature in the Fifteenth Century*, p. 275.
[67] Clifford, 'An Edition', pp. 39–40, and Stow, 'The continuation of the *Eulogium Historiarum*', p. 680, both accept Kingsford's *terminus ante quem* of 1426.
[68] Cf. Stow, 'The continuation of the *Eulogium Historiarum*', pp. 676–8.

TEXTS RELATED TO THE *CONTINUATIO*   xlix

The *Southern Chronicle*, like the *Continuatio*, is written in Latin. National Library of Wales, Aberystwyth, MS 21608 contains a Middle English chronicle which is also closely related to the *Continuatio*. Another copy of this Middle English chronicle (although it is incomplete and partially damaged) is to be found in Bodleian Library, Oxford, MS Lyell 34, from which it was first edited by John Davies in 1855–6, as a result of which it was for long known as *Davies' Chronicle*.[69] However, it has recently been re-edited by William Marx from the Aberystwyth manuscript, which is both fuller and undamaged for the reigns of Richard II and Henry IV, under the title *An English Chronicle*.[70] The *English Chronicle* covers the years 1377–1461 and is a continuation of the Middle English prose *Brut*, which by the mid-fourteenth century had established itself as the most popular account of England's history from the time of Brutus, legendary founder of Albion. It was apparently written in two parts. The section covering the years 1377–1437 was probably composed around 1438–40; this is followed by a gap of three years, and the further continuation from 1440 to 1461 was written in the 1460s. Thus, for that portion of the text which is relevant to this discussion, we are dealing with a chronicle written in the late 1430s, although since the entire text from 1377 to 1461 is written in one hand, apparently of the last quarter of the fifteenth century, it was evidently not until later that it was copied into NLW MS 21608.[71]

The compiler of the *English Chronicle*, who may well also have been its translator into Middle English, drew his material from two texts—the *Continuatio* and an existing continuation of the *Brut*—which he interwove to create his own narrative.[72] Broadly speaking, he used the *Brut* as the framework for his narrative (for example, to introduce or conclude events, or to provide chronological guidance), but then frequently switched to the livelier and fuller accounts in the *Continuatio* to flesh out episodes. Sometimes he simply copied out (and translated) material from the *Continuatio*, but at other times he added or corrected little points of detail.[73] His selection of material suggests that he was a

---

[69] *An English Chronicle of the Reigns of Richard II, Henry IV, Henry V and Henry VI*, ed. J. S. Davies (Camden Society First Series, lxiv; London, 1855–6).
[70] *An English Chronicle 1377–1461*, ed. Marx. For the manuscript and its dating, see pp. xi–xxii. The hand is 'of the fourth quarter of the fifteenth century' (p. xvi).
[71] Only one piece of internal evidence corroborates this, the description of Humphrey 'that was duke of Gloucester'; Humphrey died in 1447 (*English Chronicle*, ed. Marx, p. 41).
[72] This process of integration by the compiler is discussed in meticulous detail by Marx, *English Chronicle*, pp. xxix–lv.
[73] For example, the involvement of William Latimer and Robert Ferrers in the Hauley-Shakell case, or the fact that Richard II surrendered at Flint, not Conwy (although plenty of

compiler with a sense of purpose: especially noticeable are his omission of much of the ecclesiastical, parliamentary, and legal material to be found in the *Continuatio* (the controversies over Wyclif, the Schism, the Questions to the Judges, and much else), and his introduction, from the *Brut*, of chivalric material: thus he provided several reports of jousts held in London, giving his chronicle something of that feel of a court journal which was characteristic of *Brut* chronicles. The author of the *Continuatio* showed little interest in jousts.

Between 1397 and 1405, the compiler of the *English Chronicle* relied almost entirely on the *Continuatio*. This was to have a significant influence on English historiography, for it meant that the version of the national story as it was told in the *Continuatio* merged with the *Brut* tradition and, through the Middle English of the latter, reached a much wider audience than it would have had it remained half-forgotten in the single surviving manuscript containing the Latin continuation of a rather obscure universal chronicle. In its broad outlines, there was nothing exceptional about the *Continuatio*'s version of that story—namely, that Henry IV was a man who came in a just and popular cause, but who soon found the weight of usurpation and questionable legitimacy to be too heavy to allow the establishment of strong and stable rule—but the supporting evidence, especially that relating to greater and lesser churchmen, added both detail and nuance, modifying the dominant crown–magnate narrative. The prominence of Archbishop Arundel is central in this respect, not only in the revolution and deposition proceedings of 1399, when he acted both as the avenger of his cruelly mistreated brother (thereby providing a subsidiary wheel of fortune motif to parallel that of Henry and Richard) and as the guardian of the royal conscience—the king's 'spiritual father', as he pointed out to Henry in 1405, just at the moment when he was once again about to be betrayed, this time by the man whom he had been instrumental in putting on the throne. Also central is the account of the Franciscan trials of 1402, lifted almost wholesale from the *Continuatio*, in which lowly but learned men are deployed to highlight both the range and the indefeasible logic of the opposition to the king. The deeply sympathetic account of Archbishop Scrope's rising, which is portrayed as a popular and clerical as well as an aristocratic movement, and the dishonourable circumstances of his trial and execution are also designed to heighten the sense of moral outrage at Henry's

---

chroniclers confused Conwy and Flint in 1399: Taylor, *English Historical Literature in the Fourteenth Century*, p. 189).

conduct. Unlike the *Southern Chronicle*, the *English Chronicle* does not question the archbishop's power as a miracle-worker.

Yet it was not just for its account of the years 1397–1405 that the influence of the *Continuatio* left its imprint on the *Brut* tradition. Its generally moderate tone towards both Lollards and the 1381 rebels also found its way into later continuations of the *Brut*, thereby nuancing the attitudes of later generations of commentators, up to and including the present. Following Scrope's rising, however, the author of the *English Chronicle* reverted to the *Brut* for his summary (scarcely full enough to be termed a narrative) of the last eight years of Henry IV's reign. Chivalric exploits are his dominant theme for the years 1407–11, although for the last two years of the reign he once again quarried the *Continuatio* for material relating to the English expeditions to France of 1411 and 1412, and for Prince Henry's attempt to persuade his father to abdicate. As this demonstrates, he must have been aware of the *Continuatio*'s account of the years 1406–13,[74] but chose to deviate from its focus on papal history, which he evidently deemed to be peripheral to the national story that *Brut* chronicles traditionally told.

To summarize, the incorporation of the *Continuatio* into popular English historiography via the *English Chronicle* had the effect of bringing to the attention of a much wider audience the fact that history was more complex than the habitually patriotic and patrician narrative of the *Brut*; and it was, in large part, through the introduction of more ecclesiastical history into the predominantly secular *Brut* tradition that this was achieved. Although manifestly critical of Richard II's rule, the *English Chronicle* is far from being an unalloyed piece of Lancastrian propaganda. Rather, it marks an early stage—at a time when the Lancastrian dynasty still occupied the throne—in the synthesis of often polarized viewpoints on the significance of the events surrounding the great upheaval of 1399. To describe it as history 'from below' would be an overstatement, but its discreetly subversive viewpoint was a good deal less elevated than most of the chronicles of the time, and it was the author's use of the *Continuatio* that provided this perspective.

EDITORIAL CONVENTIONS AND ORTHOGRAPHY

Standard contractions and suspensions in the manuscript are expanded silently, as are abbreviated place names (for example, 'Cantuarie' for 'Cant'). In his Rolls Series edition, Haydon employed the classical

---

[74] Rather than using a common source that ended in 1405, as suggested by Kingsford.

diphthongs -oe and -ae throughout, but the scribe's preference is always for simple -e (for example, 'federati', not 'foederati'; 'hec', not 'haec'; and the genitive -e rather than -ae), and the original orthography of the manuscript has been retained here.

Contemporary marginals which seem to have been intended to act as headings have been treated as paragraph rubrics, inserted in italics in both the text and the translation. This includes all the dates in Arabic numerals marking the start of each new year. Marginals which are not contemporary, or which simply read 'nota' or repeat a word or phrase for emphasis, have been relegated to the footnotes in the *apparatus criticus*.

Where the scribe used feast-days of saints to indicate dates (as he usually did), these have been supplemented in the translation with day and month dates in the modern fashion, in square brackets. (But note that when the scribe wrote, for example, 'on the vigil of the feast of St John the Baptist', the date supplied in brackets is that of the feast itself (24 June, in this case), rather than the vigil (23 June).) It is also worth noting that, as far as can be gathered, the scribe reckoned 25 March as the beginning of each new year, although this is not consistently applied. Where English place names are mentioned, the county in which the place was located is also inserted in square brackets.

Manifest scribal or copyist's errors have been corrected, with a note in the *apparatus criticus* (for example, 'eos' for 'suos', 'per notam' for 'priuatam'). Yet there are a number of cases which indicate the scribe's orthographical preferences rather than errors. These have been corrected silently in the text to the accepted modern spelling, but are noted below:

(a) One consonant instead of two: *coligere* for *colligere*; *quatuor* for *quattuor*; *litera* for *littera*
(b) Verb endings: *transiuit* for *transiit*; *sciuit* for *sciit*; *exiuit* for *exiit*
(c) Two consonants instead of one: *sepellitur* for *sepelitur*
(d) 'h' omitted or inserted: *ortans* for *hortans*; *exortans* for *exhortans*; *orribiliter* for *horribiliter*; *ebdomada* for *hebdomada*; *herroneum* for *erroneum*; *archuum* for *arcuum*; *habundans* for *abundans*; *hostium* for *ostium*; *rethe* for *rete*; *caracter* for *character*; *cronicis* for *chronicis*; *ypocrisie* for *hypocrisie*; *himbrium* for *imbrium*; *trono* for *throno*; *marchas* for *marcas*; *yemauit* for *hiemauit*; *sathanas* for *satanas*
(e) 'c' for 's' or vice versa: *obcessum* for *obsessum*; *discensio* for *dissensio*; *pissium* for *piscium*
(f) 'd' for 't': *todidem* for *totidem*
(g) inserted 'c' or 'p': *nichil* for *nihil*; *ympnus* for *hymnus*; *solempnis* for *sollemnis*; *dampno* for *damno*; *uerumptamen* for *uerumtamen*

(h) miscellaneous: *assoluerunt* for *absoluerunt*; *famulia* for *familia*; *simbam* for *cymbam*; *abbissi* for *abyssi*; *ritmice* for *rhythmice*; *tirannice* for *tyrannice*; *layci* for *laici*; *ydiote* for *idiote*; *optulerunt* for *obtulerunt*; *eukaristia* for *eucharistia*; *lignium* for *ligneum*; *rubiginosis* for *robiginosis*; *hiis* for *his*; *nunquam* for *numquam*.

The scribe or copyist's rendering of place names is inconsistent, sometimes even within the same sentence. Some examples follow: *Almanniam* and *Alemanniam*; *Hispania* and *Hispannia*; *Britania* and *Britannia*; *Glouernie* and *Gloucestrie*; *Hontigdon* and *Huntyngdon*; *Notingham* and *Notyngham*; *Northumbria* and *Northhumbria*.

Finally, it is worth noting that the chronicler regularly used the word 'tallagium' to describe financial exactions, but it is clear from the context that he did not mean 'tallage' in the strict sense of an arbitrary levy on demesne lands or feudal dependants, but as a generic term for taxes or subsidies; it has therefore been translated throughout as 'tax' or 'taxes'.

CONTINUATIO EULOGII

fo. 191ʳ, line 12ᵃ Rex Cipri anno Domini millesimo trecentisimo sexagesimo quarto uenit in Franciam et Angliam petens auxilium contra Sarasenos. Reges dabant sibi aurum et homines ipsum sequi uolentes, quorum auxilio postea Alexandria Egipti capta est.[1] Rex abundans auro cepit edificare castrum insigne in insula Shipey.[2] Princeps transiit in Aquitanniam ad eam custodiendam.[3]

Anno Domini millesimo trecentisimo sexagesimo quinto rex Hispanie Petrus, homo crudelissimus, quandam Iudeam desponsauit, ut dicebatur. Papa, auditis querelis, omnes a fidelitate sua absoluit et ipsum a regno deposuit et bastardum fratrem suum regem fecit; qui bastardus misit in Franciam ad Bertrandum Kleykyn, militem probum, rogans ut ueniret et Petrum fratrem suum eiicere iuuaret, qui subdole cum magna comitiua Anglicorum uenit, et Petrus eiectus est.

Anno millesimo trecentisimo sexagesimo sexto, Petrus ille depositus uenit in Vasconiam ad principem Edwardum, rogans ut auxilio suo restitueretur ad regnum, spondens aurum et duas filias suas posuit obsides.[4] Dux Clarencie, dominus Leonellus, filius regis secundus, desponsata filia sua comiti Marchie, cum comitiua decora transiit ut filiam ducis Mediolani desponsaret, et cito ibidem moriebatur.[5]

Anno millesimo trecentisimo sexagesimo septimo princeps quesiuit assensum patris, et missi sunt ad eum dominus Iohannes de Gant, tertius filius regis, qui iure filie Henrici nuper ducis Lancastrie, quam duxerat, dux Lancastrie factus fuit, et dominus Edmundus, quartus filius regis, comes Cantibrugie, cum exercitu copioso;[6] eorum adiuncta magna comitiua, pertransiit montana Hispanie et, commisso graui prelio, bastardum fugauit et populum multum interfecit, et Petrum ad tempus potenter restituit; et recepit in auro et iocalibus quadraginta milia librarum, inter que recepit pretiosum gladium Hispanie, auro et lapidibus ornatum. Dux Lancastrie duxit primogenitam dicti Petri et

---

ᵃ *marginal in later hand*: hucusque codex archiepiscopi Ardmachani

[1] Peter of Lusignan, king of Cyprus (1359–69), took the cross at Avignon with King John II of France in Mar. 1363 and arrived in England in October. He led a crusading force which sacked Alexandria in Oct. 1365 (P. Edbury, *The Kingdom of Cyprus and the Crusades* (Cambridge, 1991), pp. 164–6).

[2] Work on Queenborough Castle, Isle of Sheppey, began in May 1361; it was completed, along with its satellite town, at a cost of some £25,000, in 1369, and named after Edward III's Queen Philippa (*The History of the King's Works*, ed. H. M. Colvin, R. A. Brown, and A. J. Taylor (London, 1963), i. 236–7).

[3] Edward, the Black Prince, was made prince of Aquitaine in 1362 and arrived there in June 1363.

[4] The mistress, possibly wife, of King Pedro of Castile (1350–69) was Maria de Padilla (d. 1361). His tolerance for Jews in Castile encouraged the rumour that she was Jewish. After his

The king of Cyprus, in the year of the Lord 1364, came to France and to England seeking help against the Saracens. The kings gave him money and those men who wished to go with him, with whose help Alexandria in Egypt was subsequently captured.[1] The king, with his abundant wealth, began to build a splendid castle on the Isle of Sheppey [Kent].[2] The prince crossed to Aquitaine to undertake its keeping.[3]

In the year of the Lord 1365, it is said that Peter, king of Spain, a most cruel man, married a certain Jewess. Complaints were made to the pope, who absolved everyone from their fealty, deposed him from the kingdom, and made his bastard brother king. This bastard appealed to France, asking that worthy knight Bertrand du Guesclin to come and help him drive out his brother Peter; [du Guesclin] arrived craftily with a great retinue of Englishmen, and Peter was driven out.

In the year 1366, this Peter, having been deposed, came to Gascony to ask Prince Edward for help to restore him to his kingdom, promising him money and handing over his two daughters as pledges.[4] Lord Lionel, duke of Clarence, the second son of the king, having married his daughter to the earl of March, set off with a suitably impressive following to marry the daughter of the duke of Milan, but soon died there.[5]

In the year 1367, after the prince had obtained his father's permission, Lord John of Gaunt, the king's third son—who by right of his marriage to the daughter of Henry, former duke of Lancaster, had been made duke of Lancaster—and Lord Edmund, earl of Cambridge, the king's fourth son, were sent to him with a substantial army;[6] having joined up with their large force, [Prince Edward] crossed the mountains of Spain and, following a fierce battle, put the Bastard to flight, killing a great number of people and reinstating Peter by force for the time being; and he acquired £40,000 in money and treasure, including a precious Spanish sword decorated with gold and rich jewels. The duke of Lancaster married the first-born daughter of this Peter and his

---

bastard brother, Enrique of Trastámara, drove him into exile in early 1366, he fled to Gascony and arrived at the prince's court with his three daughters, who were subsequently handed over to the prince as hostages. In 1362 he had made the Treaty of Windsor with Edward III, and the prince agreed to help him on condition that Pedro would pay for the campaign (W. M. Ormrod, *Edward III* (New Haven and London, 2011), pp. 437–41). Bertrand du Guesclin was a Breton mercenary, later constable of France (1370–80). Among the English mercenaries accompanying him in 1365 were Hugh Calveley and Matthew Gournay.

[5] Lionel married Violante, daughter of Gian Galeazzo, duke of Milan, in May 1368, and died in Oct. 1368; his daughter, Philippa, married Edmund Mortimer, earl of March, in early 1368 (W. M. Ormrod, 'Lionel, duke of Clarence', *ODNB*, xxxiii. 950–2).

[6] John of Gaunt became duke of Lancaster, and Edmund of Langley became earl of Cambridge, in 1362.

Edmundus frater eius secundam. Petrus postea ab Hispanis captus est et frater suus bastardus guttur eius nouacula secari fecit.[7]

Anno millesimo trecentisimo sexagesimo octauo rex Francie seisiuit in manum suam comitatum Pontiuii et Abuile, hereditatem regis Anglie, et omnes Anglicos de ea eiici fecit, fractionem pacis regi Anglie imponens.[8] Dominus Willelmus Scharshille, capitalis iusticiarius regis, factus est frater minor Oxonie, et coram conuentu in presentia notariorum iurauit quod ordinem numquam exiret; et ante professionem moriebatur.[9]

Anno millesimo trecentisimo sexagesimo nono princeps, magna tallagia et seruitia exigens, ciuitates et magnates Aquitannie offendebat. Et ipse cepit dissinteria grauiter uexari. Magnates appellabant ad curiam regis Francie ab eius grauaminibus, secundum consuetudinem terre, et ciuitates se claudebant. Bertrand Klaykyn remanentes Anglicos de magna comitiua prudenter et astute eiecit, et ciuitates ac castra in Aquitannia cepit.[10] Dominus de Clisson et alii contra Iohannem ducem Britannie rebellabant.[11] Symon Langham, archiepiscopus Cantuarie, factus est cardinalis, et transiens per Parisius uersus Auinoniam frustra nititur regem Anglie excusare.[12] Eodem anno Romani miserunt ad Vrbanum papam, rogantes ut ueniret ad ecclesiam suam, dicentes quod a tempore Benedicti undecimi nullus papa ipsam uisitauit, et ideo Roma periit, ecclesia et tituli cardinalium ceciderunt. Et ipse ascendit ad Romam et post ad Auinoniam rediit.[13]

Anno millesimo trecentisimo septuagesimo princeps, erigens se ut potuit, ciuitatem Lemouicensem cepit et in Angliam rediit. Dux Britannie similiter rediit. Et eodem anno *b*rex Anglie se regem Francie scripsit.*b* [14] Vrbanus papa moritur.*c* [15] Cardinales uenerunt ad morientem

---

b-b underlined. Marginal in later hand: nota quomodo rex Anglie scribit se regem Francie
c marginal in later hand: Vrbanus papa morietur

---

[7] The battle of Nájera, in which the prince (accompanied by Gaunt and Langley) defeated Enrique and du Guesclin, was on 3 Apr. 1367. Pedro was restored to the throne, but in Mar. 1369 he was captured by Enrique and du Guesclin at the battle of Montiel and murdered. Pedro's daughters Constanza and Isabella married John of Gaunt and Edmund of Langley in Sept. 1371 and July 1372 respectively.

[8] Ponthieu and Abbeville were overrun by French forces in Apr.–May 1369 (Ormrod, *Edward III*, p. 502).

[9] Sir William Shareshull (b. 1289–90) was Chief Justice of the King's Bench 1350 to 1361; he entered the Franciscan convent at Oxford in early 1369 (with 'great honour' according to *Monumenta Franciscana*, ed. Brewer, i. 541), died while still a novice, and was buried there early in 1370 (R. W. Kaeuper, 'Shareshull, Sir William', *ODNB*, xlix. 992–3).

[10] After Pedro of Castile failed to pay the prince what he owed him for the Nájera campaign, the prince summoned the estates of Aquitaine in Jan. 1368 to grant him a five-year fouage (hearth-tax). The lords of Armagnac, Albret, and others appealed against this to Charles V of France, thereby precipitating the renewal of the Anglo-French war in 1369

brother Edmund married the second-born. Peter was later captured by Spaniards and his bastard brother slit his throat with a dagger.[7]

In the year 1368, the king of France seized into his hands the county of Ponthieu and Abbeville, the inheritance of the king of England, and he had all the English driven out of it, blaming the king of England for breaking the peace.[8] Lord William Shareshull, chief justice of the king, was made a friar minor at Oxford and swore to the convent in the presence of notaries that he would never leave the order, but he died before making profession.[9]

In the year 1369, the prince angered the towns and nobles of Aquitaine with his demands for great taxes and services; and he began to suffer severely from dysentery. The nobles appealed against his impositions to the court of the king of France, in accordance with the custom of the land, and the towns closed their gates. Bertrand du Guesclin shrewdly and craftily dismissed the remaining Englishmen from his great retinue and seized the towns and castles of Aquitaine.[10] Lord Clisson and others rose in rebellion against John, duke of Brittany.[11] Simon Langham, archbishop of Canterbury, was made a cardinal and, travelling through Paris on his way to Avignon, tried in vain to exonerate the king of England.[12] In the same year, the Romans sent to Pope Urban asking him to return to his see, declaring that since the time of Benedict XI no pope had visited it, as a result of which Rome was dying and the churches and titles of the cardinals were failing. So he journeyed to Rome, and then returned to Avignon.[13]

In the year 1370 the prince, rousing himself as far as he was able, captured the town of Limoges and returned to England. The duke of Brittany also returned. And in the same year the king of England styled himself king of France.[14] Pope Urban died.[15] The cardinals approached

---

(Ormrod, *Edward III*, pp. 498–501). After the Nájera campaign the prince's health never fully recovered.

[11] Olivier de Clisson (constable of France 1380–92) defied Duke John of Brittany over the lordship of Château Josselin in 1370, with the support of Charles V (M. Jones, *Ducal Brittany 1364–1399* (Oxford, 1970), p. 54).

[12] Simon Langham, abbot of Westminster (1349–62), chancellor of England (1363–7), archbishop of Canterbury (1366–8), was made cardinal-priest of St Sixtus by Urban V on 22 Sept. 1368. He left for Avignon on 28 Feb. 1369 and often acted as an Anglo-French intermediary during the early 1370s (W. J. Dohar, 'Langham, Simon', *ODNB*, xxxii. 482–4).

[13] Urban V (1362–70) arrived in Rome in Oct. 1367 and returned to Avignon in Sept. 1370. Benedict XI was pope in 1303–4.

[14] The Black Prince seized and sacked Limoges in Sept. 1370 and returned to England in Jan. 1371. Duke John of Brittany did not return to England until May 1373, after French troops occupied his duchy; he had made an alliance with Edward III in the autumn of 1372 (Jones, *Ducal Brittany*, pp. 62–76). Edward III resumed the title of king of France in June 1369.

[15] Urban V died at Avignon on 19 Dec. 1370.

et ipsum rogabant concedere eis plenam remissionem omnium peccatorum secundum morem predecessorum suorum in eorum transitu obseruatum. Ipse autem respondebat: 'Nos ipsi primum peccatis nostris utinam absoluti essemus. Portetis igitur uos peccata uestra, nos portabimus nostra.' Cui successit Gregorius undecimus, inter quem et Florentinos | orta est dissensio. Florentini uolebant sibi tributum soluere sed nolebant per ipsum regi. Papa uero misit bullas per mundum mandans regnis et ciuitatibus quod post publicationem earum, ubicumque essent Florentini, diriperent omnia eorum bona et debita eis non soluerent et a finibus suis arcerent sub pena interdicti post mensem. Episcopus autem Londoniensis, W[illielmus] Curtenay, publicauit bullam istam in Cruce Sancti Pauli. Maior ciuitatis statim sigillauit ostia Florentinorum et duxit eos ad regem. Quibus ait rex: 'Estis uos homines nostri?' Qui responderunt: 'Etiam sumus uestri.' 'Et nos', inquit rex, 'protegemus uos.' Episcopus Exoniensis, cancellarius Anglie, uocauit episcopum Londoniensem coram se in cancellaria querens ab eo qua temeritate ipse publicauit bullam antedictam inconsulto rege et suo concilio, contra statuta regni. Alius respondebat: 'Quia papa mandauit.' Cui cancellarius: 'Eligatis igitur uel perdere temporalia uestra uel uerba uestra proprio ore reuocare.' Qui uix obtinuit ut per alium possit reuocare. Et unus ascendit Crucem et dixit: 'Dominus meus de interdicto hic nihil locutus est. Mirum est quod nescitis intelligere loquentes qui tot sermones hic auditis.' Et tunc rex statuit in parliamento quod papa non daret ecclesias pertinentes ad laicorum patronatum.[16]

Anno Domini millesimo trecentisimo septuagesimo uno, dux Lancastrie et dux Britannie cum exercitu magno transierunt in Franciam, et uillas inuenientes muratas sine bello sine lucro redierunt. Eodem anno Flandrenses et Gallici transierunt pro sale ad Le Bay. Rex misit comitem Herfordie ad mare, qui eos occidit et naues eorum sale oneratas duxit Hamptoniam.[17]

---

[16] This story is inserted several years too early. Gregory XI was elected pope on 5 Jan. 1371, and was at war with Milan from 1371 to 1375, but not with Florence until 1375 (the 'War of the Eight Saints', 1375–8). The interdict against the Florentines was issued on 31 Mar. 1376, reached England in mid-May, and was published by Courtenay (who only became bishop of London in Sept. 1375) in early Jan. 1377. The king reacted on 30 Jan. 1377 by declaring that the Florentines could trade in England as the king's serfs, under his protection. The mayor of London in 1376–7 was the mercer Adam Stable; the chancellor was not the bishop of Exeter (Thomas Brantingham), but either Sir John Knyvet or Adam Houghton, bishop of St David's, who replaced Knyvet on 11 Jan. 1377 (J. Najemy, *A History of Florence, 1200–1575* (Oxford, 2006), pp. 151–5; *SAC* I, pp. 53, 64–8; G. Holmes, *The Good Parliament* (Oxford, 1975), pp. 179–80). The parliamentary enactment may refer to *PROME*, v. 420–2.

the dying man and asked him to grant them full remission of all sins in accordance with the practice followed by his predecessors on their deathbed, to which he replied: 'I only wish we ourselves could first be absolved of our sins! So let you bear your sins and we will bear ours.' He was succeeded by Gregory XI, between whom and the Florentines a dispute arose; the Florentines were willing to pay tribute to him, but not to be ruled by him. The pope therefore sent bulls throughout the world instructing kingdoms and towns, once they had been published, that wherever there were Florentines, they should seize all their goods, refuse to pay debts to them, and exclude them from their territories, under penalty of interdict after a month. The bishop of London, William Courtenay, therefore published this bull at St Paul's Cross. The mayor of the city promptly sealed up the doors of the Florentines and brought them before the king. 'Are you our men?' the king asked them. 'We are indeed yours', they replied. 'And we will protect you', said the king. The bishop of Exeter, chancellor of the realm, summoned the bishop of London before him in the chancery and demanded to know why he had had the temerity to publish the aforesaid bull without consulting the king and his council, contrary to the statutes of the realm. To which he replied: 'Because the pope ordered it.' 'In which case', the chancellor responded, 'you may choose either to lose your temporalities or revoke your words in person.' Eventually, however, he was allowed to get another person to revoke them for him. Someone therefore stood up at the Cross and said: 'My lord said nothing about any interdict here. It is extraordinary that you, who hear so many sermons here, are incapable of understanding what is being said.' Whereupon the king enacted in parliament that the pope should not provide to churches belonging to lay patrons.[16]

In the year of the Lord 1371 the duke of Lancaster and the duke of Brittany crossed to France with a large army and, finding the towns to be walled, returned without either giving battle or acquiring booty. In the same year the Flemings and French sailed to the Bay for salt. The king ordered to sea the earl of Hereford, who killed them and brought their ships, loaded with salt, to Southampton.[17]

---

[17] Gaunt and John of Brittany's 'Great March' began in July 1373 at Calais and ended with a much-depleted army in Dec. at Bordeaux; it cost around £100,000. The fleet sent to the Bay of Biscay in Apr. 1373 was under the command of John de Montague, earl of Salisbury, not Hereford (J. Sumption, *Divided Houses: The Hundred Years War*, iii (London, 2009), pp. 180–96).

Anno Domini millesimo trecentisimo septuagesimo duo, dux Lancastrie transiit ad Bruges ad tractandum de pace cum duce de Berry, et ibi mansit per totam estatem in grauibus expensis regni, nihil aliud referens in reuentu nisi quod Gallici pacem habere nolunt nisi habeant omnia que habuerunt ante uendicationem hereditatis factam per regem Anglie; quo concesso, placeret eis soluere residuum redemptionis Iohannis regis Francie; et nullas gratias reportauit.[18]

1373. Anno Domini millesimo trecentisimo septuagesimo tertio, dux Lancastrie cum exercitu transiturus in Franciam uenit ad Calkewelhulle iuxta Kalesiam, contra quem ibidem uenit exercitus magnus Gallicorum. Gallici rogabant eum tractare de pace, et fuerunt ibidem tractantes quousque tota messis Francie erat in castris et ciuitatibus ac uillis muratis congregata. Comes Warwicie, existens in Anglia, admirans quid facerent, de assensu regis cum comitiua quadam transiit ad ducem, et reprehendens eum et alios qui cum illo ibidem erant, cucurrit ad Gallicos, qui uidentes eum fugierunt. Dux rediit et multi de exercitu dissinteria perierunt. Comes Warwicie, ut quidam dixerunt, ueneno Calesie periit, et quod comes Herfordie propter hoc nocte suspensus fuit iussu regis; et certum est quod ultra non comparuit.[19] Hoc anno horilogia distinguentia uiginti quattuor horas primo inuenta sunt.[20]

Anno Domini millesimo trecentesimo septuagesimo quarto Symon Langham cardinalis uenit nuntius pape in Angliam,[d] et cito post papa et cardinales per litteras suas ipsum grauiter reprehendebant pro eo quod ipse, derogando preeminentie sue et Curie Romane, suum deposuit capicium regi Anglie. Qui non potuit excusari quousque rediret, et testimonio sufficienti ostenderet quod non nisi medietatem capicii deponebat.[21] In redeundo autem ad Curiam singulis monachis Cantuarie dabat aurum.

---

[d] *marginal in later hand*: legatus

[18] The peace conference at Bruges took place between Mar. and June 1375, not 1372, and the chief French negotiator was Philip the Bold, duke of Burgundy, not Berry; he and Gaunt agreed a year-long truce on 17 June. Both sides were criticized for their lavish expenditure, and field commanders resented the timing of the truce (Sumption, *Divided Houses*, pp. 224–38).

[19] This expedition is dated four years too late, in fact taking place in the autumn of 1369. Warwick's criticism of Gaunt and the French flight following his arrival at Calais are confirmed by other chronicles. The chronicler's implication is that Warwick was poisoned because he reproached Gaunt, and that Hereford was complicit in his death; in fact Warwick probably died of the plague at Calais (on 13 Nov. 1369); Humphrey de Bohun, earl of Hereford, Essex, and Northampton, did not die until 16 Jan. 1373, and was certainly not

In the year of the Lord 1372 the duke of Lancaster crossed to Bruges for peace talks with the duke of Berry. He remained there throughout the summer, at great expense to the kingdom, but was unable on his return to report anything except that the French had no wish to make peace unless they could have everything they had had before the king of England had put forward his claim to his inheritance; once this had been agreed, they would be happy to pay the residue of the ransom of King John of France; for which he received no thanks.[18]

1373. In the year of the Lord 1373 the duke of Lancaster, having crossed to France with an army, arrived at Coquelles Hill near Calais, where a large army of Frenchmen confronted him. The French invited him to treat for peace, and they remained there deliberating until the entire harvest in France had been gathered and stored in castles and cities and walled towns. The earl of Warwick, who was in England and saw with amazement what they were doing, with the king's consent brought over a force to join the duke and, reproaching him and the others who were there with him, hastened towards the French, who fled when they saw him. The duke returned, and many of his army died of dysentery. Some people said that the earl of Warwick died of poisoning at Calais, and that on account of this the earl of Hereford was hanged at night by order of the king; what is certain is that after this he disappeared from sight.[19] This year clocks measuring twenty-four hours were first invented.[20]

In the year of the Lord 1374 Cardinal Simon Langham came to England as a papal envoy, and soon after this the pope and the cardinals sent letters severely rebuking him because, in derogation of his dignity and that of the Roman Curia, he had doffed his hat to the king of England; for which he could not obtain pardon until he returned and provided sufficient proof that he had only half removed his hat.[21] Before returning to the Curia, therefore, he distributed money to each of the monks of Canterbury.

---

hanged on the king's orders (Sumption, *Divided Houses*, pp. 41–4; A. Tuck, 'Beauchamp, Thomas, earl of Warwick', *ODNB*, iv. 597–9; *CP*, vi. 473–4).

[20] The earliest known mechanical striking clocks were made in Italy in the second quarter of the 14th c. The chronicler is doubtless referring to the mechanical clocks installed by Edward III at Windsor in 1351–3, and at Westminster, Queenborough, and King's Langley in the late 1360s (Gerhard Dohrn-van Rossum, *History of the Hour*, trans. T. Dunlap (Chicago, 1996), pp. 108–9, 129–31, 135).

[21] Although the French cardinals at Avignon objected to Langham's apparent act of deference to Edward III, Pope Gregory was not unduly worried: he promoted Langham to Cardinal-Bishop of Palestrina in 1373 (W. J. Dohar, 'Langham, Simon', *ODNB*, xxxii. 484).

Post Pentecosten rex congregauit magnum concilium prelatorum et dominorum apud Westmonasterium, et quendam magistrum in theologia, fratrem minorem Iohannem Mardisle, qui coram eo predicauerat in die Pentecostes, rogauit interesse. Sedebant enim in medio sacrarii princeps Edwardus et archiepiscopus Cantuarie, Willielmus Witlesey, in theologia magister. A latere archiepiscopi prelati omnes et a latere principis omnes domini temporales sedebant, et coram principe et archiepiscopo quattuor magistri in theologia in una forma sedebant, scilicet, prouincialis fratrum predicatorum, Iohannes Owtred monachus de Durham qui ibidem esse in concilio procurauit, frater Iohannes Mardisle, frater Thomas Asshburne Augustiniensis. Decretiste uero et legiste super tapetia in area sedebant.[22] Tunc cancellarius dixit causam conuocationis esse istam:[e] 'Papa misit domino regi bullam in qua scribit quod cum ipse sit dominus generalis omnium temporalium ex Christi uicariatu ac dominus spiritualis et capitalis regni Anglie ex dono olim Iohannis regis, mandat quod rex leuari faciat tallagium in subsidium contra sibi rebelles Florentinos | et alios, et illud sibi mittere non postponat.[23] Et ideo, uos prelati, dicatis iam an ipse sit dominus noster ex uicariatu Christi. Et cras, uos domini temporales, dicetis et respondebitis ad cartam regis Iohannis. Vos, domine archiepiscope, quid dicitis?' Qui respondebat: 'Ipse est omnium dominus; non possumus hoc negare', quod omnes prelati seriatim dixerunt. Prouincialis fratrum predicatorum rogabat se excusari de tam ardua questione et consuluit quod secundum morem ordinis sui in arduis negotiis cantaretur hymnus 'Veni Creator Spiritus', uel missa de Spiritu Sancto, ut ille Spiritus eos doceat ueritatem. Monachus de Durham respondebat per modum collationis, accipiendo pro exordio 'Ecce duo gladii hic',[24] uolens per hoc ostendere Petrum habuisse temporalium et spiritualium potestates. Mardesley assumpsit statim illud, 'Mitte gladium tuum in uaginam',[25]

---

[e] Littere Pape, *in lower margin of fo. 191ᵛ in later hand*

[22] This council was held not in 1374, but on 6–7 June 1373, when Pentecost Sunday fell on 5 June; it immediately followed the Canterbury convocation at St Paul's, which began on 30 May (J. Catto, 'An alleged Great Council of 1374', *EHR* lxxxii (1967), 764–71). Whittlesey was archbishop of Canterbury 1368–74. The provincial of the Dominicans in England was Thomas Rushook, who later became Richard II's confessor and was exiled to Ireland in 1388; Uthred (or John) Boldon was sub-prior of Durham and a noted theologian who had clashed openly with the friars at Oxford in the 1360s (D. Knowles, 'The censured opinions of Uthred of Boldon', in *The Historian and Character and Other Essays* (Cambridge, 1964), pp. 129–70; John Mardisley was a theologian from York of controversial views who became provincial minister of the Franciscans in England in 1375; Thomas Ashbourne was a theologian and

After Pentecost the king convened a great council of prelates and lords at Westminster, to which he invited a certain master in theology, a friar minor, John Mardisley, who had preached in his presence on the feast of Pentecost. In the middle of the sacristy sat Prince Edward and the archbishop of Canterbury, William Whittlesey, a master in theology. All the prelates sat on the archbishop's side, all the lords temporal on the prince's side, and facing the prince and the archbishop, seated on a bench, were four masters of theology, namely, the provincial of the friars preachers; John Uthred, a monk of Durham who had taken care to be present at the council; friar John Mardisley; and Thomas Ashbourne, an Austin friar. Canon and civil lawyers sat on carpets on the ground.[22] Then the chancellor announced the reason for the convocation as follows: 'The pope sent the lord king a bull in which he states that, since he is the universal lord of all temporal things as Christ's vicar, and the superior and spiritual lord of the kingdom of England through the grant of the former King John, he instructs the king to order a tax to be levied as a subsidy against the Florentines and others who are rebelling against him and to send it to him without delay.[23] Tell me now, therefore, you prelates, whether he is indeed our lord through Christ's vicariate, and tomorrow you lords temporal will respond and speak to the charter of King John. What do you say, lord archbishop?' The latter replied: 'He is the lord of all things; that we cannot deny', to which all the prelates in turn assented. The provincial of the friars preachers begged to be excused from answering such a hard question and advised that, according to the custom of his order in difficult matters, the hymn 'Veni Creator Spiritus' should be sung, or a mass of the Holy Spirit, so that the Spirit might show them the truth. The monk of Durham answered by way of a sermon, taking as his theme 'Behold, here are two swords',[24] by which he intended to demonstrate that Peter had both temporal and spiritual powers. Mardisley promptly responded with 'Put up thy sword into a sheath',[25]

---

prior of the Augustinian house in London. The royal wardrobe account book covering the period from 28 June 1371 to 27 June 1373 (TNA E 101/397/5) does not include any payments or gifts to those who preached to Edward III, as later account books do.

[23] The chancellor was the lawyer Sir John Knyvet. The papal subsidy, first requested in Mar. 1372, was for the war against Milan, not Florence; the English government actively resisted it (Holmes, *Good Parliament*, pp. 12–14). In his 'charter' of May 1213, in return for lifting the interdict on England and his own excommunication, King John had acknowledged that he held England as a vassal of Pope Innocent III and promised the pope an annual tribute of £666.

[24] Luke 22: 38.
[25] John 18: 11.

ostendens quod illi gladii tales potestates non significabant, et quod Christus temporale dominium non habebat, nec apostolis tradidit sed relinquere docuit, quod probauit per scripturas et euangelia, per doctorum originalia et exemplo religiosorum qui sua relinquunt, per decreta et ostendebat quod papa se fatetur generale dominium non habere. Et narrauit quomodo Bonifacius octauus statuit se dominum omnium regnorum et quomodo fuit repulsus in Francia et Anglia. Et quod Christus tradidit Petro uicariatum spiritualis regiminis non terrene dominationis. Nam dixit quod in dominatione terrena papa non succedit Petro sed Constantino, secundum Beatum Thomam.[26] Augustiniensis dicebat quod Petrus in ecclesia cognoscitur per claues, Paulus per gladium.[27] 'Papa est Petrus portans claues ecclesie in foro confessionis. Vos, domine princeps, solebatis esse Paulus portantes gladium, sed quia iam dimisistis gladium, Petrus non cognoscet Paulum. Erigatis igitur gladium et Petrus cognoscet Paulum.' Et soluta est conuocatio illo die.

Archiepiscopus dixit: 'Bona consilia fuerunt in Anglia sine fratribus.' Et dixit ei princeps: 'Propter tuam fatuitatem oportuit nos conuocare illos; per tuum consilium perdidissemus regnum.' Et in crastino archiepiscopus dixit se nescire respondere. Cui dixit princeps: 'Asine, responde! Tu deberes nos omnes informare.' Cui archiepiscopus dixit: 'Placet mihi quod non sit hic dominus', et hoc consequenter omnes prelati dixerunt. Monachus uero dixit quod non erat dominus. 'Vbi sunt ergo duo gladii?' dixit dominus princeps. 'Domine', dixit ipse, 'iam sum melius prouisus quam fui.' Tunc domini temporales respondebant dicentes quod Iohannes rex dedit regnum Curie Romane sine consensu regni et baronum, quod legitime facere non potuit, quare dixerunt quod illa carta siue donatio non ualuit. Missi sunt ergo nuntii ad papam qui hanc responsionem eidem referrent.[28]

Comes Penbrochie mittitur cum nauibus et pulchra comitiua custos Vasconie, et Hispani eum ceperunt cum nauibus suis. Rex audiens Rupellam obsessam a Gallicis parauit se cum principe et exercitu ad succursum, et iacens in nauibus apud Sandwicum usque post festum Sancti Michaelis uentum habere non potuit. Et interim Gallici ceperunt Rupellam, nobilem portum Aquitanie uinis bonis abundantem,

---

[26] The reference is to the *Summa Theologica* of Thomas Aquinas (d. 1274).
[27] Matt. 16: 19.
[28] The ambassadors to Avignon must have left shortly after the council ended, for by late Aug. 1373 they had already reached Chambéry; they were John Gilbert, bishop of Bangor; John de Sheppey; William de Burton; and Uthred Boldon. Their instructions included a request to defer the papal subsidy 'until the wars cease' (*CPL*, iv (1362–1404), pp. 125–9).

demonstrating that those swords did not signify such powers, and that Christ had not had temporal dominion, and he had not committed it to the apostles, but instructed them to relinquish it, which he proved through the Scriptures and the gospels, the early teachings of scholars, and the example of men of religion who had given up their possessions; and he demonstrated through decretals that the pope had acknowledged that he did not have universal dominion. He also related how Boniface VIII had set himself up as lord of all kingdoms and how he had been rebuffed in France and England; and that Christ made Peter his vicar for spiritual rule, but not for earthly lordship; for, he declared, according to the blessed Thomas,[26] in earthly rule the pope was not the successor to Peter but to Constantine. The Augustinian stated that Peter was known in the church for his keys, Paul for his sword:[27] 'The pope is Peter, carrying the keys of the church in matters of faith. You, lord prince, used to be Paul, the bearer of the sword, but now, since you laid down the sword, Peter does not recognize Paul. Take up the sword, therefore, and Peter will recognize Paul.' And thus ended the convocation for that day.

'Without the friars', declared the archbishop, 'there were good councils in England.' To which the prince replied: 'It was on account of your stupidity that we had to summon them; if we had followed your advice, we would have lost the kingdom.' Next day, the archbishop said that he did not know what to reply. 'Answer, you ass', the prince said to him, 'it is your responsibility to advise all of us.' The archbishop said to him: 'I am content that [the pope] should not be lord here', and all the prelates consequently said the same. Even the monk declared that he was not the lord. 'So where are the two swords?' asked the lord prince. 'My lord', he replied, 'I am better informed now than I was.' Then the temporal lords replied, saying that King John had given the kingdom to the Roman Curia without the consent of the realm and the barons, which he could not rightfully do, as a result of which they declared that charter or donation to be worthless. So messengers were sent to the pope to report this reply to him.[28]

The earl of Pembroke was sent with ships and a fine retinue to be keeper of Gascony, but the Spaniards seized him along with his ships. The king, hearing that La Rochelle was being besieged by the French, raised an army to go with the prince to relieve it, but despite remaining on board ships at Sandwich until after Michaelmas [29 September] they had no favourable wind. Meanwhile the French seized La Rochelle, a fine port in Aquitaine full of good wine, to the great detriment

ad magnum damnum regni Anglie. Dux Lancastrie transiit cum illo exercitu ad capiendum uillam Sancti Malori in Normannia, sed repulsus rediit.[29]

Tertia pestilencia. Hoc anno fuit magna pestilencia quam gentes uocabant tertiam.[30]

Anno Domini millesimo trecentisimo septuagesimo quinto, archiepiscopus Cantuarie moritur. Et monachi Cantuarie postulabant cardinalem, cui rex noluit assentire, sed offensus priorem et monachos grauiter uexauit laboribus et expensis. Cardinalis, non ualens archiepiscopatum cum bona gratia regis habere, resignauit iuri suo, et papa dedit eum Symoni Sudbury aduocato Curie.[31] Robertus Knollis, miles famosus, missus fuit cum exercitu in Franciam, sed expulsus nihil ibi profecit, sed in Angliam rediit.[32]

Fratres Predicatores comedunt carnes. Eodem anno fratres predicatores petierunt et habuerunt dispensationem a papa comedendi carnes ne secularibus, ut dixerunt, essent onerosi.[33]

Anno Domini millesimo trecentisimo septuagesimo sexto princeps Edwardus moritur et Cantuarie sepelitur.[34] Rex per comitem Sarum uocauit regem Nauarrie ad Clarendonam, quem recipiendo salutauit humaniter ad ostium aule ibidem, et postea tractauit cum eo pro certis terris inter eosdem commutandis; sed rex Nauarrie respondebat se consilium ibidem non habere sicut ipse habuit, et reuersus est.[35]

1377. Anno Domini millesimo trecentisimo septuagesimo septimo rex Edwardus moritur.[36] | Quinquaginta et uno annis regnauit in Anglia, post cuius mortem regnauit Ricardus secundus.

ʃDe Rege Ricardo Secundo.ʃ Rex Ricardus secundus, filius Edwardi principis Wallie, filii regis Edwardi tertii auo suo mortuo, cepit regnare anno Domini millesimo trecentisimo septuagesimo septimo, puer undecim annorum, coronatus apud Westmonasterium, cuius tutor

---

ʃ-ʃ *In upper margin of fo. 192ᵛ*

[29] The sea battle of La Rochelle (23 June 1372) resulted in the destruction by the Castilian fleet of an English fleet led by John Hastings, earl of Pembroke, who was held captive for nearly three years in Spain and died on 16 Apr. 1375 shortly before he was due to be released. Edward III was waiting on board ships at Sandwich and Winchelsea from 27 Aug. to 14 Oct. 1372, but was unable to sail. John of Gaunt did not besiege St Malo until 1378, but the earl of Salisbury landed a force there in 1373 (Sumption, *Divided Houses*, pp. 138–42, 180–2; Ormrod, *Edward III*, p. 630; N. Saul, *Richard II* (New Haven and London, 1997), pp. 35–6).

[30] The second and third visitations of the plague are usually dated to 1361 and 1368–9 respectively.

[31] Archbishop Whittlesey died in June 1374; Sudbury (bishop of London since 1362) replaced him in May 1375. Cardinal Langham hoped to regain the see he had held in 1366–8, but withdrew when the king opposed his election; he died in 1376 at Avignon.

of the kingdom of England. The duke of Lancaster crossed with that army to seize the town of St Malo in Normandy, but was beaten off and came back.[29]

The third pestilence. In this year there was a great pestilence which people called the third.[30]

In the year of the Lord 1375 the archbishop of Canterbury died. The monks of Canterbury put forward the cardinal, but the king would not accept him; instead, taking offence, he seriously harassed the prior and monks with burdens and expenses. The cardinal, unable to secure the archbishopric with the king's good grace, resigned his right, and the pope gave it to Simon Sudbury, a papal advocate.[31] Robert Knolles, a famous knight, was sent with an army to France, but was driven back without achieving anything and returned to England.[32]

The friars preachers eat meat. This same year the friars preachers sought and were granted a dispensation from the pope to eat meat, lest they become a burden to laymen, so they claimed.[33]

In the year of the Lord 1376 Prince Edward died and was buried at Canterbury.[34] The king, through the earl of Salisbury, summoned the king of Navarre to Clarendon [Wiltshire], and on his arrival greeted him warmly at the entrance to the hall there. Later, he discussed with him the exchange of certain territories between them, but the king of Navarre replied that he did not have his council with him there, as [King Edward] did, and so he went home.[35]

1377. In the year of the Lord 1377 King Edward died.[36] He ruled for fifty-one years in England, and after his death Richard II reigned.

Of King Richard II. His grandfather having died, King Richard II, the son of Edward, prince of Wales, son of King Edward III, began to reign in the year of the Lord 1377. A child of eleven years, he was crowned at Westminster; John, duke of Lancaster, was appointed as his

---

[32] The wealthy war-captain Sir Robert Knolles led a plundering army of around 4,000 men through northern France from Aug. to Dec. 1370, by which time most of his men had been killed or captured, for which he was widely blamed (Sumption, *Divided Houses*, pp. 84–93).

[33] This and the corresponding entry below (p. 16) for the Augustinians are oversimplifications. Numerous licences were issued to friars to eat meat in certain circumstances or at certain times, or to laymen to allow religious to eat meat when dining with them (*CPL*, iv, pp. 36, 171, 374, 501; *CPP*, i (1342–1419), index under 'meat, dispensations to eat', p. 759), but Gregory XI's pontificate does not appear to have marked a general relaxation of the accustomed prohibition on eating meat.

[34] Edward, the Black Prince, died at Kennington on 8 June 1376.

[35] Charles 'the Bad', King of Navarre, was at Clarendon for talks with Edward III in early Aug. 1370, but not thereafter (Sumption, *Divided Houses*, p. 74).

[36] Edward III died on 21 June 1377 at Sheen, having acceded to the throne on 25 Jan. 1327.

factus est Iohannes dux Lancastrie.[37] Eodem anno Romani miserunt ad papam Gregorium dicentes quod nisi ueniat et uisitet ecclesiam suam nihil habebit de Roma; qui statim Romam ascendit.[38] Eodem anno frater regis Hispanie et Iohannes de Vienna Gallicus uenerunt cum Hispanis et Gallicis in galeis, et Insulam de Wight, Rotyndene, Winchelse, Rye, Stonore, Grauysende cum manerio regis ibidem combusserunt.[39] Decima et quintadecima in parliamento Londonie tento exacte fuerunt, et rex circuiuit regnum multaque donaria a ciuitatibus, prelatis et diuersis dominis ei data fuerunt.[40]

Fratres Augustinienses comedunt carnes sub conditione. Eodem anno fratres Augustinienses obtinuerunt licentiam et dispensacionem comedendi carnes. Et sub conditione quod obseruarent ieiunium fratrum minorum ante Natale Domini.[41]

1378. Anno Domini millesimo trecentisimo septuagesimo octauo Papa Gregorius moritur Rome.[g] [42] Romani circumdabant cardinales in conclaui ad eligendum nouum papam congregatos, mortem eisdem comminantes nisi Romanum uel Ytalicum eligerent, quia, ut dicebant, Roma periit sub incuria Gallicorum. Ipsi uero elegerunt episcopum Barensem, auditorem causarum, et obtulerunt eidem electionem, quam ipse acceptauit, et coronauerunt eum, intimantes regibus, ducibus et comitibus ipsos iubar ecclesie elegisse;[43] petieruntque ab eo multa beneficia et obtinuerunt pro se et amicis suis, uocantes ipsum Vrbanum.[h] Qui post paululum ad reprimendum, ut dixit, symoniam cardinalium, statuit quod quiscunque uellet habere aliquam gratiam ueniret ad ipsum; sed cardinales, indignantes et offensi, dixerunt ei quod papa non erat, quia non libere electus, et quod elegerunt eum sperantes quod talem electionem, habita opportunitate, cassarent. Qui omnino de eis non curauit. Cardinales spoliabant Curiam de magnis thesauris una cum registro Curie et fugierunt ad ciuitatem Fundensem ubi scripserunt per mundum Vrbanum non esse papam sed electum in timore, qui potuit cadere inconstanter, et si alicubi acceptus esset pro

---

[g] *marginal in later hand*: Gregorius papa moritur [h] *marginal in later hand*: Vrbanus

[37] Richard II was born on 6 Jan. 1367 and crowned on 16 July 1377. John of Gaunt exercised great power during his nephew's minority, but Richard's tutor was Sir Simon Burley, a former retainer of the Black Prince (Saul, *Richard II*, pp. 15–16).

[38] Gregory XI visited Rome for the first time in Jan. 1377 and died there on 27 Mar. 1378.

[39] Winchelsea, Rye, Hastings, Rottingdean, Lewes, Folkestone, and the Isle of Wight were raided by a Franco-Castilian force led by Jean de Vienne, admiral of France, between late June and late Aug. 1377. Gravesend was threatened but not attacked until Aug. 1380 (Sumption, *Divided Houses*, pp. 281–6, 385–6).

tutor.³⁷ This same year the Romans sent to Pope Gregory declaring that unless he came and visited his church he would have nothing from Rome; so he immediately went to Rome.³⁸ In this same year the brother of the king of Spain and the Frenchman John de Vienne came with Spaniards and Frenchmen in galleys and burned the Isle of Wight [Hampshire], Rottingdean, Winchelsea, Rye, Stonor [all East Sussex] and Gravesend [Kent], together with the king's manor there.³⁹ At a parliament held in London a tenth and fifteenth were exacted. The king also toured the realm, and many gifts were given to him by townsmen, prelates, and various lords.⁴⁰

The Austin friars eat meat under condition. In the same year the Austin friars received a licence and dispensation to eat meat, on condition that they observe the pre-Christmas fast of the friars minor.⁴¹

1378. In the year of the Lord 1378 Pope Gregory died at Rome.⁴² The Romans surrounded the cardinals who had assembled in conclave to elect a new pope, threatening them with death if they did not elect a Roman or an Italian, for, so they said, Rome had been ruined by the negligence of the French. They therefore chose the bishop of Bari, an auditor of causes, and offered him election, which he accepted, and crowned him, announcing to kings, dukes, and counts that they had elected the splendour of the Church.⁴³ And they demanded and obtained numerous benefices from him for themselves and their friends, naming him Urban. But after a short while, in order to curb the simony of the cardinals, so he said, he decreed that anyone who wanted to obtain any grant should approach himself. The cardinals, however, indignant and offended, told him that he was not the pope, because he had not been freely elected, and that they had elected him in the hope that, once the opportunity arose, they would quash that election. He entirely ignored them. The cardinals seized great treasure from the Curia, together with the papal register, and fled to the town of Fondi, from where they wrote to announce to the world that Urban was not pope, but had been elected out of fear, which was likely to produce instability, and that if he was acknowledged as pope anywhere, then the

---

⁴⁰ The parliament of Oct.–Nov. 1377 granted two tenths and fifteenths (*PROME*, vi. 4). Apart from a loan of £5,000 from the Londoners in Oct. 1377, there was little borrowing by the exchequer until the spring of 1379 (A. Steel, *Receipt of the Exchequer 1377–1485* (Cambridge, 1954), pp. 38–9).
⁴¹ See n. 33 above.
⁴² Gregory XI died on 27 Mar. 1378.
⁴³ The election of Bartolomeo Prignano, a Neapolitan, who became Urban VI, was announced on 9 Apr. 1378; he was crowned on 18 Apr., Easter Sunday.

papa quod episcopi per ipsum ordinati episcopi non essent reputandi, nec ordines celebrare possent, et sic perirent ibi omnia sacramenta ecclesiastica. Elegerunt unum ex seipsis quem Clementem uocauerunt, miseruntque regi Francie magnam summam auri et transierunt ad Auinoniam; tunc rex Francie et omnia regna sibi alligata, uidelicet omnes reges Hispanie preter regem Portugalie, acceptauerunt Clementem, sicque fecit Scotie.[44] Dixerunt autem sapientes quod licet episcopi supradicti sic suspensi in ordine suo adinstantes, et alii presbyteri uere ordinati, bene et rite celebrantes consecrauerint, nec propter talem suspensionem perierunt sacramenta. Dixerunt insuper quod non oportet in omni casu electionem omnino esse liberam, loquendo de libertate canonica, et quod Romani bene potuerunt artare cardinales in tali casu, iusta causa subsistente, sicut omnis communitas potest artare superiorem suum propter bonum commune et utilitatem publicam; et post acceptationem electionis a tota Christianitate, quamuis aliquid defuisset de forma electionis, non licuit tamen propter hoc cardinalibus dissoluere ecclesiasticam libertatem.

Eodem anno Hispani miserunt ad regem Anglie pro liberacione comitis de Dene de Hispania, quem Iohannes Hawle et Ricardus Shakyll ceperunt antea in bello Hispanie, sed ipsi timentes perdere redemptionem sui prisonarii noluerunt ipsum producere ad domini regis mandatum. Rex per consilium suum obiecit eis quod ipsi fecerunt carcerem in domibus suis infra regnum suum contra suum mandatum et uoluntatem, et misit eos ad Turrim Londonie. Ipsi uero, prostrato eorum custode, fugierunt ad Westmonasterium.[45] Constabularius Turris uenit ut eos reduceret et Iohannes Haule resistens[i] | interfectus fuit ad illum uerbum quod legebatur per diaconum in alta missa, 'Si sciret paterfamilias qua hora fur ueniret, etcetera';[46] tamen Ricardus

---

[i] interfectus fuit *anticipated in a scroll in lower margin of fo. 192*[v]

[44] The rebel cardinals publicly challenged Urban's election on 20 July. They retired initially to Anagni, where they were offered protection by the count of Fondi, Onorato Caetani, whom Urban VI had offended, and then to Fondi itself, where on 20 Sept. they elected Robert of Geneva, cardinal-priest of the Twelve Apostles, as Clement VII. This account of the outbreak of the Great Schism is broadly correct, if favourable to the Urbanists (W. Ullmann, *The Origins of the Great Schism* (London, 1948), pp. 9–56; P. Partner, *The Lands of St Peter: The Papal State in the Middle Ages and the Early Renaissance* (London, 1972), pp. 367–8).

[45] The chronicler has confused the names of the two esquires, which were Robert Hauley and John Shakell. They had captured Alfonso de Villena, count of Denia, at Nájera in 1367 and were demanding a ransom of 60,000 crowns for his liberation; he had returned to Spain

bishops ordained by him would not be recognized as bishops, nor could they perform ordinations, and thus all the sacraments of the Church would be invalid there. They elected one of their own number whom they called Clement, sent a large sum of gold to the king of France, and went to Avignon, whereupon the king of France and all the kingdoms allied to him, that is to say all the kings of Spain except the king of Portugal, accepted Clement, as did the Scots.[44] Learned men said, however, that it was permissible for the aforesaid bishops, thus suspended, to retain their status, and for other properly ordained priests to carry out consecrations while celebrating in a proper and correct manner, and that the sacraments would not be invalid on account of such a suspension. They also declared, citing canonical privilege, that it was not necessary in every case for an election to be completely free, and that the Romans were perfectly entitled to put pressure on the cardinals in such cases if the cause was lawful, just as every community can put pressure on its lord for the common good and public utility; and that after the acceptance of the election by the whole of Christendom, even if there was something irregular with the form of election, it was nevertheless not permissible for the cardinals to go against ecclesiastical liberty because of that.

In this same year the Spanish wrote to the king of England concerning the liberation of the count of Denia in Spain, whom John Hauley and Richard Shakell had captured earlier at the battle of Spain; they, however, fearful of losing the ransom for their prisoner, defied the order of the lord king to hand him over. The king, through his council, reproved them for making a prison in their homes within his kingdom, contrary to his order and to his will, and sent them to the Tower of London, but they broke out of prison and fled to Westminster.[45] The constable of the Tower came to recapture them, and John Hauley was killed resisting him, just as these words were being spoken by the deacon at high mass: 'If the good man of the house had known what hour the thief would come, etc.';[46] however, Richard Shakell surrendered to

---

to raise this sum, leaving his son as a hostage in England. The English government, mindful of diplomatic relations, tried to moderate the esquires' demand, but they were unmoved and concealed their hostage, so in Oct. 1377 they were imprisoned in the Tower, from which they escaped in Aug. 1378 and sought sanctuary in Westminster Abbey. The so-called Hauley–Shakell affair became a cause célèbre, with blame for the violation of sanctuary falling on John of Gaunt in particular, even though he was out of the country when it was committed. The controversy over sanctuary in the Nov. 1378 parliament (see below, p. 24) was a direct result of it (Saul, *Richard II*, pp. 36–8).

[46] Luke 12: 39.

Shakill ibat cum eo. Statim monachi cessauerunt a diuinis et per multas Dominicas sequentes excommunicatos denuntiari fecerunt per archiepiscopum Cantuarie sue ecclesie et suorum priuilegiorum uiolatores, et ecclesiam reconciliare nolebant.[47] Rex autem sepe mandauit abbati per breuia sua quod ad eum ueniret et a dicta denuntiatione cessaret ac suam ecclesiam reconciliari faceret sicut iuxta fundationis sue debitum in ea Deo seruiret, promittens quod negotium erit bene reformatum. Sed abbas nec adquiescere nec comparere uolebat, asserens ecclesiam suam dedicatam fore per Beatum Petrum miraculose et alterius dedicatione non indigere, ostendens[j] chronicam dedicationis ut sequitur:[48]

'Tempore quo rex Ethelbertus, qui regnauit in Cancia, predicante Beato Augustino fidei sacramenta susceperat, nepos quoque eius Sebertus, qui Orientalibus Anglis prefuit, fidem eodem episcopo euangelisante suscepit. Hic Londonie, que regni sui metropolis habebatur, intra muros ecclesiam in honore Pauli Beatissimi construens, episcopali eam sede uoluit esse sublimem; cui Sanctus Mellitus, quem Beatus Papa Gregorius cum pluribus aliis in adiutorium miserat Augustino, merito simul et honore pontificali primus omnium prefuit.[49] Volens autem rex utrique apostolo se gratum prestare, in occidentali parte eiusdem ciuitatis extra muros in honore Beati Petri monasterium insigne fundauit, multis illud donariis ornans et ditans possessionibus. Venerat autem tempus quo ecclesia fuerat in eo dedicanda, paratisque omnibus pro loco et tempore, pro monasterii dignitate, agente episcopo ea nocte in tentoriis, dies crastina prestolabatur. Magna plebis expectatio, que adhuc rudis in fide, his sollemniis interesse non solum pro deuotione sed etiam pro admiratione[k] gaudebat.

---

[j] ostendas *MS*   [k] *Flete*; adiutorio *MS*

---

[47] The constable of the Tower was Sir Alan Buxhill. He was accompanied by some fifty men including William Lord Latimer and Sir Ralph Ferrers, who was said to have killed Hauley on the steps of the high altar on 11 Aug. 1378. The bishop of London, William Courtenay, joined Archbishop Sudbury in denouncing the perpetrators; no services were held in the abbey until Christmas (*The Anonimalle Chronicle 1333 to 1381*, ed. V. Galbraith (Manchester, 1927), pp. 121–4; *SAC* I, pp. 237–45).

[48] The abbot from 1362 to 1386 was Nicholas Litlyngton. For the 'chronicle' cited, see the following note.

[49] The foundation of Westminster Abbey is wreathed in legends, one of which dates it as far back as the time of King Lucius in the 2nd c. The ultimate source for the background to this story is Bede's Ecclesiastical History, bk. 2, ch. 3, although Bede does not mention Westminster. It is found in the 11th-c. chronicle of the monk Sulcard and the 12th-c. lives of Edward the Confessor, and incorporated in the 14th- and 15th-century histories of the abbey

him. The monks immediately suspended divine services, and for several Sundays following they ensured that all those who violated their church and their privileges were denounced by the archbishop of Canterbury as excommunicated, and they refused to reconsecrate the church.[47] The king sent several writs to the abbot ordering him to come into his presence, to cease this denunciation and to have his church reconsecrated in order to use it for serving God in accordance with the requirements of his foundation, promising that full amends would be made for this affair, but the abbot refused either to comply or to appear before him, declaring that his church had been consecrated miraculously by St Peter and did not require any other form of consecration, citing the chronicle of the consecration as follows.[48]

'At the time when King Ethelbert, who reigned in Kent, accepted the sacraments of the faith through the preaching of the blessed Augustine, his nephew Sebert, who ruled over the East Angles, also accepted the faith through the evangelizing of the same bishop. He, who was building a church in honour of the most blessed Paul within the walls of London, the chief city of his kingdom, wanted it to be an eminent episcopal see; St Mellitus, whom the blessed Pope Gregory had sent along with several others to help Augustine, was the first of all those to be raised to its episcopal status and honour.[49] The king, however, wishing to show his gratitude to each of the apostles, also founded a splendid monastery in honour of the blessed Peter outside the walls on the western side of the same city, embellishing it with many gifts and enriching it with possessions. The time came when the church there was ready to be dedicated, and when everything had been prepared for the place and time, and for the dignity of the monastery, the bishop arranged that that night should be spent in tents awaiting the following day. The great expectancy of the people, who as yet were inexperienced in the faith, rejoiced at being present at such solemnities not simply out of devotion but also in wonderment. That same night

---

(Flete, pp. 2–11). This account is confused. Sebert (d. 616) was king of the East Saxons, not of the East Angles. By the mid-12th c., he had come to be widely credited as the abbey's founder, and in 1308 his tomb was moved to a place of honour next to the Confessor's shrine. A version of this legend with slightly different wording can be found in Flete's *History* (pp. 36–7); where Flete's wording seems to be more accurate than that reproduced here, it has been adopted, with the wording of the *Continuatio* given in footnotes.

Eadem nocte piscatori cuidam in Thamasis fluuii, qui eidem monasterio subterfluit, ulteriori ripa in habitu peregrini Beatus Petrus apparens promissa mercede transponi se ab eodem et petiit et promeruit. Egressus autem a nauicula ecclesiam, piscatore cernente, ingreditur, et ecce, subito lux celestis emicuit miroque splendore collustrans omnia noctem conuertit in diem. Affuit enim cum apostolo multitudo ciuium supernorum egredientium et ingredientium,[50] et choris hymnidicis preeuntibus melodia celestis insonuit. Omnia plena lumine, omnia referta dulcedine; aures uocis angelice mulcebat iocunditas; nares indicibilis odoris fragrantia perfundebat; oculos lux etherea illustrabat. Videbantur quasi mixta terrena celestibus, humana coniuncta diuinis, et quasi in scala Iacob angeli descendentes et ascendentes in illis sacris sollemniis uisebantur.[51] Peractisque omnibus que ad ecclesie dedicationem spectant sollemniis, rediit ad piscium piscatorem piscator egregius hominum,[52] quem cum diuini luminis fulgore perterritum alienatum pene sensibus reperisset, blanda consolatione reddidit animum[*l*] proprie rationi. Ingredientes ambo cymbam simul uterque piscator interloquendum, apostolus hominem hisdem quibus se quondam magister suus conueniens uerbis: "Numquid", ait, "pulmentarium non habes?"[53] Et ille: "Timui",[*m*] inquit, "inconsuete lucis profusione[*n*] stupidus cum expectatione tui detentus nihil cepi. Sed promissam a te mercedem securus expectaui." Ad hec apostolus: "Laxa nunc", inquit, "retia in capturam." Paruit imperanti piscator et mox impleuit rete piscium maxima multitudo;[54] quibus ad ripam extractis, "Hunc", inquit apostolus, "qui ceteris magnitudine et pretio precellit, Mellito episcopo mea ex parte piscem defer. Pro nautica uero mercede cetera tibi tolle. Ego sum Petrus qui tecum loquor, qui cum meis conciuibus constructam in meo nomine basilicam dedicaui episcopalemque benedictionem mee sanctificationis | auctoritate preueni. Dic ergo pontifici que tu uidisti et audisti, tuo quoque sermoni signa parietibus impressa testimonium perhibebunt. Supersedeat igitur dedicationi. Suppleat quod omisimus, Domini scilicet corporis et sanguinis sacrosancta misteria, populumque erudiens sermone et benedictione confirmans, notificet omnibus hunc me locum crebro uisitaturum, hic me fidelium uotis et precibus affuturum." Et his dictis clauicularius celestis disparuit. Et iam nocturnis

---

[*l*] *Flete*; hominem MS   [*m*] *Flete*; Tum MS   [*n*] *Flete*; perfusione MS

[50] Luke 2: 13.
[51] Gen. 28: 12.
[52] Matt. 4: 19.
[53] John 21: 5.

the blessed Peter, appearing in the garb of a pilgrim to a certain fisherman on the far bank of the river Thames, which flowed below the said monastery, asked to be carried across from there and, having promised a reward, was granted his wish. With the fisherman looking on, he got out of the boat and went into the church, and behold, suddenly a heavenly light shone forth, illuminating everything with extraordinary brilliance and turning night into day. Also present there with the apostle was a great company of the heavenly host,[50] going in and coming out, preceding whom went choirs singing hymns with a celestial melody. Everything was filled with light and suffused with sweetness; joyfulness soothed the ears with angelic voices; an indescribably sweet fragrance flooded the nostrils; an ethereal light bathed the eyes. It seemed as if earthly things were mixed with heavenly and human affairs joined to divine, and as these sacred rites were being witnessed angels could be seen descending and ascending as if on Jacob's ladder.[51] When all the solemnities pertaining to the dedication of the church had been performed, the great fisher of men returned to the fisher of fish,[52] whom he found terrified by the brilliance of the divine light and almost driven out of his mind. With soothing words of comfort he restored his mind to its senses, and as the two fishermen got back into the boat speaking together, the apostle used those same words which his Master had once used on meeting him: "Have you nothing to eat?" he said.[53] "I was afraid", replied the other, "and amazed by the extraordinary profusion of light and, distracted by waiting for you, I have caught nothing. But I have been confidently waiting for the fare you promised me." To this the apostle said: "Now let down your nets for a catch." The fisherman obeyed the command, and quickly the net filled with a great multitude of fish.[54] On the shore, as they were taking these out, the apostle said: "Take this fish, which is the biggest in size and value, to Bishop Mellitus as a gift from me; keep the rest for yourself as your reward for my passage. I who am speaking to you am Peter, who, with my helpers, have dedicated this church built in my name, thereby anticipating the bishop's blessing by the authority of my holiness. Tell the bishop, therefore, what you have seen and heard, and the signs impressed on the walls will bear witness to what you say. Let him forgo the dedication, therefore, and supply what we have omitted, that is to say, the sacred mysteries of the body and blood of the Lord, enlightening the people with a sermon and strengthening them with a blessing, and making known to all that I shall visit this place frequently and shall be here for the wishes and prayers of the faithful"; having said which,

[54] Luke 5: 4–6.

tenebris finem dedit aurora. Cum Beato Mellito ad future dedicationis celebranda misteria processuro cum pisce piscator occurrit. Quem cum episcopo tradidisset omnia ei que ab apostolo fuerant mandata prosequitur. Stupet pontifex, reserratisque basilice sacre ualuis, uidit pauimentum utriusque alphabeti inscriptione signatum, parietem bis senis in locis sanctificationis oleo linitum, tot cereorum reliquias duodenis crucibus inherere. Et quasi recenti aspersione adhuc cuncta madescere.[55] Refert hec episcopus populo, et mox una uox omnium pulsat celos laudantium et Deum benedicentium toto corde.'

Eodem anno, uidelicet millesimo trecentisimo septuagesimo octauo, Iohannes Wyclif, magister in theologia, dictus flos Oxonie, determinando disputauit contra possessiones immobiles ecclesie, religionem fratrum minorum multum commendans, dicens eos esse Deo carissimos;[56] et quod Iohannes papa fuit grossus legista, nesciens quid diceret in theologia; item quod domini temporales et monasterium fundatores auferre possunt bona temporalia ab ecclesiasticis delinquentibus.[57]

Parliamentum Gloucestrie. Eodem anno parliamentum statuitur Glouernie in quo rex graue tallagium a populo extorquebat, dicens quod si non haberet, traylbastonem haberet; dictumque fuit ibidem quod pecunia regni fuerat in manibus opificum et laborantium, concessumque fuit quod quilibet maritus solueret grossum et quelibet uxor similiter grossum, et quod diuites in hac solutione pauperes iuuarent.[58] Westmonasterium propter contemptum regis in non ueniendo alias ad citationes suas priuabatur temporalibus ita uix ut sex solidos et octo denarios haberet pro esculentis et poculentis.[59] Declaratumque fuit ibidem quod rex potest concedere libertatem ad

---

[55] The act of consecrating or dedicating a church involved writing in the Latin and Greek alphabets in ashes on the floor, anointing the wall with twelve crosses, burning twelve candles, and asperging the interior of the building.

[56] John Wyclif (c.1324–84), taught theology at Oxford and was by the 1370s the most famous scholastic philosopher in England. His increasingly radical views drew him into conflict with the Catholic Church, but some influential laymen such as John of Gaunt encouraged him to speak out against ecclesiastical privilege and in favour of taxing the Church. For the expression at this time of his views on clerical disendowment, see Workman, *John Wyclif: A Study of the English Medieval Church*, i. 312–23.

[57] John XXII, the second Avignon pope (1316–34), came from Cahors and taught civil and canon law at Toulouse. During the 1320s, he started a debate about the Franciscan belief that Christ and the apostles owned nothing, then decided that they did, by which time the issue was in the public sphere. Ecclesiastical disendowment was favoured by many English reformers, especially the Lollards, who were much influenced by Wyclif.

[58] The second parliament of Richard II's reign met at Gloucester from 20 Oct. to 16 Nov. 1378. Poll-taxes were granted at the parliaments of January 1377 and April 1379, but not in 1378. The chronicler appears to be referring to the first poll-tax (1377), which imposed a levy of 1 groat (4 pence) on each man or woman over the age of 14, 'genuine beggars excepted'.

the keeper of the keys of heaven vanished. By now dawn was bringing an end to the darkness of night. When the blessed Mellitus was on his way to celebrate the mysteries of the dedication, the fisherman went up to him with the fish, which he handed over to him, and all the things the apostle had ordered him to do now came to pass. The bishop was dumbfounded, and when the doors of the holy basilica were unlocked he saw the pavement inscribed with writing in each alphabet, the walls anointed in twelve places with the sanctifying oil, the same number of twelve candle-ends placed in twelve crosses, and everything still moist, as if just asperged.[55] The bishop reported these things to the people, and soon the united voice of all, praising and blessing God with all their hearts, resounded to the heavens.'

In the same year, namely 1378, John Wyclif, master of theology, known as the flower of Oxford, argued in disputation against the immovable goods of the Church, greatly praising the religion of the friars minor and saying that they were especially dear to God;[56] and that Pope John was an ignorant jurist who did not know what to say on theological matters; also that the lords temporal and founders of monasteries should be allowed to deprive delinquent ecclesiastics of their temporal goods.[57]

Parliament at Gloucester. In the same year, a parliament was summoned to Gloucester in which the king extorted a heavy tax from the people, saying that if he did not receive it he would impose a trailbaston; it was also declared there that the kingdom's wealth was in the hands of workmen and labourers, and it was granted that each married man should pay 1 groat and each married woman a groat as well, and that in making this payment the rich should help the poor.[58] Westminster [abbey] was deprived of its temporalities for contempt of the king, because it had not responded to his summonses on a previous occasion; as a result, it was left with scarcely 6 shillings and 8 pence for food and drink.[59] And it was declared there that the king might grant immunity for the time being to those who by misfortune lacked the ability to pay,

---

The second poll-tax of 1379 introduced an elaborate scale of payments from dukes down to labourers (*PROME*, v. 400; vi. 115–16). A trailbaston was a special judicial commission introduced during the reign of Edward I to combat disorder, but deeply unpopular because of the heavy fines and forfeitures imposed.

[59] For the official record of the debate which follows, see *PROME*, vi. 79–80 (items 27–8), which sets out the position of the church in defence of sanctuary and the arguments of the lords against it, especially in cases of debt, and *PROME*, vi. 106 (items 7–8); see also Workman, *Wyclif*, i. 320–4. It was the murder of Robert Hauley in the abbey (see above) which sparked the controversy, which was widely discussed by chroniclers. Wyclif was invited to speak on the government side; he was a strong opponent of sanctuary and the arguments here are similar to those he expressed in his *De Ecclesia*. Wyclif's views were by now becoming heretical, and this was his last significant intervention in politics.

tempus illis qui ceciderunt a casu in impotentiam soluendi utpote per rapinam, combustionem uel submersionem usque ad tempus potentie soluendi, sed rex non potest concedere raptori uel fraudulento detentori rei aliene ut gaudeat tali libertate quod cogi non possit ad soluendum, et partiatur inde cum abbate pro domus locatione. Hoc non priuilegium sed prauilegium dici debet, quia rex non potest dispensare cum minima concupiscentia rei aliene contra mandatum Dei, uidelicet, 'Non concupisces rem proximi tui', igitur nec cum uiolentia detentione.[60] Ostendebatur etiam ibidem quod pro debito non est homo liber ibidem ex priuilegio sed ex consuetudine per reges tolerata. Et quod priuilegium loci quod continet hanc formam—'Concedimus quod quiscunque homo ueniens ad locum siue equestris siue pedestris pro quocunque delicto, etiam si in personam nostram deliquerit, gaudeat ibidem omnimoda libertate'—in diuersis casibus qui possunt contingere periculosum esset obseruare. Et quod rex priuilegium predecessoris sui possit suspendere et reuocare, cum 'non habeat imperium par in parem'.[61] Et quod ecclesia illa non magis modo polluta fuit quam quando monachus olim monachum iuxta summum altare interfecit, et tum statim reconciliata fuit. Tangebatur insuper ibidem quod in morte casuali, propter consanguineos, ordinate fuerunt olim ciuitates refugii, sed si quis de industria occideret hominem etiam 'de altare meo euelles eum, ut moriatur'.[62] Petebaturque ibidem quod abbas teneatur detinere ibi debitores ne effugiant, sub pena solutionis debitorum, si priuilegio illo gaudere uoluerit. Dictumque fuit quod priuilegium lucrosum sanctum est et inuiolabile, non lucrosum nullum est. Statutumque fuit ibidem quod priuilegium ecclesie a Deo concessum et mandatum de nundinis ab ecclesiis et cemeteriis amouendis obseruaretur, | et domus Dei sit domus orationis et non negotiationis.[63] Et nundinae Cantuarienses in uico principali statuebantur, sed statim archiepiscopus rogabat regem ut intra prioratum reuocarentur.

Ad hoc parliamentum uenerunt nuntii cum bulla utriusque pape rogantium regem ut assisteret ecclesie. Rex uero precepit archiepiscopo Cantuariensi ut audiret eos et decerneret cum quo tenendum esset et quod acciperet clericorum consilium et tempus sufficiens. Archiepiscopus, auditis partibus, uenit in parliamentum et dixit:

---

[60] Exod. 20: 17.
[61] 'Par in parem non habet imperium', a frequently quoted legal principle to express the idea that a sovereign, or sovereign power, should not interfere in the affairs of another.

for example through robbery, fire, or flood, until such time as they are able to pay. However, the king may not grant to a robber, or to someone who fraudulently detains something belonging to another, that he should enjoy immunity to the extent that he cannot be coerced into paying, so that instead it is shared with the abbot for the rent of the house. That should not be called a privilege but a depravity, because the king may not dispose of something belonging to another without arousing envy, contrary to God's command, 'Thou shalt not covet thy neighbour's goods'; nor indeed by forcible detention.[60] It was also argued there that a free man who is a debtor is permitted by kings to remain there not through immunity but through custom; and that the privilege of a place which is expressed as follows—'We grant that any man whatsoever coming to a place, whether on horse or on foot, for any kind of crime, even if he has offended against our person, shall enjoy every kind of immunity here'—would, in various cases that might arise, be dangerous to maintain; and that the king may suspend or revoke a privilege of his predecessor, since 'an equal should not have power over an equal';[61] and that the said church [Westminster] was no more polluted now than formerly, when a monk killed another monk next to the high altar, on which occasion it was promptly reconsecrated. Moreover, it was also mentioned there that in the case of accidental death, citizens used to be allowed refuge in a reasonable manner, on account of the [victim's] kindred, but that if anyone killed a man intentionally, then 'you may take him from my altar, that he may die'.[62] It was also requested there that if the abbot wished to enjoy that privilege, he should be obliged to hold debtors there to stop them escaping, under pain of paying their debts; and it was said that a lucrative privilege is holy and inviolable, one that is not lucrative is as nothing; and it was decreed there that the church's privilege, granted and ordained by God, of moving fairs from churches and cemeteries should be observed, and that the house of God should be a house of prayer, not of commerce.[63] It was also ordained that the Canterbury fairs should be in the main street, but the archbishop immediately begged the king that they be moved back within the priory.

Messengers with a bull from each pope came to this parliament to ask the king to help the Church. The king therefore ordered the archbishop of Canterbury to hear them and to decide which one to side with, and that he should take some time and deliberate with the clergy. Having heard each side, the archbishop came into parliament and said:

[62] Exod. 21: 14.
[63] Cf. Matt. 21: 13.

'Sicut respondere uolo coram Deo, recipiatis Vrbanum.' Et ibi statutum fuit quod omnes Anglici reciperent Vrbanum.[64] Vrbanus papa expulit regem Cisilie et Neapolis, de genere Anglicorum, dicens eum scismaticum et Gallicis alligatum et talis non debet regnare in spirituali patrocinio Beati Petri. Et Karolum de Pace cognatum suum cum assistentia regni regem fecit.[65] Hoc anno archiepiscopus Cantuariensis Symon Sudbury cepit edificare ecclesiam suam cathedralem et muros ciuitatis Cantuarie, et proposuit ibi edificasse pulcherimam et fortissimam ciuitatem.[66]

1379. Anno Domini millesimo trecentisimo septuagesimo nono, monachi de Bury elegerunt abbatem, contra quem uenit alius monachus eiusdem domus, magister de Roma, factus abbas a papa, et cum sibi adherentibus missam in pontificalibus celebrauit. Sed a cancellario Anglie uocatus, didicit prohibitum esse per statutum regni ne quis abbathiam capiat de prouisione pape, sub pena carceris. Et post incarcerationem gratiam habuit transfretandi.[67] Iohannes de Arundell, filius Ricardi comitis de Arundell, cum exercitu missus fuit senescallus in Vasconiam. Et luxuria et rapina exhibentibus*[o]* suscitauit Dominus spiritum de inferioribus abyssi postquam egressi sunt de portu Hamptoun qui eos compulit ad scopulos Hibernie, et naues fregit ac eos submersit; sic omnia que ibidem habebant perierunt.[68]

Eodem anno papa misit ad Oxoniam, quibus hoc procurantibus, bullam suam in qua mandauit, sub pena amissionis omnium priuilegiorum, quod magistrum Iohannem Wikcliff incarcerarent et ipsum ibidem detinerent usque ad examinationem archiepiscopi Cantuariensis et episcopi Londoniensis; et reprehendit eos de hoc quod conclusiones

---

[o] exhigentibus *MS*

[64] For the outbreak of the Papal Schism, see above, p. 16. The parliamentary record of the recognition of Pope Urban VI is in *PROME*, vi. 104.

[65] Although called the kingdom of Sicily and Naples, only Naples was ruled by the Angevins in the 14th c. In 1378, Queen Joanna of Naples recognized the Avignon pope, Clement VII, and in 1381 Urban VI declared her dethroned and awarded her kingdom to Charles of Durazzo, called Charles 'of the Peace' because his father had been obliged in 1360 to send him, then just a boy, to Queen Joanna as a hostage for the peace made between them. (For 'Charles de la Paix', see *Chronique des quatre premiers Valois*, ed. S. Luce (SHF; Paris, 1862), p. 313. I am grateful to Rob Bartlett for his help with this.) Joanna had by now adopted Louis I of Anjou as her heir; he was the son of King John II of France, and thus ultimately descended from Eleanor, daughter of Henry II. Louis invaded Naples but died in 1384 without defeating Charles. Charles subsequently fell out with Urban VI before dying in 1386. Thomas Walsingham included much detail on Charles's exploits (*SAC* I, pp. 580–2, 610–12, 668–70, 740–8, 776).

[66] The 300-year-old nave of Canterbury cathedral was demolished in 1377 and work began on the new perpendicular nave in 1378. Sudbury was a generous benefactor of the work until his death in 1381. It was completed in 1405. The rebuilding of the ruinous city walls also began in 1378 but was not completed until the mid-15th c. Both projects were initially supervised

'As I am willing to answer before God, you should recognize Urban'; and it was decreed there that all Englishmen should recognize Urban.[64] Pope Urban expelled the king of Sicily and Naples, who was a descendant of the English, declaring him to be a schismatic and allied to the French and that such a man should not reign under the spiritual protection of Saint Peter; and, with the support of the kingdom, he made his kinsman, Charles of the Peace, king.[65] In this year the archbishop of Canterbury, Simon Sudbury, began to build his cathedral church, and he planned to have built there a most beautiful and powerful city.[66]

1379. In the year of the Lord 1379, the monks of Bury [Suffolk] elected an abbot, but he was challenged by another monk of the said house, a master from Rome who was made abbot by the pope and who, together with his supporters, celebrated mass in episcopal vestments. But when he was summoned by the chancellor of England, he was made aware that it was forbidden by statute of the realm for anyone to accept an abbacy by papal provision, under pain of imprisonment; and following his imprisonment he was allowed to leave the country.[67] John de Arundel, son of Richard earl of Arundel, was sent with an army to be seneschal of Gascony. And they indulged in such extravagance and pillage that after they sailed out of the port of Southampton [Hampshire], the Lord summoned up a spirit from the depths of the sea which drove them against the rocks of Ireland and smashed their ships and drowned them; and everything they had there was lost.[68]

In the same year, after certain people requested it, the pope sent his bull to Oxford, in which he ordered them, on pain of loss of all their privileges, to arrest and detain Master John Wyclif until he could be examined by the archbishop of Canterbury and the bishop of London; and he admonished them for the fact that they had allowed the teaching of conclusions

---

by the celebrated master-mason Henry Yevele (T. Tatton-Brown, *Canterbury: History and Guide* (Stroud, 1994), pp. 43–6; *PROME*, vi. 107, item 15).

[67] The dispute at Bury St Edmunds began in 1379, after the death of abbot John Brincle, when Edmund Brounfeld, proctor-general of the Benedictines, arrived from Rome claiming that Pope Urban had provided him as abbot. Several monks of Bury, with royal support, elected their sub-prior, John Timworth, instead of Brounfeld, but the community was divided. Brounfeld was arrested for contravening the Statute of Provisors and imprisoned in the Tower for three years. Timworth's election was eventually ratified by Urban VI in 1383, and in 1385 Brounfeld became abbot of La Grande Sauve in southern France (*SAC* I, pp. lxxxiii–lxxxiv, 315–25). The chancellor of England was Richard Lord Scrope of Bolton.

[68] Arundel's force of some 650 men sailed from Plymouth and was heading for Brittany; it is usually said to have been wrecked off Ireland in mid-Dec. 1379, although a list of payments to the captains of the vessels states that they were 'submersarum et naufragatarum in le Mounkesbay in Cornubia'—Mounts Bay, between Land's End and Lizard Point (*Eulogium*, iii, p. lx n.); the chroniclers were unsympathetic, accusing Arundel and his men of widespread looting before their departure (Saul, *Richard II*, p. 44; *SAC* I, pp. 324–39).

tales que in bulla scripte erant docere permitterent.[69] Amici uero prefati magistri Iohanni Wiccliff et ipse Iohannes consuluerunt in congregatione regentium et non regentium quod non incarcerarent hominem regis Anglie ad mandatum pape, ne uideantur dare pape dominationem et potestatem regale in Anglia. Et quia oportuit aliquid facere ad mandatum pape, ut uidebatur consilio uniuersitatis, monachus quidam, uicecancellarius, rogauit dictum Wikcliff et precepit quod ipse teneret se in aula nigra et de ea non exiret, quia nullum alium eum habere uolebat;[70] et quia iuratus erat uniuersitati hoc pro conseruatione priuilegiorum uniuersitatis decuit ipsum pati. Et conclusiones in bulla assignate fuerunt singulis magistris in theologia regentibus ibidem liberate; et omnes tradiderunt cancellario determinationes suas, qui uice omnium et assensu determinauit publice in scolis eas ueras esse, sed male sonare in auribus auditorum. Et dictus Wikclif respondebat dicens quod ueritas Catholica non debet damnari propter sonum quem facere posset in auribus quorumdam, quamuis aliquando debeat taceri, quia per istam opinionem, 'Christi bonus odor sumus in Domino',[71] possit concipi quod essemus accidens non substantia.[72] Et dictus W[ikclif] probauit coram archiepiscopo Cantuariensi et episcopo Londoniensi conclusiones illas ueras esse; qui ipsum rogabant quod de materia ipsarum amplius non loqueretur.

Eodem anno miles quidam de familia regis uenit de Wodstoke ad Oxoniam. Scolares quidam nocte uenerunt et stabant coram hospitio suo facientes de eo quendam cantum rhythmice in Anglico continentem certa uerba contra honorem regis; et miserunt sagittas ad fenestram hospitii. Miles mane surgens conquestus est regi. Statim cancellarius et suus uicecancellarius uocati sunt Londonias et statuuntur coram cancellario regni et consilio regis.[73] Et querebatur a cancellario uniuersitatis quare non puniuit derisores regis. Respondebat cancellarius | quia timuit irregularitatem. Cui cancellarius regni: 'Tu probare uis

---

[69] These events took place in 1377 and early 1378, before Wyclif's appearance at the Gloucester parliament described above. Pope Gregory XI's bulls, which condemned eighteen of Wyclif's conclusions, were dated 22 May and received in England by Nov. (*SAC* I, pp. 174–212, where several of the bulls are reproduced, along with Wyclif's conclusions). The chancellor of the university was Adam Tonworth. Gregory XI's death in Mar. 1378 probably saved Wyclif from further action (K. B. McFarlane, *John Wycliffe and the Beginnings of English Non-Conformity* (London, 1952), pp. 79–83; *The History of the University of Oxford*, ii: *Late Medieval Oxford*, ed. J. Catto and R. Evans (Oxford, 1992), pp. 207–8).

[70] Probably the Black Hall in School Street (*History of the University of Oxford*, ed. Catto and Evans, p. 207).

[71] 2 Cor. 2: 15.

[72] The distinction between accident and substance was a point discussed at length by medieval philosophers, often with reference to Aristotle's *Categories* and *Metaphysics*, and

such as those written in the bull.[69] The friends of the said Master John Wyclif, together with John himself, therefore argued in a congregation of the regents and non-regents that they should not imprison a subject of the king of England on the pope's order, lest it appear that they were giving the pope dominion and royal power in England. Yet because it seemed to the council of the university that it was necessary to do something in response to the pope's order, a certain monk, the vice-chancellor, summoned the said Wyclif and ordered him to betake himself to the Black Hall and to remain there, because he did not want anyone else to arrest him;[70] and, since he had taken an oath to the university for the preservation of its privileges, it seemed right to him that he should undergo this. Whereupon the conclusions mentioned in the bull were given to each of the masters in theology lecturing there, and they all delivered their determinations to the chancellor, who, on behalf and with the assent of all, declared publicly in the schools that they were true, but that they sounded offensive to the ears of listeners. To which the said Wyclif replied by saying that catholic truth should not be condemned on account of the sense it might have to the ears of some people, even if at times it should be silenced, because according to this opinion, 'We are the incense of Christ unto the Lord',[71] it might be interpreted as meaning that we are the accident not the substance.[72] Thus the said Wyclif proved in the presence of the archbishop of Canterbury and the bishop of London that these conclusions are true, but they asked him not to speak of such matters any further.

In this same year, one of the knights of the king's household came from Woodstock [Oxfordshire] to Oxford. Some of the scholars came and stood at night outside his hostel and sang there a certain rhyme in English which included various words insulting to the king, and they fired arrows at the window of the hostel. When he got up in the morning, the knight complained to the king. Immediately the chancellor and his vice-chancellor were summoned to London and brought before the chancellor of the realm and the king's council;[73] and the chancellor of the university was asked why he had not punished those who had insulted the king. The chancellor responded that it was because he feared disorder. The chancellor of the realm replied: 'What you mean

---

was central to Wyclif's developing view of the Eucharist (A. Kenny, *Wyclif* (Oxford, 1985), pp. 80–90).

[73] The students who sang insultingly outside the knight's window were led by three monks from Gloucester, Canterbury, and Norwich. The royal summons to the university authorities was dated 22 Mar. 1378. Adam Houghton, bishop of St David's, was chancellor of the realm (*History of the University of Oxford*, ed. Catto and Evans, p. 208; Workman, *Wyclif*, i. 307).

quod Oxonia non potest regi per clericum. Rex non potest contempni Oxonie sicut nec alibi. Et si uos de Oxonia non potestis corrigere et castigare regis contemptores propter irregularitarem, ut dicit cancellarius, sequitur quod Oxonia non potest regi per clericos sed oportet regem subtrahere priuilegia. Tu deberes maxime priuilegia uniuersitatis defendere et propter officium tuum et etiam propter iuramentum tuum, et contra ipsa priuilegia tu loqueris. Nos te deponimus ab officio tuo.' Respondebat uniuersitatis cancellarius: 'Officium meum habeo a papa et a rege; quod a rege habeo rex potest auferre, sed non illud quod a papa habeo.'[p] Cui cancellarius Anglie: 'Et nos priuamus te parte regia, et tunc uideas si poteris gaudere parte pape, te ad dictum officium inhabilitantes. Rex potest ab Oxonia amouere uniuersitatem et te.' Vicecancellarius monachus adiudicatus fuit carceribus quia ad mandatum pape incarcerauerat, ut superius dictum est, Iohannem Wiccliff, qui postea ad rogatum amicorum liberatus est. Cancellarius depositus, pallians depositionem suam, resignauit sponte in conuocatione, ut dixit, non coactus. Hoc anno factum est parliamentum Londoniis, in quo decima et quintadecima exacte sunt, dicente communitate quod rex abundauit de bonis aui sui, patris sui, ac donariis multis. Statuitur etiam quod statutum Edwardi Primi de beneficiis extraneorum firmiter obseruetur.[q] [74] Hoc anno frater regis Hispanie fuit frater minor et ipse asserebat quod papa erit frater minor qui terminabit scisma ecclesie; qui transiit ad Romam cum centum equis, sed non reuenit.[75]

1380. Anno Domini millesimo trecentisimo octogesimo, factum est parliamentum apud Clarendon ubi quidam frater Carmelita, bacallaureus in theologia, accusauit ducem Lancastrie de proditione regis, sed in probatione deficiens tractus in habitu suo et suspensus est Sarum, et sepultus in cemeterio Sancti Martini ibidem.

Tallagium duodecim denarios. In hoc parliamento exactum fuit tale tallagium quod quilibet maritus solueret regi duodecim denarios et

---

[p] *marginal in later hand*: nota   [q] *marginal in later hand*: nota

[74] In the Westminster parliament of 16 Jan. to 3 Mar. 1380, the commons granted one and a half fifteenths and tenths to the king and submitted a petition deploring the number of benefices granted by papal provision to foreigners; the king agreed to write to the pope and enforce the Statute of Provisors of 1353, passed under Edward III, not Edward I (*PROME*, vi. 153, 169–71).

[75] This probably comes from the same source as the list of 'kings who became friars' in *Monumenta Franciscana*, i. pp. 539–41, which says that the Infante Pedro ('Petrus Infans'), 'of the royal line of the king of Castile', renounced the world, became Franciscan, and died in Rome, where he was buried. He has not been noticed by Spanish historians, but the story is plausible. However, it could have referred to a prophecy ascribed to Peter, the uncle of King Peter IV of Aragon, who also became a Franciscan (Catto, 'An alleged Great Council',

is that Oxford cannot be governed by a cleric. The king cannot be insulted at Oxford, nor indeed anywhere else. And if you people of Oxford cannot control or punish those who insult the king because of disorder, as the chancellor says, it follows that Oxford cannot be governed by clerics, so it is appropriate for the king to withdraw its privileges. You above all are bound to defend the university's privileges, both because of your office and also because of your oath, and what you are saying is contrary to those privileges. We depose you from your office.' The chancellor of the university replied: 'I hold my office from the pope and from the king; that which I hold from the king, the king can remove, but not that which I hold from the pope.' The chancellor of England said to him: 'And we deprive you of the royal part, and then you will see if you can still enjoy the papal part, once you have been disqualified from that office. The king is quite capable of removing the university as well as you from Oxford.' The vice-chancellor, a monk, was adjudged to be imprisoned because he had, at the pope's order, as noted above, imprisoned John Wyclif, who was subsequently released at the request of his friends. The deposed chancellor, making light of his deposition, resigned of his own accord in convocation, so he said, not through coercion. In this year a parliament was held in London in which a tenth and a fifteenth were granted, the commons declaring that the king had an abundance of goods from his grandfather, his father, and numerous gifts. It was also enacted that the statute of Edward the First concerning foreigners' benefices should be firmly observed.[74] In this year the brother of the king of Spain became a friar minor, and he declared that the pope who will bring an end to the schism in the Church will be a friar minor; he went across to Rome with a hundred horses, but did not return.[75]

1380. In the year of the Lord 1380, a parliament was held at Clarendon [Wiltshire], where a certain Carmelite friar, a bachelor of theology, accused the duke of Lancaster of treason to the king, but, failing to prove his case, he was drawn in his habit and hanged at Salisbury [Wiltshire], where he was buried in St Martin's cemetery.

A tax of twelve pence. In this parliament a tax was granted to the effect that each married man should pay the king 12 pence, and each

---

p. 766, citing Oxford, Bodleian Library, MS Bodley 703, fos. 68v–69). Either way, it is tempting to wonder whether this was inserted thirty years or more later, in the knowledge that the Franciscan Pope Alexander V was elected at the Council of Pisa, which set in motion the process that did eventually end the Schism at Constance (see below, p. 148).

quelibet uxor duodecim denarios.[76] Eodem anno uenerunt nuntii de Britannia ad ducem Iohannem de Monte Forti, rogantes ut ad eos rediret, deprecantesque amicitiam regni Anglie, hoc decere dicentes quia patres eorum nati fuerunt in Anglia et tam regnum quam ducatus uno nomine Britannia appellantur. Ordinatumque fuit quod quartus filius regis Edwardi, Thomas comes de Bokyngham, dictus de Wodstok, equitaret in Franciam cum exercitu usque in Britanniam, et inde ipse simul et dux intrarent Franciam.[77] Eodem anno archiepiscopus Cantuariensis factus est cancellarius regni, uolens de officio cancellarii domum suam tenere et prouentus archiepiscopatus in edificatione Cantuarie expendere, sed non perfecit opus suum.[78]

Iohannes Wiccliff determinauit Oxonie sacramentum eucharistie esse panem, ut dicit Apostolus, 'Panis quem frangimus',[79] et confessio Berengarii in Decretis, et illum panem esse corpus Christi sicut petra erat Christus.[80] Aliter tamen est ibi corpus quam ubi in signo, quia est ibi per gratiam sanctificantem digne sumentes, nec accidens ibi esse sine subiecto; et quia Hugo de Sancto Victore fuit primus qui illum terminum transubstantiatio inuenit;[81] et quod accidens ⸢non est⸣ sacramentum altaris sed substantia, quia tunc panis ratonum prestantior esset sacramento altaris, eo quod omnis substantia est prestantior quocumque accidente; et breuiter, oppositum non inuenitur, ut fundari potest in scriptura. Et quod omnes doctores primi millenarii post Christum, in quo, ut dicitur in Apocalypsi, ligatus fuit Satanas, sic sensierunt de sacramento, et iam solutus Satanas decepit gentes in fide sacramenti.[82] Et quod ille panis sanctus non debet aspici ut panis, sed ut corpus Christi in memoriam Dominice passionis. Discipuli eius hanc doctrinam predicabant et diuulgabant per totam Angliam, multos laicos seducentes, etiam nobiles et magnos dominos qui defendebant tales falsos predicatores.[83] Magistri

---

⸢⸣ repeated

---

[76] The chronicler has confused two parliaments here. The notorious case of John Latimer, the Carmelite friar who accused John of Gaunt of treason and was tortured to death by a group of royal household knights, occurred at the Salisbury parliament of Apr. 1384; the third poll-tax, levied at the rate of 12 pence for each man and woman, was granted at the Northampton parliament of Nov. 1380 (*The Westminster Chronicle 1381–1394*, ed. L. Hector and B. Harvey (OMT, 1982), pp. 66–80; *PROME*, vi. 191–2, 360).

[77] The Breton embassy referred to here arrived at Westminster in May 1379, and Duke John crossed to Brittany in early Aug. 1379, but it was not until July 1380, following a treaty of alliance between England and Brittany, that a force of some 5,000 men led by Thomas of Woodstock, earl of Buckingham, fifth son of Edward III, arrived at Calais. He and Duke John met near Rennes in Oct., but following Duke John's agreement with the French crown Buckingham returned to England in early May 1381 (Sumption, *Divided Houses*, pp. 359–412).

[78] Archbishop Sudbury became chancellor on 30 Jan. 1380, but died in 1381.

[79] 1 Cor. 10: 16 ('The bread which we break, is it not partaking of the body of the Lord?').

married woman 12 pence.[76] In this same year, messengers came from Brittany to Duke John de Montfort asking him to return to them, and seeking the friendship of the kingdom of England, saying that this was fitting since their forefathers had been born in England and both the kingdom and the duchy were known by the one name, Britain. And it was decided that the fourth son of King Edward, Thomas earl of Buckingham, called 'of Woodstock', should campaign in France with an army until he reached Brittany, whence he and the duke should jointly invade France.[77] In the same year, the archbishop of Canterbury was made chancellor of the realm; he wanted to maintain his household from the office of chancellor and use the archiepiscopal revenues to pay for the building of Canterbury, but he did not bring his work to completion.[78]

John Wyclif determined at Oxford that the sacrament of the Eucharist was bread, as the Apostle says, 'The bread which we break',[79] and the confession of Berengar in the Decretals;[80] and that that bread is the body of Christ, just as the rock was Christ. However, the body is there in a different way from where it is a sign, because it is there through those worthily assuming sanctifying grace, nor can an accident be there without a subject; and because Hugh of St-Victor was the first person to invent that term 'transubstantiation';[81] and that the accident is not the sacrament of the altar but the substance, since otherwise the bread of rats would be more perfect than the sacrament of the altar, because every substance is more perfect than any accident. To speak briefly, the contrary is not found, as can be established from the Scriptures. And that all the doctors of the first millennium after Christ, during which, so it is said in the Apocalypse, Satan was bound fast, conceived of the sacrament in this way, but now Satan has been let loose he has deceived people in their faith in the sacrament.[82] And that that holy bread should not be thought of as bread but as the body of Christ, in memory of the Lord's Passion. His disciples preached and disseminated this doctrine throughout England, seducing numerous laymen, including nobles and great lords who defended these false preachers.[83] However, all the

---

[80] Berengar of Tours (d. 1088), who questioned transubstantiation, recanted his views in his Confession of 1079, but subsequently withdrew his recantation.

[81] Hugh of St-Victor (d. 1141), philosopher, theologian, and head of school of the abbey of St-Victor in Paris, whose works included *De Sacramentis Christiane Fidei*.

[82] Rev. 20: 1–3 ('[An angel] laid hold of the dragon, that serpent of old, who is the Devil and Satan, and bound him for a thousand years; and he cast him into the bottomless pit, and shut him up, and set a seal on him, so that he should deceive the nations no more till the thousand years were finished. But after these things he must be released for a little while').

[83] The most notorious defender of early Lollard preachers was John of Gaunt, duke of Lancaster.

tamen omnes in theologia regentes Oxonie determinabant contra hanc doctrinam, et precipue regens fratrum minorum hanc doctrinam redarguit potenter, et ipsos Lollardos esse probauit;[84] cuius determinatio adhuc in archiuis uniuersitatis conseruatur. Archiepiscopus Cantuariensis tamen non satis de hoc curare uidebatur. Hoc anno magna glacies percussit pontem ligneum Rofe et fregit illum ita ut scapha ibidem diu haberetur.[85] In parliamento Londonie tento fuit prohibitum quod nullus portet | aurum, argentum, nec monetam extra regnum per camsores uel alio modo sine licentia regis.[86]

1381. Anno Domini millesimo trecentisimo octogesimo uno, Thomas comes Bokyngham equitando per Franciam nihil magni fecit, et ueniens in Britanniam inuenit ducem Gallicis federatum et rediit in Angliam.[87] Hoc anno duo armigeri sedentes in taberna quadam Londonie dixerunt quod summa collecte solidorum huius anni non peruenit ad summam grossorum anni precedentis, transieruntque ad cancellarium Anglie petentes iustitiarios in Canciam et in Estsexiam ad inquirendum de collectione dicte summe et offerebant regi summam auri pro residuo colligendo.[88] In Cancia autem responsum fuit quod post solutionem grossorum multi utriusque sexus mortui sunt. In Estsex uero sedebat iudex cum aliis et uocabat quondam pistorem illius loci collectorem. Pistor dixit sociis suis: 'Non sufficit istis quod collectum est, sed modo ueniunt ad nouum tallagium colligendum; si haberem assistentiam ego resisterem illis.' Et statim omnes, captis instrumentis que habebant, ad pugnam uenerunt ad locum; statim iustitiarius cum suis fugit. 'Ecce', dixit pistor, 'patet quod pro nouo tallagio uenerunt.' Tunc illa uilla transiit ad aliam proximam et ipsam fecit insurgere, et ille due tertiam et sic ultra totum comitatum et comitatum Hertfordie et postea per Erhethe transierunt in Canciam ad Maydston et Waldam, et inde Cantuariam, totam patriam eleuantes et

---

[84] Between 1379 and 1381, the last phase of his Oxford career, Wyclif fell out decisively with the friars, whom he had previously praised. His views on the Eucharist developed gradually during the 1370s; by 1380 he was arguing openly against transubstantiation, since 'to posit accidents without a substance was meaningless'. When he repeated these views in a public determination on 10 May 1381 (the event referred to here), the university authorities turned against him, and by the end of 1381 he had been obliged to leave Oxford (A. Hudson, *The Premature Reformation: Wycliffite Texts and Lollard History* (Oxford, 1988), pp. 281–90, and for 'rats' bread' see p. 290; *History of the University of Oxford*, ed. Catto and Evans, pp. 213–14). For Wyclif's views, and the refutation, or 'confession', of the Franciscan John Tissington, see *Fasciculi Zizaniorum Magistri Johannis Wyclif cum tritico*, ed. W. Shirley (RS; London, 1858), pp. 104–80. The chancellor of the university at this time was William Barton (J. Catto, 'Barton, William', *ODNB*, iv. 215).

[85] The collapse of the old bridge over the Medway at Rochester occurred following a sudden thaw in early Feb. 1381; its replacement was not completed until 1391 (R. Britnell,

masters in theology lecturing at Oxford determined against such teaching, and the regent of the friars minor in particular, whose determination is still preserved in the university's archives, strongly refuted this doctrine and showed these people to be Lollards.[84] Yet the archbishop of Canterbury did not seem to be unduly concerned about this. In this year a large ice floe struck the wooden bridge at Rochester [Kent] and broke it, so that for a long time there was a ferry-boat there.[85] In a parliament held at London it was prohibited for anyone to carry gold, silver, or money out of the kingdom, whether through money-changers or by any other method, without a royal licence.[86]

1381. In the year of the Lord 1381, Thomas earl of Buckingham campaigned through France but achieved nothing of note, and when he came to Brittany he found that the duke had allied himself to the French, so he returned to England.[87] In this year two esquires sitting in a certain tavern in London said that the total of shillings collected this year amounted to less than the total of groats of the previous year, and they approached the chancellor of England asking for justices in Kent and in Essex to enquire into the collection of the said sums, and they offered the king a sum of gold to collect the residue.[88] The answer given in Kent was that after payment of the groats many people of both sexes had died. Meanwhile in Essex a judge sat with others and summoned a certain baker who was a collector there. The baker said to his fellows: 'They are not satisfied with what has been collected, and now they are coming to collect a new tax; if I could have some help, I would resist them.' And immediately all of them, seizing the tools which they had, came to that place ready to fight, whereupon the justice and his men promptly fled. 'Look', said the baker, 'it is evident that they came for a new tax.' Then that township went to another one nearby and made it rise up, and the two together went to a third, and then they went throughout the county as well as the county of Hertford, and afterwards they crossed via Erith to Maidstone in Kent and the Weald, and from there to Canterbury, raising the whole country and forcing people to join them, breaking into

---

[85] 'Rochester Bridge, 1381–1530', in N. Yates and J. Gibson, eds., *Traffic and Politics: The Construction and Management of Rochester Bridge, AD 43–1993*' (Woodbridge, 1994), pp. 43–60).

[86] This was in the parliament of Nov. 1381 (*PROME*, vi. 260–2).

[87] John de Montfort, duke of Brittany, reached agreement with the French in Jan. 1381; Buckingham's army returned to England in May (Sumption, *Divided Houses*, pp. 409–12).

[88] The second poll-tax of 1379, at 4 pence (a groat) per head, raised around £22,000; the third poll-tax of 1380–1, at 12 pence (a shilling) per head, was expected to raise at least £60,000 but by Mar. 1381 had raised only about one-third of this sum, due to widespread evasion. Commissions to recover the residue were issued on 16 Mar. (Saul, *Richard II*, pp. 56–8).

sequi cogentes, domos penetrantes, omnia uictualia consumentes, homines occidentes et spoliantes ac domos destruentes. Et cum quereretur ab eis quis esset capitaneus eorum, quia nullum habebant, derisorie respondebant.[89]

Jak Straw. Jak Straw et Thomas Melro redeuntes ad campum qui dicitur Blacheth uocauerunt ad se episcopum Rofensem. Et cum quereret episcopus quis esset principalis qui sibi loqueretur, processit unus tegulator de Estsex qui ualde eloquens fuerat, exprimebat episcopo multa grauamina uirorum simplicium per tallagia et oppressiones maiorum, rogans ut hec narraret regi; et cogitabant, ut dixit, repatriare si debita correctio habita sit.[90] Rex et archiepiscopus uenerunt per aquam et uisis illis archiepiscopus non sinebat regem ascendere uel loqui cum illis: 'Quia', inquit, 'circumducent uos et per uos facient omnia eis placentia.' Maior et burgenses Londonie querebant a ciuitate si uelint claudere ciuitatem. Et responderunt quod non contra uicinos et amicos suos. Burgenses Londonie miserunt quosdam de ciuitate ad comitiuam ut eos prohiberent ex parte ciuitatis ne regem in sua camera inquietarent et dicerent ciuitatem contra eos esse armatum. Ipsi uero nuntii dixerunt: 'Venite ad nos, pro uobis missi sumus.' Et antequam peruenerint London, ipsi de London combusserunt Sauoye, manerium ducis Lancastrie, et iocalia sua ibidem inuenta proiecerunt in Thamisiam, dicentes: 'Nolumus esses fures.'[91] Quidam bonus uir, haraldus armorum, dixit se uidisse centum milia hominum et inter eos plures demones; qui cepit infirmari et in breui mortuus est. Venerunt tunc ad ciuitatem multitudo terribilis, senes decrepiti, iuuenes cum securibus et sagittis robiginosis cum arcubus et baculis, in festo Corporis Christi, et occiderunt illos armigeros qui iustitiarios procurabant, quorum unum a feretro Sancti Edwardi extraxerunt, quosdam etiam alios et Flamyngos circa quadringentos perimerunt.[92] Aperiebant carceres, uinctos dimittentes, uincula ferrea de Noua Porta obtulerunt in ecclesiam fratrum minorum, et marchalciam fregerunt;

---

[89] The justice forced to flee from Brentwood (Essex) on 2 June 1381 was Sir Robert Bealknap. The esquire John Bampton, one of the commissioners to raise the residue of the tax, had also fled Brentwood, probably on 30 May. Thomas Baker of Fobbing (Essex) led the local resistance, which began in the neighbouring townships of Fobbing, Corringham, and Stanford-le-Hope (*The Peasants' Revolt of 1381*, ed. R. B. Dobson (London, 1970), pp. 38, 124).

[90] Jack Straw may be confused with John Wrawe, one of the leaders of the revolt in Sussex, or his name may have been (as this chronicler appears to think) an alias for Wat Tyler (Walter the Tiler), widely acknowledged as leader of the rebels. Thomas Melro is otherwise unknown. Thomas Brinton was bishop of Rochester 1373–89. The meeting at Blackheath took place on 12 June, by which time rebel bands from both Kent and Essex had converged on London (*Peasants' Revolt*, ed. Dobson, p. 39).

houses, consuming all the provisions, killing and despoiling men and destroying homes. And when they were asked who was their captain, they replied with scorn, because they did not have one.[89]

Jack Straw. Jack Straw and Thomas Melro, returning to the field called Blackheath, called on the bishop of Rochester to meet them. And when the bishop asked them who was the leader who would speak to him, a tiler from Essex, a man of great eloquence, came forward and recounted to the bishop the many grievances of the ordinary people on account of the taxes and oppressions of the great, asking him to explain this to the king; their intention, so he said, was to return to their homes once a suitable remedy was provided.[90] The king and the archbishop arrived by water, but when he saw them the archbishop would not permit the king to disembark or speak with them: 'Because', he said, 'they will take you around and use you to get everything they want.' The mayor and burgesses of London asked the citizens if they wanted to close the city; and they replied no, not against their neighbours and friends. The burgesses of London sent some men from the city to the mob to prohibit them on behalf of the city from molesting the king in his chamber, and to tell them that the city was in arms against them. What these messengers actually said was: 'Come to us, we have been sent for you.' And before they could enter London, the Londoners burned the Savoy, the manor of the duke of Lancaster, and threw the jewels they found there into the Thames, declaring: 'We do not wish to be thieves.'[91] A certain herald at arms who was a good man declared that he had seen a hundred thousand men, among them several demons; whereupon he began to sicken and soon died. Then, on the feast of Corpus Christi [13 June], a terrible multitude entered the city, decrepit old men, young men with rusty axes and arrows and bows and clubs, and they killed those esquires who were looking after the justices, one of whom they dragged out from the shrine of St Edward, along with many others, including about four hundred Flemings who were slain.[92] They opened the prisons, releasing the prisoners, carried the iron chains from Newgate to the church of the friars minor, and broke open

---

[91] Richard II took a barge from the Tower to Rotherhithe to meet the rebels on the morning of Thursday 13 June, but he did not go ashore. John of Gaunt's Savoy palace, on the banks of the Thames, was looted and burned the same afternoon. The part played by the Londoners in admitting the rebels to the city was a matter of controversy (Saul, *Richard II*, p. 63).

[92] The number of Flemings killed by the rebels is uncertain but amounted at least to scores; other foreigners were also targeted. The esquire dragged out of Westminster abbey and beheaded was Richard Imworth, keeper of the Marshalsea prison, 'a tormentor without pity' (*Peasants' Revolt*, ed. Dobson, pp. 163, 189, 202).

domos ciuitatis penetrauerunt, comedentes et bibentes ac rapientes sine prohibitione. Rex et probissimi milites et burgenses ciuitatis ita territi erant ut nec ipsis resistere nec ipsam Turrim defendere audebant.

In crastino iuerunt ad Turrim et dixerunt regi se uelle proditores et malos consiliarios suos occidere, et eductum archiepiscopum Anglie, cancellarium, decollabant, ad quemlibet ictum dicentem: 'Hec est manus Domini.' Similiter magistrum Hospitalariorum, thesaurarium Anglie, et plures alios decollebant. Exigebantque a rege ut omnes suos regni faceret liberos, et rex tradidit eis litteras suas patentes libertatis generales.[93] Sed rex, grauiter ista ferens, et burgenses, timentes ne spoliarent ciuitatem, consulebant cum Roberto Knollis milite quo modo possent eos eiicere. Et Sabbato, iuxta consilium suum, proclamatum fuit in quattuor | partibus ciuitatis quod dux Lancastrie ueniret contra regem et comitiuam cum uiginti milibus Scotorum, et ideo comitiua conuenire deberet in Smythfeld, et ibi rex ad eos ueniret. Ipsi festinabant in Smythfeld et maior ciuitatis iussit ut ciuitas armaretur et sequatur Robertum Knollis militem.[94] Rex autem uenit in Smythfeld et Walterus tegulator capiciatus accessit ad regem, dicens se uelle emendare cartam libertatis quam rex sibi alias tradidit. Cui maior Londonie dixit: 'Quomodo loqueris tu regi? Supplica sibi, et depone capicium tuum.' 'Tu es proditor', dixit alter.

Jak Straw moritur. Et statim unus armiger regis perfodit eum pugione, deinde maior et alius burgensis, et mortuus est Walterus tegulator.[95] Clamabat autem comitiua: 'Quid facit rex cum nostro prolocutore?' Dixerunt alii: 'Facit eum militem.' Et clamauerunt omnes: 'Transite in campum Sancti Iohannis et ueniet ad uos nouus miles.' Traxeruntque ipsum miserum in quandam domum, et statim uenit ciuitas splendide armata et circumdederunt omnes in campo predicto, qui sic obsessi perdiderunt corda, nescientes quid agerent.[96] Et rex interrogabat Robertum Knollis: 'Nonne occidentur isti?' Et respondit: 'Non, domine, multi miseri sunt hic inuiti.' Quibus dixit Robertus:

---

[93] The rebels entered the Tower during the morning of 14 June, following a meeting with Richard II at Mile End, at which he agreed to give them charters of manumission from serfdom. Simon Sudbury, chancellor and archbishop of Canterbury, and Robert Hales, treasurer and Master of the Hospitallers, were dragged out to Tower Hill and there beheaded (Saul, *Richard II*, pp. 68–9).

[94] Knolles was a veteran of the wars in France who had been entrusted with leadership of an English army to France in 1370 (above, p. 14).

[95] The esquire who stabbed Tyler was Ralph Standish. Other sources give most of the credit for the ending of the revolt at Smithfield to the Londoners, especially the mayor, William Walworth, who also attacked Tyler (Saul, *Richard II*, pp. 70–3).

the Marshalsea; they entered houses in the city, eating, drinking, and stealing without hindrance. The king and the most honourable knights and burgesses of the city were so afraid that they dared not resist them nor even defend the Tower.

On the following day, they went to the Tower and told the king that they wanted to kill the traitors and his evil councillors and, carrying off the archbishop of England, the chancellor, they beheaded him; at each stroke, he declared: 'This is the hand of the Lord.' They similarly beheaded the Master of the Hospitallers, treasurer of England, and several others. And they demanded of the king that he should make all his subjects in the realm free, whereupon the king gave them his general letters patent of liberty.[93] Nevertheless, the king, who bore these matters hard, and the burgesses, who were afraid that their city would be ransacked, consulted with Sir Robert Knolles as to how they might be able to get rid of them. And on the Saturday [15 June], in accordance with his advice, it was proclaimed in the four parts of the city that the duke of Lancaster was going to come against the king and the mob with twenty thousand Scotsmen, and that it was therefore necessary for the mob to assemble at Smithfield, where the king would meet them. They hurried to Smithfield, while the mayor of the city ordered the citizens to take up arms and follow Sir Robert Knolles.[94] Thus the king came to Smithfield, where Walter the Tiler, wearing his hat, approached the king, saying that he wanted to make some changes to the charter of liberty which the king had given him before. The mayor of London said to him: 'How dare you speak to the king like that? Kneel before him, and remove your hat.' 'You are a traitor', said the other.

Jack Straw is killed. And immediately one of the king's esquires stabbed him with a dagger, following which the mayor and another burgess did likewise, and thus Walter the Tiler died.[95] At this, the mob cried out: 'What is the king doing with our spokesman?' Others declared: 'He is knighting him.' Whereupon everyone shouted: 'Go to St John's Field and the new knight will come to you.' And they carried that wretched man to a certain house, and immediately the people of the city arrived, splendidly armed, and surrounded all those who were in that field, who, being thus encircled, lost heart and did not know what to do.[96] The king asked Robert Knolles: 'Should they not all be killed?' To which he replied: 'No, my lord, many of these poor people are here against their will.' Robert said to

---

[96] Tyler was carried, mortally wounded, to St Bartholomew's priory, Smithfield, where he died (*Peasants' Revolt*, ed. Dobson, p. 167).

'Cadite, uos miseri, scindite cordas arcuum et recedite. Nullus remaneat hac nocte in ciuitate nec in regione ista sub pena capitis.' Et statim omnes fugerunt. Et illi qui redierunt Cantuariam fecerunt proclamationes ordinationum suarum, et quendam burgensem ibidem reclamantem occiderunt. Cartas, munimenta et scripturas in domo iudicii combusserunt.[97] In Southfolk insurrectores priorem de Bury et iustitiarium regis decollabant. In Northfolk, Southsex et diocesi Wintoniensi homicidia multa facta sunt. Rex transiit in Estsex et Hertfordshyram, comes Cancie in Canciam, et alii in alias partes regni, et malefactores trahi fecerunt, suspendi et decollari, quosdam in quartas diuidentes.[98]

1382.[s] Anno Domini millesimo trecentisimo octogesimo duo, Iohannes Wicclif Oxonie determinauit de religione, dicens quod sola religio meritoria est religio communis Christiana, de qua dicit apostolus: 'Religio munda et immaculata hec est', etcetera;[99] et quod omnes alie religiones priuate sunt superstitiose, impertinentes ad salutem, ab hominibus statute et inuente, traditiones, ritus et doctrinas, ac mandata hominum continentes. Et quod institutores earum, ut Benedictus, Franciscus et alii, albam parietem religionis Christiane luto suarum traditionum maculauerunt et animabus Christianorum onus Iudaicum imposuerunt;[100] et quod in statuendo suas religiones peccauerunt. Nec sancti sunt nisi forte quod in morte penituerunt. Item quod mendicatio fratrum ualidorum est illicita, et quod laborare deberent ad uictum acquirendum, secundum Apostolum et Augustinum de operibus monachorum et regulis eorundem.[101] Discipuli prefati Iohannis studuerunt in compilationibus sermonum et sermones fratrum congregauerunt, euntes per totam Angliam doctrinam huius sui magistri predicabant, corruperuntque fidem sacramenti eucharistie et deuotionem erga ecclesiam et religionem, non solum in multis popularibus et laicis, sed etiam in nobilibus et litteratis.[102] Hoc anno fratrum elemosine

---

[s] Wiclyff, *in upper margin of fo. 195ᵛ in later hand*

[97] The sheriff of Kent, Sir William Septvans, a benefactor to the Canterbury grey friars, was forced to hand these over to the rebels for burning (Cotton, *Grey Friars of Canterbury*, p. 84).

[98] John de Cambridge, prior of Bury, and Chief Justice Sir John Cavendish were beheaded in Suffolk on 14–15 June. Commissions to suppress the lingering unrest were issued by Richard II on 18 June, but it was not until mid-July that order was fully restored (*Peasants' Revolt*, ed. Dobson, pp. 40–4).

[99] Jas. 1: 27 ('religio munda et inmaculata apud Deum et Patrem haec est'). Wyclif had been obliged to leave Oxford before the end of 1381, spending the last three years of his life at Lutterworth (Leicestershire), where he suffered a series of strokes. His attacks on the friars, whom he blamed for driving him out of Oxford, began in 1379–80 and became more virulent after 1381. For his views on 'private religions' and 'sects' not grounded in the Bible,

them: 'Get down on the ground, you wretches, cut your bowstrings, and be gone. Anyone who spends the night in the city or nearby will lose his head.' And straight away they all fled. And those who came back to Canterbury issued proclamations of their ordinances, and they killed a certain burgess who defied them. They burned the charters, muniments, and records in the house of justice.[97] In Suffolk, the rebels beheaded the prior of Bury and a royal justice; many murders were also committed in Norfolk, Sussex, and the diocese of Winchester. The king went into Essex and Hertfordshire, the earl of Kent into Kent, and others into other parts of the kingdom, and they had the malefactors drawn, hanged, and beheaded, and some of them quartered.[98]

1382. In the year of the Lord 1382, John Wyclif determined at Oxford concerning religion, saying that the only religion through which merit is earned is the universal Christian religion, of which the Apostle says: 'Pure religion and undefiled is this', etcetera.[99] And that all other private religions are superstitious, irrelevant to salvation, ordained and invented by men, traditions, customs, and teachings resting upon the decrees of men. And that those who founded them, such as Benedict, Francis, and others, bespattered the pure white wall of the Christian religion with the mud of their traditions and placed the Jewish yoke upon the souls of Christians.[100] And that in setting up their religions they sinned. Nor are they saints, unless by chance they repented on their deathbeds. Also that begging by able-bodied friars is unlawful, and that they ought to labour in order to sustain themselves, according to the Apostle and Augustine concerning the tasks and rules of monks.[101] The disciples of the said John busied themselves with making compilations of sermons and collected the sermons of the friars, and going throughout England they preached the teaching of this master of theirs, and they perverted faith in the sacrament of the Eucharist and devotion to the Church and religion, not merely among many common and illiterate people but also among the well-born and the literate.[102] In this year the alms of the friars were withdrawn; the

---

published in 1381 in his *De Apostasia*, see Hudson, *Premature Reformation*, pp. 347–51; Kenny, *Wyclif*, pp. 94–9; A. Gwynn, *The English Austin Friars in the Time of Wyclif* (Oxford, 1940), pp. 262–9.

[100] St Benedict of Nursia (d. *c*.547), author of the Benedictine Rule; St Francis of Assisi (d. 1226), founder of the Franciscan order; the 'Jewish yoke', or 'yoke of the commandments' entailed acceptance of Jewish precepts.

[101] Wyclif was referring to St Paul (2 Thess. 3: 10) and St Augustine's treatise, *De opere monachorum*.

[102] Although the early Lollard preachers were inspired by Wyclif, the direct connection between him and them is difficult to prove (Hudson, *Premature Reformation*, pp. 62–70).

subtrahuntur, mendicantes laborare iubentur, predicare non sinuntur, denariorum predicatores et domorum penetrantes uocantur.[103] Scripserunt insuper libellos famosos in Anglico contra fratres, suos etiam errores in Anglico scripserunt.[104]

Hoc anno rex Annam sororem imperatoris, regis scilicet Bohemie, solutis pro ea uiginti duo milia marcis, sine consensu regni desponsauit. Oblata sibi fuit filia comitis Flandrie, quam si habuisset iure suo postea Flandriam habuisset. Dux autem Burgundie ipsam duxit qui nunc comitatum habet.[105] Hoc anno orta est dissensio in Flandria quia ciuitates uel bone uille Flandrie procurarent subtractionem priuilegiorum Gandauensium; qui rebellantes Anglicorum auxilium petierunt.[106] Eodem anno factum est parliamentum Londonie, in quo pax cum insurgentibus facta est et decima ecclesiasticorum et quintadecima laicorum concedentur.[107] | Hoc autem anno fuit magnus terremotus per totam Angliam et Flandriam, arbores, domos, ecclesias, campanilia, castra eleuans et inclinans, subito post prandium duodecimo kalendas Iunii, et in eadem hebdomada fuit alius terremotus magnus. Fuit tunc etiam eclipsis lune magna, sanguinea apparens.[108] Statutumque fuit in eodem parliamento quod statuta contra beneficiatos extraneos in Anglia edita per antea et contra ipsorum procuratores firmiter obseruentur.[109]

1383. Anno Domini millesimo trecentisimo octogesimo tertio episcopus Northwicensis, magis militari leuitate dissolutus quam pontificali maturitate solidus, procurauit a papa auctoritatem predicandi crucem Christi et debellandi antipapam ac eius fautores. Papa concessit sibi potestatem illam et indulgentiam concessam euntibus in Terram Sanctam omnibus qui crucis assumpto charactere cum eo uellent uel de bonis suis ei aliquid conferrent. Deditque ei*t* potestatem

---

t interlined

---

[103] Apparently a reference to the prohibition on unlicensed preachers (although friars were not specifically mentioned) tacked on to the acts of the parliament of May 1382 as a result of discussions held at the church council held at Blackfriars in the same month (*PROME*, vi. 275; Kenny, *Wyclif*, pp. 94–5).

[104] For examples of scurrilous poems against the friars written around this time, see *Monumenta Franciscana*, i. 591–608.

[105] Richard II married Anne of Bohemia, daughter of Emperor Charles IV (d. 1378), at Westminster on 20 Jan. 1382, when he agreed to lend Emperor Wenzel £12,000 (18,000 marks). Negotiations for his marriage had been ongoing almost since his accession, and included offers from France, Navarre, Scotland, and Milan, but not from Flanders. The chronicler is confusing these negotiations with those of the mid-1360s, when Edward III's son Edmund came close to marrying Margaret, daughter of Count Louis de Mâle of Flanders; instead, Margaret married Philip the Bold, duke of Burgundy and count of Flanders (d. 1404) (Saul, *Richard II*, pp. 83–90).

mendicants were ordered to work, prohibited from preaching, and labelled as preachers of pennies and intruders into homes.[103] They [Wyclif's disciples] also wrote slanderous libels against the friars in English, as well as setting down their own errors in English.[104]

In this year the king married Anne, sister of the emperor—that is to say, the king of Bohemia—having paid twenty-two thousand marks for her, without the consent of the realm. The daughter of the count of Flanders was offered to him, and if he had accepted her he would subsequently have held the county of Flanders in his own right. However, the duke of Burgundy who now holds the county married her.[105] In this year a quarrel erupted in the county of Flanders because the cities or good towns succeeded in having the privileges of the men of Ghent withdrawn; the latter, rebelling, asked for help from the English.[106] In the same year a parliament was held in London in which peace was made with the insurgents and a tenth was conceded from the clergy and a fifteenth from the laity.[107] Also in this year, after lunch on 21 May, there occurred without warning a great earthquake throughout England and Flanders which damaged and brought down trees, houses, churches, bell-towers and castles, followed in the same week by another great earthquake. Then there also occurred a great eclipse of the moon, which appeared blood-red.[108] It was also enacted in this parliament that the statutes previously issued against foreigners holding benefices in England and against those who sought to procure them should be firmly kept.[109]

1383. In the year of the Lord 1383 the bishop of Norwich, more given to military recklessness than attentive to his episcopal duties, procured from the pope authority to preach a crusade and to make war on the antipope and his supporters. The pope granted him that power and, to all those who, having taken the sign of the Cross, either wished to go with him or gave him a contribution from their goods, the indulgence that is granted to those who go to the Holy Land. He also gave him the power to take

---

[106] The Flemish revolt broke out in 1379, leading to a sharp drop in English wool exports to Flanders (Sumption, *Divided Houses*, pp. 413–18).

[107] Pardons were issued for the 1381 revolt in the parliament of Nov. 1381, with many named exceptions, and again in Oct. 1382; the latter assembly also granted a fifteenth and tenth (*PROME*, vi. 223–4, 240–7, 278, 295).

[108] According to the *Westminster Chronicle*, pp. 27–8, the earthquake occurred 'an hour after noon' on Wednesday 21 May 1382; at noon on the following day 'a very dark hazy ring of enormous width appeared around the sun', and early in the morning of 24 May there was a second earthquake.

[109] *PROME*, vi. 255–6.

assumendi secum quoscumque religiosos inuitis suis prelatis.[110] Hoc anno domini in parliamento proposuerunt mittere exercitum in Franciam. Episcopus ostendebat bullam pape et petiit licentiam exequendi. Rex laborare noluit; communitas uoluit quod episcopus transiret. Episcopus manucepit bellum ecclesie et Francie in necessitate. Domini obtulerunt sibi quod transiret sub uexillo alterius domini quem rex missurus est. Sed dixit episcopus quod uexillum ecclesie foret principale. Item domini dixerunt quod non erat licitum episcopo pugnare. Respondebat quod in causa Domini et pape bene potuit.[111] Predicabat autem ipse et sui et promittebant indulgentiam uiuis et stabant supra sepulcra mortuorum et eos absoluebant, precipientes angelo Michaeli ut animas eorum in celum deduceret; sicque magnam summam pecunie collegerunt. Homines cruce se signabant et insolentes omnem quasi domum religiosorum perturbabant et in quibusdam locis silentium et a cultu diuino recesserunt sub colore, ut dixerunt, expugnandi antipapam, qui de facto castitatem expugnabant.[112]

Transiit igitur episcopus cum pecunia congregata et stipendio accepto a rege cum armatis, sacerdotibus et falsis religiosis; ueniensque in Flandriam textores quosdam de Dunkirc sibi obuios occidit et Conquestorem Westflandrie se uocauit.[113] Scripsitque regi Francie uocans eum scismaticum et regni Francie iniustum occupatorem, mandauitque sibi scismaticum papam dimittere. Et uillam Iprensem obsedit; uillani uiriliter se defendebant et plures interficiebant, percussitque eos Deus in posteriora et sanguinis fluxu moriebantur. Post paruum tempus uenit rex Francie cum magno exercitu, et qui uenerant ad predandum sacerdotesque et apostate ad mare currebant. Episcopus et milites in uillis se clauserunt et intercedente pro eis duce Britannie Iohanne, de indulgentia regis Francie uix redierunt, sanguine fluentes et patriam inficientes. Benedictus Deus qui confundit insolentes! Rex precepit episcopo dicere psalterium pro his quos occidit, et priuauit eum temporalibus suis donec persoluisset sibi stipendium quod ab

---

[110] For the 'Flemish Crusade' of 1383, see M. Aston, 'The Impeachment of Bishop Despenser', *BIHR* xxxviii (1965), 127–48; N. Housley, 'The Bishop of Norwich's Crusade', *History Today*, xxxiii (1983), 15–20; Saul, *Richard II*, pp. 101–7. Louis de Mâle, count of Flanders, may have supported the Avignonese 'antipope', but most of his subjects supported the Roman pope, one of many controversial aspects of the expedition.

[111] For the debates in the Oct. 1382 and Feb. 1383 parliaments, see *PROME*, vi. 280–2, 311–13. John of Gaunt in particular was strongly opposed to the bishop's plans, since he wanted to use English resources for a campaign in Spain (*Westminster Chronicle*, pp. 31–7).

[112] For documents relating to the preaching and organization of the expedition, see *The Reign of Richard II: From Minority to Tyranny 1377–1397: Selected Sources*, ed. A. McHardy (Manchester, 2012), pp. 96–7, 102–4.

with him any religious whatsoever, even if their superiors were unwilling.[110] In this year the lords in parliament proposed to send an army to France. The bishop produced the papal bull and asked for permission to act upon it. The king did not wish to exert himself; the commons wanted the bishop to go. The bishop undertook war on behalf of the Church and, of necessity, against France. The lords suggested to him that he should go under the banner of another lord whom the king would send. However, the bishop said that the banner of the Church should be the principal one. The lords also said that it was not lawful for a bishop to wage war. He replied that in the cause of God and the pope he certainly could.[111] Thus he and his followers preached and promised an indulgence to the living and stood upon the graves of the dead and absolved them, praying to the Angel Michael to bring their souls into heaven; and in this way they collected a great sum of money. Men took the sign of the cross, and in their presumption they disrupted almost every religious house, and in some places they withdrew from silence and from divine worship on the pretext, so they said, of fighting against the antipope, although in fact what they were resisting was chastity.[112]

With the money he had collected and with the payment he had received from the king, therefore, the bishop crossed to Flanders with armed men, priests, and false religious; and when he arrived in Flanders, he killed some weavers from Dunkirk who challenged him, whereupon he styled himself 'Conqueror of West Flanders'.[113] He also wrote to the king of France calling him a schismatic and the wrongful occupier of the realm of France and ordering him to dismiss the schismatic antipope. And he besieged the town of Ypres; however, the townsmen defended themselves with vigour and killed many men, and God smote them in the posterior, so that many men died of the bloody flux. After a short while the king of France arrived with a large army, and those who had come to plunder, and the priests and the apostates fled to the sea. The bishop and the knights shut themselves away in towns, but Duke John of Brittany interceded on their behalf, so that, through the indulgence of the king of France, they just about managed to return, flowing with blood and infecting the country. Blessed be God who confounds the presumptuous! The king ordered the bishop to recite the psalter for those whom he had killed, and he deprived him of his temporalities until he had given him back the payment he had

---

[113] Despenser crossed from England to Flanders on 16 May 1383 with about 5,000 men, having been issued two months earlier with £29,404 from the royal treasury; Dunkirk was stormed on 24 May (Aston, 'The Impeachment of Bishop Despenser', p. 140).

ipso recepit.¹¹⁴ Eodem anno rex Armenie uenit in Franciam et Angliam petens auxilium, et ipsum bene ditatum rex Anglie dimisit.¹¹⁵ In parliamento tunc tento Londonie statuitur quod raptor mulieris et mulier assentiens raptori ipso facto erunt inhabiles ad hereditatem et dotem et tam hereditas quam dos ad proximos reuertentur.*ᵘ* ¹¹⁶

1384. Anno Domini millesimo trecentisimo octogesimo quarto Gallici cum Scotis federati tres exercitus in Angliam ordinarunt: unum qui cum Scotis duce Iohanne de Vienna, probatissimo milite Francie, et alios duos exercitus*ᵛ* qui in oriente et occidente Angliam simul intrarent. Rex tunc accepto prudentium et ueteranorum militum consilio exercitum non diuisit, sed cum toto exercitu suo, centum milia armatorum continente, in Scotiam perrexit. Et sic Scoti nec Gallici cum rege pugnare audebant, sed de fenestris castrorum Anglicos aspiciebant. Alii autem duo exercitus non uenerunt. Et rex, combusta uilla de Edinburgh, rediit in Angliam | et auunculum suum Edmundum ducem Eborum et alium auunculum suum Thomam ducem Glouernie uocari precepit.¹¹⁷

Anno Domini millesimo trecentisimo octogesimo quinto, dux Lancastrie, qui quondam filiam Petri regis Hispanie duxerat in uxorem, collecta etiam magna pecunia per indulgentiam papalem, cum iuuentute regni transfretauit in Hispaniam iure uxoris ibi regnare disponens.¹¹⁸ Rex autem Hispanie dixit se nolle pugnare cum eis, sed solus pro eo pugnabit. Collegit omnia uictualia preter nouellos fructus in uineis et arboribus intra castra et uillas muratas. Et rex Francie, propter ligam cum rege Hispanie et armorum suorum uendicationem, collegit classem magnam in portu de Sclusa, fecitque sibi nauem rubiam in signum sanguinis effundendi, ibidem diu iacens et expectans uentum uoluit, ut dixit, in Angliam transfretare.

ᵘ marginal in later hand: nota   *ᵛ interlined*

[114] The siege of Ypres began on 9 June and was raised on 10 Aug., in part due to a severe outbreak of dysentery; the French army arrived in Flanders at the end of the month (Sumption, *Divided Houses*, pp. 493–510). The bishop and most of his men returned to England in early Oct. For John of Brittany's mediation, see *Reign of Richard II*, ed. McHardy, p. 109. Despenser was impeached in the parliament of Oct. 1383, and his temporalities confiscated for two years; some of his captains were tried and briefly imprisoned (*PROME*, vi. 327–41; *Westminster Chronicle*, pp. 51–5).

[115] Leo VI, titular king of Armenia (1373–93), had been driven out of his kingdom by Muslims and was seeking Western help to recover it. After spending several months in Paris, he arrived in England around Christmas 1385 but seems to have been widely disliked. On 3 Feb. 1386 Richard II controversially granted him £1,000 a year from the exchequer, shortly after which he returned to France (*Westminster Chronicle*, pp. 154–61).

[116] *PROME*, vi. 296 (parliament of Oct. 1382).

received from him.[114] In the same year the king of Armenia visited France and England seeking help, and the king of England sent him back well rewarded.[115] In the parliament then held in London, it was enacted that the ravisher of a woman, and a woman who assented to her ravisher, shall automatically be debarred from the inheritance and dower, and that both the inheritance and the dower shall revert to the nearest heirs.[116]

1384. In the year of the Lord 1384 the French, having allied themselves to the Scots, planned to send three armies against England: one under the leadership of John de Vienne, the most experienced knight in France, to join up with the Scots, while the other two armies would simultaneously invade England from the east and west. Whereupon the king, taking the advice of wise and experienced knights, did not divide his forces, but marched with his whole army, containing a hundred thousand armed men, into Scotland. And thus neither the Scots nor the French dared to join battle with the king, merely watching the English from castle windows. The other two armies never arrived. So the king, having set fire to the town of Edinburgh, returned to England, and ordered that his uncle Edmund be called duke of York and his other uncle Thomas duke of Gloucester.[117]

In the year of the Lord 1385, the duke of Lancaster, who had previously taken to wife the daughter of King Peter of Spain, and after collecting a large sum of money through a papal indulgence, crossed by ship with the youth of the kingdom to Spain, intending to reign there in right of his wife.[118] However, the king of Spain declared that he had no desire to do battle with them, but would fight for himself, alone. He gathered together inside castles and walled towns all the provisions apart from the young fruit on the vines and trees. And the king of France, because of his alliance with the king of Spain and in order to vindicate his arms, assembled a large fleet in the port of Sluys and had his ship coloured red to signify the shedding of blood; he remained there for a long time, hoping for wind, since he wished, so he declared, to cross to England.

---

[117] For this campaign, Richard II's first, he led an army of some 14,000 soldiers into Scotland in Aug. 1385. He created his uncles Edmund and Thomas dukes of York and Gloucester respectively on 6 Aug., the day he crossed the border, but the English only spent two weeks there before returning; several Scottish abbeys were burned as well as Edinburgh. Meanwhile a Scottish force accompanied by Jean de Vienne, admiral of France, ravaged the West March and burned the suburbs of Carlisle (Sumption, *Divided Houses*, pp. 547–51).

[118] The events described in this paragraph took place in 1386, not 1385. For John of Gaunt's marriage to Constanza of Castile, see above, p. 4. He left England in July 1386 with an army of around 3,000 men, with about £26,000 from Richard II and the English exchequer to fund his expedition, but probably not much from his papal indulgence (A. Goodman, *John of Gaunt* (Harlow, 1992), pp. 116–18).

Feretrum Sancti Thome. Nihil tamen contra eum ordinatum fuit nisi quod domini circa Londoniam morarentur et feretrum Sancti Thome Cantuariensis Symoni de Burley constabulario Douerie tradebatur custodiendum in castro Douerie, et ordinatum fuit quod omnes homines recederent cum bonis suis ab insula Thaneti et eam uacuam dimitterent; sed hoc monachi Cantuarienses et insulani non patiebantur. Et tum sapientes de impedimento regis Francie satis prudenter consulebant. Rex tunc, in absentia ducis Lancastrie consiliis, comitis Oxonie, iuuenis quem ducem Hibernie uocari preceperat, Michaelis de la Pole cancellarii, Symonis predicti, et aliorum adulatorum consiliis adhesit. Cum autem rex Francie uentum habere non posset et equi eius in mari mortui essent, reuersus est, Deo regnum Anglie protegente, non homine.[119] Eodem anno, ut supradictum est, dominus Iohannes de Gaunt, dux Lancastrie, profectus est in Hispaniam cum magna iuuentute militari ad uendicationem ius suum in regno Hispanie contingens eum ex parte uxoris sue, ducens secum ducissam, uxorem suam, et tres filias suas. Et post aliquantulum ibidem moram, postque habito tractatu inter regem Hispanie pretensum et dictum ducem, conuentum est quod prefatus rex seniorem filiam ducis, que erat heres et proxima regno Hispanie, desponsaret, soluendum duci magnam auri et argenti summam in manibus, et postmodum omni anno durante uita ducis rex solueret aut solui faceret eidem duci decem milia librarum que ad onus et expensas regis Hispanie adduci et deferri deberent ad Bayonam per sufficientem securitatem inde dicto duci et assignatis suis factam. Quo etiam tempore dux ille maritauit alteram filiarum suarum regi Portugalie.[120]

1386. Anno Domini millesimo trecentisimo octogesimo sexto post festum Sancti Michaelis factum est parliamentum Londoniis in quo, cum propositum fuit ex parte regis que fuit causa conuocationis parliamenti, uidelicet ut ordinetur remedium contra regem Francie et inimicos exteriores, et dux Gloucestrie et comites Arundellie ac Warwici, et eis assistentes responderunt quod prius oporteret ordinare contra inimicos intraneos, uidelicet Michaelem de la Pole, cancellarium, et

---

[119] For the 'great invasion scare' of 1386, see J. Palmer, *England, France and Christendom 1377–99* (London, 1972), pp. 67–87, and Saul, *Richard II*, pp. 152–6. A large French fleet began gathering at Sluys (Flanders) in the spring, and the planned invasion of England was not called off until Nov. The English government in fact put considerable effort into preparing a plan to resist an invasion. The unpopular 'sycophants' identified by the chronicler were Simon Burley, Richard's under-chamberlain since the start of the reign; Robert de Vere, earl of Oxford, created marquis of Dublin in 1385 and duke of Ireland in 1386; and Michael de la Pole, chancellor of England 1383–6, created earl of Suffolk in 1385.

[120] It was agreed in July 1387 that Catherine of Lancaster, Gaunt's daughter by Constanza of Castile, would marry Henry, son of King Juan of Castile; this was ratified in the Treaty of

The shrine of St Thomas. Yet nothing was done to resist him, except that the lords remained in the vicinity of London and that the shrine of St Thomas of Canterbury was delivered to Simon Burley, constable of Dover, to be kept in Dover castle, and that an order was issued that all men should evacuate and withdraw from the Isle of Thanet [Kent], taking their possessions with them; however, neither the monks of Canterbury nor the islanders were prepared to do this. Whereupon wise people consulted together sensibly about how to resist the king of France effectively. Then the king, in the absence of the duke of Lancaster's counsel, looked for advice to the earl of Oxford, a young man whom he had promoted to be duke of Ireland, to Michael de la Pole, chancellor, to the aforesaid Simon, and other sycophants. Yet when the king of France was unable to get a favourable wind, and his horses had died at sea, he turned back; thus it was God, not man, who saved the kingdom of England.[119] In this same year, as noted above, Lord John of Gaunt, duke of Lancaster, crossed over into Spain with a great force of young men in order to assert the claim to the kingdom of Spain which belonged to him through his wife, taking with him his wife the duchess and his three daughters. And after he had been there for a short while, and once discussions had been held between the self-styled king of Spain and the said duke, it was agreed that the aforesaid king would marry the elder daughter of the duke, who was the heir and next in line to the kingdom of Spain, for which he would pay to the duke a large sum of gold and silver in hand, and subsequently, each year while the duke remained alive, the king would either pay or arrange to be paid to him ten thousand pounds, which were to be dispatched and carried to Bayonne at the arrangement and expense of the king of Spain, under sufficient security to be given there to the said duke or his assignees. At the same time, the said duke also married another of his daughters to the king of Portugal.[120]

1386. After Michaelmas [29 September] in the year of the Lord 1386, a parliament was held in London in which, once the cause of the summons to parliament was announced on the king's behalf, namely to ordain a remedy against the king of France and hostile foreigners, and both the duke of Gloucester and the earls of Arundel and Warwick, as well as their supporters, replied that first of all it was necessary to deal with enemies within, that is to say, Michael de la Pole, the chancellor,

---

Bayonne and they married in Sept. 1388. When Juan died in 1390 they became king and queen of Castile. Gaunt and Constanza abandoned their own claims to the Castilian throne, and Juan promised Gaunt 600,000 francs (£100,000) immediately and 40,000 francs (£6,666) a year for life (Goodman, *John of Gaunt*, pp. 127–8). Philippa of Lancaster, Gaunt's daughter by his first wife Blanche, married King João of Portugal in Feb. 1387.

alios multos,[121] rex de consilio Michaelis parliamentum dissoluit et omnes abire precepit; qui iam congregati pro salute regni in periculo existentis tractare se uelle dicebant. Rex ad parliamentum uenire noluit; illi autem miserunt pro statuto pro quo medius Edwardus fuit adiudicatus, et sub pena illius statuti regem uenire compellebant.[122] Et Michaelem, obiectis criminibus diuersis et precipue quod colligi fecisset collectam Sancti Antonii Vienne in regno prohibitam, quam collectam sumpsisset in usus suos; item quod cartas albas sigillasset; et contra regem Francie nihil ordinasset; et quod officio suo ad detrimentum regni usus fuisset; de officio cancellarie et honore comitis deponebant et perpetuo carceri in castro de Corf adiudicabant, et loco eius Thomam de Arundellie, episcopum Eliensem, statuerunt cancellarium. Rex autem misit Michaelem ad castrum de Windelsore.[123]

De Commissione. Deinde, quia in anterioribus parliamentis dictum est quod prouentus | corone non sufficiebant congruo honore domus regie, et sub isto colore semper tallagia exacta fuerunt, exigebant a rege quod concederet episcopis Cantuarie, Eborum, Wintonie, Eliensis, ducibus Eborum et Gloucestrie, comitibus Arundellie et Warwici, abbati de Waltham et Iohanni de Cobham, baroni, et commissionem eis faceret usque ad Natale Domini, nisi parliamentum interueniret, recipiendi omnes corone prouentus, disponendique de[w] eis, castra et maneria eius intrandi, officiales amouendi et nouos instituendi, domumque regiam et regni negotia ordinandi. Concessitque eis parliamentum quod si necesse uiderent tallagium leuarent. Huic commissioni oportuit regem consentire, precepitque Thome cancellario predictam commissionem sigillare, quod et factum est ad mandatum suum sub suo signeto. Comes de Arundellie factus est custos maris. Et, soluto parliamento, Rex Michaelem de la Pole Londonie per[x] preconem comitem Suffolchie uocari fecit atque eum libertati restituit.[124]

---

[w] *interlined*   [x] *interlined*

[121] The 'Wonderful Parliament' met at Westminster from 1 Oct. to 28 Nov. 1386 (*PROME*, vii. 31–54). Opposition to the government was led by Thomas, duke of Gloucester, Richard, earl of Arundel, and Thomas, earl of Warwick, with the support of the commons.

[122] Faced with demands for the dismissal of de la Pole and the treasurer (John Fordham), Richard II withdrew angrily to Eltham manor for several days or perhaps weeks (*Knighton's Chronicle 1337–1396*, ed. G. Martin (OMT, 1995), pp. 353–88). The 'middle Edward' was King Edward II; this 'statute' was probably the appointment of twenty-one Lords Ordainers to govern the realm for eighteen months, forced upon Edward in the parliament of Feb.–Mar. 1310, although the *English Chronicle* (p. 9) evidently thought that it was the act by which Edward II was deposed.

and several others,[121] the king, on the advice of the said Michael, dissolved the parliament and told them all to go away; but, since they were now assembled together, they declared that they wanted to discuss the safety of the realm, which was in peril. The king refused to come to the parliament, but they sent for the statute by which the middle Edward was adjudged, and forced the king to attend on pain of that statute.[122] And after Michael had been accused of various crimes, especially the fact that he had organized a collection for St Anthony of Vienne, which was forbidden in the realm, which sum of money he had appropriated to his own use; also that he had sealed blank charters; and that he had made no arrangements to resist the king of France; and that he had discharged his office to the detriment of the kingdom; they removed him from the office of chancellor and the dignity of an earldom and adjudged him to perpetual prison in Corfe castle [Dorset], and in his place they appointed Thomas of Arundel, bishop of Ely, as chancellor. However, the king sent Michael to Windsor castle [Berkshire].[123]

Concerning the commission. After this, since it had been stated in previous parliaments that the revenues of the crown were not sufficient to maintain the royal household in suitable style, and upon this pretext taxes were always being raised, they obliged the king to concede and draw up a commission to the bishops of Canterbury, York, Winchester, and Ely, the dukes of York and Gloucester, the earls of Arundel and Warwick, the abbot of Waltham, and John de Cobham, baron, to last until Christmas, unless a parliament was held before then, to receive and disburse all the revenues of the crown, enter the king's castles and manors, remove his officers and appoint new ones, and make ordinances for the royal household and the business of the realm. Parliament also granted to them the power to raise a tax if they deemed it necessary. To this commission the king was obliged to consent, and he ordered Thomas, the chancellor, to seal the said commission, which was done, at his order, under his signet. The earl of Arundel was made keeper of the sea. And once the parliament was over, the king had it proclaimed publicly in London that Michael de la Pole should be called earl of Suffolk, and restored him to liberty.[124]

---

[123] For the charges against de la Pole see J. Roskell, *The Impeachment of Michael de la Pole Earl of Suffolk in 1386* (Manchester, 1984); *PROME*, vii. 37–46. Thomas Arundel, bishop of Ely since 1373, would become archbishop first of York and then of Canterbury.

[124] The Commission of Government, which was formally conceded by the king on 19 Nov. 1386 and placed executive power in the hands of these lords until Christmas 1387, also included the bishop of Exeter, Richard Lord Scrope, and Sir John Devereux. The earl of Arundel was made admiral of the north and west on 10 Dec. 1386 (Saul, *Richard II*, p. 167). De la Pole was at liberty again by Christmas 1386.

Anno autem nono huius regis Ricardi, rex tenuit magnum parliamentum apud Westmonasterium in quo Edmundum de Langley, auunculum suum, tunc comitem Cornubie, fecit ducem Eborum; Thomam de Wodstok, alterum auunculum suum, tunc comitem Bokyngham, fecit ducem Gloucestrie; Robertum Veer, comitem Oxonie, fecit marchionem Dublenensem.[125] Henricum de Bolynbrok, filium ducis Lancastrie, fecit comitem Derbeie;[126] Edwardum, filium ducis Eborum, fecit comitem Ruthlandie; Iohannem Holand, fratrem comitis Kancie, fecit comitem Hontingdonie; Thomam Mowbray, comitem Notingham, fecit marescallum Anglie; et Michaelem de la Pole, militem, fecit comitem Suffolchie. In eodem etiam parliamento, in communi audientia omnium dominorum et communitatis, rex comitem Marchie heredem fore proximum ad coronam Anglie post ipsum publice fecerat proclamari; qui quidem comes modico tempore post in Hibernia interemptus fuit.[127] Comes Arundellie omnes nauos regis Francie alias preparatas in Angliam de Rupella reuertentes bonis uinis oneratas cepit et, hominibus occisis, duxit in Angliam ad portum de Winchelse.[128]

1387. Anno Domini millesimo trecentisimo octogesimo septimo rex in castro de Notingham uicesimo quinto die mensis Augusti conuocatis capitalibus iusticiariis suis et uno seruiente ad legem proposuit has questiones que sequuntur, precipiens eis firmiter in fide et ligeantia sua quod fideliter secundum leges Anglie ad eas responderent.[129]

---

[125] The parliament which met in the ninth year of Richard's reign was that of 20 Oct. to 6 Dec. 1385, here wrongly inserted after the account of the 1386 parliament. As noted above by the chronicler, Edmund, earl of Cambridge (not Cornwall), and Thomas, earl of Buckingham, were elevated to the dukedoms of York and Gloucester on 6 Aug. 1385, during Richard's Scottish campaign. It was probably on this day too that Robert de Vere was made marquis of Dublin (the first marquisate in England), but his promotion was controversial and only confirmed after some delay in the 1385 parliament, when York's and Gloucester's dukedoms were also confirmed (C. Given-Wilson, 'Richard II and the higher nobility', in *Richard II: The Art of Kingship*, ed. A. Goodman and J. Gillespie (Oxford, 1999), pp. 107–28).

[126] The promotions noted in this paragraph occurred at different dates between 1377 and 1390. Henry of Bolingbroke was styled earl of Derby from the date of Richard's coronation, 16 July 1377; Edward of York was created earl of Rutland on 25 Feb. 1390; John Holand was created earl of Huntingdon on 2 June 1388; Thomas Mowbray became Earl Marshal for life on 30 June 1385; Michael de la Pole was created earl of Suffolk on 6 Aug. 1385 and his promotion confirmed in the 1385 parliament.

[127] The chronicler's statement that Richard had Roger Mortimer, earl of March (b. 1374) proclaimed as his heir at this time has been the subject of much speculation and is not confirmed by any other contemporary source. It is possible that some such proclamation was

Then, in the ninth year of this King Richard, the king held a great parliament at Westminster in which he made his uncle Edmund of Langley, then earl of Cornwall, duke of York; he made his other uncle Thomas of Woodstock, then earl of Buckingham, duke of Gloucester; Robert de Vere, earl of Oxford, he made marquis of Dublin.[125] Henry of Bolingbroke, son of the duke of Lancaster, he made earl of Derby;[126] Edward, the son of the duke of York, he made earl of Rutland; John Holand, the brother of the earl of Kent, he made earl of Huntingdon; Thomas Mowbray, earl of Nottingham, he made marshal of England; and he made Michael de la Pole, a knight, earl of Suffolk. Also, in the same parliament, before a general audience of all the lords and commons, the king had it publicly proclaimed that the earl of March was the next heir to the crown of England after himself; but not long afterwards, this earl was killed in Ireland.[127] The earl of Arundel seized all the ships of the king of France which had previously been intended for England while they were returning from La Rochelle loaded with good wine, and, having killed the men, brought them to England, to the port of Winchelsea [East Sussex].[128]

1387. On the twenty-fifth day of the month of August in the year of the Lord 1387 the king, having summoned his chief justices and a sergeant-at-law to Nottingham castle, put to them these questions that follow, firmly ordering them on their faith and allegiance that they should reply to them faithfully according to the laws of England.[129]

---

made in the 1386 rather than the 1385 parliament, or that it did not happen at all. It was not until July 1398 that March was killed in Ireland: cf. I. Mortimer, 'Richard II and the succession to the Crown', *History*, xci (2006), pp. 320–36.

[128] For Arundel's seizure of some fifty ships of the French wine-fleet off Cadzand in Mar. 1387, see Saul, *Richard II*, pp. 167–9. He returned to Orwell (Suffolk), not Winchelsea.

[129] The notorious 'Questions to the Judges' were Richard's response to his humiliation in the 1386 parliament. They were probably drafted by Sir Robert Tresilian, Chief Justice of the King's Bench, and the apprentice-at-law John Blake, and presented to the justices first at Shrewsbury at the beginning of Aug. 1387 and secondly at Nottingham on 25 Aug. The justices involved were: Tresilian; Sir Robert Bealknap, Chief Justice of the Common Bench; Sir Roger Fulthorpe; Sir John Holt; Sir William Burgh; Sir John Cary; and the sergeant-at-law John Lockton. When brought to trial in the parliament of Feb. 1388, they claimed to have been coerced to answer in the manner they did, but Tresilian was executed for treason (as was John Blake) while the others were convicted and exiled to Ireland for life (*PROME*, vii. 117–18). The Questions to the Judges are among the most widely copied texts of the 14th c. and 'together comprise the most remarkable statement of the royal prerogative ever made in England in the middle ages' (Saul, *Richard II*, pp. 173–5). The chronicler has made changes to the text in order to avoid repetition and prolixity, but has preserved the essence of the ten questions and responses, largely in the language of the official version, which was enrolled on the Statute Roll and is reproduced in *Select Documents of English Constitutional History 1307–1485*, ed. S. Chrimes and A. Brown (Edinburgh, 1961), pp. 137–9.

Mirabiles questiones.[y] In primis querebatur ab eis an illa nouum statutum et ordinacio atque commissio facta in ultimo parliamento derogent regalie et prerogatiue regis.[130] Qui unanimiter respondebant dicentes quod derogant, eo quod fuerant edita contra uoluntatem regis.

Item querebatur qualiter illi essent puniendi qui regem excitauerunt ad consentiendum commissioni. Responderunt quod pena capitali sunt merito puniendi.

Item querebatur qualiter illi qui commissionem predictam fieri procurarunt sunt puniendi. Responderunt quod pena capitis, si rex eis gratiose non indulgeat.

Item querebatur ab eis qualem penam merentur illi qui compulerunt regem ad consentiendum commissioni. Responderunt quod sunt ut proditores merito puniendi.

Item querebatur ab eis quomodo etiam sunt illi puniendi qui impediuerunt regem quominus exercere potuit que ad regaliam suam pertinent. Responderunt quod sunt ut proditores puniendi.

Item quesitum fuit ab eis an, postquam parliamento congregato negotia regni et causa congregationis parliamenti de mandato regis fuerint exposita et declarata, ac certi articuli limitati per regem super quibus domini et ceteri communes regni in eodem parliamento procedere debeant, si domini et communitas super aliis articulis uoluerint omnino procedere et nullatenus super articulis per regem ministratis donec super articulis per eosdem expressatis fuerit per ipsum regem primo responsum, non obstante quod fuerat eis iniunctum per regem in contrarium, numquid rex debeat habere in ea parte regimen parliamenti, et de facto regere ad effectum quod super articulis limitatis per regem primo debeant procedere, uel quod domini et communes primo debeant habere responsum a rege super articulis per ipsos ministratis antequam ulterius procedatur. Responderunt unanimiter quod rex in ea parte haberet regimen, et sic seriatim in omnibus aliis articulis tangentibus parliamentum usque ad finem eiusdem parliamenti; et si quis contra huiusmodi regimen regis faceret, tanquam proditor est puniendus.

Item querebatur ab eis numquid rex quandocumque sibi placuerit poterit dissoluere parliamentum et suis dominis ac communibus precipere quod recedant, an non. Responderunt quod potest, et si quis extunc contra uoluntatem regis procedat ut in parliamento, tanquam proditor est puniendus.

---

[y] *although abbreviated from the official text (PROME, vii. 364–5), this version of the 'Questions to the Judges' preserves the essential points of the text. Only significant errors are noted*

[130] The 'Commission of Government' established in the Oct. 1386 parliament; see above, p. 52.

The extraordinary questions. First, they were asked whether that new statute and ordinance and commission made in the last parliament derogated from the regality and prerogative of the king.[130] They replied unanimously, saying that they do so derogate, since they were promulgated against the king's will.

Also, they were asked how those who called for the king to consent to the commission should be punished. They replied that they deserved capital punishment.

Also, they were asked how those who were responsible for having the said commission drawn up should be punished. They replied, capital punishment, unless the king should grant them mercy.

Also, they were asked what type of penalty was deserved by those who compelled the king to consent to the commission. They replied that they deserved to be punished as traitors.

Also, they were asked how those people who prevented the king from being able to exercise what pertains to his regality should be punished. They replied that they should be punished as traitors.

Also, they were asked whether—once parliament has assembled, after the business of the realm and the reason for summoning parliament have, by the king's command, been explained and announced, and certain articles have been defined by the king upon which the lords and the other commons of the realm ought to deliberate in the said parliament, if the lords and the community wish to deliberate entirely upon other articles and not at all on the articles specified by the king until they have first of all been given a response by the king concerning the articles which they have put forward, notwithstanding that they have been ordered by the king to do the opposite—the king ought to have the rule of parliament in this matter, and in fact to rule to the effect that they must first deliberate on the articles defined by the king, or whether the lords and commons should first have a response from the king concerning the articles put forward by them, before proceeding further. They replied unanimously that the king should rule in this matter, as well as successively concerning all the other articles relating to the parliament up until the end of the same parliament; and if anyone should do anything contrary to the king's ruling in this way, he should be punished as if he were a traitor.

Also, they were asked whether or not the king can dissolve parliament whenever he pleases and order his lords and commons to depart. They replied that he can, and if anyone continues to act as if he were in parliament, contrary to the king's will, he should be punished as if he were a traitor.

Item querebatur ex quo rex potest quandocumque sibi placuerit remouere quoscumque officiarios et iusticiarios suos[z] ac ipsos pro delictis eorum punire, numquid domini et communes possunt absque uoluntate regis officiarios ipsos impetere super delictis eorum in parliamento, an non. Responderunt quod non possunt, et si quis contrarium fecerit est ut proditor puniendus.

Item querebatur qualiter ille est puniendus qui mouebat in parliamento quod mitteretur pro statuto pro quo Rex Edwardus secundus erat alias adiudicatus in parliamento, per cuius statuti inspectionem[a] nouum statutum et ordinatio ac commissio predicta fuerunt in parliamento concepta. Responderunt quod tam ille qui sic mouebat in parliamento quam ille alius qui pretextu huius motionis statutum illud portauit ad parliamentum sunt ut proditores puniendi.[131]

Item querebatur an iudicium in ultimo parliamento redditum contra comitem Suffolchie fuerit erroneum et reuocabile, an non. Responderunt quod si esset reddendum, ipsi non redderent, quia uidetur eis quod esset iudicium reuocabile tanquam erroneum in sua parte.[132]

In quorum omnium testimonium iusticiarii et seruiens predicti sigilla sua responsionibus suis apposuerunt coram[b] testibus ad premissa uocatis, reuerendis patribus dominis Alexandro archiepiscopo Eborum, Roberto archiepiscopo Dublinie, Iohanne episcopo Dunolmensi, Thoma Cicestrie episcopo, Iohanne Bangorensi episcopo; Roberto duce Hibernie, et Michaele comite Suffolchie; Iohanne Rypon clerico ac Iohanne Blake scutifero.[133] Isti autem iustitiarii fuerunt de consilio dominorum in parliamento preterito, et unus eorum postquam recesserat de castro dixit: 'Iam meruimus cordas quibus suspendamur, quia timore mortis hec dicta fuerunt et non de ueritate.'[134]

Rex misit pro duce Gloucestrie, comitibus Arundellie et Warwici, ponens insidias in uiis ad capiendum eos; ipsi uero, his per amicos auditis, cum forti comitiua in silua de Haryngay iuxta Londoniam conuenerunt.[135] Rex, de consilio unius burgensis Londonie, uenit ad

---

[z] *PROME*; eos *MS*   [a] *PROME*; imposicionem *MS*   [b] *interlined (omitted in PROME)*

---

[131] See above, n. 122.
[132] See above, p. 52.
[133] Alexander Nevill, archbishop of York, condemned to exile and forfeiture in the Feb. 1388 parliament; Robert Wikeford, archbishop of Dublin; John Fordham, bishop of Durham, dismissed as treasurer in Oct. 1386; Thomas Rushook, bishop of Chichester, exiled to Ireland along with the justices and translated to the see of Kilmore in 1389; John Swaffham, bishop of Bangor; Michael de la Pole, earl of Suffolk, and Robert de Vere, duke of Ireland; John Ripon, king's clerk, imprisoned in 1388 but pardoned in 1393; John Blake, executed for treason in 1388.

Also, they were asked, since the king can remove any of his officers and justices whenever it pleases him and punish them for their crimes, whether or not the lords and commons can impeach those same officers for their crimes in parliament without the king's assent. They replied that they cannot, and if anyone acts to the contrary he is to be punished as a traitor.

Also, they were asked how that person should be punished who proposed in parliament that the statute by which King Edward the second was formerly adjudged in parliament should be sent for, by the inspection of which statute the aforesaid new statute and ordinance and commission were drafted in parliament. They replied that both he who proposed this in parliament and the other person who, on the pretext of this motion, brought that statute into parliament should be punished as traitors.[131]

Also, they were asked whether or not the judgment pronounced in the last parliament against the earl of Suffolk was erroneous and revocable. They replied that if it was up to them to pronounce it, they would not do so, because it seems to them to be a revocable judgment, since in their opinion it is erroneous.[132]

In testimony of all of which the aforesaid justices and sergeant affixed their seals to their replies in the presence of the following who had been summoned to witness the above: the reverend fathers lords Alexander, archbishop of York, Robert, archbishop of Dublin, John, bishop of Durham, Thomas, bishop of Chichester, John, bishop of Bangor; Robert, duke of Ireland, and Michael, earl of Suffolk; John Ripon, clerk, and John Blake, esquire.[133] Yet these justices had given counsel to the lords in the previous parliament, and after they withdrew from the castle one of them declared: 'Now we deserve ropes with which to hang ourselves, because these words were not spoken in truth, but out of fear of death.'[134]

The king sent for the duke of Gloucester, the earl of Arundel, and the earl of Warwick, placing snares in their way to seize them, but they were forewarned about these by friends and arrived with a large following at Harringay wood near London.[135] The king, on the advice of a burgess from London, came to Westminster, hoping to crush them

---

[134] Knighton attributes a similar remark to Justice Sir Robert Bealknap, who had refused to put his seal to the judges' answers until threatened by de Vere and de la Pole with death (*Knighton's Chronicle*, pp. 394–5).

[135] Richard II tried to have the earl of Arundel arrested at Reigate in early Nov. 1387, but he evaded capture and joined Gloucester and Warwick at Harringay Park on 13 Nov. (Saul, *Richard II*, p. 186).

Westmonasterium, sperans auxilio Londoniensium ipsos debellare.¹³⁶ Archiepiscopus Cantuariensis supplicabat regi quod placeret sibi admittere eos ad presentiam suam sine nocumento et cum eis de pace tractare; et, accepto iuramento a rege, iuit et adduxit eos coram rege sedente in magna aula.¹³⁷ Exercitus eorum foris erat. Et ait rex: 'Qua temeritate audetis uos insurgere et contra pacem regni mei uos armare?' Respondit dux Gloucestrie: 'Nos non insurgimus neque nos armamus nos contra pacem regni, sed ad tuitionem uite contra inimicos nostros et regni, in quo casu quilibet homo potest arma portare. Petimusque et uos requirimus quod fiat parliamentum statim post Purificationem Beate Virginis, et in iudicio parliamenti nos ponemus nos; et custodiatis inimicos nostros, uestros adulatores, faciatisque ibidem esse presentes.' Et ait rex: 'Parliamentum habebis et eis non nocebis, et te faciam ita*c* infimum sicut minimum garcionem coquine tue.'¹³⁸ Cui dux: 'Non me inferiorem facietis quam filium regis', et genuflectens se dixit: 'Filius sum regis.' Archiepiscopus Cantuariensis supplicauit regi quod admitteret eos in crastino in eodem loco et reformationi consentiret; concessitque rex. Sed in crastino, mutans propositum, transiit ad Turrim.

In crastino uero domini uenerunt cum exercitu suo in campum Sancti Iohannis et miserunt pro | maiore Londonie, qui duxit eos in aulam communem ciuitatis, et amicitiam ciuitatis susceperunt.¹³⁹ Rex uero misit pro eis ut loquerentur cum eo in Turri, qui respondentes dixerunt locum non esse tutum, sed extra Turrim cum eo loqui parati fuerunt. Rex iussit maiorem uenire, cui mandauit armare ciuitatem. 'Absit, domine', dixit maior, 'ligei et fideles uestri sunt et amici regni.' Rex eum eiecit et misit ducem Hibernie cum litteris suis patentibus et uexillo suo ut Cestrenses et ceteros occidentales adduceret. Et domini, adiunctis sibi comite de Derby filio ducis Lancastrie, comite de Notyngham marescallo, et adaucto exercitu, transeundo obuiauerunt duci uenienti cum uexillo regis expanso prope Oxoniam.¹⁴⁰ Quidam

---

c *interlined*

¹³⁶ The burgess referred to was probably Nicholas Brembre, former mayor of London.
¹³⁷ William Courtenay, archbishop of Canterbury 1381–96; this meeting in Westminster Great Hall was on 17 Nov., when Gloucester, Arundel, and Warwick formally presented their Appeal of Treason against the king's supporters, from which they were known as the Appellants or Lords Appellant.
¹³⁸ This echoes Richard's comment in the 1386 parliament, when asked to dismiss de la Pole, that 'he would not dismiss the humblest of his kitchen staff from his post at their request' (*Knighton's Chronicle*, pp. 354–5).

with the help of the Londoners.[136] The archbishop of Canterbury begged the king to allow them to come into his presence unharmed and to treat peaceably with them; whereupon, having been given the king's word, he went and brought them into the presence of the king, who was sitting in the Great Hall.[137] Their army remained outside. And the king said: 'How dare you have the temerity to rise up and arm yourselves against the peace of my realm?' 'We are not rising up', replied the duke of Gloucester, 'nor are we arming ourselves against the peace of the realm, but to defend ourselves against our enemies and those of the realm, in which situation any man may bear arms. And we ask you, and insist, that a parliament be held immediately after the Purification of the Blessed Virgin [2 February], and we will submit ourselves to the judgment of parliament; and you will keep our enemies, your toadies, in custody, and you will ensure that they are present.' And the king replied: 'You shall have a parliament, and you shall not harm them, and I will deal with you as basely as the lowliest servant in your kitchen.'[138] To which the duke replied: 'You shall treat me no more basely than as the son of a king', and then declared, kneeling: 'I am the son of a king.' The archbishop of Canterbury begged the king to meet them again in the same place on the following day and agree to reform, and the king agreed. When the next day came, however, he changed his mind and went to the Tower.

On the morrow, therefore, the lords came with their army to St John's Field and sent for the mayor of London, who led them to the common hall of the city, and they received the friendship of the city.[139] Then the king sent for them to talk with him in the Tower, but they replied by saying that it was not a safe place, although they were willing to talk to him outside the Tower. The king sent for the mayor and ordered him to arm the city. 'God forbid, my lord!' declared the mayor; 'these men are your faithful lieges and friends to the kingdom.' The king threw him out and sent the duke of Ireland with his letters patent and his banner to collect the Cheshiremen and other westerners. And the lords, now joined by the earl of Derby, son of the duke of Lancaster, the marshal, the earl of Nottingham, and an ever-growing army, set out and came up with the duke, who was approaching with the king's banner unfurled, near to Oxford.[140] A certain prudent knight rode out

---

[139] This meeting was at the London Guildhall; the mayor was the fishmonger Nicholas Exton.

[140] Bolingbroke and Mowbray openly joined the three senior Appellants at Huntingdon on 12 Dec. (Saul, *Richard II*, p. 187).

miles prudens exiit de exercitu ducis Hibernie ut uideret qui essent, et reuersus dixit duci: 'Hic sunt constabularius et marescallus Anglie et precipui domini regni. Quomodo habuistis litteras uestras?' Cui ait dux: 'Nonne uultis pugnare contra eos?' Respondit miles: 'Absit.'[141] Et dux urgebat equum ultra Thamisiam cum suo confessore de ordine minorum, magistro in theologia, et fugit.[142] Cestrenses, scissis cordis arcuum, et cum arcubus suis, uerberati, turpiter redierunt, militemque principalem ducis Hibernie consiliarium decollebant, et tulerunt ab eis uexillum regis et ipsum uoluentes plicabant.[143] Dux autem Hibernie festinauit in insulam de Shipeye et inde in Alemaniam fugit, et Michael de la Pole similiter euasit; item, Alexander Neuyle, archiepiscopus Eborum, ad partes iuit transmarinas; et numquam reuersi sunt.[144] Et predicti quinque domini, uidelicet, dux Gloucestrie, Ricardus comes Arundellie, [Thomas][d] comes Warwici, Henricus Bolyngbrok comes Derbeie, et Thomas Mowbray comes Notingham, in destructionem predictorum rebellium et aliorum cum eis uenientium apud Rotcotbrigge ceperunt et interfecerunt multos, et quasi omnes, exceptis fugientibus.

Et tunc predicti quinque domini statuerunt parliamentum apud Westmonasterium, ubi Robertus Tresylian, iustitiarius, Nicholas Brembre miles, ciuis Londonie, et alii plures morti adiudicantur et ob proditionem eis impositam tracti et suspensi sunt.[145] Et in eodem parliamento Symon de Berle, ualens miles de Iartero, et Iohannes Beauchamp miles, senescallus hospitii regis, Iacobus Berniers miles et alii capti fuerunt et apud Turrim Londonie decollati. Deinde dicti quinque domini coram iustitiariis se statuerunt et in omnibus eis impositis iustificantur; et ne aliqui eorum aduersarii se excusare possent per hoc quod nihil fecissent dignum mortis secundum legem Anglie, uel per mandatum regis, statuerunt legem de assensu parliamenti pro tempore eiusdem parliamenti tantummodo ualituram, uidelicet, si parliamentum aliquem appellaret de crimine, quia cum

---

[d] Ricardus *MS*

---

[141] The duke of Gloucester was constable of England, and Mowbray marshal.

[142] The 'battle' of Radcot Bridge, near Witney (Oxfordshire) was on 20 Dec. De Vere's confessor was Thomas Roughton; his brother Richard was the queen's confessor (C. Given-Wilson, *The Royal Household and the King's Affinity, 1360–1413* (New Haven and London, 1986), p. 178).

[143] Sir Thomas Molyneux, de Vere's lieutenant, was killed just before the battle by Sir Thomas Mortimer, the captain of the Appellants' army (Saul, *Richard II*, p. 188).

[144] De la Pole died abroad in 1389, de Vere and Nevill both died abroad in 1392.

from the duke of Ireland's army to see who they were, and when he returned he said to the duke: 'The constable and marshal of England and the greatest lords of the realm are here. How did you get hold of your letters?' The duke said to him: 'Do you not want to fight against them?' 'God forbid!' replied the knight.[141] And the duke, accompanied by his confessor, a minorite and a master in theology, spurred his horse across the Thames and fled.[142] The Cheshiremen, having cut their bowstrings, also withdrew in shame with their bows, beaten men. And [the lords] beheaded the knight who was the principal adviser to the duke of Ireland, and they seized the king's banner from them, rolled it up, and folded it.[143] Meanwhile the duke of Ireland sped to the Isle of Sheppey [Kent] and fled from there to Germany, and Michael de la Pole likewise escaped. Alexander Nevill, archbishop of York, also went abroad; and they never came back.[144] And the aforesaid five lords, that is to say, the duke of Gloucester, Richard earl of Arundel, Thomas earl of Warwick, Henry Bolingbroke earl of Derby, and Thomas Mowbray earl of Nottingham, in the process of destroying the aforesaid rebels and the others who had come with them to Radcot Bridge [Oxfordshire], seized and killed a great many, indeed nearly all of them apart from those who fled.

And then the aforesaid five lords held a parliament at Westminster where Justice Robert Tresilian, Nicholas Brembre, knight, citizen of London, and several others were condemned to death and, because of the treason imputed to them, drawn and hanged. And in the same parliament Simon de Burley, a worthy knight of the Garter, John Beauchamp, knight and steward of the king's household, James Berners, knight, and others were seized and beheaded at the Tower of London.[145] Whereupon the aforesaid five lords came before the justices and declared themselves innocent of all the things alleged against them. And lest any of their enemies be able to excuse himself on the grounds that he had done nothing worthy of death according to the law of England, or [had acted] on the king's orders, they introduced a law, with the assent of parliament, which would remain in force only as long as this parliament continued, namely, that if parliament appealed any person of a crime, since he could not do battle with parliament, he

---

[145] Eight of the king's supporters were put to death during the 'Merciless Parliament' of 1388, including Chief Justice Tresilian (above, p. 129), and Nicholas Brembre, former mayor of London, who was accused *inter alia* of trying to raise the Londoners against the Appellants. The king and Queen Anne pleaded for the life of Simon Burley, but unsuccessfully; Beauchamp and Berners were both knights of the king's chamber (Saul, *Richard II*, pp. 191–5; for the official record of the parliament, including the trials, see *PROME*, vii. 55–120).

parliamento pugnare non posset, sine ratione damnaretur.[146] Et fecerunt parliamentum appellare quosdam de certis criminibus, ut de tractatibus habitis cum rege Francie de terris ultramarinis reddendis, et aliis de quibus rei non fuerunt.[147] Et ducem Hibernie, Michaelem, et alexandrum archiepiscopum Eborum perpetuo damnabant exilio. Iohannem Blake trahi et suspendi fecerunt.[148] Episcopus insuper Cicestrensis, frater predicator, et alii iustitiarii cum seruiente ad legem exilio in Hiberniam relegantur.[149] Et durauit hoc parliamentum a festo Purificationis usque ad festum Sancti Iohannis Baptiste, contendente cum eis rege et dicente quod feloniam non commiserunt et appellationem interpositam fuisse, sed non potuit quemquam saluare.[150] Statuta huius parliamenti obseruare omnes iurare fecerunt et burgenses ciuitatum, et quod nullus illis statutis contraueniat uel ad reuocationis alicuius intercedat. Tandem regem iurare fecerunt nouiter quod leges regni obseruaret et quod non adulatorum sed parliamenti et dominorum consiliis adhereret; nec aliqui eorum pro his ita gestis malum inferret;[151] in cuius rei testimonium patentes litteras plene indulgentie rex fieri fecit. Qui tamen ista grauiter semper ferebat, et domini dixerunt inter se numquam omnes tres simul in presentia sua conuenire.[152]

Hoc anno magister Iohannes | Wikklif moritur, cuius corpus apud Lutterworth sepelitur.[e] Sed postea per sententiam uniuersalem ecclesie fuit exhumatum et ossa sua fuerunt combusta.[153] Eodem anno archiepiscopus Cantuarie in conuocatione cleri Londonie statuit nullos sacerdotes debere predicare nisi fuerint per diocesanos admissi.[154]

1388. Anno Domini millesimo trecentisimo octogesimo octauo Robertus Knolles edificauit et construi fecit pontem Rofensem.[155] Hoc

---

[e] M[agister] I[ohannes] Wikklif moritur et in Angliam humatur et combussitur, *in upper margin of fo. 198ᵛ in later hand*

---

[146] The process of Appeal of Treason, never previously used in parliament, normally allowed for judicial combat between the appellant and the defendant. Its employment in 1388 was highly controversial, but the Appellants declared that a case of such importance could only be tried according to the law of parliament. 'The implication of this lofty if somewhat ambivalent statement was that parliament could make up the rules as it went along; which is precisely what it did' (Saul, *Richard II*, p. 192).
[147] John Salisbury, a royal chamber knight, was convicted of treason for his dealings with the French and suffered a traitor's death.
[148] De la Pole and de Vere were condemned to death *in absentia*. For Blake, see above, p. 55, n. 129.
[149] The justices and the sergeant (John Lockton) who had responded to the Questions to the Judges (above, p. 54 and n. 129) were found guilty of treason but, pleading coercion, were sentenced to exile. The bishop of Chichester was the Dominican Thomas Rushook, Richard II's unpopular confessor.
[150] The Merciless Parliament opened on 3 Feb. and was dissolved on 4 June.
[151] Richard II renewed his coronation oath at high mass in Westminster abbey on 3 June. A schedule for the oath to uphold the acts of the parliament, dated 4 June, lists 35 clerics,

should be condemned without argument.[146] And they made parliament appeal various people of certain crimes, such as holding talks with the king of France about restoring overseas territories, and other things of which they were not guilty.[147] And they condemned the duke of Ireland, Michael [de la Pole], and Alexander, archbishop of York, to perpetual exile. They had John Blake drawn and hanged.[148] Furthermore, the bishop of Chichester, a friar preacher, and the other justices and the sergeant-at-law, were exiled to Ireland.[149] And this parliament lasted from the feast of the Purification [2 February] until the feast of St John the Baptist [24 June], while the king argued hotly with them, saying that they had not committed any felony and that the appeal was specious, but he could not save any of them.[150] They made everyone, including the burgesses of the towns, swear to observe the statutes of this parliament and that no one should disobey these statutes or attempt to get any of them revoked. Finally, they made the king swear anew that he would abide by the laws of the realm, and that he would govern with the advice of parliament and the lords, not that of sycophants; nor would he bear ill will towards any of them for what they had done;[151] in testimony of which they obliged the king to draw up letters patent of full pardon. Yet he always bore these things hard, and the lords agreed among themselves that all three of them would never again come into his presence simultaneously.[152]

In this year master John Wyclif died, and his body was buried at Lutterworth. Later, however, by universal decree of the Church, it was exhumed and his bones were burned.[153] In the same year, in a convocation of the clergy at London, the archbishop of Canterbury ordered that no priests should be permitted to preach unless they were admitted by the diocesans.[154]

1388. In the year of the Lord 1388 Robert Knolles built and had constructed Rochester bridge [Kent].[155] In this year, England's youth

---

95 gentry, and 40 burgesses in Sussex, suggesting that some 5,000 Englishmen in all were obliged to swear it (TNA C 49/96). For the Appellants' pardons and sureties, see *PROME*, vii. 72–82.

[152] The three lords referred to here were the senior Appellants, Gloucester, Arundel, and Warwick.

[153] Wyclif died on 31 Dec. 1384; he spent the last three years of his life at Lutterworth (Leicestershire), a living he had been granted in 1374. He was declared a heretic at the Council of Constance in 1415, and it was ordered that his remains be burned, but this was not done until 1428.

[154] Convocations of Canterbury diocese were held in London in Feb. and Oct. 1388, and in Jan. and Dec. 1391. Restrictions on preaching were issued by Archbishop Courtenay in 1387 and 1389 (*Concilia Magnae Brittaniae et Hiberniae*, ed. D. Wilkins (London, 1737), iii. 202, 210). It is not clear to which of these the chronicler is referring.

[155] The new Medway bridge at Rochester was completed in 1391 (above, p. 36).

anno iuuentus et heredes nobilium Anglie perierunt in Hispania, et rex Hispanie statuit cum duce preliari. Dux autem transiit in Portugaliam et tradidit filiam suam in matrimonio regi Portugalie, diuulgauitque per Hispaniam quod ipse misisset in Angliam pro alio exercitu. Rex Hispanie, hoc credens, quibusdam interuenientibus pro certa summa pecunie composuit cum duce, qui statim post rediit in Angliam.[156]

1389. Anno Domini millesimo trecentisimo octogesimo nono, in parliamento tento Londonie, rex retraxit quedam priuilegia Londoniensium et ut mercatores extrinseci possent diuidere merces suas et per partes uendere in ciuitate concessit. Post hoc rex misit Londoniensibus ut aurum sibi accommodarent; et ipsi se excusabant, dicentes se non esse aliis mercatoribus potentiores. Tunc rex uocauit ad Wodstok maiorem Londonie, uicecomites et alios ciuitatis rectores, qui coram iustitiariis statuti sunt. Quibus sic ait: 'In ciuitate Londonie pistores in decem quarteriis frumenti sex solidos octo denarios excessiue lucrantur. Similiter brasiatores in decem quarteriis ordei sex solidos octo denarios excessiue lucrantur. Et sic carnifices in decem bobus.' Si maior et uicecomites ista negassent, duodena miserorum ipsa affirmassent, ideo secundum consilium eis datum posuerunt se in gratia regis. Et iustitiarius dixit: 'Iuxta statuta regni non solum in ciuitate uestra sed in aliis rex aufert a uobis regimen ciuitatis pro uestro malo regimine.' Posuitque tunc rex in ciuitate nouos officiarios suos. Postea Londonienses magnam summam auri collegerunt ita quod quidam propter illam collectam fugerunt de ciuitate. Et regem uenientem cum maxima sollemnitate tanquam angelum Dei susceperunt, tradideruntque sibi claues ciuitatis et in auro quadraginta milia libras ei obtulerunt. Et sic regimen ciuitatis receperunt.[157] Hoc anno Vrbanus papa moritur, et Bonifacius eligitur.[158]

1390. Anno Domini millesimo trecentisimo nonagesimo Bonifacius uocauit archiepiscopum Eborum ad cardinalatum, et omnes ditiores episcopos Anglie transferre nitebatur ut primos fructus suarum

---

[156] This is the third time that the chronicler has repeated similar information about Gaunt's Spanish campaign (above, pp. 48–50).

[157] The act granting foreign merchants access to the retail trade in London was passed in the parliament of Feb. 1388 and much resented by the Londoners (*PROME*, vii. 71). Richard II's celebrated quarrel with London occurred in 1392. Having refused a loan to the king, the London officers were summoned to Nottingham (not Woodstock) on 24 June; the city's charter was revoked and the king's knight Edward Dallingridge made keeper of the city in place of mayor John Hende on 25 June. Following a further meeting with the king at Windsor on 22 July, the citizens organized a splendid civic reception for Richard on 21 Aug., and on 19 Sept. the city's liberties were restored on payment of a fine of £10,000 (C. Barron, 'The

and noble heirs died in Spain, and the king of Spain resolved to do battle with the duke [of Lancaster]. However, the duke crossed over into Portugal and gave his daughter in marriage to the king of Portugal, and he put it about throughout Spain that he had sent to England for another army. The king of Spain, believing this, made an agreement with the duke through certain intermediaries for a certain sum of money, whereupon the duke promptly returned to England.[156]

1389. In the year of the Lord 1389, at a parliament held in London, the king withdrew certain privileges from the Londoners and granted foreign merchants the right to divide up their wares and sell them at retail within the city. After this, the king sent a request to the Londoners to lend him some money, but they declined, saying that they were no richer than other merchants. Whereupon the king summoned the mayor of London, the sheriffs, and other officials of the city to Woodstock [Oxfordshire], where they were brought before the justices. 'In the city of London', he said to them, 'the bakers overcharge by 6 shillings and 8 pence on every ten quarters of wheat; similarly, the brewers overcharge by 6 shillings and 8 pence on every ten quarters of barley; and the butchers do the same on every ten oxen.' If the mayor and sheriffs had denied these things, a jury of paupers would have affirmed them, so, acting on the advice given to them, they placed themselves at the king's mercy. Whereupon the justice said: 'In accordance with the statutes of the kingdom, because of your bad governance, the king removes the government of the city from you not only in your city but elsewhere'. Whereupon the king appointed his own new officers in the city. Following this, the Londoners collected such a large sum of money that some people fled the city on account of this levy. And when the king arrived, they received him with tremendous pomp, like an angel of God, and they handed him the keys of the city and presented him with forty thousand pounds of money. Thus did they recover the governance of the city.[157] In this year Pope Urban died, and Boniface was elected.[158]

1390. In the year of the Lord 1390, Boniface promoted the archbishop of York to the office of cardinal, and he attempted to translate all the wealthier bishops in England so that he could lay his hands on the

---

quarrel of Richard II with London, 1392–7', in F. Du Boulay and C. Barron, eds., *The Reign of Richard II* (London, 1971), pp. 173–201.

[158] The Roman pope, Urban VI, died in Oct. 1389; Boniface IX was elected in Nov.

ecclesiarum perciperet.¹⁵⁹ Summe sacerdotum Romam peregrinantium pro beneficiis acquirendis in portu Douerie et summe pecunie tradite per escambium mercatorum ad parliamentum Wintonie deferentur. Et ibi statutum fuit firmiter tenendum quod papa non sinatur transferre episcopos nec extra regnum nec infra sine assensu regis; et quod nullus a modo capiat beneficium a papa, sed ecclesiastici patroni conferant sua beneficia iuxta intentionem laicorum qui ius patronatus eis contulerunt. Et super hoc omnes promiserunt regi assistentiam sicut pro corona.¹⁶⁰ Hoc*ƒ* anno fuit in Anglia magna pestilentia quam quintam Pestilentiam uocabant.¹⁶¹

Anno Domini millesimo trecentisimo nonagesimo uno nihil hic scribitur quia regnum Anglie fuit in malo statu.

Anno Domini millesimo trecentisimo nonagesimo duo rex splendide pauit capitulum fratrum minorum apud Sarum, et comedit cum eis ibidem in refectorio, habens secum reginam Annam, episcopos et alios dominos, in festo Assumptionis Beate Marie, et ibidem utebatur regalibus et corona.¹⁶²

Quid autem actum est in regno annis Domini millesimo trecentisimo nonagesimo tertio et millesimo trecentisimo nonagesimo quarto hic non scribitur propter uarietatem regni Anglie.

Anno Domini millesimo trecentisimo nonagesimo quinto dux Lancastrie de mandato regis transiit in Franciam et tractauit de pace cum rege Francie Ambianis; et rex fecit omnes expensas et dedit sibi et cuilibet de sua familia magna donaria.¹⁶³

Anno Domini millesimo trecentisimo nonagesimo sexto factum est parliamentum Londoniis, ad quod rediens dux Lancastrie formam pacis in tractatu habitam expressit, uidelicet quod Rex Ricardus Anglie arma Francie, Calesiam et omnia conquesta per Edwardum dimitteret, et omnia que Edwardi erant ante uendicationem regni Francie, cum residuo redemptionis Iohannis regis Francie, possideret. Et dixit quod

---

ƒ *a new and fainter nib begins to be used at this point*

---

¹⁵⁹ Thomas Arundel was translated from Ely to the archbishopric of York in Apr. 1388, but there is no record of him being made a cardinal. The only archbishop of York who became a cardinal in the 14th c. was John de Thoresby in 1361. There were translations to or from eight of the seventeen English bishoprics in 1388–9, several of which followed from the exile of Alexander Nevill and Thomas Rushook.

¹⁶⁰ There is confusion here between the parliaments of 1390 and 1393. Parliament was held at Winchester in Jan.–Feb. 1393, and passed the 'Great Statute of Praemunire', which reinforced the Statute of Provisors enacted at the Jan. 1390 Westminster parliament. The Winchester parliament also granted one and a half fifteenths and tenths (*PROME*, vii. 151–3,

first fruits of their churches.[159] The sums at the port of Dover from priests going on pilgrimage to Rome in order to acquire benefices, and all the money handed over in exchange by merchants, were brought to the parliament at Winchester [Hampshire]. And it was enacted there that it should be firmly ordered that the pope is not permitted to translate bishops either outside the realm or within the realm without the assent of the king; and that henceforth no one should accept a benefice from the pope, but that ecclesiastical patrons should confer their benefices in accordance with the intention of the laymen who granted them the right of patronage. Whereupon they all promised assistance to the king, as to the crown.[160] In this year there was a great plague in England which they called the Fifth Pestilence.[161]

For the year of the Lord 1391 nothing is recorded here, because the kingdom of England was in a poor state.

In the year of the Lord 1392 the king sumptuously paved the chapter-house of the friars minor at Salisbury [Wiltshire], and he dined with them in the refectory there together with Queen Anne, various bishops, and other lords on the feast of the Assumption of the Blessed Mary [15 August], and he wore his regalia and crown there.[162]

What was done in the realm in the years 1393 and 1394 is not recorded here, however, on account of the vicissitudes of the kingdom of England.

In the year of the Lord 1395, the duke of Lancaster crossed to France on the king's orders and treated for peace with the king of France at Amiens; and the king paid all the expenses and gave splendid gifts to him and each member of his household.[163]

In the year of the Lord 1396 a parliament was held at London, to which the duke of Lancaster on his return presented the peace proposal drawn up in negotiations, that is to say, that King Richard of England would give up the arms of France, Calais, and all the conquests of Edward [III], and would continue to hold everything that belonged to Edward before his challenge to the kingdom of France, together with the residue of the ransom of King John of France. And he declared that to bear the arms of France was not helpful, and that

---

223–4, 228). Boniface IX had declared 1390 to be a Jubilee year, which brought great numbers of pilgrims to Rome.

[161] The chronicler has evidently reckoned the 1375 plague as the fourth and that of 1390 as the fifth.

[162] This was in 1393, when Richard was at Salisbury 14–18 Aug. (Saul, *Richard II*, p. 472).

[163] These were the sumptuous negotiations of 1392, held at Amiens, led by John of Gaunt on the English side (Saul, *Richard II*, pp. 213–15).

arma Francie portare non prodest, et Calesia plus nocet regno Anglie in expensis quam prodest; sed dux Gloucestrie, comites Arundellie et Warwici omnino contradixerunt.[164] In hoc parliamento dux Lancastrie petiit quod filius suus Henricus iudicaretur heres | regni Anglie, cui contradixit comes Marchie, asserens se descendisse a domino Leonello, secundo filio Edwardi regis. Econtrario dux dicebat quod Rex Henricus tertius habuit duos [filios], Edmundum seniorem et primogenitum, et Edwardum. Qui tamen Edmundus dorsum habuit fractum, et propter hoc iudicauit seipsum indignum esse ad coronam, quare pater eorum eos sic componere fecit, quod Edwardus regnaret, et post eum heredes Edmundi; et dedit Edmundo comitatum Lancastrie, et ab eo descendit Henricus filius eius iure matris, que fuit filia dicti Edmundi. Cui respondit comes, dicens hoc non esse uerum: 'Sed Edwardus fuit primogenitus, et Edmundus uir elegantissimus et nobilis miles, prout in chronicis patenter continetur.' Rex autem imposuit eis silentium.[165] Item, in hoc parliamento dux Lancastrie petiit regem dare sibi ducatum Aquitannie sub certa annua pensione, et ipse pro posse totum acquireret, sicut et rex Francie dedit illum cuidam militi sub eadem conditione. Sed dux Gloucestrie, comites Arundellie et Warwici omnino contradixerunt, dicentes pertinentia ad coronam esse satis pauca. Rex tamen concessit.[166]

Hoc anno Hibernici ueri Anglici auxilium contra puros Hibernicos petierunt. Quibus rex dixit se uelle Hiberniam adire, et ideo exegit decimam cleri et quintamdecimam laicorum ut in parliamento solebat, statuens quod omnes natiui de Hibernia in Hiberniam remearent,[g] dicens paucos Hibernicos esse ibidem, quare dicti puri Hibernici preualent ibidem. Dotati uero Hibernici in Anglia et ecclesiastici promoti, dato auro, ab hoc statuto sunt exempti. Et rex cum exercitu transiit in Hiberniam, ubi, agente quodam fratre de ordine predicatorum,

---

[g] -earent *written over an erasure*

[164] The terms mentioned here summarize the proposal put to the parliament of 1394, which was rejected; in 1393 and 1394 the negotiations were held at Leulinghem, not Amiens (Saul, *Richard II*, pp. 213–15). John II of France had been captured at the battle of Poitiers in 1356 and put to ransom for £500,000, little over half of which had been paid before the renewal of war in 1369.

[165] This discussion refers to the notorious 'Crouchback Legend', which as March said was palpably untrue (Given-Wilson, *Henry IV*, pp. 96–7). Both Gaunt (probably in the Jan. 1394 parliament) and his son Henry (at the time of his usurpation in 1399) hoped to use this legend to support Henry's claim to be the heir to Richard II, asserting as stated here that Edmund 'Crouchback' was the elder son of King Henry III, but it was firmly rejected; the name 'Crouchback' in fact came from Edmund's having taken the crusaders' cross. Henry's

Calais was more harmful than beneficial to the kingdom of England because of the costs involved; but the duke of Gloucester and the earls of Arundel and Warwick completely disagreed.[164] In this parliament the duke of Lancaster petitioned for his son Henry to be acknowledged as heir to the kingdom of England, but the earl of March opposed this, claiming that he was descended from Lord Lionel, the second son of King Edward. In response, the duke declared that King Henry III had two [sons], Edmund who was the elder and firstborn, and Edward. However, this Edmund had a broken back, on account of which he judged himself unworthy of the crown, as a result of which their father made them come to an agreement that Edward would reign, and would be succeeded by the heirs of Edmund; and he granted Edmund the earldom of Lancaster, and it was from him that his son Henry was descended, by right of his mother, who was the daughter of the aforesaid Edmund. To which the earl replied by saying that this was not true: 'But Edward was the firstborn, and Edmund was a most comely man and a noble knight, as can clearly be seen in the chronicles.' However, the king told them to be quiet.[165] Also in this parliament the duke of Lancaster petitioned the king to grant him the duchy of Aquitaine for a certain annual pension, and he would strive to acquire all of it, just as the king of France granted it to a certain knight under the same condition. But the duke of Gloucester, the earls of Arundel and Warwick disagreed entirely, saying that what pertained to the crown was little enough. Yet the king granted it.[166]

In this year the loyal Anglo-Irish asked for help against the native-born Irish. The king told them that he wanted to come to Ireland, whereupon he demanded a tenth from the clergy and a fifteenth from the laity, as was customary in parliament, ordering that all the inhabitants of Ireland should stay in Ireland, declaring that there were only a few [Anglo-]Irish there, as a result of which the aforesaid native-born Irish were in the ascendant there. However, those Irish who were beneficed in England, and churchmen who were promoted, offered money and were exempted from this order. And the king crossed to Ireland with his army, where, at the doing of a certain friar of the order of Preachers, he was

---

mother Blanche was not the daughter but the great-granddaughter of Edmund, first earl of Lancaster (d. 1296).

[166] Gaunt was granted the duchy of Aquitaine for life in the parliament of Jan. 1390 but continued through the 1390s to try, against much opposition from the lords and commons, to have this converted into a hereditary grant of the duchy, only finally abandoning his claim in 1398 (Given-Wilson, *Henry IV*, pp. 88–92, 103).

fuit ipse in periculo aduersariorum. Sed frater captus missus est ad Turrim Londonie, qui postea ad preces prouincialis carceri sui ordinis est liberatus.[167]

Titulus Regis ad Aquitanniam. Hoc autem anno dux Lancastrie transiit in Aquitanniam ut ducatum sibi adquireret; sed Burdegalia et alie ciuitates ipsum excluserunt, dicentes quod a tempore secundi Henrici, qui iure sue uxoris illum ducatum possedit, semper iste ducatus tenuit de rege Anglie: 'Et si rex Anglie nos noluerit habere, tenebimus de nobismet ipsis.'[168] Hoc anno Makamor et quidam alii principales purorum Hibernicorum capti fuerunt, quos rex duxit in Angliam et honorifice satis tractauit.[169] Dux uero Lancastrie, spe frustratus, rediit.[170]

Anna Regina moritur. Hoc etiam anno moritur Domina Anna, regina Anglie, in manerio de Shene, et apud Westmonasterium sepelitur; quod factum fuit anno octauodecimo regni regis Ricardi; qua quidem regina mortua, rex obtulit regi Francie treugas triginta annorum, petens filiam suam in uxorem.[171] Hoc anno archiepiscopus Cantuariensis moritur et Thomas de Arundell a monachis Cantuarie postulatur. Et rex, uocato duce Lancastrie et multis comitibus et nobilibus, installationi sue sollemniter affuit, estimans quod frater suus uenisset ad sollemnitatem; quem de facto ibidem cepisset si uenisset.[172]

1397. Noua Regina. Anno Domini millesimo trecentisimo nonagesimo septimo et anno regni regis Ricardi uicesimo, rex transiit ad Calesiam et cum rege Francie extra Calesiam loquebatur et desponsauit filiam suam in Calesia cum magna gloria et pompa in ecclesia Sancti Nicholai ibidem, Isabellam nomine, tunc nouem annorum existentem; quam sollemniter et in magnis expensis duxit in Angliam, que fuit cito post coronata apud Westmonasterium.[173] Et post aduentum suum in Angliam, uocauit archiepiscopum Cantuariensem, rogans eum ut adduceret ad se comitem Arundellie, fratrem suum. Cui archiepiscopus dixit: 'Facietis sibi malum si uenerit?' Cui rex, hoc negans,

---

[167] Richard II crossed to Ireland with an army of about 8,000 men on 1 Oct. 1394, returning in May 1395. The chronicler's use of the term 'Irish' in this paragraph is confusing, reflecting the ethnic situation in the lordship (Saul, *Richard II*, pp. 281–5). The name of the Dominican friar is not known.

[168] The first king of England to hold Aquitaine was Henry II (1154–89), following his marriage to Eleanor of Aquitaine. John of Gaunt went there in Oct. 1394 and managed to quell the revolt, but not to gain acceptance for his hereditary title to the duchy (Goodman, *John of Gaunt*, pp. 188–200).

[169] Art MacMurrough, self-styled king of Leinster, was the leading native Irishman to submit to Richard during his campaign, but he was not brought over to England or imprisoned.

[170] Gaunt arrived back in England in late Dec. 1395.

[171] Anne of Bohemia died at Sheen on 7 June 1394; in his grief, Richard is said to have had the manor burned to the ground. Negotiations for the marriage of Richard and the French

placed in danger from his enemies. But the friar was seized and sent to the Tower of London, although later, at the request of the provincial, he was handed over to the prison of his order.[167]

The king's title to Aquitaine. In this year also the duke of Lancaster crossed to Aquitaine to acquire the duchy for himself, but Bordeaux and other cities would not admit him, saying that since the time of Henry II, who held the same duchy by right of his wife, this duchy was always held from the king of England: 'And if the king of England should not wish to have us, we will hold it from our very own selves.'[168] This year MacMurrough and various other leaders of the native-born Irish were captured, and the king brought them to England and treated them quite honourably.[169] The duke of Lancaster returned, his hopes dashed.[170]

Queen Anne dies. In this year also Lady Anne, queen of England, died at the manor of Sheen [Surrey] and was buried at Westminster; this occurred in the eighteenth year of the reign of King Richard. And once this queen was dead, the king offered the king of France a truce for thirty years, asking for his daughter in marriage.[171] In this year the archbishop of Canterbury died, and Thomas Arundel was put forward by the monks of Canterbury. And the king, having summoned the duke of Lancaster and a large number of earls and nobles, attended his solemn installation, thinking that his brother would come to the ceremony; and if he had come, he would have seized him there by force.[172]

1397. A new queen. In the year of the Lord 1397 and the twentieth year of the reign of King Richard, the king crossed to Calais and spoke with the king of France outside Calais, and he married his daughter, named Isabella, who was nine years old at the time, in the church of St Nicholas there at Calais with great pomp and glory; and he brought her, with much solemnity and great expense, to England, and soon afterwards she was crowned at Westminster.[173] After his return to England, he summoned the archbishop of Canterbury, asking him to bring his brother the earl of Arundel into his presence. The archbishop said to him: 'If he comes, will you do him harm?' The king, denying this,

---

king's daughter began in July 1395 following his return from Ireland and were concluded in the spring of 1396 (Saul, *Richard II*, pp. 225–7, 455–6).

[172] Archbishop Courtenay died on 31 July 1396. Thomas Arundel was provided to Canterbury on 25 Sept. and received his temporalities on 11 Jan. 1397.

[173] Richard II met Charles VI of France at Ardres, eight miles south of Calais, on 27–30 Oct. 1396, and married Isabella in Calais on 4 Nov., five days before her seventh birthday. She was crowned on 7 Jan. 1397 (Saul, *Richard II*, p. 230).

assecurauit eum, iurando super corpus Christi statim post missam archiepiscopi. Archiepiscopus autem cum magna instantia fratrem suum timentem duxit ad presentiam regis apud Westmonasterium. Quo uiso, dixit rex comiti de Notyngham: 'Curam habeas de comite isto Arundellie', et statim transiit in cameram. Comes uero de Notyngham duxit comitem Arundellie in aliam cameram et clausit ostium. Archiepiscopus autem expectauit usque ad uesperam, et tristis rediit ad domum suum apud Lambhith. In crastino rex tradidit comitem cuidam inimico suo ut in castro de Wight ipsum custodiret, et statim omnia bona sua confiscauit. Comitem uero Warwici cepit in curia sua, quem misit in Turrim. Et statim cum turba magna transiit ad mansionem ducis Gloucestrie in Exsex uocatam Plasshe; quo capto, dixit sibi rex: 'Tu non uis ad me uenire pro aliquo nuntio, ego igitur ad te uenio, et te aresto.' Cui ait dux: 'Gratiose agatis mecum, saluando uitam | meam.' Cui rex: 'Illam gratiam habebis quam prestitisti Symoni de Burley, cum regina pro eo coram te genuflecteret. Legas ista!', tradens sibi cedulam accusationis sue. Et cum dux legisset: 'Ad ista respondebimus.' Et rex commisit eum comiti de Notingham, capitaneo Calesie, ut in castro ibidem ipsum custodiret.[174] Et postea transiit in partes occidentales Anglie et collegit exercitum, uocauitque Gallos in auxilium, qui cum lanceis eleuatis uenerunt per medium regni. Misitque ad singulos episcopos, abbates et generosos atque mercatores, et sub colore mutui aurum ipsorum, numquam persoluendum, extorsit, in tanta quantitate quod unus simplex generosus soluit quadraginta libras.[175] Ibi autem processerunt comites Rutlandie, Cancie, Huntingdonie, Sarum, Notingham, marchio Dublunie et alii, appellantes ducem Gloucestrie, comites Arundellie et Warwici de criminibus lese magestatis perpetratis anno regni regis decimo et undecimo.[176] Et rex misit unum iustitiarium ad ducem Gloucestrie ut ab eo quereret quomodo ad appellationes responderet. Et dux manu propria scribendo

---

[174] Arundel, Warwick, and Gloucester were arrested without warning by the king on 10–11 July 1397. Warwick was apprehended near Temple Bar (London) and imprisoned at Tintagel (Cornwall); Arundel was imprisoned at Carisbrooke (Isle of Wight), of which the earl of Rutland, presumably the 'enemy' mentioned here, was the keeper; and Gloucester at Calais, where Thomas Mowbray, earl of Nottingham, was captain of the town.

[175] This passage is confused. Although Richard visited Woodstock (Oxfordshire) in Aug. 1397, he did not go to 'the western side of England' until Feb./Mar. 1398, when he spent several weeks near the Welsh border (Saul, *Richard II*, p. 473). Moreover, no other chronicler says he summoned French troops, and it may be that the chronicler meant to write 'Wallicos' (Welshmen) rather than 'Gallos'. For the king's forced loans of 1397–8, see C. Barron, 'The Tyranny of Richard II', *BIHR* xli (1968), 1–18.

guaranteed his safety, swearing on the body of Christ straight after the archbishop had said mass. With much urging, therefore, the archbishop brought his fearful brother into the king's presence at Westminster. On seeing him, the king said to the earl of Nottingham: 'Take charge of this earl of Arundel', and promptly withdrew to his chamber; whereupon the earl of Nottingham took the earl of Arundel into another chamber and closed the door. The archbishop waited until the evening, when he returned downcast to his residence at Lambeth. On the following day, the king handed the earl over to one of his enemies to be kept in custody in a castle on [the Isle of] Wight, and immediately confiscated all his goods. He also arrested the earl of Warwick at his court, and sent him to the Tower. Then, accompanied by a great crowd, he set off without delay for the duke of Gloucester's residence in Essex called Pleshey and, having seized him, the king said to him: 'You would not come to me, despite my summonses, so I have come to you; and I arrest you.' The duke said to him: 'Deal mercifully with me, and spare my life.' The king replied: 'You shall have as much mercy as you showed to Simon de Burley, when the queen went down on her knees before you on his behalf. Read these!', and he handed him a schedule of the charges against him. 'We shall reply to these', said the duke when he had read them. Whereupon the king handed him over to the earl of Nottingham, captain of Calais, to hold him in custody in the castle there.[174] After this, he crossed over to the western side of England and collected an army, and he summoned the French to help him; and they passed through the heart of the kingdom, their lances raised high. And he sent messages to each of the bishops, abbots, gentlemen, and merchants, and on the pretext of a loan—never to be repaid—he extorted money from them in such quantities that even a mere gentleman paid 40 pounds.[175] Then the earls of Rutland, Kent, Huntingdon, Salisbury, Nottingham, the marquis of Dublin, and others came forward to appeal the duke of Gloucester and the earls of Arundel and Warwick of crimes of lèse-majesté committed in the tenth and eleventh year of the king's reign.[176] The king also sent one of his justices to the duke of Gloucester to ask him how he would respond to the appeals. And the duke wrote his reply in his own hand in English, sealed the letter, and

---

[176] The 'Counter-Appellants' were the five earls named here plus the earl of Somerset (shortly to become marquis of Dorset, not Dublin), William Lord Scrope, and Thomas Lord Despenser. These eight lords first presented the appeal against Gloucester, Arundel, and Warwick at Nottingham on 5 Aug. 1397 and subsequently in the parliament at Westminster in Sept., accusing them of treason for their part in the events of 1386–8.

in Anglico respondebat, litteram sigillabat et regi mittebat. Iustitiarius prudenter ita litteram regi tradidit quod *h*habuit penes se copiam sigillo*h* regis consignatam. Cumque responsio ducis regi non placeret, mandauit sub pena mortis comiti de Notingham quod ipsum occideret. Et ipse transiit ad Calesiam et ibidem famuli comitis, *i*cum lecti plumali*i* super ducem posito, ipsum uiliter suffocabant occulte, diuulgantes ipsum morte naturali obiisse.[177]

Parliamentum. Deinde post Exaltationem Sancte Crucis uenit ad parliamentum rex, equitans terribiliter per medium Londonie cum centum milibus armatorum, quorum tamen multi ficti sunt.*j*[178] Et tenuit parliamentum cum confederatis suis in magno tentorio quod in pauimento Westmonasterii statuerat; et ne episcopi, abbates uel clerici intromitterent se in parliamento, fecit eos et clerum compromittere uices suas in dominum Thomam Percy militem, senescallum sui hospitii. Et in hoc parliamento non secundum legem Anglie sed secundum iura ciuilia processerunt, nec leges periti Anglie se ibi intromittebant.[179] Et primo rex, ad supplicationem et petitionem sui parliamenti, reuocauit commissionem alias factam anno decimo et statuit quod si quis talem commissionem procurauerit sit ut proditor puniendus. Reuocauitque omnia statuta in parliamentis anno decimo et undecimo edita, et similiter indulgentias extortas, et etiam cartam indulgentie quam sponte comiti obtulerat Arundellie, quia illa carta, ut dicebat, fuit concessa in preiudicium regis, et quia rex tunc ignorabat quod materie fuerant ita odiose et corone sue preiudiciales.[180] Item statuit, ad petitionem parliamenti, quod magnum parliamentum uocabatur, quod si quis procurauerit mortem regis alicuius de cetero, uel deponere, uel sursum reddere homagia, siue de huiusmodi locutus fuerit, uel populum suscitauerit, uel contra regem equitauerit, adiudicabitur ut proditor regis et exheredabitur pro se et heredibus in perpetuum;[181] et quod filii iam nati adiudicatorum in hoc parliamento, nec eorum filii, ueniant de cetero ad parliamentum, tum nec sint de concilio regis.[182]

---

h–h underlined   *i–i* underlined   *j* marginal in a later hand: 100,000 armati

---

[177] This was William Rickhill, Justice of the Common Bench. Gloucester was murdered in Calais castle on the night of 8 Sept. 1397. His confession was read out to the Sept. 1397 parliament, but the details of his death were only revealed in the parliament of Oct. 1399, when Rickhill was exculpated for his part in it (*PROME*, vii. 411–14; viii. 43–7, 87–9).

[178] The manuscript of the English Chronicle used by Davies gives the more realistic 'one thousand' men (*An English Chronicle of the Reigns of Richard II, Henry IV, Henry V and Henry VI*, ed. Davies, p. 130).

[179] Parliament met on 17 Sept. 1397. Westminster Great Hall was being rebuilt, so proceedings were held in a marquee set up in the palace yard (*PROME*, vii. 331–40; and for Thomas Percy's appointment as proctor for the clergy, ibid., 344).

sent it to the king. Wisely, the justice handed the letter to the king on condition that he kept a copy for himself authenticated with the king's seal. And since the duke's reply did not please the king, he ordered the earl of Nottingham, under threat of death, to kill him. Whereupon the latter crossed to Calais, where some of his servants wickedly and secretly suffocated the duke by placing a featherbed on top of him, putting it about that he had died of natural causes.[177]

Parliament. After this, following the Exaltation of the Holy Cross [14 September], the king came to parliament, riding fearsomely through the heart of London with a hundred thousand armed men, although many of them were false.[178] And he held his parliament with his accomplices in a great marquee which had been set up in the courtyard at Westminster; and in order that the bishops, abbots, and clerks should not be allowed into the parliament, he obliged them and the clergy to delegate their authority to Thomas Percy, knight, the steward of his household. And the proceedings in this parliament were not conducted according to the law of England but according to civil law, and men learned in the law of England were not permitted there.[179] And the king first, at the request and petition of his parliament, repealed the Commission formerly made in the tenth year and decreed that anyone who proposed such a commission would be punished as a traitor. He also repealed all the statutes issued in the parliaments of the tenth and eleventh years, along with the pardons extorted, including the charter of pardon which he had of his own accord granted to the earl of Arundel, since that charter was granted, so he claimed, to the prejudice of the king, and because the king had been unaware at the time that its contents were so hateful or prejudicial to his crown.[180] He also decreed, at the petition of the parliament, which was known as the Great Parliament, that if in future anyone were to plot to kill the king, or to depose him, or to withdraw homage, or if he should talk of such things, or raise up the people, or ride against the king, he would be adjudged as the king's traitor and disinherited, both himself and his heirs in perpetuity.[181] And that neither those sons already born to those who were adjudged in this parliament, nor their sons, should in future come to parliament, nor indeed should they be of the king's council.[182]

---

[180] *PROME*, vii. 345–9. Arundel had received a second charter of pardon in 1394.

[181] The chronicler is abridging the 'four points of treason' decreed by Richard II (*PROME*, vii. 350–1).

[182] The chronicler has somewhat garbled the king's decree, which was that 'neither the male heirs engendered of the bodies of those who are adjudged and convicted in the present parliament, nor the male heirs of their body to be engendered, shall ever come to parliaments or councils of the king, nor be of the king's council nor that of his heirs' (*PROME*, vii. 352).

Item ad supplicationem parliamenti indulsit comitibus Derbie et Notingham equitationem cum duce Gloucestrie contra ducem Hibernie,[k] qui duo humiliter se posuerant in regis gratiam; et similiter indulsit illis qui positi fuerant in commissione et eam non fuerunt executi.[183]

Deinde adduxerunt comitem Arundellie,[184] et dux Lancastrie fuit iustitiarius ibidem, qui sibi exposuit appellationem dominorum et accusationem parliamenti et iussit respondere. Qui dixit quod respondere non expedit: 'Quia scio quod ordinastis mortem meam propter bona mea.' Et notificauerunt sibi penam tacentis, et dixit dux: 'Quia parliamentum te accusauit, meruisti damnari sine responsione secundum legem tuam.' Cui comes respondens dixit: 'Ista feci propter circumstantias que tunc erant, et si errores fuerunt, habeo indulgentiam regis.' 'Illa indulgentia', dixit dux, 'reuocata est per parliamentum quia extorta eo tempore quo tu fuisti rex.' 'Adhuc habeo indulgentiam quam mihi rex sponte obtulit', dixit comes, 'et mihi misit, non rogatus, quinque annis elapsis.' 'Et similiter illa est reuocata', dixit dux, 'ex statuto parliamenti.' Et comes dixit: 'Maxima prerogatiua regis est quod ipse potest concedere indulgentiam cuiuscunque delicti, et si uos statuistis quod ipse non potest uel non debet concedere indulgentiam, plus fecistis contra prerogatiuam suam quam ego. Et si tu, Iohannes, bene esses examinatus, plura fecisti tu contra regem quam ego.' Dux et alii consulebant quod poneret se in gratia regis, et dixit comes: 'Pono me in gratia Summi Regis. Pro legibus et utilitate | regni mori non recuso.' Et dux tulit sententiam: 'Rex tibi condonat tractionem et suspensionem, sed decollaberis in monte Turris ubi Symon de Burley fuit decollatus, et filii tui exheredabuntur, et eorum filii excludentur a parliamento nec erunt de concilio regis in perpetuum.' Et in festo Sancti Matthei apostoli et euangeliste, morte adiudicatus, in dicto monte decollatus est.[185]

Et in crastino comes Warwici, in parliamento ductus, simili morti adiudicatur,[186] qui secundum consilium sibi datum confessus est se omnia fecisse, confidens in sapientia ducis et comitis ac in sanctitate

---

[k] interlined

[183] This royal pardon applied especially to Alexander Nevill, former archbishop of York, Edmund of Langley, duke of York, and William Wykeham, bishop of Winchester, all of whom had been members of the 1386 commission (*Usk*, p. 27).

[184] Arundel was tried and executed on 21 Sept. His trial was widely reported by the chroniclers, who stressed his courage and defiance of the king, treating his death as a quasi-martyrdom (*Usk*, pp. 27–31; *SAC* II, pp. 87–95).

At the request of the parliament, he also pardoned the earls of Derby and Nottingham for their riding with the duke of Gloucester against the duke of Ireland, whereupon these two humbly submitted themselves to the king's grace; and he similarly pardoned those who had been appointed to the Commission and had not been involved in enforcing it.[183]

Then they brought in the earl of Arundel,[184] and the duke of Lancaster, acting as justice there, read out to him the appeal of the lords and the accusation of parliament and ordered him to respond. He declared that it would be pointless to respond, 'because I know that you have decided to put me to death, because of my possessions'. Then they warned him of the penalty for remaining silent, and the duke said: 'Since parliament has accused you, then according to your own law you deserve to be condemned without right of reply.' The earl said to him in response: 'I did those things because of the circumstances at the time, and if there were mistakes, I have the king's pardon.' 'That pardon', said the duke, 'has been revoked by parliament, because it was extorted at a time when you were acting as king.' 'I still have the pardon which the king granted me of his own accord', said the earl, 'and which he sent me, unsolicited, five years ago.' 'That has similarly been revoked by statute of parliament', replied the duke. To which the earl said: 'It is the greatest prerogative of a king that he can grant a pardon for any offence, and if you have decreed that he cannot or should not grant a pardon, you have acted more against his prerogative than I have. And if you, John, were to be interrogated closely, you have done more against the king than I have.' The duke and others advised him to submit himself to the king's mercy, but the earl replied: 'I submit myself to the mercy of the Supreme King. For the laws and welfare of the kingdom, I am quite prepared to die.' Whereupon the duke passed sentence: 'The king pardons you the drawing and hanging, but you will be beheaded on Tower Hill, where Simon de Burley was beheaded, and your sons will be disinherited, and their sons will be excluded from parliament and from the king's council for ever.' Thus, on the feast of St Matthew the Apostle and Evangelist [21 September], having been condemned to death, he was beheaded on that same hill.[185]

And on the following day the earl of Warwick, having been brought into parliament, was condemned to the same fate;[186] in accordance with the advice given to him, he confessed to having done everything he did

---

[185] For Burley's execution, see above, p. 62.
[186] Warwick was tried and sentenced on 28 Sept., a week after Arundel (*PROME*, vii. 415–16).

abbatis Sancti Albani et reclusi in Westmonasterio, qui dixerunt illa sibi licere.[187] Et dixit: 'Verumtamen si iudicaueritis me errasse, pono me in gratia regis.' Tunc adiudicatus fuit perpetuo carceri in insula Mannie, prece et intercessione dominorum, quia longeuus fuit. Similiter dux Gloucestrie adiudicatus fuit exheredationi consimili et post mortem, quia, ut dixerunt, facta eius ita notoria fuerant, et uiuens responderat per scripturam.[188] Cernens etiam rex quod ipsi eiecerunt archiepiscopum Eborum, et quod pacem non haberet cum archiepiscopo Cantuariensi, fecit parliamentum accusare Cantuariensi archiepiscopum. Et cum incepisset prolocutor proponere contra archiepiscopum, dixit rex: 'Non proponas contra cognatum meum. Recede, pater, securus.'[189] Qui, cum recessisset, habuit post se nuntium qui prohibuit ne amplius intraret parliamentum, et adiudicatus est perpetuo exilio et priuationi omnium bonorum suorum, quia procurauerat se poni in commissione, et eam executus fuerat, et eam sigillauit quando erat cancellarius. Item, in die Lune proximo sequenti, *Iohannes Cobham et Iohannes Cheyny,* milites, perpetuis carceribus adiudicantur.[190] Item rex et parliamentum statuerunt quod omnes annue pensiones, priuilegia ac dona concessa quibuscunque ab adiudicatis in hoc parliamento a die proditionis perpetrate adnullentur; et similiter idem fiat de beneficiis per eos collatis, et quod presentationes et collationes sint in manu regis. Item statuerunt quod quiscunque procurauerit et consuluerit ad cassandum statuta huius parliamenti proditor sit censendus.[191] Quod quidem parliamentum inceptum fuit die Lune septimodecimo die Septembris.[192]

Archiepiscopus dixit se recedere nolle: hic se fuisse natum, et hic se uelle mori. Rex cum duce Lancastrie intrauit ad eum in cameram cum aliis comitibus, in qua tristis sedebat, et dixit sibi rex: 'Ne tristeris, nec recedere recuses, quia te assecuro quod post breue tempus reuocaberis, et nullus erit archiepiscopus Cantuariensis nisi tu quamdiu nos duo uixerimus.' Cui dixit archiepiscopus: 'Ante recessum meum aliqua

---

i-l underlined

[187] The abbot of St Albans 1349–96 was Thomas de la Mare, the duke of Gloucester's godfather (Saul, *Richard II*, pp. 371–2; *Usk*, pp. 34–5).

[188] For the condemnation of Gloucester, see *PROME*, vii. 411–14.

[189] The Speaker of the Commons was the king's councillor Sir John Bussy. For Archbishop Arundel's exile, see *PROME*, vii. 349–50.

[190] John Lord Cobham, a member of the 1386 Commission, was condemned at the second session of the parliament, which met at Shrewsbury on 28 Jan. 1398; Cheyne, a follower of the duke of Gloucester, was probably condemned at the same time (*PROME*, vii. 418–20; Saul, *Richard II*, p. 381 n. 54).

[191] *PROME*, vii. 351–3.

because he trusted in the wisdom of the duke [of Gloucester] and the earl [of Arundel], and in the holiness of the abbot of St Albans and a recluse at Westminster, who told him that these things were lawful.[187] 'Nevertheless', he said, 'if you adjudge me to have done wrong, I submit myself to the king's mercy.' Whereupon, at the prayer and intercession of the lords, he was condemned to perpetual imprisonment on the Isle of Man, because he was an old man. In the same way, the duke of Gloucester was also condemned posthumously to disinheritance, because, so they declared, his deeds were so notorious, and since he had, while still alive, made answer in writing.[188] Mindful also of the fact that these were the men who had driven out the archbishop of York, and that he would never have peace with this archbishop of Canterbury, the king also made parliament bring charges against the archbishop of Canterbury. Once the Speaker had begun to put the case against the archbishop, however, the king said: 'Do not proceed against my kinsman. You may leave in safety, father.'[189] Yet when the archbishop had left, he found that a messenger had been sent after him who ordered him not to reappear in parliament, and he was condemned to perpetual exile and deprivation of all his possessions, on the grounds that he had procured his own appointment to the Commission, and enforced it, and that he sealed it when he was chancellor. Also, on the Monday following, John Cobham and John Cheyne, knights, were sentenced to perpetual imprisonment.[190] The king and the parliament also decreed that all annuities, privileges, and gifts granted to any persons by those who were condemned in this parliament should be annulled with effect from the day the treason was committed; and, likewise, that the same should be done concerning benefices collated by them, and that the presentations and collations should remain in the hands of the king. They also decreed that anyone who proposed or advised that the statutes of this parliament should be repealed would be accounted a traitor.[191] And this parliament began on Monday the seventeenth of September.[192]

The archbishop declared that he did not wish to depart: this was where he had been born, and this was where he wanted to die. The king and the duke of Lancaster went into the chamber where he was sitting, downcast, with some other earls, and the king said to him: 'Do not be sad, and do not refuse to depart, because I assure you that in a short while you will be recalled, and that for as long as we two are both alive nobody except you will be archbishop of Canterbury.' The archbishop said to him: 'Before I depart, there are things I want to say to you',

---

[192] The first session of the parliament met from 17 to 29 Sept.

uobis dicam', et protraxit sermonem de luxuria que regnabat in personis eorum, et in curiis auaritia atque superbia, quibus inficiunt totum regnum. Et in die sibi assignata, in uigilia Sancti Michaelis, in portu Douerie recessit.[193] Statuunt insuper quod super feretrum Sancti Edwardi omnes domini iurarent se totis uiribus statuta huius parliamenti obseruare, ad maiorem securitatem, et quod omnes heredes et successores dominorum tam spiritualium quam temporalium prestabunt idem iuramentum omnibus futuris temporibus quando eis liberabuntur hereditates et possessiones in faciendo homagia et fidelitates suas. Et, ad requisitionem parliamenti, omnes episcopi excommunicauerunt in Cruce Sancti Pauli omnes facientes contra statuta et ordinationes huius parliamenti.[194] Post hoc comites appellantes rex ordinauit duces, uidelicet:[m] Henricum de Bolyngbrok, comitem Derbeie, fecit ducem Herfordie; comitem Rutlandie fecit ducem Albemarlie; comitem Cancie fecit ducem Surreie; comitem Hontingdon fecit ducem Excestrie; et comitem Notyngham fecit ducem Northfolchie; ac comitem Somersetie fecit marchionem Dorsetie. Insuper dominum Le Spensier fecit comitem Gloucestrie; dominum de Neuile de Raby fecit comitem Westmorlandie; dominum Thomam Percy fecit comitem Wigornie; dominum Willielmum Scrope, tunc thesaurarium Anglie, fecit comitem Wilts; et dominum Iohannem Montageu fecit comitem Sarum. Rex itaque dedit comitatum Arundellie comiti Notingham quando ipsum in ducem ordinauit.[195] Eodem anno rex scripsit ad papam ut quemdam laicum litteratum, Rogerum Walden, in archiepiscopum Cantuariensem promoueret, asserens, ut quidam dicebant, Thomam esse mortuum. Fecitque parliamentum hoc compromittere[n] in duodecim personas, que continuando parliamentum ubicunque et quandocunque regi placeret sibi placita secum ordinarent. Quibus omnis peractis, in partes occidentales est reuersus.[196] Nuntius festinanter rediens de Curia Romana portauit bullas, et rex

---

[m] *marginal in later hand*: Comes Derbei   [n] com *interlined*

[193] Michaelmas is an error for Martinmas here, probably copied from the parliament roll, which makes the same mistake (*PROME*, vii. 350, which also states erroneously that the archbishop was obliged to leave England by Friday, the eve of Michaelmas [*recte* Martinmas], whereas 10 Nov., the eve of Martinmas, fell on a Saturday in 1397.

[194] These oaths were sworn on 30 Sept. on the Confessor's shrine in Westminster Abbey (*PROME*, vii. 359–62).

[195] For the king's promotions at the close of parliament on 29 Sept., see PROME, vii. 358–9. The chronicler is wrong to say that Henry of Bolingbroke had been one of the *Counter*-Appellants. He has also omitted to note the creation of Margaret Marshall as duchess of Norfolk in her own right, and is wrong in stating that Montague was created earl of

whereupon he delivered a lengthy sermon concerning the extravagance which reigned among those about him, and the rapacity and arrogance of the court, through which they corrupted the whole realm. Then, on the day assigned to him, the vigil of Michaelmas [29 September], he departed from the port of Dover.[193] They also decreed, for greater security, that all the lords should swear upon the shrine of St Edward to uphold the statutes of this parliament with all their strength, and that all the heirs and successors of the lords, both spiritual and temporal, should take the same oath on all future occasions when inheritances or possessions are delivered to them and they do homage and fealty. Also, at the request of parliament, all the bishops excommunicated at St Paul's Cross all those who acted contrary to the statutes and ordinances of this parliament.[194] Following this, the king promoted the appellant earls to dukes, as follows: Henry of Bolingbroke, earl of Derby, he made duke of Hereford; the earl of Rutland he made duke of Aumale; the earl of Kent he made duke of Surrey; the earl of Huntingdon he made duke of Exeter; and the earl of Nottingham he made duke of Norfolk; he also made the earl of Somerset marquis of Dorset. Furthermore, he made Lord Despenser earl of Gloucester; he made Lord Nevill of Raby earl of Westmorland; he made Lord Thomas Percy earl of Worcester; he made Lord William Scrope, then treasurer of England, earl of Wiltshire; and he made Lord John Montague earl of Salisbury. And when the king created the earl of Nottingham a duke, he also gave him the earldom of Arundel.[195] In this same year the king wrote to the pope asking him to promote a certain literate layman, Roger Walden, to the archbishopric of Canterbury, claiming, according to some people, that Thomas was dead. And he made parliament delegate this power to twelve persons, who, by continuing the parliament in whatever place and at whatever time it suited the king, would, together with him, enact statutes pleasing to him. Having done all this, he returned to the western parts.[196] A messenger came hurrying back from

---

Salisbury at this time, since he had inherited his earldom from his uncle William in July 1397. Thomas Mowbray, earl of Nottingham, was not given the earldom of Arundel, but the former earl's lordship and castle of Lewes; Arundel itself was given to John Holand (A. Dunn, *The Politics of Magnate Power: England and Wales 1389–1413* (Oxford, 2003), p. 63).

[196] The 'parliamentary committee' was appointed on 31 Jan. 1398, the last day of the Shrewsbury session of parliament. It consisted of eighteen members, of whom any nine could make a quorum. Its powers were later extended and it was widely seen as an instrument of Richard's tyranny (*PROME*, vii. 389; J. Edwards, 'The parliamentary committee of 1398', *EHR* xl (1925), 321–33). Following the Shrewsbury session, Richard II remained close to the Welsh border until late Mar. (Saul, *Richard II*, p. 473).

fecit Rogerum consecrari, et cito post idem Rogerus celebrauit ingressum suum Cantuarie sumptuose.[197] Et post hoc rex in diebus sollemnis in quibus utebatur de more regalibus iussit sibi in camera parari tronum, in quo post prandium | se ostentans sedere solebat usque ad uesperas, nulli loquens sed singulos aspiciens; et cum aliquem respiceret, cuiuscumque gradus fuerit, oportuit ipsum genuflectere.[198]

Rex uult habere securitatem pacis. Albe Carte. Rex autem, apud Notyngham conuocatis archiepiscopo et episcopis ac consiliariis suis, dixit se non posse secure equitare per regnum propter odium Londoniensium et septemdecim comitatum adiacentium, et ideo uoluit eos, collecto exercitu, exstirpare nisi signum securitatis sibi prestarent.[199] Ordinauerunt igitur quod ciuitas et quilibet comitatus illorum magnam summam auri colligeret et in signum pacis sibi offeret; quod et factum est. Ordinauit etiam rex, cum compromisso parliamento et reliquo consilio suo, uniuersos et singulos in ciuitatibus et uicis sigilla sua cartis apponere albis, in quibus postea protestabantur se statuta huius parliamenti imperpetuum obseruare, et contrarios, si qui fuerint, statim regi uel suo consilio intimare. Hoc idem omnes episcopi iurauerunt, et singulos de clero iurare compulerunt. Ordinauerunt insuper quod archiepiscopi, episcopi, abbates, priores, domini, communes in ciuitatibus et uillis singuli cartis albis sigilla sua apponerent, quod et fecerunt, per episcopos maxime artati. In quibus postea huiusmodi sententiam rex, ut dicitur, scribere intendebat: 'Quia magestatem uestram retroactis temporibus grauiter offendimus, nos et omnia bona nostra uobis damus ad libitum uestre uoluntatis.' Familias dominorum, ducis Gloucestrie et comitum et omnium cum eis equitantium, pecuniis denudauit.

1398. Anno Domini millesimo trecentisimo nonagesimo octauo et anno regni regis Ricardi uicesimo primo, dux Northfolchie, prius comes de Notingham, secrete dixit sub sigillo confessionis Henrico filio ducis Lancastrie, tunc duci Herfordie: 'Rex ordinauit te et me interficere pro equitatione cum duce Gloucestrie; et ideo dispone quid acturus sis, et ego me disponam.'[200] Et alius dixit: 'Rex hoc indulsit

---

[197] Walden, a former king's secretary (1393–5) and treasurer of England (1395–8), was provided to Canterbury on 8 Nov. 1397 and received his temporalities on 21 Jan. 1398 (*HBC*, p. 233).

[198] This famous description of Richard's absolutist tendencies has been questioned, but is in keeping with the chronicler's portrayal of the king: see G. Stow, 'Richard II in the *Continuatio Eulogii*: Yet another alleged historical incident?', in N. Saul, ed., *Fourteenth Century England V* (2008), pp. 116–29; see also above, p. xl.

[199] The council met at Nottingham on 30 June 1398. For Richard's deeply unpopular 'blank charters', see Barron, 'The Tyranny of Richard II'.

the Roman Curia bringing bulls, and the king had Roger consecrated, and soon after this the aforesaid Roger lavishly celebrated his entry to Canterbury.[197] And after this, on solemn festivals when, by custom, the king used his regalia, he ordered a throne to be made ready for him in a chamber, on which he liked to sit ostentatiously from after dinner until the evening, talking to no one but watching everyone; and when his eye fell on anyone, regardless of their rank, that person had to kneel.[198]

The king desires a guarantee of peace. Blank charters. Then the king, having summoned the archbishop and the bishops and his councillors to Nottingham, declared that he was unable to ride safely through the kingdom on account of the hatred of the people of London and its seventeen adjoining counties, and that he wished therefore to gather an army and destroy them, unless they would give him guarantees of safety.[199] They decreed, therefore, that the city and each of those counties should collect a large sum of money and hand it over to him as a token of peace; and this was done. The king also decreed, along with his delegated parliament and the rest of his council, that each and every person in the cities and towns should put their seals to blank charters, in which they subsequently declared their willingness to uphold the statutes of this parliament for evermore and to inform the king or his council immediately of any persons acting to the contrary, if indeed there were any. All the bishops swore this too, and they compelled every one of the clergy to swear it. Moreover, they decreed that the archbishops, bishops, abbots, priors, lords, and each of the commoners in the cities and the towns should put their seals to blank charters, which was duly done, under the greatest pressure from the bishops; upon which, so it was alleged, the king planned subsequently to write the following sentence: 'Because we gravely displeased your majesty in the past, we place ourselves and all our goods freely at your disposal.' He also stripped of their money the followers of the lords, the duke of Gloucester and the earls, and all who had ridden with them.

1398. In the year of the Lord 1398 and the twenty-first year of the reign of King Richard, the duke of Norfolk, formerly earl of Nottingham, said secretly, under seal of confession, to Henry, son of the duke of Lancaster, then duke of Hereford: 'The king has ordered you and me to be killed for riding with the duke of Gloucester. Decide what you are going to do, therefore, and I shall do likewise.'[200] To which

---

[200] For the dispute between the dukes of Hereford and Norfolk, which erupted in Jan. 1398 and led to both men being exiled in the autumn, see C. Given-Wilson, 'Richard II, Edward II and the Lancastrian Inheritance', *EHR* cix (1994), 553–71. The abortive duel at Coventry (Warwickshire) took place on 16 Sept.

nobis.' Cui dux Northfolchie dixit: 'Rex non est fidelis, sicut patet in duce Gloucestrie et comitibus.' Dux autem Herfordie retulit ista dicta suo patri, et pater regi; requisitus, dux Northfolchie negauit. Dux Herfordie ipsum de dictis illis et de occisione ducis Gloucestrie appellauit, quare cirothecas proiecerunt, et erat eis dies pugne apud Couentriam assignatus; ubi cum ad duellum forent parati, rex tunc presens ipsorum causam in manus suas assumpsit et ducem Herfordie ad terminum decem annorum, ducem uero Northfolchie, et Thomam Arundell archiepiscopum Cantuariensem, perpetuo relegauit. Dux uero Northfolchie apud Venetias diem suum clausit extremum. Concessitque rex duci Herfordie certam summam annuatim percipiendam de regno Anglie, sed prohibuit quod non loqueretur cum Thoma de Arundell, ad quod iuramento astrictus est; rex prudentiam eius atque consilium timebat.[201] Rex itaque dedit comitatum Arundellie Iohanni Holand comiti Hontingdonie.[202] Thomas de Arundell transiit ad papam et, procurante rege, cum magno periculo uite sue uix euasit malendrinos per uiam latitantes. Papa non audebat consolari eum timore regis.[203] Hoc insuper anno comes Marchie occiditur in Hibernia.[204]

1399. Anno Domini millesimo trecentisimo nonagesimo nono et anno regni regis Ricardi uicesimo secundo, rex, conuocato concilio suo, dixit quod uolebat transfretare in Hiberniam, sed desiderabat prius uisitare Sanctum Thomam; sed non bene confidebat in ciuitate Londonie nec in comitatu Cancie. Archiepiscopus autem assecurauit eum et duxit eum ad Cantuariam stipatum magna multitudine Cestrensium, qui nocte ac die uigilabant super eum, et singulis diebus sex denarios cuilibet dabat. Hos pascebat archiepiscopus apud Cantuariam sumptuose, et reduxit regem ad London.[205]

Aquila. Rex intrauit Turrim et omnia iocalia pretiosa a predecessoribus suis ibidem reposita tulit secum; ubi et inuenit aquilam auream et ampullam lapideam in ea clausam, cum quadam scriptura dicente

---

[201] Norfolk died at Venice on 22 Sept. 1399 on his return from the Holy Land. Richard granted Hereford £2,000 a year from the treasury during his exile (Given-Wilson, *Henry IV*, p. 123).

[202] Holand had been granted the lordship, but not the earldom, of Arundel following Earl Richard's execution in Sept. 1397, to which the castles and lordships of Lewes (Sussex) and Reigate (Surrey) were added following Norfolk's exile (Dunn, *Politics of Magnate Power*, p. 63; *CP*, v. 198).

[203] Thomas Arundel spent about a year of his exile in Italy, first in Rome and then in Florence; he asked Pope Boniface IX to restore him to Canterbury (A. Brown, 'The Latin letters in MS All Souls 182', *EHR* lxxxvii (1972), 565–73).

the other replied: 'The king pardoned us for that.' The duke of Norfolk said to him: 'The king cannot be trusted, as is plain from what happened to the duke of Gloucester and the earls.' The duke of Hereford therefore repeated these words to his father, who told the king; when questioned about it, the duke of Norfolk denied it. The duke of Hereford appealed him for saying these things and for the murder of the duke of Gloucester, whereupon they threw down their gauntlets, and a day was assigned for them to do battle at Coventry; but when they appeared there, ready to duel, the king, who was present, took their quarrel into his own hands and declared that the duke of Hereford should be exiled for a term of ten years, and the duke of Norfolk, like Thomas Arundel, archbishop of Canterbury, in perpetuity. The duke of Norfolk later died at Venice. And the king granted to the duke of Hereford a certain sum of money to be taken each year from the kingdom of England, but he prohibited him from speaking with Thomas Arundel, obliging him to swear an oath not to do so; the king feared the latter's wisdom and counsel.[201] The king therefore gave the earldom of Arundel to John Holand, earl of Huntingdon.[202] Thomas Arundel went to see the pope, encountering great danger, for he barely escaped with his life from bandits who, at the king's prompting, lay in wait for him on the road. The pope, for fear of the king, dared not offer him any consolation.[203] Also in this year the earl of March was killed in Ireland.[204]

1399. In the year of the Lord 1399 and the twenty-second year of the reign of King Richard, the king, having summoned a council, announced that he wished to take ship for Ireland, but first he wanted to visit Saint Thomas; however, he did not fully trust either the city of London or the county of Kent. The archbishop thus gave him assurances and conducted him to Canterbury, surrounded by a great multitude of Cheshiremen who watched over him day and night, to each of whom he gave 6 pence every day. The archbishop fed these men lavishly at Canterbury and escorted the king back to London.[205]

The eagle. The king went into the Tower and carried off with him all the precious jewels which his predecessors had deposited there; he also found there a golden eagle with an ampulla made of stone enclosed in

---

[204] Roger Mortimer, earl of March, died in battle in Ireland on 20 July 1398.
[205] Richard was at Canterbury in early Apr. 1399. Several chroniclers testify to the unpopularity of the king's Cheshire bodyguard (Saul, *Richard II*, pp. 393–4, 444–5, 474).

quod Beata Virgo tradidit illam Sancto Thome Cantuariensi archiepiscopo tunc exulanti, dicens quod 'de oleo huius ampulle boni reges futuri Anglorum ungerentur, et unus eorum terram a parentibus amissam sine ui recuperabit, et erit magnus inter reges, et edificabit multas ecclesias in Terra Sancta; et fugabit omnes paganos a Babilonia, ubi plures ecclesias edificabit; et quotiens portabit aquilam in pectore suo, uictoriam habebit de inimicis suis, et regnum eius semper augmentabitur. Et inuenietur in tempore opportune; et unctio regum Anglorum in caput paganorum erit, causa inuentionis huius aquile.'[206] Istam aquilam portabat rex[o] | semper in collo suspensam. Quidam eremita de partibus borealibus, sacerdos, uenit ad archiepiscopum Cantuariensem et dixit: 'Deus misit me ad uos ut dicerem uobis quod accedere debeatis ad regem et sibi dicere quod restituat hereditates exheredatis, alioquin utrique uestrum euenient magna mala in breui.' Cui archiepiscopus dixit: 'Tu ipse dices ista regi.' 'Libenter', dixit ipse, et archiepiscopus misit ipsum ad regem. Rex de consilio astantium misit ipsum ad Turrim.[207] Deinde rex fecit testamentum suum, regno ualde preiudiciale, ut dixerunt qui uiderunt; et ducem Eborum fecit custodem regni, et transfretauit cum magno exercitu in Hiberniam.[208]

Iohannes Dux Lancastrie moritur. Eodem anno factus fuit terremotus magnus sub ecclesia Sancti Pauli Londonie, et postea dux Lancastrie de graui langore moritur et in ea sepelitur.[209] Quod audiens, filius eius exul applicuit in litore boreali Anglie una cum Thoma Arundell et filio comitis de Arundell, qui fugerat de regno; ad quos uenit comes Northumbrie, dominus de Percy, cum tota potentia boreali, nec aliquis uoluit contra eos sequi ducem Eborum aut consiliarios regis, quamuis Willielmus le Scrope, thesaurarius Anglie, abundantissime aurum offerret.[210] Henricus scripsit ciuitati Londonie, uocans se ducem Lancastrie et regni senescallum, dicens se uelle regnum ad debitum regimen et pristinam reducere libertatem. Consenseruntque Londonienses, et omnia castra regis duci tradita sunt. Thesaurarius regis et duo regis consiliarii maximi, in parliamento milites, uersus Hiberniam

---

[o] *in a scroll in lower margin of fo. 200ᵛ:* semper in collo; *in upper margin of fo. 201ʳ:* Ricardi Secundi

[206] For the full meaning of this inscription, which the chronicler's habit of abridging his written sources has somewhat obscured, see *SAC* II, pp. 238–9. According to the St Albans account, Richard asked Archbishop Arundel to anoint him for a second time with the oil, but Arundel refused.

[207] The northern hermit was William Norham, who approached Archbishop Walden in the spring of 1399; he was imprisoned but released after Richard's deposition (*SAC* II, pp. 118–21, and below, p. 117).

it, together with some writing saying that the Blessed Virgin gave this to Saint Thomas of Canterbury, the then exiled archbishop, saying that 'with the oil from this ampulla, the good kings of the English will in future be anointed, and one of them shall recover without violence the land lost by his progenitors, and he will be great among kings, and he will build many churches in the Holy Land; and he will drive all the pagans from Babylon, where he will build many churches; and whenever he wears the eagle on his breast, he will overcome his enemies, and his kingdom will continually increase. And when the time is right, this will be found; and it will be the balm of the kings of the English in the chief city of the pagans, as a result of the discovery of this eagle.'[206] The king wore this eagle continuously, hung around his neck. A certain hermit from the northern parts, a priest, approached the archbishop of Canterbury and said: 'God has sent me to you to tell you that you must go to the king and tell him that, unless he restores their inheritances to those who have been disinherited, great misfortunes will shortly befall both of you.' The archbishop replied: 'You go and tell this to the king yourself.' 'Willingly', he replied, and the archbishop sent him to the king. The king, on the advice of those who were standing around, sent him to the Tower.[207] Then the king made his will, which according to those who saw it was greatly prejudicial to the realm; and he made the duke of York keeper of the realm, and crossed with a great army to Ireland.[208]

John duke of Lancaster dies. In this same year, there was a great earthquake underneath St Paul's church in London, following which the duke of Lancaster died of a serious illness and was buried there.[209] Hearing this, his son, an exile, landed on the north coast of England, together with Thomas Arundel and the son of the earl of Arundel, who had fled the realm; they were joined by the earl of Northumberland, Lord Percy, with all the power of the north, and nobody wanted to follow the duke of York or the king's councillors in opposing them, even though William le Scrope, treasurer of England, offered abundant quantities of money.[210] Henry wrote to the city of London, calling himself duke of Lancaster and steward of the realm, saying that he wanted to restore the kingdom to its accustomed form of government and ancient liberty. The Londoners agreed, and all the king's castles were delivered up to the duke. The king's treasurer and the two foremost

---

[208] Richard's will was the subject of one of the deposition charges against the king (*CR*, pp. 181–2; it is printed in *Foedera*, viii. 162). He landed with his army at Waterford (County Waterford) on 1 June 1399.

[209] John of Gaunt died at Leicester on 3 Feb. 1399.

[210] Henry returned to England on or just after 30 June, landing first at Ravenspur (Spurn Head, at the mouth of the Humber), then at Bridlington (Yorkshire). For the progress of the revolution which won him the throne, see *CR*, pp. 32–41.

fugientes, in castro Bristollie se clauserunt, sed dux uenit et castrum expugnauit et eos decollari fecit.[211] Rex hoc audiens cepit consilium: et unus dixit melius esse ibi expectare quousque communitas attediaretur de eorum peruagatione per regnum, alius autem dixit quod primo obstandum esset, quodque sibi melius esse credens, applicuit in Wallia Boreali; sed exercitus eius, ad diuersos portus diuertens, ipsum sequi nolebat. Thomas Percy, senescallus domus sue, in castro de Conwey fregit uirgam in aula, dicens: 'Dominus rex non tenet domum amplius', et omnes domestici deseruerunt regem; ipse autem exprobrabat infidelitatem Anglie.[212] Dux scripsit senescallo archiepiscopi Cantuariense quod omnia seruaret Thome de Arundell sub pena capitis. Roggerus Walden omnia iocalia sua amouit de palacio Cantuarie, et omnia capta sunt apud Rofam et posita in castro.[213]

Dux et Thomas de Arundell uenerunt ad regem in castrum de Conwaye, dicentes sibi post pauca quod ulterius non regnaret.[214] Thomas de Arundell dixit sibi: 'Pulcher homo es, sed falsissimus inter omnes. Tu promisisti mihi, iurando super corpus Christi, quod non noceres fratri meo, et cum duxissem ad presentiam tuam, non uidi eum amplius. Promisisti mihi fallaciter quod me ab exilio reuocares, et alium archiepiscopum ordinasti et mortem meam procurasti. Regnum non rexisti sed spoliasti, theolonia notabiliter eleuando, tallagia annuatim extorquendo, non ad utilitatem regni, quam numquam procurasti, sed ad auaritiam tuam satiandam et superbiam ostendendam. Adulatorum tuorum infimorum, tua semper donaria postulantium, consiliis adhesisti et eos promouisti. Sanum consilium, dominos precipuos, consanguineos tuos, quia uolebant tuam proteruiam compescere, sicut per statuta potuerunt et in periculo regni debuerunt, iniuste occidisti, et posteritatem eorum tyrannice extinguere quoque statuisti; sed statuta tua non stabunt. Incontinenter uixisti, et fedo exemplo tuo curiam tuam et regnum maculasti.' Cum talia multiplicaret, dux dixit: 'Sufficit.' Et rex, non habens quomodo se defenderet, duci se reddidit et renuntiare promisit, et ipsi duxerunt illum ad Turrim Londonie,

---

[211] William le Scrope (treasurer), Sir John Bussy, and Sir Henry Green, all deeply unpopular royal councillors, were beheaded outside Bristol castle on 29 July.

[212] Richard arrived back from Ireland around 24 July, landing at Milford Haven (Pembrokeshire). On 31 July, he decided to abandon what remained of his army at Carmarthen and hastened to Conwy castle in North Wales. It was at Carmarthen that Thomas Percy broke his staff of office and disbanded the royal household (*CR*, pp. 121–2).

[213] The reinstatement of Arundel as archbishop of Canterbury was done without papal approval, but was not resisted by Boniface IX. For the seizure of Walden's goods, many of which he had appropriated from Arundel, see *Usk*, pp. 78–82. However, he became bishop of London in 1404.

councillors of the king, knights of parliament, fleeing to Ireland, shut themselves up in Bristol castle, but the duke arrived and captured the castle and had them beheaded.[211] Hearing this, the king took counsel: one person said that it would be better to wait there until the people grew weary of this marching about the kingdom, but another said that it was important to resist, and because this seemed to him to hold out more hope, he landed in North Wales; his army, however, having been dispersed to various ports, did not want to follow him. Thomas Percy, steward of his household, broke his staff of office in the hall of Conwy castle [Gwynedd], saying: 'The king no longer keeps a household', and all his servants abandoned the king; he for his part cursed England's faithlessness.[212] The duke wrote to the steward of the archbishop of Canterbury telling him under pain of death to preserve unharmed everything belonging to Thomas Arundel. Roger Walden removed all his jewels from the palace at Canterbury, and they were all seized at Rochester and deposited in the castle.[213]

The duke and Thomas of Arundel came to the king in Conwy castle, telling him that in a short time he would cease to reign.[214] Thomas of Arundel said to him: 'You are a fine-looking man, but you are the falsest of men. You promised me, and swore upon the body of Christ, that you would not harm my brother. Yet after I brought him into your presence, I never saw him again. You falsely promised me that you would recall me from exile, but you appointed another archbishop and tried to have me killed. You did not rule your kingdom but despoiled it, imposing great tolls, extorting taxes annually, not for the benefit of the kingdom, which you never cared about, but to satisfy your own greed and flaunt your vainglory. You followed the counsels of your low-born sycophants, who constantly demanded gifts from you, and you promoted them. Those who offered good counsel, the great lords, your kinsmen, you unlawfully put to death, because they wanted to curb your extravagance, as they are entitled by the statutes of the realm to do and indeed ought to do when the kingdom is in danger, and like a tyrant you also commanded that their progeny be destroyed; but your statutes will not endure. You lived a life of debauchery, and by your foul example you besmirched your court and the kingdom.' When he had added further such comments, the duke said: 'That is enough.' Whereupon the king, having no means to defend himself, surrendered and promised to resign, and they brought him to the Tower of London

---

[214] Henry and Richard met not at Conwy but at Flint castle (Flintshire), probably on 16 Aug. 1399.

custodes et uigiles circa eum posuerunt.[215] Postea in uigilia Sancti Michaelis[216] missi sunt ad eum episcopi, comites, barones, notarii et milites ut quererent ab eo si renuntiare uellet ut promiserat. Primo negauit, sed post ostenderunt sibi quod oportebat eum renuntiare, et hoc absolute et sine conditione, tradideruntque sibi cedulam, quam legebat presente duce et magna multitudine procerum et magnatum.

Renuntiatio Regni per Ricardum Regem facta. 'Ego Ricardus, rex Anglie, renuntio omni iuri quod habeo in corona Anglie cum pertinentiis, id est, in regnis Anglie et Francie, Hibernie et Scotie, et in ducatibus Aquitannie et Normannie, et in comitatu de Pontif, ac in uilla Calesie, et in omnibus aliis castris et fortaliciis que in presenti habeo aut habere debeo de iure, ultra mare et citra, ac in quacumque parte eorumdem, pro me [et] heredibus meis imperpetuum.'[217] Et testes requisierunt notarios facere super ista renuntiatione instrumenta publica. Et confessus est se multum deliquisse contra Deum et regnum, et se non esse dignum regnare, quia bene sciebat, ut dixit, quod populus ipsum numquam dilexit, nec ipse populum.

Post hec uenit dux Lancastrie ad Westmonasterium,[218] et sollemni fo. 201ᵛ processione episcoporum ac monachorum susceptus est; et | celebrata sollemni missa de Spiritu Sancto, uenit in aulam. Et ante eum portabatur principalis gladius regius, auro et lapidibus pretiosis ornatus; et ponebat se in sede patris sui, id est, iuxta episcopum Carleoli. Et sedebant ibi omnes episcopi et omnes comites, etiam qui dominos antea appellabant,[219] ac ceteri domini de regno et populus multus, inter quos lecta fuit renuntiatio regis, et ab omnibus erat acceptata. Postea legebantur plures excessus quos Ricardus fecerat contra statum, suum iuramentum, ac leges regni, et mortes dominorum parium regni et exilia, ac testamentum suum;[220] pro quibus ipsum ibidem deponebant, et uice omnium de regno, procuratores assignati reddiderunt sursum homagia sua. Et Thomas de Arundell de assensu omnium damnauit eum perpetuo carceri.[221] Tunc surrexit dux Lancastrie. Signo crucis se

---

[215] Richard and Henry arrived in London on 1 Sept. Richard was imprisoned in the Tower the next day.
[216] This account of Richard's deposition agrees in its essentials with 'The Manner of King Richard's Renunciation', which also dates this meeting to 28 Sept. (*CR*, pp. 162–4).
[217] This renunciation is severely abridged; for the full text, see *PROME*, viii. 12–13.
[218] On 30 Sept. (*CR*, pp. 165–6).
[219] That is, the 'Counter-Appellants' who had appealed the king's opponents in the parliament of Sept. 1397.

and set guards and watchmen about him.[215] Afterwards, on the eve of Michaelmas [29 September],[216] bishops, earls, barons, notaries, and knights were sent to him to ask him whether he wished to resign as he had promised. At first he refused, but later they explained to him that he had to resign, and to do it absolutely and unconditionally, and they gave him a schedule which he read out in the presence of the duke and a large gathering of great men and magnates.

The renunciation of the kingdom made by King Richard. 'I, Richard, king of England, renounce all right that I have to the crown of England with its appurtenances, namely, in the kingdoms of England and France, in Ireland and Scotland, and in the duchies of Aquitaine and Normandy, and in the county of Ponthieu, and in the town of Calais, and in all the other castles and fortresses which I hold at present or ought by right to hold, either overseas or on this side of the sea, and in any part whatsoever of them, on behalf of myself and my heirs, in perpetuity.'[217] Whereupon witnesses ordered the notaries to draw up public instruments based on this renunciation. And he admitted that he had committed many crimes against God and the kingdom, and that he was not worthy to reign, for he knew well, so he said, that the people had never loved him, nor he them.

Following this, the duke of Lancaster came to Westminster,[218] where he was received by a formal procession of bishops and monks; and after a solemn mass of the Holy Spirit had been said, he entered the hall. Before him was carried the principal royal sword, embellished with gold and precious jewels; and he sat down in his father's seat, that is, next to the bishop of Carlisle. And all the bishops and all the earls were seated there, including those who previously appealed the lords,[219] as well as the other lords of the realm, and a multitude of people, before whom the king's renunciation was read out, and by all of whom it was accepted. Then the numerous crimes which Richard had committed against the estates, his oath, and the laws of the realm were recited, and the death and banishment of lords who were peers of the realm, and his will;[220] on account of which they there deposed him, and proctors assigned to represent all the people of the realm withdrew their homage. And Thomas Arundel, with the assent of all, condemned him to perpetual imprisonment.[221] Then the duke of Lancaster stood up. Making the

---

[220] The deposition charges against Richard were set out in the 'Record and Process' (*CR*, pp. 168–84; for criticism of the king's will, see pp. 181–2).
[221] Richard was not sentenced to imprisonment until 27 Oct. (*PROME*, viii. 34–5).

signans, legebat quamdam cedulam in qua ostendebat quod ipse descendebat de rege Henrico, filio Iohannis, et proximus masculus erat de sanguine suo, et istis de causis regnum uendicabat; ad quod omnes domini singulatim assenserunt, et communitas communiter hoc clamabat.[222] Tunc surrexerunt archiepiscopi Cantuarie, Thomas, et Eborum, et osculabant manus eius et duxerunt eum ad sedem regiam sumptuose ornatam.[223] Ac archiepiscopus Thomas Arundell fecit collationem bonam de themate, 'Vir fortis dominabitur populo',[224] et postea cancellarius sigillum, et alii officiarii sua officia, sibi reddebant, et rex eis iterum ea tradebat. Et archiepiscopus Cantuarie, Thomas, pronuntiabat quod rex coronaretur in festo Sancti Edwardi apud Westmonasterium, mandans omnibus quod conuenirent ad parliamentum die Lune sequenti.[225]

Rex Ricardus in diuitiis omnes predecessores suos studuit excedere et ad Salomonis gloriam peruenire, cepitque plus illis infra regnum post annum eius undecimum formidari,[226] quamuis prole careret et animo bellicoso. In thesauris et iocalibus, in uestibus et ornamentis regalibus, in quibus uehementer excessit, in splendore mense, in palaciis que edificauit, nullus in Regibus eo gloriosior diebus suis. Et in maxima altitudine sue glorie subito, appensus et inuentus minus habens, deponitur potens de sede, et statua percussa miserabiliter est contrita, arborque procera in medio terre, omnibus opulentiis priuata, uigili iubente celesti, succiditur,[227] et in carcere perpetuo, uidelicet castro Pontis Fracti, fit habitatio eius.[228]

Coronatio Regis Henrici Quarti. Rex Henricus quartus coronatur a Thoma de Arundell, unctus cum oleo aquile innotate; et erat primus qui cum oleo illo ungebatur. Continuauit parliamentum, in quo assistentes regi Ricardo examinauit, sed de pernicioso consilio nullus tunc conuinci potuit. Prohibuitque rex cum parliamento imperpetuum ne sine responsione aliquis damnaretur.[p] Parliamentum ultimum Ricardi, iudicia sua et ordinationes factas ibidem irritauit, et iuramenta atque excommunicationes non obseruantium euanuerunt. Filium

---

[p] *marginal in later hand*: nota

[222] For the wording of Henry's claim to the throne, see the 'Record and Process' in *CR*, p. 186. However, the 'Record and Process' does not include the claim that he was the nearest male heir to the throne, which is taken from 'The Manner of King Richard's Renunciation' (*CR*, p. 166).

[223] The archbishop of York was Richard Scrope (1398–1405).

[224] 1 Kgs. (1 Sam.) 9: 17.

[225] Parliament was summoned for Monday 6 Oct.; 13 Oct. was the Translation of Edward the Confessor.

sign of the Cross, he read out a certain schedule in which he explained that he was descended from King Henry, son of King John, and was the nearest male heir by blood, and for these reasons he claimed the kingdom; to which all the lords individually assented, and the commons collectively cried out in agreement.[222] Then Thomas, archbishop of Canterbury, and the archbishop of York stood up, and they kissed his hands and led him to the magnificently decorated throne.[223] And Archbishop Thomas Arundel delivered a fine sermon on the theme 'A strong man shall rule over the people',[224] following which the chancellor surrendered the seal to the king, and other ministers their offices, and he handed them back to them again. And Thomas, archbishop of Canterbury, announced that the king would be crowned at Westminster on the feast of St Edward [13 October], ordering them all to assemble for parliament on the following Monday.[225]

King Richard strove to outdo all his predecessors in riches and to rival the glory of Solomon, and from his eleventh year he began to be more feared within the realm than them,[226] albeit that he lacked offspring and a warlike nature. In treasure and jewels, in kingly robes and adornments, which he accumulated inordinately, in the splendour of his table, in the palaces that he built, no one in [the Books of] Kings was more glorious in his time than he. And at the very height of his glory, suddenly, having lost respect and support, the great man was deposed from his throne, and his image was smashed and wretchedly ground down, and, at the command of the Heavenly Watchman, the mighty tree in the middle of the land, stripped of all its riches, was cut down,[227] and his dwelling-place became a perpetual prison, that is, the castle of Pontefract.[228]

The coronation of King Henry IV. King Henry IV was crowned by Thomas Arundel and anointed with the oil of the aforementioned eagle; and he was the first to be anointed with that oil. Parliament reconvened, in which it interrogated those who had supported King Richard, but no one could be convicted of evil counsel at that time. And the king, together with parliament, ordered that in future, for evermore, no person should be condemned without right of reply. He abolished Richard's last parliament, its judgments and the ordinances decreed there, and the oaths and excommunications sank into unheeded

---

[226] That is, the eleventh year of Richard's reign (1387–8). For the splendour of Solomon, see 1 Kgs. (1 Sam.) 10.

[227] Cf. Dan. 4: 19–23.

[228] Richard was moved from London to Pontefract castle in early Dec. 1399 (Saul, *Richard II*, p. 424).

comitis Arundell comitem Arundell fecit.²²⁹ Comitem Warwici de carcere et Iohannem de Cobham de exilio reuocauit. Cartas omnes quas a regno sigillari exegerat Londoniis patenter comburi fecit. Primogenitum suum Henricum principem Wallie fecit, et omnes duces ordinatos a rege Ricardo in ultimo parliamento deordinauit.²³⁰ Rogerum Walden omnia que receperat de episcopatu Cantuariensi Thome de Arundell restituere fecit, et ad preces eiusdem Thome uitam sibi concessit. Bonifacius*q* papa iudicium Ricardi contra Thomam Arundell cassum fuisse declarauit per bullam, et quod ecclesia Cantuariensis non uacauit nec pastore destituta fuit.²³¹

Rex tenuit Natale Domini apud Windesore, et quidam armiger de Circestre, in armis multum exercitatus, secundum consuetudinem suam misit unum de sua familia ad curiam regis ut sibi referret gesta fortia hastiludiensium.²³² Archiepiscopus autem Cantuariensis post Circumcisionem Domini mouit a Cantuaria usque Windesore ut esset cum rege in die Epiphanie. Quidam de familia regis interim iacebat una nocte cum una meretrice Londonie, que mane dixit sibi: 'Vale, amice, quia amplius te non uidebo.' Et ille quesiuit quare, que et dixit: 'Comites Huntyngdonie et Cancie ac Sarum et multi alii milites iacent in insidiis in partibus de Kyngeston ut regem, archiepiscopum Cantuariensem et omnes uos uenientes de Wyndesore occidant et regem Ricardum restituant.' Et ille quesiuit: 'Vnde hoc nosti?' Et illa respondens dixit: 'Vnus de familia eorum dormiuit mecum altera nocte qui hoc dixit mihi.' Festinauit ergo ipse ad regem narrans sibi sermonem hunc; et statim cessabant ludere. Et qui uenerat de Circestre, hoc audiens, narrauit magistro suo. Rex uero premuniuit archiepiscopum per nuntium, et ipse reuersus est ad Reygate. Rex etiam, diuertens per aliam uiam, nocte festinauit ad London, mandans omnibus de comitatibus ad se festinanter conuenire.²³³

---

q there is a change of nib here

²²⁹ Thomas, born in 1381, was restored to his father's possessions in Nov. 1399 but not formally restored to his earldoms of Arundel and Surrey until Oct. 1400 (*CPR 1399–1401*, p. 134).

²³⁰ For these trials and other acts of the Oct. 1399 parliament, which reconvened on 14 Oct., see *PROME*, viii. 2–90. The dukes of Exeter, Surrey, and Aumale, created in 1397, were demoted to the rank of earl, as was John Beaufort, marquis of Dorset; Thomas Despenser was demoted from his earldom of Gloucester. The new king's eldest son, the future Henry V, was made prince of Wales, duke of Lancaster, duke of Aquitaine, duke of Cornwall, and earl of Chester (*PROME*, viii. 33–7).

²³¹ Arundel was formally reinstated to Canterbury on 19 Oct. Neither he nor the king persecuted Walden, who in Dec. 1404 was provided to the see of London. For some firsthand comments on Walden, see *Usk*, pp. 78–82.

oblivion. The son of the earl of Arundel, he made earl of Arundel.[229] He recalled the earl of Warwick from prison and John de Cobham from exile. He ordered all the charters which [Richard] had ordered to be sealed by the kingdom to be publicly burned in London. He made his eldest son, Henry, prince of Wales, and demoted all the dukes created by King Richard in the last parliament.[230] He made Roger Walden restore everything which he had received from Thomas Arundel's see of Canterbury, but, at the request of the said Thomas, granted him his life. Pope Boniface decreed by bull that Richard's judgment against Thomas Arundel was annulled, and that the church of Canterbury was neither left empty nor deprived of a pastor.[231]

The king held Christmas at Windsor, and a certain esquire from Cirencester [Gloucestershire], a great practitioner of arms, sent a member of his household to the king's court, as was his custom, so that he could report back to him on the warlike deeds at the jousts.[232] Following the Circumcision of the Lord [1 January], the archbishop of Canterbury also moved from Canterbury to Windsor so that he could be with the king on the feast of Epiphany [6 January]. Meanwhile, a member of the king's household lay one night with a London prostitute, who said to him in the morning: 'Farewell, my friend, for I shall not be seeing you again.' And he asked why, and she said: 'The earls of Huntingdon and Kent and Salisbury and many other knights are lying in wait near Kingston [Surrey] to kill the king, the archbishop of Canterbury, and all of you who are coming from Windsor, and to restore King Richard.' And he asked: 'How do you know this?' And she replied: 'A member of one of their households slept with me the other night, and he told me.' Hurrying to the king, therefore, he told him about this conversation, and they immediately brought the festivities to an end. And the man who had come from Cirencester, hearing this, reported it to his master. The king therefore sent a messenger to forewarn the archbishop, who turned back to Reigate [Surrey], and then hastened back to London at night by a different route, sending out orders to all the men of the shires to join him as soon as possible.[233]

---

[232] This was probably a former esquire of Thomas of Woodstock, duke of Gloucester, called John Cosyn, who a few days later led the townsmen of Cirencester in resisting the rebel earls and was rewarded by Henry IV with an annuity of 100 marks (Given-Wilson, *Henry IV*, p. 427).

[233] King Henry left Windsor for London on 4 Jan. For the 'Epiphany Rising', see Given-Wilson, *Henry IV*, pp. 160–5.

CONTINUATIO EULOGII

Quidam uir de familia archiepiscopi transiit per Kyngeston, et comes Cancie, | uidens eum de fenestra hospitii, iussit eum adduci ad se et interrogauit eum, dicens: 'Vbi est magister tuus?' Qui respondit: 'In castro de Reygate.' At ille, 'Vbi est rex?' Qui respondit: 'Londonie.' Et dixit comes: 'Verum dicis. Ipsi fugerunt timore nostro. Si obuiassem domino tuo, rasissem sibi coronam.' Et iussit famulis suis spoliare eum equo et pecunia sua. At ipse et comes Sarum cum familia sua equitabant ad Circestre per uiam proclamantes quod Rex Ricardus transiret. Cum autem uenissent in hospitia sero apud Circestre, quos cum dicte uille communitas arestasse uoluisset, restiterunt fortiter dimicantes; quibus tamen debellatis et captis, ipsi duo cum multis aliis decapitati sunt et uinculis mancupantur, quia quidam de eorum familia miserunt ignem in tecta diuersarum domorum ibidem, et multos in cippis et compedibus seruauerunt, quos postea regi Oxonie presentarunt, ubi multi tracti, suspensi et decapitati sunt.[234] Postmodum apud Prytwell in Excexc in quodam molendino Iohannes Holand, dux Exonie, frater regis Ricardi ex parte matris, se transformans in simplicem, per patrie illius communitatem captus et usque Plasshe adductus, decollatur.[235] Interea apud Bristolliam dux Gloucestrie capitur et in foro ibidem a populo decapitatus est, dolens et malam uitam suam deplorans.[236] Capita autem comitum super pontem Londonie posita sunt. Alii insurrectores clerici et laici, inter quos Rogerus Walden et episcopus Carleoli, Londonie inuenti, coram iustitiariis statuuntur, et solus Rogerus Walden excusatur. Laici trahuntur et suspenduntur; clerici trahuntur et decollantur. Episcopus Merk incarceratur et episcopatu priuatur; postea tamen rex gratiose egit cum eo, uisa conuersatione eius.[237] Ricardus olim rex, in carcere hoc audiens, cepit omnino de auxilio desperare et confessus est eos de consilio suo dato in castro de Conway ista fecisse; et, ut dicebatur, pro tristitia comedere nolens, moriebatur. Corpus eius delatum est ad Sanctum Paulum Londonie et

---

[234] The earls of Kent and Salisbury and their fellow rebel, Ralph Lord Lumley, reached Cirencester on 6 Jan., and were beheaded by the townsmen, led by John Cosyn, two days later. Henry IV tried the other conspirators at Oxford on 12 Jan., by which time the rising had collapsed. Twenty-seven men were convicted of treason, most of whom were beheaded, although four knights and esquires suffered the full penalties of a traitor's death.

[235] John Holand was handed over to Joan, countess of Hereford (Henry IV's mother-in-law) at Pleshey castle, and executed on 9 or 10 Jan.

[236] Thomas Despenser, not duke but earl of Gloucester, was beheaded at Bristol on 13 Jan.

[237] Sir Bernard Brocas and Sir Thomas Shelley were executed on 5 Feb., and two of Richard II's clerks, Richard Maudeleyn and William Ferriby, on 29 Jan. Thomas Merks, bishop of Carlisle, was sentenced to death and kept in prison until 28 Nov. 1400, when the

A member of the archbishop's household was passing through Kingston when the earl of Kent spotted him from the window of his lodgings and, ordering him to be brought to him, asked him: 'Where is your master?' He replied: 'In Reigate castle.' 'Where is the king?' he went on. 'In London', replied the man. And the earl said: 'You are telling the truth. They have fled for fear of us. If I had encountered your lord, I would have shaved off his crown.' And he ordered his servants to take the man's horse and money. Then he and the earl of Salisbury and their followers rode to Cirencester, proclaiming along the way that King Richard was coming. However, once they had arrived at a late hour at a lodging-house in Cirencester, when the people of the said town tried to apprehend them, they resisted strongly and fought against them; but, having been overcome and captured, these two and many others were beheaded or placed in chains, because some of their followers had set fire to the roofs of various houses there, and they placed many of them in the stocks and in shackles, whom they later handed over to the king at Oxford, where many of them were drawn, hanged, and beheaded.[234] Following this, John Holand, duke of Exeter, the brother of King Richard on his mother's side, who had adopted the disguise of a poor man, was captured by local people in a certain mill at Prittlewell in Essex and, having been taken to Pleshey, was beheaded.[235] Meanwhile, the duke of Gloucester was seized at Bristol and beheaded by the people in the marketplace there, lamenting and bewailing his evil life.[236] And the heads of the earls were placed on top of London bridge. Other clerks and laymen who had risen up, including Roger Walden and the bishop of Carlisle, were discovered in London and brought before the justices, and Roger Walden was the only one to be acquitted. The laymen were drawn and hanged; the clerks were drawn and beheaded. Bishop Merks was imprisoned and deprived of his see, but later the king, having observed his conduct, treated him mercifully.[237] Richard, the former king, hearing of these events in prison, began to despair utterly of help, and admitted that they had done these things on the advice he had given them at Conwy castle; and it was said that he died after refusing to eat because of his despondency. His body was brought to St Paul's in London, and his face displayed to the

---

king pardoned him, though he lost his bishopric of Carlisle. Also suspected of involvement in the rising were Henry Despenser, bishop of Norwich, and William Colchester, abbot of Westminster, but, like Walden, they were not brought to trial (Given-Wilson, *Henry IV*, pp. 163, 349–50).

facies sua ostensa est populo; et, celebratis ibidem exequiis eius per regem, apud Langley sepultum est.[238]

Isabella Regina. Isabella, secunda uxor regis Ricardi, dote sua nudata, multis tamen muneribus dotata, ab Anglia in Franciam pulsa est; qua repatriante, Gallici treugas prius initas soluunt.[239] Tunc rex misit Londoniensibus ut aurum sibi mutuarent; ipsi autem ad eum accesserunt querentes an ipsa missio de uoluntate sua processit, referentes quomodo ipse promisit se ab huiusmodi mutuis et tallagiis abstinere. Qui eis respondens dixit se omnino egere et pecuniam ab eis tunc habere oportere.[240] Hec omnia facta sunt anno primo regis huius et anno uicesimosecundo Ricardi, et anno Domini millesimo trecentisimo nonagesimo nono.[241]

1400. Anno Domini millesimo quadringentesimo et regni Henrici quarti secundo, rex, congregato exercitu, transiit in Scotiam, sed illis non comparentibus, uictualibusque deficientibus, in Angliam est reuersus. Tunc comes de Dunbar effectus est Anglicus et datus est sibi comitatus Richmundie.[242] Hoc anno factum est parliamentum Londoniis, in quo decimam cleri et quintamdecimam laicorum rex exegit.[243] In hoc parliamento archiepiscopus Cantuariensis quendam hereticum, dicentem accidens non esse sine subiecto in sacramento altaris et panem manere, degradauit; qui Smythfeld combustus est. Hoc exemplo terribili alii complices sui hereses suas in Cruce Sancti Pauli personaliter reuocabant.[244] Ad hoc parliamentum uenit Audoenus de Glendour, Wallicus qui fuerat armiger comitis Arundellie, conquerens quod dominus de Gray Ruthyn quasdam terras suas in Wallia usurpauit; sed contra dominum de Gray nihil profecit. Episcopus de Sancto Assaf consuluit in parliamento quod non omnino contempnerent prefatum Audoenum ne forte Wallici insurgerent; et illi de parliamento

---

[238] Richard died around 14 Feb., in Pontefract castle; it is more likely that he was murdered on Henry's orders, perhaps by starvation, than that he starved himself to death. His obsequies were performed at St Paul's on 6–7 Mar.; initially buried at King's Langley, his remains were exhumed and reburied in Westminster abbey by Henry V in Dec. 1413.

[239] After much negotiation, Isabella was returned to the French via Calais on 31 July 1401. Her jewels, gold, and silver were valued at £9,364, but Henry declined to return the £33,333 of her dowry given to Richard at their wedding in 1396. Her father, Charles VI, had agreed on 29 Jan. to respect the Anglo–French truce agreed in 1396, but by the winter of 1401–2 Anglo–French hostilities were escalating (Given-Wilson, *Henry IV*, pp. 165–73).

[240] For the king's financial problems at this time, see Given-Wilson, *Henry IV*, pp. 174–9.

[241] The chronicler is dating his calendar years from 25 Mar., not 1 Jan. In fact, 21 June 1399 marked the start of Richard II's 23rd regnal year.

[242] Henry's army of some 13,000 men spent the last two weeks of Aug. 1400 in Scotland, reaching Leith but failing to provoke the Scots into fighting or persuading them to do homage to him (A. Curry, A. Bell, A. King, and D. Simpkin, 'New regime, new army? Henry IV's

people; and once his obsequies had been celebrated there by the king, he was buried at Langley [Hertfordshire].[238]

Queen Isabella. Isabella, the second wife of King Richard, was dispatched from England to France, stripped of her dowry but provided with many gifts. Once she had arrived home, the French cancelled the truces previously agreed.[239] Then the king sent to the Londoners asking them to loan him money, but they approached him to ask whether this message proceeded from his will, reminding him how he had promised to abstain from loans and taxes of this kind. He told them in reply that he was completely destitute and must have some money from them straight away.[240] All these things happened in the first year of this king and the twenty-second year of Richard, and the year of the Lord 1399.[241]

1400. In the year of the Lord 1400 and the second year of King Henry IV, the king, having gathered an army, marched into Scotland, but the Scots failed to appear and, lacking provisions, he returned to England. Then the earl of Dunbar declared himself to be English and was given the earldom of Richmond.[242] In this year a parliament was held at London, in which the king exacted a tenth from the clergy and a fifteenth from the laity.[243] In this parliament the archbishop of Canterbury degraded a certain heretic who stated that there could not be any accident without substance in the sacrament of the altar and that the bread must remain; and he was burned at Smithfield. Following this terrible example, his accomplices personally recanted their heresies at St Paul's Cross.[244] Owain Glyndwr, a Welshman who had been an esquire of the earl of Arundel, came to this parliament to complain that Lord Grey of Ruthin had seized certain of his lands in Wales, but he was unable to obtain any remedy against Lord Grey. The bishop of St Asaph advised the parliament not to treat the said Owain with complete disdain, lest the Welsh should rise up; to which the people in the

---

Scottish expedition of 1400', *EHR* cxxv (2010), 1382–1413). George Dunbar, earl of the Scottish March, did defect to the English cause in 1400, but there is no evidence that he was given the earldom of Richmond, the lands of which (though not the title) were held by Ralph, earl of Westmorland.

[243] Parliament met at Westminster from 20 Jan. to 10 Mar. 1401 (*PROME*, viii. 93–153). Parliament granted a fifteenth and tenth, and Canterbury convocation granted a clerical tenth.

[244] The relapsed heretic William Sawtre was interrogated on several occasions by convocation, found to be incorrigible, and degraded on 26 Feb. 1401; he was burned at Smithfield on 2 Mar., defiant to the last. Within a few days his fellow heretic John Purvey had recanted, acknowledging the sacrament of the Eucharist (P. McNiven, *Heresy and Politics in the Reign of Henry IV* (Woodbridge, 1987), pp. 81–6).

dixerunt se de' scurris nudipedibus non curare.²⁴⁵ Hoc anno ˢimperator Constantinopolitanusˢ uenit in Angliam ostendens indulgentiam pape omnibus sibi de bonis suis conferentibus, et petiit auxilium a rege contra Turcos et infideles. Qui habebat cotidie missam [priuatam]ᵗ in camera sua ab episcopis suis ritu Grecorum; et cotidie imperator et omnes sui communicabant. Quem rex honorifice recepit et omnes expensas suas in Anglia persoluit. Et collectis in Anglia quattuor milia libris per indulgentiam, rex addidit alia quattuor milia et ipsum dimisit.²⁴⁶

Anno Domini millesimo quadringentesimo uno Wallici contra regem Henricum quartum rebellant et bona Anglicorum undique diripiunt.²⁴⁷ Rex autem transiit in Walliam Borialem et insulam de Anglesey, ubi fratres minores de conuentu Lamasie et Wallici cum aliis regi resistebant, et ideo exercitus regis fratres occidebant et captiuabant ac conuentum spoliabant; et, Audoenoᵘ non comparente, reuertitur rex, et dominus le Gray manucepit tuitionem patrie. Rex uero tradidit ministerio ordinis fratres captiuatos, et iussit omnia restitui conuentui, et uoluit quod conuentus ille inhabitaretur ab Anglicis fratribus.²⁴⁸ | Hoc anno quidam frater minor de Northfolch in suo sermone recommendauit regem Ricardum, dicens quod uiueret; et ille de carcere regis traditur ministerio ordinis corrigendus. Audoenus de Glendour dominum le Gray in bello cepit.²⁴⁹ Et eodem anno capitulum generale fratrum minorum celebratur Leycestrie in festo Assumptionis,²⁵⁰ in quo prohibitum est sub pena perpetui carceris ne aliquis fratrum loquatur uerbum quod possit sonare in preiudicium regis; et quod quilibet presidens haberet potestatem talem incarcerandi

---

ʳ *interlined*   ˢ⁻ˢ *underlined*   ᵗ *per notam MS*   ᵘ *underlined, and marginal in later hand*: 'Audoenus de Glendour'

---

²⁴⁵ For Owain Glyndwr and the Welsh revolt of 1400–9, see R. R. Davies, *The Revolt of Owain Glyndwr* (Oxford, 1995). Owain, a descendant of the princes of Powys and Deheubarth who had served in the retinue of the earl of Arundel in 1387, had risen against the king in Sept. 1400, claiming to be rightful prince of Wales, and was subsequently outlawed, so it is impossible to believe that he came to this parliament; however, the spark that ignited his revolt probably was a dispute with his neighbour, Reginald Grey of Ruthin, lord of Dyffryn Clwyd. The bishop of St Asaph was John Trevor, who defected to the Welsh cause in 1404.

²⁴⁶ The Byzantine Emperor Manuel II spent nearly two months with Henry, from 11 Dec. 1400 to early Feb. 1401. Constantinople was blockaded by the Ottomans at this time. Adam Usk also comments favourably on his and his men's religious observance. He probably left England with about £2,000, not £8,000 (D. Nicol, 'A Byzantine emperor in England: Manuel II's visit to London in 1400–1401', *University of Birmingham Historical Journal*, xii (1969–70), 204–25; *Usk*, pp. 118–20).

²⁴⁷ The Welsh revolt was rekindled by the seizure of Conwy castle by the Tudor brothers in Apr. 1401. However, the rest of this paragraph refers to events in Sept. 1400, not to the king's second Welsh expedition of Oct. 1401.

parliament replied that they cared naught for barefooted buffoons.[245] In this year, the emperor of Constantinople came to England, offering an indulgence from the pope to all those who gave him contributions from their goods, and he begged the king for help against the Turks and infidels. Each day he had a private mass said in his chamber by his bishops, according to the rite of the Greeks; and each day the emperor and all his men took communion. The king received him with great honour and paid all his expenses while he was in England. And when he had collected four thousand pounds in England through his indulgence, the king added a further four thousand and sent him away.[246]

In the year of the Lord 1401, the Welsh rose up against King Henry IV, plundering English possessions everywhere.[247] The king therefore marched into North Wales and the Isle of Anglesey, where the friars minor in the convent of Llanfaes and the Welsh, along with others, resisted the king, as a result of which the royal army killed and captured the friars and plundered the convent. However, since Owain remained in hiding, the king returned, and Lord Grey undertook to defend the country. Thus the king handed over the friars who had been captured to the official of the order and commanded that everything be restored to the convent, and he declared that the convent should be filled with English friars.[248] In this year a certain friar minor from Norfolk praised King Richard in his sermon, saying that he was still alive; and he was transferred from prison to the official of the order for correction. Owain Glyndwr captured Lord Grey in battle.[249] And in this same year the general chapter of the friars minor was held at Leicester on the feast of the Assumption [15 August],[250] at which it was forbidden on pain of perpetual imprisonment for any of the friars to say anything which might redound to the prejudice of the king, and

---

[248] For the king's order regarding Llanfaes priory (near Beaumaris, Anglesey), dated 28 Jan. 1401, see *CPR 1399–1401*, p. 418.

[249] Grey was captured in Apr. 1402 and carried off to Snowdonia (Davies, *Revolt*, p. 107).

[250] Little, *Franciscan Papers*, p. 215, assumes that the chronicler was correct in assigning this provincial chapter at Leicester to 1401, but Whitfield, 'Conflicts of personality', pp. 360–2, argues that it was in Aug. 1402. The chronicler's chronology is certainly confused at this point, but Whitfield's argument rests largely on his dating of the trials of the friars in 1402 to July or Aug. 1402, whereas it is now known that the trials and executions took place in late May/early June (R. L. Storey, 'Clergy and common law in the reign of Henry IV', in R. F. Hunnisett and J. B. Post, eds., *Medieval Legal Records in Memory of C. A. F. Meekings* (London, 1978), pp. 341–61, at 353–7). It thus seems more likely that the chapter was held on 15 Aug. 1401, thereby making sense of the provincial minister's remark to the king, and the king's riposte, in early June 1402: Zouche told Henry that 'he had forbidden all the friars from doing or saying anything prejudicial or offensive to the king, and he begged for mercy for them. "They refuse to be disciplined by you", replied the king, "so they will have to be disciplined by me"' (below, p. 108).

qui ausus esset in hoc culpari. Hoc insuper anno post Natale Domini apparuit quadam stella comata aspectu terribilis in occidente, cuius flamma magna sursum ascendebat.[v] [251] Hoc anno Rogerus Claryndon, miles, et prior de Lande ac octo fratres ordinis Sancti Francisci suspensi sunt.[w] [252] Item, mulier quadam accusabat fratrem minorem de conuentu Cantibrugie senem de certis uerbis dictis contra regem; qui statuitur coram iustitiario, qui dedit sententiam quod pugnaret cum muliere una manu post dorsum ligata. Sed ad suggestionem amicorum mulier pacificata ab accusatione cessauit, et archiepiscopus Cantuariensis, amicus fratris, regem pacificauit.

1402. Anno Domini millesimo quadringentesimo duo et anno huius regis tertio, populus cepit regem grauiter ferre et regem Ricardum desiderare, quia dicebant quod ipse cepit bona eorum et non soluebat. Littere insuper uenerunt ad amicos regis Ricardi tanquam ab eodem misse, quibus scribebatur quod ipse uiueret, et hoc diuulgatum fuit per Angliam.[253] Quod multi audientes gauisi sunt et ipsum restitui desiderabant. Quidam frater minor laicus de conuentu de Aylesbury uenit ad regem accusans fratrem eiusdem conuentus, sacerdotem, dicens quod ipse de uita Ricardi regis ualde exultauit, qui etiam adductus est[x] coram rege. Cui rex sic ait: 'Tu audisti regem Ricardi uiuere et cor tuum exultauit?' Frater respondit: 'Ita, domine, exultaui sicut homo exultat de uita amici sui; teneor sibi et tota parentela mea, quia ipse promouit illam.' Et dixit rex: 'Tu diuulgasti quod ipse uiueret, et sic excitasti populum contra me?' Frater respondit: 'Non certe, domine.' Et rex ait: 'Dic mihi in ueritate, sicut est in corde tuo, si uideres ipsum et me in campo pugnantes, cum quo teneres?' Frater respondit: 'Certe ego tenerem cum eo, quia sibi plus teneor.' Et rex ait: 'Pugnares tu pro eo?' Respondit frater: 'Ita, uere.' Et rex: 'Cum quo?' Respondit frater: 'Cum eo quod haberem; forte cum baculo.' Et rex conclusit: 'Ergo tu uelles quod ego essem mortuus et omnes domini de regno mei complices?' Respondit frater: 'Non.' Et rex: 'Quid faceres

---

[v] *marginal in later hand*: stella comata fratres suspenduntur [w] *marginal in later hand*: prior quidem et octo [x] *interlined*

[251] This was Halley's comet, visible for several weeks in the spring of 1402, and widely remarked upon.

[252] Roger of Clarendon was the bastard son of the Black Prince (and thus half-brother to Richard II) by his mistress Edith de Willesford. He was indicted for murder in 1398 and seems to have spent the next few years as a fugitive (C. Given-Wilson, 'Sir Roger Clarendon', *ODNB*, xi. 770). The former prior of the Austin canons at Launde was Walter of Baldock; he was dismissed for misgovernment, but secured appointment as a papal chaplain (J. H. Wylie, *History of England under Henry the Fourth* (4 vols., London, 1884–98), i. 276). The 'aged friar' from the Cambridge convent was John Lakenheath, who was eventually pardoned (Storey, 'Clergy and common law').

that each presiding officer should have the power to imprison any such person bold enough to be blameworthy in this regard. Also in this year, a comet appeared in the west after Christmas, a terrifying sight, with its great flame ascending upwards.[251] In this year, Roger of Clarendon, a knight, and the prior of Launde [Leicestershire] and eight friars of the Franciscan order were hanged.[252] Also, a certain woman accused an aged friar minor of the Cambridge convent of saying various things against the king; and he was brought before a justice, who passed sentence that he must fight with the woman with one hand tied behind his back. However, at the prompting of some friends, the woman was appeased and dropped her accusation, and the archbishop of Canterbury, a friend of the friar, placated the king.

1402. In the year of the Lord 1402 and the third year of this king, the people began to complain greatly about the king, because they said that he took their goods without paying for them; and they yearned for King Richard. Moreover, letters were sent to the friends of King Richard purporting to come from him, saying that he was alive, and this news spread throughout England.[253] Many people who heard this were overjoyed and wanted to restore him. A certain friar minor from the convent at Aylesbury [Buckinghamshire], a lay brother, approached the king to accuse a friar of the same convent, a priest, of rejoicing greatly that King Richard was alive, and the latter was brought into the king's presence. The king therefore said to him: 'Did your heart rejoice when you were told that King Richard was alive?' The friar replied: 'Indeed, my lord, I rejoiced in the same way as a man rejoices at the life of his friend; I am beholden to him, as are all my kinsmen, because he supported them.' And the king said: 'Did you spread it around that he was alive and thus incite the people against me?' 'Certainly not, my lord', replied the friar. 'Tell me truthfully', said the king, 'from the bottom of your heart, if you saw him and me fighting in a field, which of us would you support?' The friar replied: 'I would undoubtedly support him, because I am more beholden to him.' 'Would you fight for him?' asked the king. 'I would indeed', replied the friar. 'What with?' asked the king. 'With whatever I had', replied the friar, 'with a staff, perhaps.' 'In that case', declared the king, 'what you would like is to see me dead, along with all the lords of the realm who support me.'

---

[253] Rumours that Richard II was alive and living in Scotland reached a crescendo in Apr.–May 1402 (*Foedera*, viii. 255, 261–2; *CPR 1401–5*, pp. 126–9; Wylie, *Henry the Fourth*, i. 274–9). The letters purporting to come from Richard were written by William Serle, an esquire of the former king's chamber who had fled to Scotland in 1399 and forged the royal signet (Given-Wilson, *Henry IV*, p. 205); for his fate, see below, p. 126.

mecum si super me haberes uictoriam?' Cui frater: 'Facerem uos ducem Lancastrie.' Tunc rex ait: 'Tu non es amicus meus. Per hoc caput meum, tu perdes caput tuum.' Et statutus est frater coram iustitiario apud Westmonasterium cum quodam seculari sacerdote conspiratore apud quem littere conspiratorie inuente sunt, et iustitiarius dixit fratri: 'Tu exultasti quia audiuisti regem Ricardum uiuere, et diuulgasti hoc in populo.' Frater respondit: 'Non diuulgaui uerbum.' Et iustitiarius, audita duodena, tulit sententiam, dicens: 'Tu traheris per medium Londonie super claiam usque ad Tyburn, et ibidem suspenderis, ibique decollaberis, et caput tuum ponetur super pontem Londonie.' Quod et de utroque factum est, atque per uiam praeco clamabat causas eorum.

Post hec autem uenit alius frater minor,[y] per socium suum ad iram concitatus, ad regem, petens misericordiam et gratiam, dicens quod quingenti homines seculares, ecclesiastici et religiosi parant se ut conueniant super planitiem Oxonie in uigilia Sancti Iohannis Baptiste, ut inde procedant ad querendum regem Ricardum: 'At ego et decem socii mei in conuentu Leicestrie parauimus nos ad conueniendum cum illis.[254] Et est in illo conuentu unus magister in theologia senex qui male loquitur de uobis, et dixit quod Ricardus bellabit contra uos, et dicit quod hoc est prophetatum.' Octo ergo fratres et magister ducti sunt ad London ligati; duo alii accusati non sunt inuenti.[255] Accusauit autem frater ille plures alios fratres de aliis conuentibus, sed fugierunt. Rex uero uocauit archiepiscopum et alios dominos, et fratres istos adduci iussit, et quidam eorum, iuuenes et senes, fuerunt parum litterati. Stabatque accusator eorum et constanter singulos accusabat; ipsi uero incaute respondebant. Magister confessus est se exposuisse prophetiam que dicitur cuiusdam canonici de Bridlington, iuxta imaginationem suam.[256] Et dixit rex magistro: 'Isti sunt fatui et idiote, nec legere sciunt nec intelligunt. Tu deberes sapiens esse. Dicis tu quod Rex Ricardus uiuit?'

---

[y] *marginal in later hand*: alius frater

[254] The friar from Aylesbury who was initially brought before the king, and subsequently hanged, was Henry Forster, although the name of the lay friar who betrayed him is not known. The friar from Leicester who approached the king was Walter Walton, who turned approver, although it did not save him; the records of their trials on the coram rege roll are printed by I. D. Thornley, 'Treason by words in the fifteenth century', *EHR* xxxii (1957), 556–61, and Storey, 'Clergy and common law', pp. 357–8. It has been suggested that the chronicler may have used the roll as the basis of his account of the trials, but the accounts are in many ways different.

[255] The friars were brought to the Tower on 1 June 1402 to await trial (Wylie, *Henry the Fourth*, i. 277–8).

'No', replied the friar. 'So what would you do with me if you were victorious over me?' asked the king. 'I would make you duke of Lancaster', replied the friar. Whereupon the king declared: 'You are no friend of mine. By this head of mine, you shall lose your head.' And the friar was taken before a justice at Westminster, along with another conspirator, a secular priest, who had been found in possession of incriminating letters, and the justice said to the friar: 'You rejoiced because you heard that King Richard was alive, and you broadcast that news to the people.' 'I did not broadcast a word', replied the friar. Whereupon the justice, having heard the jury, passed sentence as follows: 'You will be drawn through the middle of London on a hurdle as far as Tyburn, where you will be hanged, and you will also be beheaded there, and your head will be placed upon London Bridge.' And this is what was done to both of them, and all along the road a crier called out their crimes.

After this, however, another friar minor, moved to anger by one of his fellows, approached the king to ask for mercy and favour, saying that five hundred men, seculars, ecclesiastics, and religious, were preparing to assemble on the plain at Oxford on the vigil of St John the Baptist [24 June] in order to proceed from there to seek out King Richard, 'and I and ten of my fellows in the convent at Leicester are preparing to join them.[254] And there is in that convent an aged master of theology who speaks badly of you and declares that King Richard will make war against you, and he says that this has been prophesied.' Eight friars and the master were therefore bound and brought to London; two others who were accused could not be found.[255] This friar also accused several other friars from different convents, but they fled. The king therefore summoned the archbishop and other lords and ordered that these friars be brought in, some of whom, both young and old, were barely literate. Their accuser stood there and calmly accused each one, to which they gave imprudent replies. The master admitted that he had expounded, in accordance with his interpretation, the prophecy said to be that of a certain canon of Bridlington [Yorkshire].[256] Whereupon the king said to the master: 'These others are foolish and unintelligent, they cannot read and lack understanding. You must be

---

[256] The master of theology was Roger Frisby, warden of the Franciscan convent at Leicester; his brother Richard was also a friar there and involved in this conspiracy (Whitfield, 'Conflicts of personality', p. 328; for the trial records, including the names of most of the conspirators, see Storey, 'Clergy and common law', pp. 357–61); the Bridlington Prophecies were attributed to John Thweng, prior of Bridlington, who died in 1379 and was canonized in 1401.

Magister respondit: 'Non dico quod uiuit, sed dico si uiuit ipse est uerus rex Anglie.' Et rex opposuit, dicens: 'Ipse resignauit.' Et dixit magister: 'Resignauit sed inuitus et coactus in carcere, qua resignatio nulla est de iure.' Cui rex: 'Ipse resignauit cum bona uoluntate.' Et magister: 'Non resignasset si fuisset | liber, et resignatio facta in carcere non est libera.' 'Adhuc', dixit rex, 'ipse fuit depositus.' Et magister, per modum conquestus, dixit: 'Dum esset rex, ui armorum captus fuit, incarceratus et regno spoliatus, et uos inuasistis coronam.' Cui rex: 'Non inuasi coronam, sed fui rite electus.' Magister dixit: 'Electio nulla est, uiuente possessore legitimo. Et si mortuus est, per uos mortuus est. Et si per uos mortuus est, perdidistis titulum et omne ius quod habere potestis ad regnum.' Cui rex dixit: 'Per caput istud, tu perdes caput tuum.' Magister dixit: 'Numquam dilexistis ecclesiam, sed multum illi detraxastis antequam fuistis rex, et nunc illam destruetis.' 'Mentiris', dixit rex, 'recede.' Et reducti sunt omnes ad Turrim.

Rex cepit consilium, et unus qui numquam dilexit ecclesiam, miles eius, dixit: 'Numquam extinguemus clamorem istum de uita Ricardi nisi fratres extinguantur.' Minister fratrum accessit ad regem, dicens se inhibuisse fratribus omnibus ne aliquid facerent uel loquerentur in preiudicium aut offensam regis, et gratiam pro eis petiit. Rex respondit: 'Ipsi nolunt per te castigari, oportet igitur ut per me castigentur.' Tunc ducti sunt ad Westmonasterium, compedibus colligati, et coram iustitiariis statuuntur, unacum fratre regis Ricardi, milite ex concubina genito, et uno de familia eius, ac priore de Launde, canonico, magistro in theologia, qui litteras de uita Ricardi fatebantur se recepisse.[257] Et iustitiarius dixit fratribus: 'Indictati estis quod uos in hypocrisie et adulatione et falsa uita predicastis falsos sermones in quibus false dixistis quod Rex Ricardus uiuit, et excitastis populum ad querendum eum in Scotia. Similiter uos in hypocrisie, adulatione et falsa uita audiuistis falsas confessiones in quibus iniunxistis populo pro penitentia ut quererent regem Ricardum in Wallia. Vos etiam in hypocrisie, adulatione et falsa uita collegistis magnam summam pecunie mendicando et misistis ad Audoenum Glendour proditorem ut ueniat et destruat totam linguam Anglicanam. Vos etiam misistis in Scotiam pro quingentis hominibus, ut sint parati super planitiem Oxonie in uigilia

---

[257] Roger Clarendon and his chaplain, John Calf, were arrested on 19 May 1402. See above, n. 252, for him and Walter Baldock, prior of the house of Augustinian canons at Launde.

intelligent. Do you say that Richard II is alive?' The master replied: 'I do not say that he is alive, but I say that if he is alive he is the rightful king of England.' The king contradicted him, saying: 'He resigned.' To which the master said: 'He resigned, but unwillingly and under coercion in prison, so his resignation has no validity in law.' The king said: 'He resigned of his own free will.' The master responded: 'He would not have resigned if he had been at liberty, and a resignation made in prison is not free.' 'He was also deposed', said the king. To which the master said, by way of objection: 'While he was king, he was captured by force of arms, imprisoned, and deprived of his kingdom, and you usurped the throne.' The king replied: 'I did not usurp the throne, I was properly elected.' The master said: 'An election is invalid if the rightful holder is still alive. And if he is dead, he was killed by you. And if you killed him, you lose your claim and any right that you might have to the kingdom.' To which the king responded: 'By this head of mine, you shall lose your head.' The master said: 'You never loved the church, but disparaged it greatly before you became king, and now you are destroying it.' 'You are lying', said the king, 'go away!' And they were all taken back to the Tower.

The king took counsel, and one of his knights, a man who never loved the Church, said to him: 'We shall never silence this clamour about Richard being alive unless the friars are done away with.' The friars' official approached the king to tell him that he had forbidden all the friars from doing or saying anything prejudicial or offensive to the king, and he begged for mercy for them. 'They refuse to be disciplined by you', replied the king, 'so they will have to be disciplined by me.' Then they were led to Westminster, bound together with shackles, and brought before the justices, along with the knight who was a brother of King Richard by a concubine, and a member of his household, and the prior of Launde, a canon, a master of theology, who admitted that they had received letters saying Richard was alive.[257] And the justice said to the friars: 'You are indicted on the grounds that in your hypocrisy, your sycophancy, and your false way of life you preached false sermons in which you falsely stated that King Richard was alive and incited the people to seek him out in Scotland. Similarly, in your hypocrisy, your sycophancy, and your false way of life, you heard false confessions, during which you instructed people that for their penance they should go and seek out King Richard in Wales. Also, in your hypocrisy, your sycophancy, and your false way of life, you collected a large sum of money through begging, which you sent to the traitor Owain Glyndwr so that he could come and utterly destroy the English language. You also sent to Scotland for five hundred men so that they could be ready on the plain of Oxford on the vigil of St John to search for King

Sancti Iohannis ad querendum regem Ricardum. Quomodo excusabitis uos? Consulo uobis quod ponatis uos in gratia domini regis.' Fratres uero responderunt: 'Ponimus nos in testimonio patrie.'[258] Nec Londonienses nec illi de Holbourn uoluerunt testes esse, et ideo fecerunt uenire duodenam de Hysildon et Heygate, qui dixerunt fratres reos esse. Et iustitiarius dixit: 'Vos debetis trahi a Turri Londonie usque ad Tyburn et ibi suspendi per diem naturalem[259] et postea decollari, et capita uestra super pontem poni'; quod et factum est, uidentibus et sequentibus multis milibus hominum.[z] Et magister apud Tyburn deuotum sermonem predicauit de themate 'In manus tuas, Domini',[260] iurauitque per salutem anime sue quod contra regem Henricum non deliquit, et deuote recommendauit omnes qui causa mortis sue erant. Et alius frater moriturus dixit: 'Non fuit intentionis nostre, ut dicunt inimici nostri, occidere regem et filios eius, sed ut faceremus eum ducem Lancastrie, ut esse deberet.' In crastino, hora uesperarum, uenit quidam ad gardianum fratrum minorum dicens quod posset tollere corpora, et ipsi uenientes inuenerunt corpora iacentia in sepibus et fossis, capitibus abscisis, que detulerunt ad conuentum cum merore. Viri de Hisildon et Heygate uenerunt flentes ad fratres precantes ueniam et dicentes quod nisi dixissent ipsos reos esse, ipsimet occisi fuissent. In quodam conuentu custodie Bristollie frater minor,[261] magister in theologia, et quidam naturaliter fatuus simul infirmabantur et simul moriebantur. Et cum fatuus moreretur, dixit: 'Magister et ego moriemur. Sapiens et magnus clericus fuit ille, et ego fatuus. Nunc uideamus quis celum citius possidebit.' Hoc autem anno duo alii fratres de conuentu Leycestrie capti fuerunt in partibus Lichfeld per familiam principis,[262] et ibidem tracti et suspensi sunt et decollati.[a] Caput magistri delatum est Oxonie in uigilia Sancti Iohannis Baptiste, et coram processione uniuersitatis clamabat praeco: 'Iste magister, frater minor de conuentu Leicestrie, in hypocrisie et adulatione et falsa uita predicauit multotiens, dicens quod Rex Ricardus uiuit, et excitauit populum ut quererent eum in Scotia.' Et caput eius ibi super palum

---

[z] *marginal in later hand*: hic publice frater (*additional words cropped*)   [a] *marginal in later hand*: hic alii duo fratres (*additional words cropped*)

[258] That is, trial by jury.

[259] A *dies naturalis* was a solar day, 24 hours. The hangings took place between 9 and 14 June. The jurors' later claims that they were coerced by threats into convicting the friars cannot be entirely true, since at least three of the accused were acquitted; but a total of sixteen conspirators were eventually executed, eleven of whom were Franciscans (Storey, 'Clergy and common law', pp. 356–61).

[260] Luke 43: 26 ('In manus tuas, domine, commendo spiritum meum').

Richard. How will you excuse yourselves? My advice is to throw yourselves on the mercy of the lord king.' However, the friars replied: 'We place ourselves on the country.'[258] Neither the Londoners nor the people of Holborn wished to act as jurors, so they summoned a jury from Islington and Highgate, who pronounced the friars to be guilty. Whereupon the justice declared: 'You are to be drawn from the Tower of London as far as Tyburn, and there hanged for an entire day,[259] after which you will be beheaded and your heads placed on the bridge'; and so it was done, with many thousands of men following and watching. At Tyburn, the master preached a devout sermon on the theme 'Into thy hands, O Lord',[260] and he swore upon the salvation of his soul that he had not transgressed against King Henry, and he humbly commended all those who had been the cause of his death. And another friar, as he was about to die, said: 'It was not our intention, as our enemies have stated, to kill the king and his sons, but that we should make him duke of Lancaster, as he should be.'

The next day, at the hour of vespers, someone approached the warden of the friars minor to tell him that he could take the bodies away. And when they arrived, they found the corpses lying in hedges and ditches, their heads severed, and they bore them sorrowfully to the convent. The men of Islington and Highgate came to the friars in tears, begging forgiveness and telling them that if they had not pronounced them guilty, they themselves would have lost their lives. In one of the convents of the custody of Bristol,[261] a friar minor, a master of theology, and another man who was an innate fool became ill and died at the same time. And as the fool was dying, he said: 'The master and I are dying. He is a wise man and a great churchman, and I am a fool. Now let us see who reaches heaven soonest.' Also in this year two other friars from the Leicester convent were captured in the vicinity of Lichfield [Staffordshire] by a servant of the prince,[262] and were drawn and hanged and beheaded there. The head of the master was carried to Oxford on the vigil of St John the Baptist [24 June], and in the presence of a university procession a crier called out: 'This master, a friar minor of the Leicester convent, in his hypocrisy, his sycophancy, and his false way of life, preached on many occasions that King Richard

---

[261] The English Franciscan province was divided into seven custodies, based in London, York, Cambridge, Bristol, Oxford, Newcastle, and Worcester. Canterbury was within the London custody, as were Salisbury and Ware, the Franciscan houses about which the chronicler reports unusual items of news (above, p. 68, and below, p. 146).

[262] Henry, prince of Wales. The two renegade friars were hanged at Lancaster (Wylie, *Henry the Fourth*, i. 278).

positum est.²⁶³ Hoc anno, rex Scotie misit litteras regi Francie dicens quod quidam uenit in Scotiam, et duo Iacobite dixerunt ipsum fuisse regem Ricardum; sed rumor ille magis augebatur, sicque dicebatur quod fuisset in Scotia.²⁶⁴

Hoc insuper anno, Audoenus*ᵇ* de Glendour cepit Edmundum de Mortuo Mari, multis Anglicis de marchia Wallie interfectis. Et rex, congregato exercitu, transiit in Walliam, ubi, prohibentibus maximis tempestatibus in Septembri tonitruorum, imbrium et grandinis, equitare non potuerunt, et multi de exercitu frigore mortui sunt.²⁶⁵ Ibi frater iste qui fratres suos regi accusauit captus est a Wallico, et quia fatebatur se esse de familia regis qui accusabat fratres, a Wallico occisus est.*ᶜ* | Hoc autem anno, rege existente in Wallia, Scoti irruperunt in Angliam, sed comes Northumbrie et filius eius Henricus Percy, ualens miles, pugnabant cum eis, et ceperunt comites eorum et decem milia interfecerunt de Scotis.²⁶⁶ Item hoc anno, rex desponsauit relictam Iohannis de Monte Forti, ducissam Britannie, filiam regis Nauarrie, et eam coronari fecit.²⁶⁷ Hoc anno dominus le Gray, graui redemptione soluta, liberatus est.²⁶⁸ Post festum Sancti Michaelis, factum est parliamentum Londoniis, ubi decima cleri et quintadecima populi exacte sunt, dicente rege se nihil habere.²⁶⁹ Communitas quesiuit ubi fuit thesaurus Ricardi regis. Tandem responsum fuit quod comes Northumbrie, qui regem introduxit, et alii illum habuerunt. Rogauit etiam communitas regem quod, quia multa sibi tribuunt et ipse nihil habet, sinat officiales suos super hoc examinari; sed rex non assentiit. Hoc anno, dux Aurelianensis, uir ualde suberbus et malus, misit regi Anglie litteras prouocans ipsum ad duellum. Rex respondit quod non pugnaret cum minore se, nec cum consanguineo pugnare licet. Dux dixit: 'Dignitatem quam iniuste inuasisti in te non ueneror, et ita decenter

---

ᵇ underlined; marginal in later hand: Audoenus Glendour   *ᶜ marginal in later hand*: hic alius frater

---

²⁶³ The 'master' was Roger Frisby (see above, pp. 106–8).

²⁶⁴ Jacobites were Dominican friars. For the 'pseudo-Richard' in Scotland (in reality Thomas Ward of Trumpington), see Given-Wilson, *Henry IV*, pp. 204–5.

²⁶⁵ Edmund Mortimer was captured at the battle of Bryn Glas, or Pilleth, on 22 June 1402. The king's army was in Wales during the first two weeks of Sept., but driven back by the weather (Davies, *Revolt*, pp. 107–9).

²⁶⁶ The battle of Humbleton (or Homildon) Hill, near Wooler (Northumberland), was fought on 14 Sept. 1402; a resounding victory for the English, it led to the capture of the earl of Douglas and many other Scottish leaders (Given-Wilson, *Henry IV*, pp. 199–201).

²⁶⁷ Joan of Navarre was the widow of John de Montfort, duke of Brittany (d. 1399); she married Henry IV (whose first wife, Mary de Bohun, had died in 1394), on 7 Feb. 1403 at Winchester, and was crowned at Westminster on 26 Feb.

was alive, and he incited the people to search for him in Scotland.' And his head was placed upon a stake there.²⁶³ This year, the king of Scotland sent letters to the king of France telling him that a man had come to Scotland whom two Jacobites declared to be King Richard; indeed, this rumour spread widely, and thus it was said that he was in Scotland.²⁶⁴

Also in this year, Owain Glyndwr captured Edmund de Mortimer, with many Englishmen of the march of Wales being killed. And the king, having gathered an army, marched into Wales, where, since they were prevented by tremendous thunderstorms, rain, and hail in September, they were unable to make any progress, and many people in the army died of cold.²⁶⁵ That friar who had made accusations about his fellows to the king was captured by a Welshman there, and because the man who had accused the friars admitted that he was a member of the king's household, the Welshman put him to death. Also in this year, while the king was in Wales, the Scots invaded England, but the earl of Northumberland and his son Henry Percy, a vigorous knight, fought against them, capturing their earls and killing ten thousand of the Scots.²⁶⁶ Also in this year, the king married the duchess of Brittany, widow of John de Montfort and daughter of the king of Navarre, and had her crowned.²⁶⁷ In this year Lord Grey was released after paying a heavy ransom.²⁶⁸ After the feast of Michaelmas [29 September], a parliament was held in London, where a tenth was exacted from the clergy and a fifteenth from the people, the king declaring that he had nothing.²⁶⁹ The commons asked what had happened to King Richard's treasure. The reply eventually given was that the earl of Northumberland, who had maintained the king, and others had it. The commons also asked the king whether, since much had been granted to him yet he himself had nothing, his ministers might be questioned about this, but the king would not agree to this. In this year, the duke of Orléans, an exceedingly arrogant and evil man, sent letters to the king of England challenging him to a duel. The king replied that he would not fight with someone of inferior status to himself, nor was it appropriate to fight with a kinsman. The duke said: 'I do not acknowledge in you that status which you unjustly usurped, so it is perfectly appropriate for you

---

²⁶⁸ Reginald Grey of Ruthin paid Glyndwr £6,666 to be released, probably in Nov. 1402 (*PROME*, viii. 162; *CP*, vi. 156).

²⁶⁹ Parliament met at Westminster from 30 Sept. to 25 Nov. 1402 (*PROME*, viii. 154–220; for the grant of the subsidy, pp. 175–6).

mecum pugnare potes, sicut occidisti regem cognatum tuum'; et multa alia conuicia scripsit regi.[270]

1403. Anno Domini millesimo quadringentesimo tertio et anno Henrici tertio,[271] Britones subito uenerunt ad Plymmoth ipsumque spoliant et comburunt; sed dominus de Berkley, custos maris, reddidit talionem.[272] Comes Northumbrie rogauit regem ut solueret sibi aurum debitum pro custodia marchie Scotie, sicut in carta sua continetur: 'Egomet et filius meus expendimus nostra in custodia illa.' Rex respondit: 'Aurum non habeo, aurum non habebis.' Comes dixit: 'Quando regnum intrastis, promisistis regere per consilium nostrum. Iam multa a regno annuatim accipitis et nihil habetis, nihil soluetis, et sic communitatem uestram irritatis. Deus det uobis bonum consilium.' Venit similiter filius eius, Henricus Percy, qui sororem Edmundi, captiui in Wallia, habebat uxorem, rogans regem ut permitteret Edmundum redimi de proprio.[273] Rex dixit quod cum pecunia regni non fortificaret inimicos suos contra se. Henricus dixit: 'Debet homo sic exponere se periculo pro uobis et regno uestro, et non succurretis sibi in periculo suo?' Et iratus dixit sibi rex: 'Tu es proditor! Vis ut succurram inimicis meis et regni?' Cui Henricus dixit: 'Proditor non sum, sed fidelis, et ut fidelis loquor.' Rex traxit contra eum pugionem. 'Non hic', dixit Henricus, 'sed in campo', et recessit.

Henricus Percy et auunculus eius, Thomas Percy, quem rex Ricardus fecit comitem Wigornie et domus sue senescallum, collegerunt exercitum in marchia Scotie, dicentes quod contra Scotos bellare oporteret, et uenerunt ad comitatum Cestrie et Cestrenses secum assumpserunt.[274] Miseruntque ad Audoenum ut ueniret, sed Audoenus, cognoscens quod callidi erant, non confidebat in illis. Wallicos tamen multos assumpserunt, et uenerunt omnes in Lichfeld insignati signis regis Ricardi, uidelicet ceruis.[275] Et fecit ibi Henricus proclamari, dicens

---

[270] Louis, duke of Orléans, was the younger brother of Charles VI of France. For his exchange of insulting letters with Henry IV in 1402–3, see C. Given-Wilson, 'The quarrels of old women: Henry IV, Louis of Orléans, and Anglo-French chivalric challenges in the early fifteenth century', in G. Dodd and D. Biggs, eds., *The Reign of Henry IV: Rebellion and Survival, 1403–1413* (York, 2008), pp. 28–47.

[271] It is at this point that the chronicler begins to confuse his regnal years; he has already stated that 1402 was 'Henry's third year' (above, p. xxviii, n. 37).

[272] The Breton raid on Plymouth of 10–11 Aug. 1403 was led by Guillaume de Chastel, a follower of Orléans; an English retaliatory raid was led by William Wilford, mayor of Exeter. Thomas Lord Berkeley was not appointed admiral of the south and west until 5 Nov. 1403 (*SAC* II, pp. 384–7; *CPR 1401–5*, p. 328).

[273] For the growing animosity between the king and the Percys, see J. Bean, 'Henry IV and the Percies', *History*, xliv (1959), 212–17; Given-Wilson, *Henry IV*, pp. 195–6, 214–24. Henry Percy (Hotspur) was married to Elizabeth, sister of Edmund Mortimer, and argued strongly for his brother-in-law to be ransomed from Glyndwr.

to fight with me, just as you murdered the king, your cousin'; and he wrote many other insulting things to the king.[270]

1403. In the year of the Lord 1403 and Henry's third year,[271] the Bretons suddenly descended on Plymouth [Devon] and plundered and burned it; but Lord Berkeley, keeper of the sea, repaid them in kind.[272] The earl of Northumberland asked the king to pay him the money owed to him for the wardenship of the Scottish march, as set out in his letters: 'I myself and my son have used our own goods to pay for that wardenship.' The king replied: 'I have no money, so you can have no money.' The earl said: 'When you took over the kingdom, you promised to rule with our advice. Now you receive great sums every year from the kingdom, yet you have nothing, you pay for nothing, and that is why you have alienated your people. May God grant you good counsel!' His son Henry Percy, who was married to the sister of the captive Edmund in Wales, similarly approached the king to ask him if he would allow Edmund to be ransomed with his own money.[273] The king replied that he had no intention of allowing the kingdom's money to be used to strengthen his enemies against him. 'Must a man expose himself to danger in this way for you and your kingdom', said Henry, 'and then when he is in danger you will not help him?' Whereupon the enraged king said to him: 'You are a traitor! Do you want me to succour the enemies of myself and of the kingdom?' Henry replied to him: 'I am not a traitor but a loyal man, and it is as a loyal man that I speak.' The king drew a dagger on him. 'Not here', said Henry, 'but on the battlefield', and withdrew.

Henry Percy and his uncle, Thomas Percy, whom King Richard had made earl of Worcester and steward of his household, collected an army in the march of Scotland, saying that they needed to make war on the Scots, then marched to the county of Chester and recruited Cheshiremen to join them.[274] They also sent messages to Owain to come, but Owain, knowing them to be untrustworthy, did not believe them. However, they recruited a great number of Welshmen, and they all arrived at Lichfield [Staffordshire] displaying the badges of King Richard, that is to say, harts.[275] And Henry had it proclaimed there that

---

[274] Thomas Percy, earl of Worcester from 1397, was steward of Richard II's household 1393–9 and of Henry IV's household 1401–2. For the build-up to the battle of Shrewsbury, see Given-Wilson, *Henry IV*, pp. 216–25. Hotspur marched from Scotland and arrived at Chester on 9 July 1403. His army at Shrewsbury was 'a predominantly Cheshire army' (P. Morgan, *War and Society in Medieval Cheshire 1277–1403* (Chetham Society, 3rd ser., 34; Manchester, 1987), pp. 212–16).
[275] Richard II's famous badge of the White Hart, as seen on the Wilton Diptych.

quod ipse fuit unus de illis qui maxime agebat ad expulsionem regis Ricardi et introductionem Henrici, credens se bene fecisse; et quia nunc cognouit quod peius regit Henricus quam Ricardus, ideo intendit corrigere errorem suum. Rex collegit similiter exercitum et obuiauit illi iuxta[d] Salopiam, ubi rex tractauit cum eo, querens causam suam. Cui Henricus dixit: 'Nos te introduximus contra regem Ricardum, et peius regis tu quam ipse. Tu regnum spolias annuatim, et semper dicis te nihil habere. Thesaurarius tuus nihil habet. Solutiones nullas facis, domum non tenes, heres regni non es; ideo, sicut damnificaui regno, ita paratus sum damnum reformare.' Rex respondit se tallagia recipere pro negotiis regni, et se regem electum esse per regnum: 'Consulo tibi ut ponas te in gratia mea, et habebis.' Cui Henricus dixit: 'In gratia tua non confido.' 'Precor Dominum', dixit rex, 'quod tu habeas respondere pro sanguine hic hodie effundendo, et non ego. Procede, signifer', quod est dictu, *"Auant baner!"*[e] [276] Et commissum est durum prelium, et ceciderunt ex utraque parte multi. Quod cernens, Henricus Percy, in spiritu feruoris, assumptis secum triginta hominibus, irrupit in exercitum regis et fecit deambulatorium in medio exercitus usque ad fortissimos regis custodes, interficiens comitem Staffordie et alios multos in fortitudine exercitus regis.[277] Et ipse in fine, quasi solus stans et conclusus, trucidatur; ac exercitus eius, hoc uiso, fugiit. Baro de Podyngton in parte Henrici occiditur in bello;[278] Thomas Percy capitur et decollatur; Henricus mortuus decollatur, | ne sui dicere eum uiuere, et caput eius super portam Eborum ponitur.[279]

Luna. Luna eclipsata apparuit sanguinea.[280] Heremita ille qui predixit infortunium regi Ricardo uenit ad regem et dixit sibi secreta multa que ignorantur; quem rex iussit decollari, quod et factum est.[f] [281]

---

[d] exta *MS*   [e-e] underlined in red   [f] marginal in later hand: heremita decollatus

[276] The battle of Shrewsbury was on 21 July 1403. For an account, see E. Priestley, *The Battle of Shrewsbury 1403* (Shrewsbury, 1979).

[277] Edmund, earl of Stafford, was appointed constable of England a few hours before the battle and commanded one of the royalist divisions. He died in the battle, aged 25 (*CP*, xii/i. 180). The king's standard-bearer, Sir Walter Blount, also died, indicating how close the rebels got to the king himself.

[278] Sir John Mascy of Puddington, sheriff of Cheshire, died fighting not for Henry Percy (the chronicler uses 'Henry' here to indicate Henry Percy) but for the king (Morgan, *War and Society in Medieval Cheshire*, p. 215; *SAC* II, pp. 372–3).

he was one of those people who had worked hardest to get rid of King Richard and bring in King Henry, believing that he was doing a good thing; however, since he now realized that Henry was a worse ruler than Richard, he intended to make amends for his mistake. The king likewise gathered an army, and confronted him near Shrewsbury [Shropshire], where the king spoke to him to ask him what his grievance was. Henry said to him: 'We supported you against King Richard, and you rule worse than he did. Every year you despoil the kingdom, yet you always say you have nothing. Your treasurer has nothing. You never make payments, you do not maintain your household, you are not the heir to the kingdom. Therefore, in the same way that I caused damage to the kingdom, so am I ready to repair that damage.' The king replied that he received taxes in order to deal with the business of the kingdom, and that he had been elected as king by the kingdom: 'I advise you to place yourself in my mercy, and you shall have it.' To which Henry responded: 'I have no faith in your mercy.' 'I pray the Lord', said the king, 'that it is you, not I, who will have to answer for the blood that will be shed here today. Go forward, standard-bearer', which is to say, 'Banners advance!'[276] Whereupon hard battle was joined, and many died on both sides. Perceiving this, Henry Percy, in a rush of ardour, took thirty men with him and charged at the king's army, pressing forward through the middle of the army until he came to the hardiest of those who were protecting the king, killing the earl of Stafford and many others of the king's bodyguard.[277] Eventually, however, becoming isolated, he was surrounded and killed, and when his army saw this it fled. On the side of Henry, the baron of Poddington was killed in the battle;[278] Thomas Percy was captured and beheaded; and the dead Henry himself was beheaded and his head placed atop the gate at York, lest his followers claim that he was still alive.[279]

The moon. A bloody eclipse of the moon could be seen.[280] That hermit who had foretold misfortune for King Richard approached the king and told him many secret things that were not known; and the king ordered him to be beheaded, which was done.[281]

---

[279] Thomas Percy was executed at Shrewsbury on 23 July. Hotspur's body was quartered and displayed at Shrewsbury for several days before his head was taken to York and the four quarters of his body sent to London, Bristol, Newcastle, and Chester (*CPR 1401–5*, p. 293).

[280] The eclipse of the moon lasted from around 8.30 p.m. until midnight (Wylie, *Henry the Fourth*, i. 363). The crescent moon was one of the Percy livery badges.

[281] William Norham, the northern hermit, was executed by the king when he arrived at York on 8 Aug. (*SAC* II, p. 381; for his imprisonment by Richard II, see above, p. 88).

Istud factum est in nocte Sancte Marie Magdalane, et ceciderunt, ut dictum est, mille et sescenti uiri, et rex fuit in magno periculo, *g*et princeps Wallie uulneratus in facie cum sagitta.*g* [282]

Versus. De quo quidem conflictu quidam metrice sic scripsit:

> 'Anno milleno quater et centesimo bino
> Bellum Salopie fuit in Mag. nocte Marie.'

Super caput Henrici Percy apparuit stella comata, malum significans euentum.

Boriales milites et armigeri qui fuerunt in bello Henrici Percy redierunt in Northhumbriam, claudentes se in castris ibidem, non confidentes in gratia regis.[283] Hoc anno rex transiit in Walliam, et quia terra est inequitabilis cito reuertitur.[284] Comites Scotie quos Henricus Percy tenuit captiuos misit Londoniis, qui dixerunt regem Ricardum in Scotia uiuere. Rex Anglie dixit quod non erat ipse sed quidam simulator similis sibi.[285] Edmundus*h* de Mortuo Mari in Wallia, non ualens se redimere, dixit se numquam uelle subesse sub Henrico rege, *i*sed filiam Audoeni cum magna sollemnitate duxit in uxorem.*i* [286] In natiuitate autem huius Edmundi mirabile accidit portentum. In area stabuli sui patris sanguis manabat ita alte ut pedes equorum cooperiret. Vagine omnes gladiorum et pugionum sanguine plene erant. Secures sanguine rubuerunt. Puer iacens in cunis dormire non poterat nec a uagitu cessare nisi gladius sibi ostenderetur, et in sinu nutricis positus non poterat quietari nisi aliquod instrumentum bellicum sibi traderetur.

Rex uero misit in Northumbriam pro comite Northumbrie, patre Henrici Percy; ille autem respondit se paratum uenire si rex prestaret iuramentum quod sibi non noceret quousque excusasset se in parliamento. Et ita uenit ad regem, dicens quod filius suus hec et multa alia fecit sine suo consilio.[287] Dux Aurelianensis, post festum Sancti

---

g-g underlined   *h* underlined; marginal in later hand: Edmundus   *i-i* underlined; a hand is drawn in the margin with the finger pointing to this

[282] The number who died at Shrewsbury was variously put by contemporaries at between around 1,500 and 3,500 (Given-Wilson, *Henry IV*, p. 226). Prince Henry's arrow-wound in the face was undoubtedly severe; the royal surgeon, John Bradmore, provided a detailed account of the methods he used to treat it, but it took the prince several months to recover (M. Strickland and R. Hardy, *The Great Warbow* (London, 2005), pp. 284–5).

[283] Some of the Percy retainers, the leader of whom was Sir William Clifford, refused to surrender the northern castles to the king until about a year after Shrewsbury (Given-Wilson, *Henry IV*, p. 230).

[284] The king's third campaign in Wales lasted less than a fortnight, from about 20 Sept. to 2 Oct. 1403; its main objective was the relief of Carmarthen (Davies, *Revolt*, pp. 113–14).

[285] The main Scottish prisoner recovered after Shrewsbury was Archibald, earl of Douglas, who had fought there on Hotspur's side. For the pseudo-Richard II in Scotland, see above, p. 104.

These things happened on the eve [21 July] of St Mary Magdalen, and it is said that 1,600 men died, and the king was in great danger, and the prince of Wales was wounded in the face by an arrow.[282]

Verses. And concerning this battle someone wrote the following in verse:

> 'In the one thousand four hundred and second year,
> On the eve of Mary Magdalen, was the battle of Shrewsbury.'

A comet was visible above the head of Henry Percy, foreshadowing grim events.

The northern knights and esquires who were in Henry Percy's army returned to Northumberland, shutting themselves away in castles there, since they did not trust in the king's mercy.[283] In this year the king crossed into Wales, but soon returned owing to the difficulty of the terrain.[284] He sent to London the Scottish earls whom Henry Percy held captive; they told him that King Richard was alive in Scotland. The king of England replied that it was not him but some impostor bearing a likeness to him.[285] Edmund de Mortimer, unable to ransom himself in Wales, declared that he had no desire ever to be a subject of King Henry, and in a solemn ceremony took as his wife the daughter of Owain.[286] At the birth of this Edmund there occurred an extraordinary portent. On the floor of his father's stables, blood welled up so high that it covered the feet of the horses; the scabbards of all the swords and daggers were full of blood; the axes grew red with blood. The boy, lying in his cradle, would not sleep or stop crying unless he was shown a sword, and when he was placed at his nurse's breast he could not be quietened unless some weapon of war was given to him.

Then the king sent to Northumberland for the earl of Northumberland, the father of Henry Percy, but he replied that he would only come if the king swore an oath not to put him to death without allowing him to put his case in parliament. And thus did he come to the king, declaring that his son had done these and many other things without consulting him.[287] After the feast of Michaelmas

---

[286] For the dispute on Edmund de Mortimer's ransom, see above, p. 114, n. 273. He married Owain's daughter Catherine and declared his allegiance to Glyndwr before the end of Oct. 1402 (Davies, *Revolt*, pp. 179–80). The story which follows of the 'extraordinary portent' at his birth is also mentioned, though in less detail, in *Historia Vitae et Regni Ricardi Secundi*, ed. G. B. Stow (Philadelphia, 1977), p. 173.

[287] Northumberland surrendered to the king at York on 11 Aug. 1403 and was kept in custody until Feb. 1404, when he was brought before parliament (Given-Wilson, *Henry IV*, pp. 229–31).

Michaelis, iacuit prope Burdegaliam cum exercitu, arcens portantes uictualia per terram ad ciuitatem; comes Sancti Pauli iacuit in mari impediens uictualia per mare et naues Anglicanas cum uino ne redirent. Tandem naues Anglicane, onerate hominibus, comitem fugere faciunt, et dux Aurelianensis, non habens uictualia, recedit. Et rediens comes irrupit in insulam de Wight et, emens uictualia, scripsit regi litteras inimicitie et in Franciam recessit infra octabas Natalis Domini. Tunc naues Anglicane, onerate uino, uenerunt, ducentes secum proditorem[j] ciuitatis Burdegalie, qui postea Londoniis tractus et suspensus est.[288]

Hoc anno clerus Anglie concessit regi petenti medietatem unius decime. Post festum Sancti Hillarii inceptum est parliamentum,[289] et durauit usque ad Pascha, quia rex exigebat magnum tallagium, dicens se habere bellum cum Wallicis, Scotis, Hibernicis et Gallicis in Vasconia; insuper custodia Calesie magna fuit et maris Anglicani. Communitas respondit dicens quod 'isti non inquietant Angliam multum, et si inquietarent, adhuc rex habet omnes prouentus corone, ducatus Lancastrie, ac theolonia notabiliter excessiue eleuata per regem Ricardum, ita ut prouentus theoloniorum lanarum et aliarum mercium excedant prouentus corone.[k] Habet similiter wardas quasi omnium comitum, baronum et nobilium Anglie; que theolonia et warde olim erant concesse regi in subsidium communitatis pro guerris ut a tallagiis exoneretur regnum.' Rex autem dixit se nolle perdere terras patrum suorum in diebus suis, et ideo omnino tallagium habere oportuit.[l] Tunc communitas petiit a rege ut, si tallagium habere omnino uelit, quod theolonia minueret. Rex respondit quod theolonia habere uellet, sicut habuerunt sui predecessores. Et cum mansissent Londoniis in grauibus expensis usque ad Pascha taliter disputando, tandem exegit ab eis quod pro omni parte terre in Anglia ualente annuatim uiginti solidos, soluerentur duodecim denarios, exceptis terris quas ecclesiastici habuerunt ante annum octauum Edwardi primi, filii Henrici, in quo ordinatum fuit quod ecclesiastici in possessionibus non crescerent.[290]

---

[j] *proditores MS* [k] *marginal in later hand*: nota [l] *marginal in later hand*: nota responsum

---

[288] This paragraph is chronologically confused. There was a brief attempted blockade of Bordeaux by land and sea in 1404, orchestrated by the duke of Orléans as captain-general in the duchy, but the duke's own assault on the Bordeaux region did not take place until the winter of 1406–7 (Oct.–Jan.), when he besieged Bourg and Blaye but failed to take either before withdrawing on account of bad weather and lack of provisions. (G. Pepin, 'The French offensives of 1404–1407 against Anglo-Gascon Aquitaine', in A. Curry and A. Bell, eds., *Soldiers, Weapons and Armies in the Fifteenth Century* (Woodbridge, 2011), pp. 1–40). However, the chronicler is correct in dating the attack on the Isle of Wight by Waleran, Count of Saint-Pol, to Dec. 1403, shortly after the count had sent a letter to Henry IV accusing him of being a usurper and a regicide (Given-Wilson, *Henry IV*, pp. 237–9).

[29 September], the duke of Orléans camped outside Bordeaux with an army, preventing those who were bringing provisions by land from reaching the city; the count of Saint-Pol lay at sea, preventing the arrival of provisions by sea and stopping the English ships from returning home with wine. Eventually the English ships, fully manned, forced the count to flee, and the duke of Orléans, having no provisions, withdrew. On his way back, the count attacked the Isle of Wight and, acquiring provisions, he sent insulting letters to the king before returning to France within the octave of Christmas. Then the English ships arrived, loaded with wine, bringing with them a traitor from the city of Bordeaux who was subsequently drawn and hanged at London.[288]

In this year, at the king's request, the clergy of England granted him a half of one tenth. After the feast of St Hilary [13 January],[289] a parliament was held, and it lasted until Easter, because the king demanded a large tax, declaring that he was at war with the Welsh, the Scots, the Irish, and the French in Gascony; the keeping of Calais was also a great burden, and the English Sea. The commons replied by saying that 'these things do not trouble England greatly, and if they should prove troublesome, the king still has all the issues of the crown, the duchy of Lancaster, and the remarkably heavy levies raised by King Richard, as a result of which the issues of the levies on wool and other merchandise are greater than the issues of the crown. Moreover, he has the wardships of almost all the earls, barons, and nobles of England; which levies and wardships were formerly granted to the king as an aid from the commons for the wars in order that the kingdom should be relieved of taxes.' The king, however, said that he would be loath to lose during his time the lands of his forefathers, and that it was thus imperative that he have taxes. Whereupon the commons asked the king whether, if he must have taxes, he might reduce the levies. The king replied that he wished to retain the levies just as his predecessors had. And when they had remained in London arguing in this way up until Easter, at great expense, eventually he demanded from them that from every parcel of land in England worth 20 shillings a year, 12 pence would be paid, with the exception of lands held by churchmen since before the eighth year of Edward the First, son of King Henry, in which it was decreed that churchmen should not increase their possessions.[290]

---

[289] Parliament met at Westminster from 14 Jan. to 20 Mar. 1404 (*PROME*, viii. 221–80).
[290] For the first Statute of Mortmain (1279), which prohibited the granting of land to an ecclesiastical corporation without the king's assent, see M. Prestwich, *Edward I* (Berkeley, 1988), pp. 251–3.

CONTINUATIO EULOGII

Ipsi tandem, attediati de mora, hoc concesserunt, sub hac tamen conditione, quod eligerent certas personas qui tallagium reciperent et pro guerris totum expenderent, et inde compotum parliamento darent; et rex auctoritatem recipiendi et expendendi per cartam suam eis daret.

fo. 204ᵛ Rex uidebatur assentire, ac electe sunt | persone et carta scripta; sed non sigillata, et solutum est parliamentum.[291] In hoc autem parliamento comes Northhumbrie excusatur a bello filii sui et iurauit super crucem Sancti Thome coram parliamento quod fidelis semper foret regi Henrico.[292] In hoc insuper parliamento eiiciuntur a regno due filie regine et omnes alienigine qui uenerant cum ea, quia domum regiam onerabant.[293] Hoc parliamentum ualde reprehendit regios milites et alios eius officiales, probans quod ipsi regem et regnum spoliant, per hoc quod ditissimus ipsorum in aduentu regis uix expendere potuit centum marcas, et iam quidam ipsorum expendere possunt quingentas marcas, quidam mille marcas, et quidam plus, et cum sint armigeri et bachalarii baronibus in diuitiis equipollent. Et rex dixit se nihil habere et alii crescunt annuatim.[294] Ad hoc parliamentum uenerunt littere quasi a rege Ricardo misse ita euidenter apparentes, quod totum parliamentum et rex obstupuerunt; et uocauerunt custodem illius in carcere et quesierunt quomodo ad litteras responderet. Ipse dixit se uelle pugnare in duello cum quocumque dicente regem Ricardum uiuere.[295] Dum hoc parliamentum teneretur, Wallici combusserunt magnam partem comitatus Salopie.[296]

1404. Anno Domini millesimo quadringentesimo quarto, ᵐet anno quarto regis,ᵐ Audoenus Glendor ⁿpartes australesⁿ Wallie incendit et uillam de Kaierdiefᵒ et castrum obsedit.[297] Qui uero intus erant miserunt ad regem petentes auxilium, sed ipse nec uenit neque succursum misit. Audoenus uillam cepit et incendit, preter unum uicum in quo

---

ᵐ⁻ᵐ interlined   ⁿ⁻ⁿ underlined   ᵒ underlined

[291] The sharp exchanges between the king and the speaker of the commons, Sir Arnold Savage, are confirmed in the 'Durham newsletter' (*PROME*, viii. 279). The 'new and extraordinary' tax on land and income, which was not recorded on the parliament roll so that it would not be taken as a precedent, specified 20 shillings from each knights' fee or, from those who held no knights' fees, 12 pence from every 20 pounds' worth of goods and chattels, as well as 12 pence for every 20 shillings' worth of land or rent, but it was a resounding failure and yielded only about £9,000. The war-treasurers appointed to receive and spend the tax were John Hadley, Thomas Knolles, Richard Merlawe (all citizens of London), and John Oudeby, a chamberlain of the exchequer (Given-Wilson, *Henry IV*, pp. 282–3).

[292] For his examination in parliament in Feb. 1404, see *PROME*, viii. 231–2.

[293] For the expulsion of aliens in the Jan. 1404 parliament, see *PROME*, viii. 239–40, 243 (but the queen's daughters and a few other named individuals were specifically permitted to remain).

Wearying of staying there, they eventually granted this, but on this condition, that they would choose certain persons to receive the tax and spend it wholly on the wars, for which they would present an account to parliament; and that the king would give them his charter authorizing them to receive and spend it. To this, the king appeared to agree, and persons were chosen and the charter written out; but it was not sealed, and the parliament was dissolved.[291] Also in this parliament, the earl of Northumberland was exculpated from his son's uprising, and he swore upon the cross of St Thomas in parliament that he would always be loyal to King Henry.[292] Furthermore, in this parliament the two daughters of the queen and all the aliens who had arrived with her were expelled from the kingdom, since they were a burden on the royal household.[293] This parliament strongly rebuked the king's knights and other officials of his, demonstrating that they were despoiling the king and kingdom, as shown by the fact that, at the king's accession, the wealthiest of them barely had a hundred marks to spend, and now some of them had five hundred marks, some a thousand marks, and some even more, so that, although esquires and bachelors, they were equal in wealth to barons. And the king declared that while he had nothing, others grew richer by the year.[294] Letters arrived at this parliament purporting to come from King Richard, so authentic-seeming that the king and parliament were astonished; and they summoned the person who had guarded him in prison and asked him what he had to say about the letters. He declared that he would willingly fight a duel with anyone who claimed that King Richard was alive.[295] While this parliament was sitting, the Welsh burned a large part of the county of Shropshire.[296]

1404. In the year of the Lord 1404 and the king's fourth year, Owain Glyndwr burned the southern parts of Wales and laid siege to the town and castle of Cardiff [Glamorgan].[297] The people in the town sent to the king asking for help, but he neither came nor sent assistance. Owain seized the town and burned it, apart from one quarter in which the

---

[294] Cf. *SAC* II, pp. 394–7.

[295] These letters were presumably sent by William Serle (see below, p. 126). Richard II's principal gaolers in 1399–1400 were Robert Waterton, constable of Pontefract castle, and Thomas Swynford, knight of the royal chamber (Given-Wilson, *Henry IV*, p. 163).

[296] For the devastation of western Shropshire, see Davies, *Revolt*, p. 115.

[297] An English force attempted to relieve Cardiff in Nov.–Dec. 1404 (Davies, *Revolt*, pp. 116, 254).

fratres minores habitabant, quem amore fratrum cum conuentu stare permisit. Cepit insuper castrum et destruxit, multasque diuitias ibi repositas abstulit. Et cum fratres minores peterent ab eo libros et calices quos in castro deposuerant, respondit: 'Quare posuistis bona uestra in castro? Si ea retinuissetis apud uos, salua uobis fuissent.' Hoc anno comes Sancti Pauli uenit subito cum exercitu et obsedit castrum de Marc iuxta Calesiam, et fecit fossam circa illud. Sed cum uidit Calesianos uenire, turpiter fugiit, omnibus rebus suis et tunicam armorum suorum pre festinantia ibi dimissis. Calesiani plures occiderunt et captiuabant multos.[298] Flandrenses dixerunt se iniuriatos a nautis Anglicis et ideo pacem cum Anglicis habere noluerunt, sed quos poterant captiuabant.[299] Tunc Thomas filius regis factus est custos maris, qui incendit quasdam uillulas iuxta portum de Sclusa et insula de Cagent. Qui etiam cepit tres caracas de Ianua, quia noluerunt sua uela deponere sed pugnare, et in Angliam reuersus est.[300]

Adhuc rumor de uita regis Ricardi inualuit in Anglia, et quod ipse moraretur in Scotia in castro ducis Roseye quod Albion dicitur.[301] Quidam uir uenit ad comitissam Oxonie et affirmauit regem Ricardum uiuere, que, ex hoc gaudens, arestata fuit et posita in Turri Londonie; que insuper post grauem redemptionem liberata est. Similiter abbates Sancte Osithe et Colcestrie, accusati, pro pecuniis gratiam regis Henrici habere meruerunt.[302] Hoc anno Bonifacius papa moritur, et eligitur Innocentius, iurans quod laboraret ad unionem ecclesie.[303] Quo insuper anno statuitur parliamentum apud Couentriam statim post festum Sancti Michaelis; et rex mandauit quod nullus iurisperitus ad illud ueniret, et notificauit uicecomitibus quos milites et comitatum procuratores uoluit illuc mitti. Et ibi exegit duas decimas cleri et duas quintasdecimas laicorum.[304] Hoc anno *p*filius Audoeni*p* ab Anglicis capitur *q*et in Turri Londonie*q* captiuatur.[305]

---

p–p underlined   *q–q* underlined

[298] Waleran of Saint-Pol attacked Marck on 12 May 1405 but was ignominiously driven off (*SAC* II, pp. 436–7).

[299] Anglo-Flemish negotiations were frequent during these years, eventually leading to a mercantile truce in 1407; in 1405 the Flemings and Bretons jointly attacked Humberside (*SAC* II, p. 460; Given-Wilson, *Henry IV*, pp. 458–60).

[300] Thomas, the king's second son, was appointed as admiral on 20 Feb. 1405 (*CPR 1401–5*, p. 496). He and the earl of Kent raided Sluys in late May 1405, in retaliation for St-Pol's attack on Marck, following which they seized the Genoese carracks (*SAC* II, pp. 436–9).

[301] David, duke of Rothesay, eldest son of King Robert III of Scotland, had died in Mar. 1402 at Falkland, probably murdered on the orders of his uncle, the duke of Albany. The name Albion is probably a confusion with Albany.

[302] This conspiracy was hatched in the winter of 1403–4: see J. Ross, 'Seditious activities: The conspiracy of Maud de Vere, Countess of Oxford, 1403–4', in L. Clark, ed., *Fifteenth-Century England III: Authority and Submission* (Woodbridge, 2003), pp. 25–41.

friars minor lived, which he spared, along with their convent, out of love for the friars. He also seized and destroyed the castle, carrying off many of the valuables which had been deposited there. And when the friars minor tried to recover from him their books and chalices which they had deposited there, he replied: 'Why did you put your valuables in the castle? If you had held on to them yourselves, they would have been safe with you.' In this year the count of Saint-Pol arrived suddenly with an army to besiege the castle of Marck near Calais, and had a ditch dug around it. However, when he saw the townsmen of Calais approaching, he fled in shame, leaving all his things behind there in his haste, including a coat of his arms. The men of Calais killed several people and captured many others.[298] The Flemings declared that, since they had suffered damage from English ships, they did not wish to make peace with the English, but instead seized any that they could.[299] Whereupon Thomas, the king's son, was made keeper of the sea, and burned a number of villages near the port of Sluys on the island of Cadzand. He also seized three carracks from Genoa which had preferred to fight rather than to strike their sails, and then he returned to England.[300]

The rumour continued to spread in England that King Richard was alive, and that he was living in Scotland in the duke of Rothesay's castle which is called Albion.[301] A man approached the countess of Oxford and affirmed that King Richard was alive, at which she rejoiced, so she was arrested and sent to the Tower of London; however, she was released after paying a large fine. The abbots of St Osyth and Colchester [Essex] were similarly accused, but managed to obtain King Henry's pardon in return for money.[302] In this year, Pope Boniface died, and Innocent was elected, swearing that he would work for the union of the Church.[303] Also, straight after the feast of Michaelmas [29 September] this year, a parliament was held at Coventry; and the king ordered that no person who was learned in the law should come to it, and he notified the sheriffs as to which knights and representatives of the shires he wished to have sent there. And he extracted two tenths from the clergy and two fifteenths from the laity there.[304] In this year the son of Owain was captured by the English and imprisoned in the Tower of London.[305]

[303] Boniface IX died on 1 Oct. 1404; Innocent VII was elected on 17 Oct.
[304] Parliament met at Coventry from 6 Oct. to 14 Nov. 1404; the grant of two tenths and fifteenths was one of the most generous made by a medieval parliament (*PROME*, viii. 281–317).
[305] Gruffudd, eldest son of Glyndwr, was captured at the battle of Pwll Melyn after an unsuccessful raid on Usk castle, probably in early May 1405. He died of plague in the Tower of London in 1411 (Davies, *Revolt*, pp. 226, 311; *Usk*, pp. 212–13).

Tunc heredes comitis Marchie, duo filii existentes in warda regis, quos quidam dixerunt ueros esse heredes regni de proxima linea de stirpe domini Leonelli, abducti fuerunt a curia regis per quondam damicellam de camera regine; et ipsa accusauit de hoc ducem Eborum, et dux in castro de Peuenesey aliquandiu detentus est. Dux tamen excusauit se, dicens quod ipse sciit quod allicerentur et premuniuit de hoc regem.[306] Hoc anno quidam Iohannes Cerle, qui ducem Glouernie occiderat priuiter, captus fuit ab Anglicis in Scotia, et in multis locis Anglie tractus, suspensus et uiuus depositus, et tandem, ductus Londonie, tractus ibidem et suspensus, demum decollatus est atque in quartas diuisus. Iste confessus est quod quando rex Ricardus tradidit se duci Lancastrie in Wallia, ipse furatus fuit signetum regis Ricardi. Et cum rex Henricus inquireret de occisoribus ducis Gloucestrie, ipse fugiit in Scotiam et inde misit litteras dicto signeto signatas ad amicos regis Ricardi, dicens quod ipse uiueret, et sic fuit causa mortis multorum. Dixit etiam quod est unus in Scotia similis regi Ricardo, sed non est ipse Ricardus. Tamen adhuc non quieuit rumor ille de uita eius; semper Scoti illum rumorem | auxerunt.[307]

Hoc anno uenit imperator Constantinopolitanus, ut supradictum est.[308] Et domina Iohanna, ducissa Britannie, uenit in Angliam, quam rex Henricus apud Wintoniam in abbatia Sancti Suthinii sollemniter desponsauit, uiuente adhuc Willielmo Wikham, Wintoniensi episcopo, apud Waltham. Et Henricus Beauford, tunc episcopus Lincolniensis, dictum matrimonium sollemnisauit.[309] Quo insuper anno domina Blancha, senior filia regis Henrici, nupsit filio ducis Bauarie apud Coloniam, quorum nuptias Ricardus Clifford, episcopus Wigorniensis tunc, celebrauit, presente comite Somersetie; qui post nuptiarum sollemnisationem in Angliam sunt reuersi.[310] Eodem anno in Somersetia uisi sunt corui multi uenire de partibus transmarinis, et sturni

r marginal in a later hand: prodigium

[306] The sons of Roger Mortimer, earl of March (d. 1398), were Edmund, aged 13, and Roger, aged 11. They were abducted from Windsor castle on 13 Feb. 1405 but recaptured a few days later near Cheltenham (Gloucestershire). The intention seems to have been to take them to Wales to join their uncle Edmund and Glyndwr. It was Constance, Lady Despenser, brother of Edward, duke of York, who was behind the plot, but she claimed that her brother was the real instigator. She and Edward were imprisoned at Pevensey (Sussex), but both pardoned some months later. Others were also suspected of involvement (Given-Wilson, *Henry IV*, pp. 264–5). Because of their descent from Lionel of Clarence, second son of Edward III, the Mortimer boys' claim to the throne was a controversial issue throughout Henry IV's reign, and they continued to be held under house arrest by Henry, although not mistreated.

[307] William Serle made the mistake of crossing into England in June 1404 and was arrested and handed over to the king. His death pains, extending over several weeks between Pontefract and London, were, as the king himself noted, 'more severe than other traitors heretofore' (Given-Wilson, *Henry IV*, pp. 263–4; *CCR 1402–5*, pp. 203, 352–7).

Then the heirs of the earl of March, two sons who were in the king's wardship—whom some people said were the true heirs to the kingdom, coming from the stock of Lord Lionel, the nearest line of descent—were abducted from the king's court by a certain lady-in-waiting of the queen's chamber; she accused the duke of York of this, and the duke was detained for some time in Pevensey castle [Sussex]. However, the duke acquitted himself, saying that he knew that they would be lured away and warned the king of this.[306] In this year a certain John [*recte* William] Serle, who had secretly killed the duke of Gloucester, was captured by Englishmen in Scotland and was drawn, hanged, and taken down while still alive in several places in England, before eventually being taken to London, where he was drawn and hanged and finally beheaded and quartered. This man confessed that, when King Richard surrendered to the duke of Lancaster in Wales, he had stolen King Richard's signet. And when King Henry made enquiries about the murderers of the duke of Gloucester, he fled to Scotland, from where he sent letters authenticated with the said signet to the friends of King Richard saying that he was still alive; and thus he caused the death of many people. He also said that there was someone in Scotland who looked like King Richard, but that it was not Richard himself. Yet still the rumour that he was alive would not be silenced; the Scots never ceased to spread that rumour.[307]

In this year the emperor of Constantinople arrived, as noted above.[308] Lady Joan, duchess of Brittany, also arrived in England, and King Henry solemnly married her in St Swithun's abbey at Winchester [Hampshire], at which time William Wykeham, bishop of Winchester, was still alive and living at Waltham [Hampshire]. And Henry Beaufort, then bishop of Lincoln, celebrated the said marriage.[309] Moreover, in this same year, Lady Blanche, elder daughter of King Henry, married the son of the duke of Bavaria at Cologne, whose nuptials Richard Clifford, the bishop of Worcester, celebrated, in the presence of the earl of Somerset; and after the celebration of the nuptials they returned to England.[310] In Somerset, in the same year, numerous crows from foreign parts could be seen arriving, and starlings attacked and killed

---

[308] This is noted above, p. 102, in its correct year (1400).
[309] Henry married Joan of Navarre in Winchester cathedral on 7 Feb. 1403; William of Wykeham, bishop of Winchester since 1366, died on 27 Sept. 1404; Henry Beaufort replaced him at Winchester in Nov., having been bishop of Lincoln since 1398.
[310] Blanche, Henry IV's eldest daughter, was betrothed to Louis, son of Emperor Rupert of Bavaria, in Feb. 1401 and left England in June 1402 to marry him at Cologne, accompanied by Richard Clifford, bishop of Worcester since 1401 (translated to London in June 1407), and John Beaufort, earl of Somerset. Henry never saw his daughter again; she died in 1409, aged 17.

ueniebant contra eos et eos occidebant.[r] Postea uenerunt Britones illuc ad predandum, et pauperes plebei occiderunt illos, ubi unus auriga uerberauit militem armatum, quod multotiens ibi uisum est.[311]

Hoc anno magnum scisma ualde scandalosum fuit in ordine fratrum minorum in Anglia.[312] Nam minister ordinis, turbulentorum fratrum consilio instigatus, et promotorum suorum imperitorum numero roboratus, plures conuentus et principales, plures etiam fratres et eorum amicos, grauiter offendebat per subtractionem priuilegiorum et antiquarum consuetudinum, omnia intendens ad libitum suum noua ordinare; et precipue priuilegia conuentus London, auctoritate potestatis generalis, reuocauit, assignans eis gardianum ac lectorem, et fratres a conuentu qui priuilegium defenderent remouere nitebatur. Conuentus autem appellauit ab eo ad papam, dicens quod priuilegium loci concessum est non auctoritate generali sed a cardinali uicario ordinis, auctoritate papali. Et cum nollet eis gardianum electum ab eis confirmare, inuocabant contra eum auxilium maioris Londonie.[313] Maior precipit sibi quod non turbaret pacem ciuitatis; uidebat quosdam de ciuitate insurgere uolentes contra eum amore fratrum. Minister condescendit illis tunc, et transiit in partes aquilonares ad uisitandum. Interim congregauerunt se aduersarii sui mittentes nuntium cum litteris contra eum ad generalem; feceruntque sibi amicos in curia regis, qui ita informauerunt regem, quod rex etiam tradidit nuntio litteras suas ad generalem. Nuntius transfretauit, et fuit ipse frater callidus, bacularius Cantibrugie. Minister uenit ad regem, et rex dixit quod ipse turbauit regnum. Minister ostendebat sibi litteras <generalis>[s] ordinis testimoniales de pacifico regimine. Sed dixit: 'Fratres Londonienses sunt uitiosi', et uellet eorum uitia corrigere, et ideo insurgunt contra eum. Et rex concessit sibi litteras reuocatorias premissarum. Conuentus accepit testimonium coram rege a burgensibus ciuitatis, quod numquam scandalum accidit in ciuitate per aliquem fratrem in conuentu manentem, sed omnia scandala uenerunt per aduentitios forenses et illis similes qui fuerunt ibi suspensi,[314] et minister uellet fratres natiuos

---

[s] *word obscured by fire damage*

[311] This Breton raid on Dartmouth (Devon) took place in May 1404. It was led by Guillaume de Chastel, who was killed along with several of his followers, while many others were captured. The resistance of the local people—'common people, or rustics' according to Walsingham—was widely praised by contemporaries (*SAC* II, pp. 399–407). The battle of the 'foreign' crows and local starlings was obviously seen by the chronicler as a portent for the success of the Dartmouth peasants against the Bretons.

[312] For this dispute, see pp. xxiii–xxvi, 128–30, and Whitfield, 'Conflicts of personality', *passim*. In this passage, the chronicler uses the term 'minister' to denote the provincial minister (head of the English Franciscan province, in this case, John de la Zouche) and 'general' to denote the minister-general of the Franciscan order.

them. Later, Bretons arrived there looking for plunder, and poor common people killed them; a carter gave an armed knight a beating, something which was witnessed many times there.[311]

In this year, there was a great and truly shameful dispute within the order of the friars minor in England.[312] For the minister of the order, acting on the advice of some troublesome friars and encouraged by a number of their inexperienced supporters, greatly offended several convents and principals, as well as many friars and their friends, by withdrawing their privileges and ancient customs, planning to reissue them all according to his own liking; and in particular, on the authority of the power of the general, he revoked the privileges of the London convent, assigning to them a warden and a lector, and endeavouring to expel from the convent those friars who defended the privilege. However, the convent appealed from him to the pope, saying that the privileges there had been granted not by general authority but by the cardinal-protector of the order, on papal authority. And when he refused to confirm the warden chosen by them, they invoked the help of the mayor of London against him.[313] The mayor warned him that he must not disturb the peace of the city; he could see that some people in the city wanted to rise up against him, out of love for the friars. The minister deferred to them on this occasion, and set off to the north to undertake a visitation. Meanwhile, his opponents joined forces against him, sending a messenger with letters against him to the general; and they got their friends at the king's court, who had informed the king about this, to get the king also to send a messenger with letters to the general. The messenger, who was a crafty friar, a bachelor of Cambridge, set off abroad. The minister went to the king, and the king told him that he was disturbing the realm. The minister showed him letters from the general of the order testifying to his peaceful rule. He said, however, that 'the London friars are wicked', and he wished to correct their faults, and that was why they were opposing him. Whereupon the king gave him letters revoking those which he had previously sent. The convent produced testimony in the presence of the king from the burgesses of the city to the effect that no scandal in the city had ever been caused by any friar residing in the convent, but that all the scandals were caused by incomers from abroad and others such as those who were hanged there,[314] and the minister wanted to remove the local friars

---

[313] The cardinal-protector of the Franciscan order was Franciscus Carbonarius, cardinal-bishop of Sabina. The mayor of London in 1404–5 was the draper John Hende.
[314] Presumably the friars hanged in 1402.

ibidem amouere et tales aduentitios ibidem ordinare. Nuntius missus, inueniens generalem mortuum,³¹⁵ transiit ad Curiam, et celeriter rediens portauit litteras iustitie directas duobus magistris in theologia a quodam cardinali qui asseruit quod papa fecit ipsum commissarium in hac causa uiua uoce; et dedit cardinalis eis potestatem uisitandi prouinciam, et absoluendi ministrum si excessus eius reperirent, et statuendi capitulum ac procedendi ad electionem alterius, et uices agendi ueri ministri donec minister in prouincia haberetur; et sub pena excommunicationis prohibuit ne quis resisteret illis.³¹⁶ Qua quidem commissione recepta, commissarii uisitabant quosdam conuentus, et notificauerunt regi commissionem suam et quod excessus quosdam reperierunt, et obtinuerunt a rege prohibitionem ne transfretaret, citantes eum quod compareret coram eis in castro Colchestrie. Ipse autem noluit parere, sed transfretauit. Ipsi uero absoluebant, et absolutum denuntiabant, statuentes capitulum Oxonie in Inuentione Sancte Crucis. Ac fratres informauerunt archiepiscopum Cantuariensem contra ministrum grauiter, et similiter regem, qui crediderunt eis. Vicarius autem ministri inhibuit omnibus fratribus quod ad capitulum Oxonie non accederent. Et commissarii supplicabant regi quod preciperet fratribus pro reformatione religionis ad capitulum Oxonie conuenirent, inhibens ne quis capitulum impediret; et de his breuia regia habuerunt.³¹⁷

1405.[1] Anno Domini millesimo quadringentesimo quinto et regis anno quinto, dominus Ricardus Scrop, archiepiscopus Eborum, et dominus de Mowbray, qui etiam comes marescallus uocabatur, apud Eborum decollantur. Deus enim omnipotens per ipsum archiepiscopum usque hodie mirabiliter operatur;³¹⁸ et, ut quidam dicunt, rex in hora mortis dicti presulis lepra percussus erat, quam nemo medicorum curare potuit, sed ex eadem postea mortuus est infirmitate.³¹⁹

---

[1] *marginal in later hand*: archiepiscopus Eboracum decollatus

---

³¹⁵ Enrico Alfieri, minister-general of the Franciscan order since 1387, deposed Zouche shortly before he died in 1405, but he was reinstated on 8 Mar. 1406 by the new minister-general, Antonio de Pereto (1405–8): Whitfield, 'Conflicts of personality', pp. 339–40.

³¹⁶ The two masters of theology were Nicholas of Fakenham and John Malet (Little, *Franciscan Papers*, p. 198).

³¹⁷ This was not the end of the dispute. In July 1407, minister-general Antonio de Pereto had to visit England in order to try to restore peace to the province. Despite having reinstated Zouche in the previous year, he now forced the latter to resign. Zouche was replaced by his arch-rival, William Butler, and promoted to the bishopric of Llandaff (1407–23), but he continued to seek retribution against those who had opposed him (Whitfield, 'Conflicts of personality', *passim*; and see above, pp. xxiii–xxvi).

³¹⁸ Richard Scrope was bishop of Coventry and Lichfield (1386–98) and archbishop of York (1398–1405); Thomas Mowbray was the son of the Thomas Mowbray, earl of

and appoint incomers of that sort there. The messenger who had been dispatched, discovering that the general had died,[315] went to the Curia, whence he hastily returned bearing judicial letters addressed to two masters of theology from a certain cardinal who claimed that the pope had appointed him by word of mouth as a commissioner for this case; and the cardinal gave them authority to visit the province and to dismiss the minister if they found him to be at fault, and to convene a [provincial] chapter and proceed to the election of a replacement, and to act in place of the real minister until such time as the province should have a minister; and he ordered under pain of excommunication that no one should oppose this.[316] Having received this commission, the commissioners visited several convents, and they told the king about their commission and that they had discovered a number of faults, and they obtained from the king a prohibition to prevent [the minister] from going abroad, summoning him to appear before them in Colchester castle. However, he had no wish to appear, and went abroad. They therefore dismissed him, and announced their decision, convoking a chapter at Oxford on the feast of the Discovery of the Holy Cross [3 May]. And the friars complained strongly about the minister to the archbishop of Canterbury, and likewise to the king, who believed them. Nevertheless, the minister's vicar ordered all the friars not to attend the chapter at Oxford. Whereupon the commissioners begged the king, for the sake of religious reform, to tell the friars to assemble for the chapter at Oxford, and to forbid any person to obstruct it; and they received royal writs to this effect.[317]

1405. In the year of the Lord 1405 and the king's fifth year, Lord Richard Scrope, archbishop of York, and Lord Mowbray, who was also known as earl marshal, were beheaded at York. Truly, Almighty God continues to this day to work wonders through this archbishop;[318] and, according to what some say, at the hour of this bishop's death the king was struck down by leprosy, which none of the doctors was able to cure, and it was from this illness that he later died.[319]

Nottingham and duke of Norfolk, whose quarrel with Henry had led to the exile of both men in 1398 (see above, p. 84). The younger Thomas was born in 1385 and thus 19 years old when he and Scrope were executed outside York on 8 June 1405. For their rising, see Given-Wilson, *Henry IV*, pp. 262–77. For Scrope's afterlife as a martyr and putative saint, see J. McKenna, 'Popular canonization as political propaganda: The cult of Archbishop Scrope', *Speculum*, xlv (1970), 608–23.

[319] It is extremely unlikely that Henry IV suffered from leprosy, although he did apparently have a severe skin condition which first afflicted him in his youth and continued to do so for the rest of his life (P. McNiven, 'The problem of Henry IV's health', *EHR* c (1985), 747–72; Given-Wilson, *Henry IV*, p. 533).

Quod sic contigit: heres comitis de Notyngham, dominus de Mowbray, conqueritur archiepiscopo Eborum quod cum[a] | patres sui solebant esse marescalli Anglie et terras pro illo officio assignatas possidere, rex officium et terras dedit comiti Westmerlandie.[320] Archiepiscopus, communicato cum prudentibus, predicauit in ecclesia cathedrali Eborum, hortans populum ut assisteret ad correctionem mali regiminis regni, ut scilicet depauperatio mercatorum, in quibus esse deberent substantiales diuitie regni, per excessiuas eleuationes theoloneorum et custumarum, ac confiscationes pecuniarum suarum sub colore mutui; et quod pro uictualibus et artificiis debite solutiones fiant; et quod releuetur clerus et populus ab illo assueto onere importabilium tallagiorum; et quod heredibus nobilium restituantur hereditates integre et honores secundum conditionem natalium suorum.

Articuli contra regem. Item, quod consiliarii auari et cupidi circa regem, suggentes ab eo bona ad commune subsidium ordinata, semetipsos ditantes, amoueantur. Item, quod iurisperiti ad parliamenta ueniant, et sua sapientia consulant; quod milites comitatuum et burgenses ciuitatum mittendi ad parliamenta per comitatus et ciuitates eligantur et non per regem assignentur; et quod parliamentum statuatur Londoniis, qui locus est magis publicus, et ubi hec melius corrigi possunt; que si correcta sint, habemus firmam spem quod Wallia erit subiecta Anglie sicut fuit temporibus Edwardi et Ricardi.[321] Hec in Anglico scripta appendi fecit in portis ciuitatis, et curatis similiter in uillis circumiacentibus misit predicanda. Et, collecto exercitu de burgensibus, uillanis, presbyteris et religiosis, armauit se et cum domino de Moubray processit uersus comitem Westmerlandie; et comes Westmerlandie cum exercitu uenit contra eum.[322] Qui cum appropinquarent, comes Westmerlandie rogauit archiepiscopum et dominum de Moubray ut conuenirent coram eo in medio exercituum et tractarent de pace. Archiepiscopus uero, et dominus de Moubray ac unus miles, de eorum consilio principalis, exiit ad eum.[323] Comes Westmerlandie habebat ibi flascones cum uino, et dabat eis bibere. Et dum fraudulenter simularet se tractare, quidam miles suus transiit ad exercitum archiepiscopi et dixit: 'Domini sunt concordati, et simul biberunt. Dominus archiepiscopus precipit omnibus uobis redire, quia ipse cenabit cum

---

[a] Henrici Quarti *in upper margin of fo. 205ᵛ*.

---

[320] Ralph Nevill, earl of Westmorland 1397–1425.
[321] Another version of the schedule of complaints against the king is in *SAC* II, pp. 442–5.
[322] This meeting between the armies took place on Shipton Moor, outside York, on 29 May 1405.

This happened as follows: Lord Mowbray, the heir to the earldom of Nottingham, complained to the archbishop of York that, whereas his ancestors used to be marshals of England and to hold the lands belonging to that office, the king gave the office and the lands to the earl of Westmorland.[320] The archbishop, after consulting with prudent people, preached in the cathedral church of York, urging the people to help in remedying the evil government of the kingdom, such as the impoverishment of the merchants, in whom the material wealth of the kingdom ought to reside, through the excessive levies of tolls and customs and the seizure of their money in the guise of loans; and that payment should be made for provisions and goods; and that the clergy and people should be relieved from that habitual burden of unendurable taxes; and that their full inheritances and honours should be restored to the heirs of nobles in accordance with their birthright.

The articles against the king. Also, that the greedy and rapacious councillors who surround the king, sucking out of him the goods ordained for the common profit, enriching themselves, should be removed. Also, that those who are learned in the law should come to parliaments and offer advice according to their wisdom; that the knights of the shires and the burgesses of the towns to be sent to parliaments should be elected by the shires and towns, and not appointed by the king; and that parliament should be held in London, which is a more public place and where these matters can more readily be remedied; and if these things are remedied, we have the firm hope that Wales will be subjected to England as it was in the time of Edward [III] and Richard [II].[321] These things, written in English, he had posted up on the gates of the city, and similarly sent them to priests in the surrounding villages to be promulgated. Then, having gathered together an army of townsmen, villeins, priests, and monks, he armed himself and set out with Lord Mowbray against the earl of Westmorland; and the earl of Westmorland advanced against him with an army.[322] When they drew near, the earl of Westmorland asked the archbishop and Lord Mowbray to meet with him in the middle ground between the armies to treat for peace. Whereupon the archbishop and Lord Mowbray and a knight, their chief adviser, went out towards him.[323] The earl of Westmorland had some flagons of wine there, and he gave them a drink. And while he craftily pretended to negotiate with them, one of his knights crossed over to the archbishop's army and said: 'The lords have come to an agreement and are having a drink together. The lord archbishop orders all of you to retire, since he will dine with

---

[323] The knight was Sir William Plumpton, executed along with Scrope and Mowbray.

comite hac nocte.' Et omnes erant timidi, quia erat terre mirabilis tumor propter quem tractantes ab eis uideri non poterant; et nimis creduli cito recesserunt. Quibus recedentibus et dispersis, rediit miles ille ad suos et, facto signo, ceperunt archiepiscopum, dominum de Moubray et militem; et exercitus comitis persequebatur exercitum archiepiscopi fugientem et dispersum, quosque spoliabant et grauiter uerberabant quos capere potuerunt. Fratres uero quattuor ordinum comprehensos, inter quos erant circiter octodecim fratres minores, nudabant omnes uestes suas et femoralia detrahebant et currere dimiserunt. Presentaueruntque domino regi archiepiscopum et dominum de Moubray, qui tunc fuit in castro Pontis Fracti ordinans se contra illos qui castra sua in Northumbria detinebant. Rex uenit Eboracum, et exierunt ad eum burgenses discalceati, discincti et simplicibus induti, cordas in collis gerentes, et prostrati coram rege misericordiam et gratiam eius implorantes.[324] Archiepiscopus Cantuariensis, his auditis, uenit cum festinatione ad regem, et quidam miles aulicus regis, uidens eum, dixit regi: 'Si iste archiepiscopus Eborum uiuet, omnes nos a uobis recedemus.'

Consilium archiepiscopi Cantuariensis.[325] Et archiepiscopus Cantuariensis, in presentia cuiusdam notarii, dixit regi: 'Domine, ego sum pater uester spiritualis et secunda persona post uos in regno, et nullius consilium plus acceptaretis quam meum si bonum sit. Consulo uobis quod si archiepiscopus tantum deliquerit[v] sicut uobis suggestum est, reseruetur iudicio domini pape, qui talem satisfactionem uobis ordinabit quod eam iudicabitis sufficientem. At si hoc non uultis, consulo ut reseruetur iudicio parliamenti. Absit quod iudicio uestro manus uestre eius sanguine polluantur.' Rex respondit: 'Non possum, propter astantes.'[w] Et archiepiscopus Cantuariensis requisiuit notarium super hac responsione publicum conficere instrumentum, pape si oporteat presentandum.

Moritur archiepiscopus Eborum. Rex uero intrauit aulam archiepiscopi ad prandendum, et habuit secum archiepiscopum Cantuariensem et totam familiam suam. Et dum pranderent, adiudicati sunt archiepiscopus Eborum, dominus de Moubray, et quidam miles predictus, et extra ciuitatem decollantur in festo Sancti Willielmi.[326] Et archiepiscopus decollandus dixit: 'En morior pro legibus et bono regimine regni Anglie'; et aliis dixit secum decollandis: 'Hanc penam patienter sustineamus,

---

[v] deliqit MS   [w] interlined

[324] These details of the abject surrender of the York citizens on 6 June are confirmed by other chroniclers (Given-Wilson, *Henry IV*, p. 269).

[325] Archbishop Arundel arrived in York on the morning of Monday 8 June, the day of the executions.

[326] St William, archbishop of York, had died on 8 June 1154.

the earl tonight.' They were all afraid, since there was a steep incline in the ground which made it impossible for them to see those who were negotiating; so, trusting completely, they soon retired. Once they had departed and dispersed, the aforesaid knight returned to his own side and, at a given signal, they seized the archbishop, Lord Mowbray, and the knight. Whereupon the earl's army set off in pursuit of the archbishop's fleeing and scattered army, and despoiled and severely beat those whom they could capture. Indeed, those friars of the four orders whom they caught, among whom were about eighteen friars minor, they stripped of all their clothes, pulled down their trousers and sent them scurrying on their way. Then they handed over the archbishop and Lord Mowbray to the lord king, who was at that time in Pontefract castle [Yorkshire] preparing to move against those who were occupying his castles in Northumberland. The king came to York, and the citizens came out to meet him barefoot, ungirded, and dressed in rags, with ropes around their necks, and prostrated themselves in front of the king begging his mercy and grace.[324] The archbishop of Canterbury, hearing of these events, hastened to the king, whereupon a certain knight of the royal court, seeing him, said to the king: 'If this archbishop of York is allowed to live, we shall all leave you.'

The advice of the archbishop of Canterbury.[325] Then the archbishop of Canterbury said to the king, in the presence of a certain notary: 'My lord, I am your spiritual father and the second person in the kingdom after you, and there is no one whose advice you should take more readily than mine, if it is good. I advise you that if the archbishop has transgressed so gravely, as has been suggested to you, judgment should be committed to the lord pope, who shall give you such satisfaction as you shall judge to be sufficient. And if you do not wish to do this, I advise you to commit judgment to parliament. Heaven forbid that his blood be on your hands through your own judgment.' The king replied: 'I cannot do this, because of those here present.' And the archbishop of Canterbury asked a notary public to draw up an instrument recording this response, to be presented to the pope should it prove necessary.

The death of the archbishop of York. Then the king went into the archbishop's hall to have a meal, and with him were the archbishop of Canterbury and all his household. And while they were eating, sentence was passed on the archbishop of York, Lord Mowbray, and the aforesaid knight, and they were beheaded outside the city on the feast of St William [8 June].[326] And as he was about to be beheaded, the archbishop said: 'Behold, I am dying for the laws and good government of the kingdom of England'; and to those about to be beheaded with

fo. 206ʳ et hac nocte in paradiso erimus.'³²⁷ | Et rex incontinenti quasi leprosus apparere cepit; qui statim bona ciuium ciuitatis Eborum confiscauit, deinde transiit ad aquilonem contra eos qui castra sua ibidem tenebant. Comes Northumbrie et dominus Bardolf de castro Berwici recesserunt in Scotiam.³²⁸ Rex autem uenit ad Berwicum et expugnando castrum multos lapides iactari fecit cum bombardis ad muros castri, sed frangebantur lapides per murorum duritiam. Tandem accidit quod lapis quidam percussit ferramentum cancellatum cuiusdam fenestre in quodam tenui muro, et hominem*ˣ* ibidem ascendentem occidit; et ex tunc omnes inclusi amiserunt corda et, uecordes effecti, exierunt, gratiam regis implorantes; quos rex iussit decollari.³²⁹ Et reuersus transiit in Walliam australem et castrum de Coyfy, diu a Wallicis obsessum, liberauit. Et in redeundo cariagium suum et iocalia sua Wallenses spoliabant.³³⁰ Papa autem, audita morte archiepiscopi, excommunicauit omnes occisores archiepiscopi Eborum et consilium ad hoc dantes, mandans archiepiscopo Cantuariensi quod denuntiaret eos excommunicatos. Sed archiepiscopus nolebat hoc facere solus. Tunc rex misit ad papam dicens quod timor seditionis in populo non sinebat eum uiuere, mittens pape loricam episcopi, dicens: 'Pater, uide si tunica hec filii tui sit, an non.' Et quieuit materia.³³¹

Hoc anno factum est parliamentum post Dominicam primam Quadragesime, et durauit usque ad Natiuitatem Domini.³³² Clerus autem in conuocatione concessit regi unam decimam, et sex solidos octo denarios a quolibet annuario sacerdote.³³³ Sed laici nihil soluere uolebant nisi eis daretur compotus de receptis, sicut prius ordinatum fuit et per regem promissum. Rex breuiter respondebat quod 'Reges non solebant compotum dare'.*ʸ* Officiales dixerunt quod nullus eorum

---

ˣ homines *MS*   *ʸ* *a hand is drawn in the margin pointing to this passage*

³²⁷ Cf. Luke 23: 43.

³²⁸ Northumberland, disaffected and marginalized since the Percy rebellion of 1403, had tried to seize Westmorland at the beginning of May, but when this failed he and Thomas, Lord Bardolf, fled to Northumberland and ultimately to Scotland (Given-Wilson, *Henry IV*, pp. 266–7).

³²⁹ Berwick surrendered to Henry on 6 July and at least eight defenders were beheaded (Given-Wilson, *Henry IV*, pp. 270–1).

³³⁰ Coety (or Coity) castle in Glamorgan was besieged by the Welsh twice in 1404–5, and relieved in Nov. 1404 and Sept. 1405 (Davies, *Revolt*, p. 246). According to *SAC* II, p. 462, the king's baggage-train was carried away by flood waters as he returned from Wales.

³³¹ Innocent VII's bull of excommunication against those responsible for Scrope's death was sent to Archbishop Arundel in the spring of 1406; although it did not name the king, Arundel held back from publishing it. According to the *English Chronicle* (p. 37), Innocent's response to Henry's message was 'Siue hec sit tunica filii mei an non, scio quia fera pessima deuorauit filium meum' ('whether this be my son's tunic or not, I know that a wild beast has

him, he said: 'Let us bear this suffering with patience, and this night we will be in Paradise.'[327] And immediately the king began to take on the appearance of a leper. Straight away, he confiscated the goods belonging to the citizens of the city of York, then set off northwards against those who were holding his castles there. The earl of Northumberland and Lord Bardolf fled from Berwick castle [Northumberland] into Scotland.[328] Nevertheless, the king came to Berwick and, investing the castle, ordered several stones to be fired from cannons at the castle walls, but the cannonballs shattered because of the strength of the walls. At length, one of the cannonballs happened to strike the iron framework of a window at a weak spot in the wall and killed a man walking up there; whereupon all those who were inside lost heart and, stupefied, came out of the castle, begging for mercy from the king; the king ordered them to be beheaded.[329] Then, coming back, he made his way to South Wales and relieved Coety castle [Glamorgan], which the Welsh had been besieging for a long time. And as he was returning the Welsh plundered his baggage-train and jewels.[330] Meanwhile the pope, hearing of the archbishop's death, excommunicated all those who had put the archbishop of York to death, along with those who had assented to it, ordering the archbishop of Canterbury to declare them excommunicated. But the archbishop had no wish to act alone in doing this. Whereupon the king sent to the pope telling him that fear of sedition from the people meant that he could not be allowed to live, and sent the pope the bishop's hauberk with the words, 'Father, know now whether this be thy son's coat or no'. And so the matter was dropped.[331]

In this year a parliament was held after the first Sunday in Lent [28 February], and it lasted until Christmas.[332] The clergy in convocation therefore granted to the king one tenth as well as 6 shillings and 8 pence from each stipendiary priest.[333] However, the laity did not wish to make any grant unless they were shown accounts of the receipts, as had been agreed previously and promised by the king. The king responded curtly that 'kings are not accustomed to giving account'. The officers declared that none of them knew how to render account. Those who had been deputed to receive what had been collected in the

---

devoured my son'). The quotes are from Gen. 37: 32–3 (the story of Joseph). After Innocent's death in November 1406, the bull was withdrawn by Gregory XII in April 1408 (Given-Wilson, *Henry IV*, pp. 351, 357–8).

[332] Parliament met on Monday 1 March 1406. Divided into three sessions, it was only dissolved on 22 December.

[333] Convocation met from 10 May to 16 June. The grant of 6s. 8d. from stipendiary vicars caused much grumbling (*SAC* II, pp. 470–2).

sciit compotum reddere. Ordinati ad recipiendum collectam anni precedentis dixerunt se auctoritatem recipiendi non habere, nec aliquid acceperunt; et sic negotium remansit imperfectum hoc anno.[334]

1406. Anno Domini millesimo quadringentesimo sexto et anno regni regis Henrici quarti sexto, Innocentius papa moritur, et cardinales conuenientes ad electionem iurauerunt singillatim quod quiscunque eorum foret electus cederet quando a cardinalibus foret requisitus, pro unione pacis ecclesie. Et elegerunt ex se unum quem uocabant Gregorium, in theologia doctorem, senem, qui etiam post coronationem idem prestitit iuramentum in presentia plurium notariorum.[335] Cuius etiam temporibus ordinatum est quod nullus minister prouincialis fratrum minorum stabit in illo statu ultra septennium, super qua ordinatione bullam suam tradidit generali. Hoc anno rex dedit filiam suam regi Dacie.[336] Et communitas Anglie dedit regi unam quintamdecimam.[337] Hoc insuper anno duo pape componunt et assentiunt conuenire in Sapona et resignare, et papa misit generalem fratrum minorum ad regem Anglie et per totam Almanniam, et alios episcopos et nobiles cum litteris credentie, ut intimarent eis propositum suum de cessione facienda.[338]

1407. Mors ducis Aurelianensis. Anno Domini millesimo quadringentesimo septimo et anno regis Henrici quarti septimo, dux Aurelianensis, multum odiosus in Francia, propter turbam cum qua semper equitabat interfici non potuit, ideo in ciuitate Paris, ubi cum paucis ambulabat tanquam securus, occiditur hoc modo: unus inimicus suus sero incendit quandam domum, et socii sui occiderunt ducem et abierunt festinanter clamantes: 'Ad ignem ite, ad ignem!' Familia autem ducis clamabat: 'Proditio, proditio!' Sed populus transiit ad ignem. Rex autem Francie turbatus est, et omne concilium suum cum illo, inquirentes quis hoc fecit. Dux Burgundie dixit: 'Iuretis michi quod tenebitis consilium per tres dies, et dicam uobis quis hoc fecit'; et iurauerunt. Et ipse confessus est de scientia sua hoc factum fuisse. Tunc excluserunt eum a concilio. Ipse uero transiit in Flandriam et Alemanniam, colligens exercitum copiosum. Inuocauitque auxilium

---

[334] For the request from the commons to audit the war-treasurers' accounts, see *PROME*, viii. 348–9. In fact, this parliament did grant taxation, but not until later in the year.

[335] Pope Innocent VII died on 6 Nov. 1406. The cardinal of Venice, Angelo Corraro, was elected on 30 Nov. and crowned as Pope Gregory XII on 19 Dec., aged about 80. For the agreement made in conclave, see *SAC* II, pp. 482–94.

[336] Henry IV's younger daughter Philippa (born in 1394) had been betrothed to Erik, king of Denmark in 1402; she left England in early Aug. 1406 and married Erik at Lund on 26 Oct.

previous year said that they had no authority to receive it, nor had they received anything; and thus matters remained undecided that year.[334]

1406. In the year of the Lord 1406 and the sixth year of the reign of King Henry IV, Pope Innocent died, and when the cardinals convened for the election, they individually swore an oath, in order to unite the Church in peace, that whichever of them was elected would resign when asked by the cardinals to do so. Whereupon they elected one of their number, an old man, a doctor of theology, whom they called Gregory, who also swore the same oath following his coronation, in the presence of several notaries.[335] During his time it was decreed that no provincial minister of the friars minor should remain in that office for more than seven years; and he sent his bull concerning this decree to the [minister] general. In this year the king gave his daughter to the king of Denmark.[336] And the commons of England granted the king a fifteenth.[337] Also in this year, the two popes came to an agreement to meet together at Savona and resign, and the pope sent the general of the friars minor to the king of England, and throughout Germany, as well as other bishops and nobles, with written credentials, so that they could inform them of their proposal to resign.[338]

1407. The death of the duke of Orléans. In the year of the Lord 1407 and the seventh year of King Henry IV, the duke of Orléans, who was greatly hated in France [but] could not be killed because of the great throng that always accompanied him when he travelled, was therefore killed in the city of Paris, where he went about sparsely attended as if safe, in the following manner: late at night, one of his enemies set fire to a certain house, while his companions murdered the duke and quickly rushed out, shouting: 'Go to the fire, to the fire!'. The duke's household cried 'Treason, treason!', but the people went towards the fire. The king of France was greatly disturbed by this, and all his council along with him, wondering who had done it. The duke of Burgundy said: 'Promise me you will hold a council for three days, and I will tell you who did it'; and they promised. Whereupon he admitted that this deed had been done with his knowledge. Then they excluded him from

---

[337] The commons only agreed to grant taxation at the end of parliament, on 17 Dec. (*PROME*, viii. 322–3).

[338] Savona is in Liguria, about 40 miles west of Genoa; the rival popes agreed to meet there on 29 Sept. 1407 (J. H. Smith, *The Great Schism* (London, 1970), p. 167; for the letters between the rival popes, see *SAC* II, pp. 500–16). The visit of the Franciscan minister-general, Antonio de Pereto, was mainly connected with the dispute within the English province described above, pp. 128–30.

regis Anglie; rex autem pro illo murdro contempsit eum. Rex uero Francie misit pro duce. Dux respondit quod non ueniret nisi approbaret mortem hominis morte dignissimi, quia fuit homo luxuriosissimus, iactans se uiolasse uxores multorum dominorum et nobilium Francie [et] reginam, et totam prolem regiam suam esse affirmauit. Et minabatur consiliariis regis, si contrarium consulerent, quod morerentur.[339] Hoc anno fuit magna pestilentia in Anglia, maxime in partibus occiduis.[340] Papa Gregorius, propter clamorem cardinalium, fingens se transiturum ad resignandum, promisit regi Neapolitano quod faceret ipsum imperatorem | si ipse interim Romam custodiret ad papatum suum contra alium eligendum.[341] Hoc etiam anno domina Lucia, soror ducis Mediolani, uenit in Angliam et domino Edmundo Holand comiti Cancie matrimonialiter copulatur.[342] Hoc insuper anno obiit nobilis ille miles Robertus Knollys, qui Londoniis apud Carmelitas fratres honorifice sepelitur.[343]

fo. 206ᵛ

Rex itaque per magnum tempus non soluerat soldariis custodibus Calesie sua uadia, quare ipsi detinuerunt lanas mercatorum que fuerunt ibidem; unde mercatores conquesti sunt regi, et rex petiit ut mutuarent sibi pecunias. Mercatores autem se excusabant. 'Vos habetis aurum', dixit rex, 'et ego uolo habere aurum. Vbi est?' Tandem post longam moram mercatores concesserunt sibi aurum ea conditione, quod cancellarius, archiepiscopus Cantuariensis, et dux Eboracensis manucaperent pro resolutione; quod et factum est.[344] Tunc proceres Scotorum deduxerunt comitem Northumbrie et dominum Bardolf ac abbatem de Hayles usque ad aquam Twede, dicentes eis: 'Iam procedatis. Vos habetis Angliam uobiscum.' Qui uenerunt cum parua comitiua usque

---

[339] Louis, duke of Orléans, was murdered near the Porte Barbette in Paris by agents of John the Fearless, duke of Burgundy, on the night of 23 Nov. 1407. He was only accompanied by about six valets when he was set upon by some eighteen assassins; the 'certain house' to which they set fire was the one in which they had been staying for the past few weeks. Burgundy admitted his involvement on 25 Nov. and was refused admission to the royal council on the following day. He fled to Flanders, but four months later returned to Paris and presented an elaborate justification for the murder, based in part on Louis's immorality. Rumours circulated in France about his involvement with Queen Isabeau (F. Lehoux, *Jean de France, duc de Berri: Sa vie, son action politique* (3 vols., Paris, 1966–8), iii. 106–7; R. Vaughan, *John the Fearless* (London, 1966), pp. 66–102).

[340] The plague of 1407 was not restricted to the west of England; it forced the closure of the London law courts from 24 Oct. 1407 to 20 Jan. 1408 (*SAC* II, pp. 500–1).

[341] Ladislas of Durazzo, king of Naples from 1386 to 1414, dominated central Italian politics at this time, acting at different times as protector and adversary of the Roman popes. For his attacks on Rome in 1407–8 and a colourful account of his death in 1414, see *SAC* II, pp. 516–19, 534–5, 642–3.

the council. So he went to Flanders and Germany, collecting a large army. He also appealed for help from the king of England, but the king despised him for this murder. Then the king of France sent for the duke; the duke answered that he would not come unless [the king] would agree to endorse the death of a man who very much deserved to be killed, for he was the most licentious of men, bragging about how he had dishonoured the wives of numerous lords and nobles [and] the queen of France; and he claimed that all the royal offspring were his. He also threatened the king's councillors that if they went against his wishes they would die.[339] There was a great plague in England this year, especially in the western parts.[340] Pope Gregory, at the insistence of the cardinals, pretending that he was going forth to resign, promised the king of Naples that he would make him emperor, if in the meantime he would defend Rome for his papacy against any other person who was elected.[341] Also in this year, Lady Lucia, sister of the duke of Milan, came to England and was joined in marriage to Lord Edmund Holand, earl of Kent.[342] In this year, moreover, that noble knight Robert Knolles died, and he was buried with honour at the Carmelite friars in London.[343]

For a long time, the king had not paid the wages of the soldiers who guarded Calais, as a result of which they seized the wool of the merchants which was there; the merchants therefore complained to the king, and the king asked them to loan him some money. However, the merchants declined. 'You have money', said the king, 'and I want money. Where is it?' Eventually, after a long delay, the merchants granted him money on this condition, that the chancellor, the archbishop of Canterbury, and the duke of York would act as guarantors for its repayment; which was done.[344] Then the Scottish leaders brought the earl of Northumberland and Lord Bardolf and the abbot of Hailes as far as the river Tweed, saying to them: 'Go forward from here; you have England with you.' And they came with a small retinue as far as

---

[342] Lucia Visconti married Holand and became countess of Kent on 24 Jan. 1407 in London (Given-Wilson, *Henry IV*, p. 302).
[343] Knolles, a Cheshireman and one of England's most famous war-captains, died on 15 Aug. 1407.
[344] For the 1407 crisis at Calais, where arrears of wages amounted to some £30,000, see D. Grummitt, 'The financial administration of Calais during the reign of Henry IV, 1399–1413', *EHR* cxiii (1998), 277–99.

ad Tadcastre, et uicecomes Eborum uenit cum exercitu et trucidauit eos; capita eorum posita [sunt] super pontem Londoniensem. 1408.[z][345]

1408. Anno Domini millesimo quadringentesimo octauo et anno regis Henrici quarti octauo, Gregorius papa descendebat de partibus Romanis cum cardinalibus ut de unione ecclesie tractaret et resignaret. Interim rex Neapolitanus uenit cum exercitu ad Romam et partem eius cepit et spoliauit. Quod audiens, Gregorius, cum uenisset ad ciuitatem Lucanam, nec procedere[a] uoluit ad locum assignatum nec resignare, dicens tempus non esse congruum nec locum esse tutum; sed redire intendebat. Vndecim igitur cardinales dicebant eum periurum et recesserunt ab eo in ciuitatem Pisanam.[346] Ipse autem excommunicauit eos ac omni dignitate, officio et beneficio priuauit, aliosque cardinales creauit; ipsi uero appellabant a papa Gregorio male informato ad eundem melius informandum; appellabant etiam ad consilium generale, appellabant insuper ad Summum Iudicem, Christum Iesum.[347] Et custodire fecerunt uias ne se posset a ciuitate Lucana mouere nec alicubi litteras mittere. Alter uero papa, expulsus de dominio Francie, transiit in Arrogoniam, patriam suam, et nouem cardinales sui transierunt ad Pisam et iunxerunt se ibi cardinalibus Romanis.[348] Alii uero undecim cardinales scripserunt regibus et pontificis ac ecclesie prelatis, petentes ipsorum [consensum][b] et auxilium contra Gregorium periurum.[349] Archiepiscopus uero Cantuariensis conuocauit clerum exemptum et non exemptum, exceptis mendicantibus, ad Oxoniam, in qua conuocatione fuit rex; ubi clauserunt manus suas, uidelicet papales, ut non posset aliquod beneficium dare in Anglia nec aliquid ab Anglia recipere; ordinantes insuper quod omnia que sunt debita camere pape seruabuntur in Anglia quousque fuerit unum tantummodo caput in ecclesia Domini.[350] Post paucos uero dies cardinalis uenit in Angliam, Franciscus

---

[z] *inserted in text, rubricated* [a] procede *MS* [b] *some such word seems to have been omitted here*

[345] The last invasion of Northumberland and Bardolf was abruptly halted on 19 Feb. 1408 at Bramham Moor near Tadcaster, where the sheriff, Thomas Rokeby, leading a local force, overwhelmed them; their heads were sent to Henry IV at Stony Stratford (Northamptonshire), then despatched to London for impalement on the bridge. The abbot of Hailes (Gloucestershire) was probably Henry Alcester, whose arrest as a fugitive from his house was ordered on 20 Nov. 1403; he was said to have been taken in arms at Bramham Moor (*CPR 1401–5*, p. 359). For a detailed account of the battle, see *SAC* II, pp. 530–4. It is not clear why '1408' has been inserted in the text as well as the margin.

[346] These events took place in late Apr.–early May 1408, when Gregory XII was at Lucca. For a detailed, hostile account of Gregory's behaviour at Lucca, see the speech made by Cardinal-archbishop Francesco Uguccione of Bordeaux to the meeting of lords and prelates

Tadcaster [Yorkshire], and the sheriff of York arrived with an army and killed them; their heads were placed on top of London bridge. 1408.[345]

1408. In the year of the Lord 1408 and the eighth year of King Henry IV, Pope Gregory departed from the region of Rome with the cardinals so that he could treat for the union of the Church and resign. Meanwhile, the king of Naples approached Rome with an army and seized and plundered part of it. Hearing this, when Gregory arrived at the city of Lucca, he said that he would neither proceed to the designated place nor resign, declaring that the time was not propitious nor the place safe; but that he planned to return. Eleven cardinals therefore declared him to be a perjurer and departed from him to the city of Pisa.[346] Whereupon he excommunicated them and deprived them of every honour, office, and benefice, and created other cardinals; they therefore appealed from the badly informed Pope Gregory to a better-informed one; they also appealed to a general council and, moreover, they appealed to the Supreme Judge, Jesus Christ.[347] And they made sure to guard the roads so that he could not move from the city of Lucca nor send letters anywhere. Meanwhile the other pope, having been expelled from the kingdom of France, went to Aragon, his homeland, while nine of his cardinals travelled to Pisa and joined up with the Roman cardinals there.[348] And the other eleven cardinals mentioned above wrote to kings and bishops and prelates of the Church asking for their advice and support against the perjured Gregory.[349] The archbishop of Canterbury therefore summoned the clergy, both exempt and non-exempt, apart from the mendicants, to Oxford, where the king attended the convocation; and here they tied his (that is, the pope's) hands, so that he could not grant out any benefice in England, nor receive anything from England; and they ordained also that everything that was owed to the papal chamber should be retained in England until such time as there would be only one head of the Lord's Church.[350] Then, after a few days, a cardinal came to England, Francesco,

---

at Westminster on 28–9 Oct. in *SAC* II, pp. 540–56; see also Smith, *The Great Schism*, pp. 169–70.

[347] This is quoting from the cardinals' letter: Smith, *The Great Schism*, p. 170.

[348] The Avignonese 'antipope' was the Aragonese Pedro de Luna, Benedict XIII; the French withdrew support from him in 1398, restored their allegiance to him in 1403, but withdrew it again in 1408. From 1408 to his death in 1423 he lived first at Perpignan, then at Peñiscola.

[349] In particular, the disaffected cardinals invited lords and prelates throughout Europe to attend the general council they had summoned to meet at Pisa on 25 Mar. 1409.

[350] In other words, convocation placed a restriction on papal patronage in England until the Schism was resolved: see *SAC* II, p. 536.

archiepiscopus Burdigalensis, pro pace tractaturus.[351] Clerus hoc anno ibidem statuit quod nullus curatus admitteret aliquem secularem sacerdotem uel religiosum ad predicandum in ecclesia sua sub pena excommunicationis et priuationis, nisi ostenderet litteras licentiales episcopi eiusdem diocesis aut archiepiscopi Cantuariensis, quas litteras, si quis habere uellet, presentaret se episcopo illius diocesis ubi predicare intendebat, et licentiam peteret et sine pecunia acciperet. Hoc autem statutum erat ordinatum contra Lollardos et limitatores illitteratos ac fratres uitiosos.[352]

Sedente uero rege in throno suo coronatus apud Westmonasterium, intrauit cardinalis supradictus Burdigalis, qui in introitu deposuit capellam*c* suum, et procedens ad medium aule deposuit capicium suum,*d* et, appropinquans regi, deposuit medietatem capicii sui, se inclinans.*e* [353] Rex autem surrexit et cepit manum eius et osculatus est eum. Post paucos uero dies conuocauit concilium episcoporum Anglie, Scotie et Hybernie, et clerum; in presentia regis faciens collationem, accepit pro themate*f* 'Verbum ad te, o principe',*f* [354] et notabiliter causam ecclesie perorauit. Cui conclusionaliter responsum est quod Anglici promiserunt suam assistentiam ecclesie Romane ad eius unionem, et tam ire quam mittere ad concilium generale.[355] Verumtamen post paucos dies papa euasit de ciuitate Lucana, scribens regi Anglie, archiepiscopo Cantuariensi et duci Eborum quod uerbis illius qui uenerat tanquam cardinalis fidem non darent, et de calumnia sibi imposita prout potuit se excusare nitebatur. Et uenit ad Cenas, faciens cardinales, quorum unus erat de ordine fratrum predicatorum.[356]

fo. 207*r*   Hoc anno, comes | Cancie, dominus Edmundus Holand, admirallus maris Anglicani, in obsidione castri de Briat in Britannia, occisus est.[357] Hoc insuper anno fuit magnum gelu in Anglia, quod durauit per quindecim septimanas.[358] Aque insuper fluminum in partibus borialibus

---

c capellum MS   *d* sue MS   *e* marginal in later hand: nota   *f-f* underlined

[351] The chronicler appears here to conflate at least two meetings. Canterbury convocation met at Oxford on 28 Nov. 1407, while the king was holding a parliament at Gloucester, and again at St Paul's from 23 to 28 July 1408, where it decided to withhold the payment of annates to the papal chamber. On 28 Oct. 1408 a meeting of lords and prelates was held at Westminster, attended by the king and addressed by Cardinal-archbishop Francesco Uggucione of Bordeaux, who urged the English to send a delegation to the council summoned to meet at Pisa (*SAC* II, pp. 538–64).

[352] 'Limiters' were friars given the task of going around the houses in their region to collect gifts (Moorman, *Franciscans in England*, p. 35).

[353] The zucchetto (skullcap), as distinct from the biretta.

[354] 2 Kgs. (2 Sam.) 9: 5.

archbishop of Bordeaux, in order to treat for peace.[351] In this year the clergy decreed there that no curate should allow any secular priest or member of a religious order to preach in his church, under pain of excommunication and deprivation, unless he was able to produce authorizing letters from the bishop of that diocese or from the archbishop of Canterbury, and if anyone wished to acquire such letters, he must present himself to the bishop of that diocese where he intended to preach and request a licence, which he would receive without payment. And this statute was directed against the Lollards and illiterate limiters and malicious friars.[352]

Then, with the king crowned and sitting on his throne at Westminster, the aforesaid cardinal of Bordeaux entered, and upon entering he removed his cape; then, advancing to the middle of the hall, he removed his hat, and, approaching the king and bowing, he removed the middle part of his hat.[353] The king therefore rose and took his hand and kissed him. Then, a few days later, he summoned a council of the bishops of England, Scotland, and Ireland, and the clergy; and in the king's presence he delivered a sermon, taking as his theme 'O prince, the word is for you',[354] and he gave a memorable summation on the subject of the Church. And when he had finished, the reply given to him was that the English promised their assistance to the Roman Church, to unify it, and that they would both go and send [a delegation] to the general council.[355] Some days later, however, the pope escaped from the city of Lucca and wrote to the king of England, the archbishop of Canterbury, and the duke of York saying that they should put no trust in the words of that person who had arrived in the guise of a cardinal, and that he would do all that he could to excuse himself from the falsehoods imputed to him. Whereupon he went to Siena and created cardinals, one of whom was from the order of friars preachers.[356]

In this year, the earl of Kent, Lord Edmund Holand, admiral of the English sea, was killed while besieging the castle of Bréhat in Brittany.[357] Also in this year there was a great frost in England which lasted for fifteen weeks.[358] At the beginning of September, the rivers in the northern

---

[355] This assembly of lords and prelates was held at Westminster on 28–9 October 1408; for Ugguccione's speech, see *SAC* II, pp. 538–56.
[356] Gregory created ten new cardinals at Siena in September 1408 (Smith, *The Great Schism*, pp. 170–1).
[357] Holand was killed during a raid on the island of Bréhat, off the Breton coast, on 15 Sept. 1408.
[358] The harsh winter of 1407–8 lasted from December to March (*SAC* II, p. 530).

Anglie uehementer inundauerunt super terram in principio Septembris, et in nocte Natiuitatis Beate Marie tantus impetus aque descendit de montibus in uillam de Ware ut domos prosternebat, et homines pre timore clamauerunt per totam uillam, credentes se submergi. Et conuentus fratrum minorum ibidem ita replebatur aqua ut ea die nec missa aut officium diuinum ibidem diceretur.[359] Hoc anno dux Burgundie cum magno exercitu reuertebatur in Franciam, et rex Francie recessit a ciuitate Parisiensi; que quidam ciuitas, apertis portis, ducem cum exercitu cum gaudio recepit.[360] Hoc insuper anno, transfretauerunt uersus concilium generale episcopus Sarum, Robertus Halum, episcopus Sancti Dauid, abbas monasterii Sancte Marie de Eborum [et] prior ecclesie Cantuariensis, quorum quilibet habebat a clero Anglie mille marcas, ut dicebatur, pro expensis.[361]

1409. Anno Domini millesimo quadringentesimo nono et anno regni regis Henrici quarti nono, conuenit concilium generale apud Pisam in festo Annunciationis Beate Marie; quod postea translatum est ad Constanciam.[362] Transfretauit insuper ad concilium generale episcopus Dunelmie cum magno apparatu. Item, comes de Dunbar, factus Anglicus et comes Richmundie, ut predicitur, fugiit iterum in Scotiam, dicens quod ipse finxit se Anglicum ut comitem Northumbrie, Henricum Percy, et alios inimicos regni Scotie occidi procuraret uel destrui.[363] Hoc etiam anno, domini apud concilium in Pisa probabant papas periuros, hereticos et scismaticos, et eos recusabant. Gregorius uero stipatus cognatione sua et aliis armatis, in quodam castro iuxta Venetias se tenebat, dicens se periurum non esse, quia de plenitudine potestatis apostolice absoluit seipsum ab illo iuramento, et alteri similiter commisit potestatem sufficientem ut ipsum absolueret; consimiliter et alter in Arrogonia dicebat, qui tamen misit ambaxiatores ad concilium, dicens quod si concilium statueretur in alio loco ipse ueniret et resignaret. Concilium autem respondit se resignatione non indigere, remittens nuntios uacuos.[364]

---

[359] Ware was on the River Lea.

[360] John of Burgundy re-entered Paris in triumph on 28 February 1408; Queen Isabeau and the Dauphin left the city two weeks later, but King Charles VI remained there (J. Sumption, *Cursed Kings: The Hundred Years War*, iv (London, 2015), pp. 241–5).

[361] Robert Hallum, bishop of Salisbury, was the leader of the English delegation to Pisa; his chief companions were Henry Chichele, bishop of St David's; Thomas Spofforth, abbot of St Mary's, York; Thomas Chillenden, prior of Canterbury; and Thomas Langley, bishop of Durham, noted below by the chronicler. For the English delegation as a whole, and the delegates' expenses, see M. Harvey, *Solutions to the Schism* (St Ottilien, 1983), pp. 151–9.

[362] The Council of Constance, which finally ended the Schism, opened in November 1414.

parts of England violently burst their banks and flooded the land; and on the eve of the Nativity of the Blessed Mary [8 September], such a flood of water came down from the mountains into the town of Ware [Hertfordshire] that houses were flattened, and men cried out in fear throughout the town, thinking they would be submerged. And the convent of the friars minor there was so inundated with water that neither mass nor the divine office was said there that day.[359] In this year, the duke of Burgundy returned to France with a large army, and the king of France withdrew from the city of Paris; whereupon that city, opening its gates, joyfully welcomed the duke.[360] In this year, moreover, the bishop of Salisbury, Robert Hallum, the bishop of St David's, the abbot of the monastery of St Mary in York, [and] the prior of the church of Canterbury went abroad to the general council, and it was said that each of them received a thousand marks from the English clergy for their expenses.[361]

1409. In the year of the Lord 1409 and the ninth year of the reign of King Henry IV, the general council met at Pisa on the feast of the Annunciation of the Blessed Mary [25 March]; later it was transferred to Constance.[362] The bishop of Durham went across to the council as well, with a great deal of equipment. Also, the earl of Dunbar, who, as noted above, had declared for the English and become earl of Richmond, fled once more to Scotland, saying that he had pretended to be English in order to ensure that the earl of Northumberland, Henry Percy, and other enemies of the kingdom of Scotland were either killed or ruined.[363] Also in this year, the lords at the council in Pisa declared the popes to be perjurers, heretics, and schismatics, and rejected them. However, Gregory, accompanied by his kinsmen and other armed men, took refuge in a certain castle near Venice, declaring that he was not a perjurer since through the plenitude of his papal power he had absolved himself from that oath, and he granted the other [pope] sufficient power so that he could similarly absolve himself; and the other one, in Aragon, did the same, although he sent ambassadors to the council declaring that if the council was held in a different place he would come and resign. However, the council replied that it did not need a resignation, sending the messengers back empty-handed.[364]

---

[363] For George Dunbar, earl of March, see above, p. 100. He returned to Scotland in 1409, having spent nine years allied to England, although there is no record of him being made earl of Richmond (Given-Wilson, *Henry IV*, pp. 322–3).

[364] The Council of Pisa deposed both Gregory XII and Benedict XIII on 5 June 1409; Gregory had left for Rimini, in the Romagna, the previous autumn (Smith, *The Great Schism*, pp. 171–5).

Cardinales intrauerunt conclauem palatii et per scrutinium ibidem undecim diebus permanentes in electione et artati concordare non ualebant. Tandem in festo Sanctorum Johannis et Pauli unus prudens cardinalis antiquus, ante scisma ordinatus, surrexit, dicens: 'Italici nolunt Gallicum, Gallici nolunt Romanum nec Italicum eligere, ergo eligamus unum indifferentem. Hic est unus ualentissimus clericus qui plus egit in hoc concilio sua sapientia quam omnes nos: Petrus de Candia, frater minor, cardinalis et archiepiscopus Mediolanensis, qui prius fuit episcopus Pisanus, sollemnis et nominatissimus doctor in theologia, sicut satis ostendunt facta sua. Pro Deo eligamus illum. Ego uero eligo ipsum. Quid dicitis uos, patres?' Qui omnes singillatim assenserunt. Qui sic electus, ductus fuit in ecclesiam et in Translatione Sancti Thome sollemniter coronatus.[365] Hoc tempore dux Andigauie, qui et dux Prouencie fuit, supplicabat pape ut daret sibi regnum Cisilie et Neapolitanum, quod olim antecessor suus possedit, et ipse regem Neapoli expugnaret. Et papa concessit, ita ut regnum ipsum, quod speciale patrimonium Beati Petri esse dinoscitur, ab eo teneret, soluendo annuum redditum consuetum.[366] Iste papa uocatus est Alexander quintus; hic autem fuerat studens Northwici et Oxonie, eratque iocundus uir et eloquens in Latina lingua et Greca, in qua natus et nutritus fuit. Frater autem minor quidam legebat euangelium in Greco in die coronationis sue. Auditaque electione predicta, rex Francie et omnis ciuitas Parisius sollemnes processiones faciebant, et similiter alie ciuitates. In Anglia uero non ita cito fecerunt, sed plurimi murmurabant. Quidam de Anglia intendebant proposuisse in hoc concilio quod capitulum Dudum foret reuocatum, sed uisa fratris electione tacebant.[367] Papa, receptis obedientiis prelatorum et homagiis temporalium dominorum de papatu tenentium, in dignitate papali plenarie confirmatus, in presentia omnium dixit: 'Dolemus de istis duobus contendentibus pro papatu. Dicunt quod iam est error peior priore, quia prius fuerunt duo pape, modo sunt tres. Veniant ad nos, et non erit error. Veniant et resignent, et nos prius resignabimus, et alius eligatur.'

---

[365] These dates are too late: conclave met at Pisa from 15 June, and Peter of Candia was elected and crowned on 26 June. He was Peter Philargi, born on Crete (Candia) in 1339; he became a Franciscan and studied law at Padua and Paris as well as in England. He had been archbishop of Milan since 1402 and a cardinal since 1405 (Smith, *The Great Schism*, p. 176).

[366] Louis II, son of Louis I of Anjou, became count of Provence in 1387 and had been crowned king of Naples in 1389, but he was expelled in 1399. His claim was recognized by Alexander V in July 1409, and he defeated his rival, Ladislas, at the battle of Roccasecca in May 1411, but was driven out again a few months later and soon returned to Provence (Smith, *The Great Schism*, pp. 178–9).

The cardinals entered the chamber of the palace, remained there closely confined for eleven days throughout the election, and were unable to come to an agreement. At length, on the feast of SS John and Paul [26 June], an old and wise cardinal who had been ordained before the schism rose and said: 'The Italians do not want to elect a Frenchman, the French do not want a Roman or an Italian, therefore let us elect someone who is neutral. Here is Peter of Candia, a friar minor, cardinal-archbishop of Milan, formerly bishop of Pisa, an established and renowned doctor of theology, a most vigorous cleric who, through his wisdom, has achieved more in this council than all of us, as has been amply demonstrated by his deeds. For God's sake, let us elect him. I certainly choose him. What do you say, fathers?' Whereupon they unanimously agreed. And he, having been elected, was led to the church and, on the feast of the Translation of St Thomas [3 July], solemnly crowned.[365] At this time the duke of Anjou, who was also duke of Provence, begged the pope to give him the kingdom of Sicily and Naples, which an ancestor of his once possessed, and he would wage war on the king of Naples. And the pope granted it, on condition that he would hold that kingdom from him, paying the customary annual rent, since it was known to belong to the special patrimony of St Peter.[366] This pope was called Alexander V. He had been a student at Norwich and Oxford, and was an agreeable man and well-versed in the Latin language and in Greek, his language of birth and childhood. And a friar minor read the gospel in Greek on the day of his coronation. Hearing of this election, the king of France and the entire city of Paris organized solemn processions, as did other towns. In England, however, they did not do this straight away; instead many people grumbled. Some of the English planned to have proposed in this council that the article 'Dudum' should be revoked, but when they saw that a friar was elected they kept quiet.[367] The pope, having received the obedience of the prelates and the homage of those temporal lords who held from the papacy, and been more fully confirmed in the papal dignity, said in the presence of all: 'We grieve for these two contenders for the papacy. They say that now the error is worse than it was before, because formerly there were two popes, now there are three. Let them come to us, and there will be no error. Let them come and resign, and we will be the first to resign, and let another be elected.'

---

[367] The bull known as Dudum granted friars the right to hear confessions with the same powers as parish priests, a controversial privilege frequently criticized in anti-fraternal literature (Harvey, *Solutions to the Schism*, p. 175).

fo. 207ᵛ | Hoc anno sanguis uisus est ebullire de fontibus in diuersis partibus Anglie, et consequenter de dissinteria multi moriebantur. Papa remisit omnia arreragia debita Curie Romane ab initio Curie usque ad electionem suam. Quidam autem frater minor uenit ad papam petens ab eo episcopatum in Hibernia; cui papa dixit: 'Vade ad illam ecclesiam et seruias illi, ut ipsi ibidem te petant in episcopum, et cum electus fueris nos confirmabimus tuam electionem.' Episcopus Sarum, rediens de consilio, narrauit regi acta concilii, modum electionis, commendans personam electi, et quomodo rex Francie et ciuitates ultramarine sollemnes processiones fecerunt laudantes Dominum pro ecclesie unitate. Et, de mandato regis, archiepiscopus Cantuariensis conuocauit processionem magnam Londoniis feria sexta sequenti, et factus est sermo in Cruce Sancti Pauli ubi narrata sunt omnia predicta, et intrantes post sermonem in ecclesiam Sancti Pauli cantauerunt sollemniter ymnum *g*'Te Deum Laudamus'.*g* Vbi insuper archiepiscopus concessit omnibus presentibus quadraginta dies indulgentie, et similiter episcopi qui ibi fuerunt totidem concesserunt. Misitque archiepiscopus omnibus suffraganiis suis hec consimiliter in suis ecclesiis facere; deinde nuntiata fuerunt hec, ut predictum est.[368] Dux Prouincie et dominus Balthasar, antipapa et cardinalis Bononie, cum grandi exercitu contra regem Neapolitanum ascenderunt.[369]

Hoc tempore factum est parliamentum Londonie post festum Sancti Hillarii, in quo rex dixit cistas suas fore uacuas et se grauiter indebitatum, petens decimam et dimidiam a clero et quintamdecimam et dimidiam laicorum; durauitque parliamentum usque ad Pascha, et nihil actum est tunc.[370] In hoc parliamento combustus fuit hereticus laicus qui dicebat quod corpus Christi non erat in altari, sed panis benedictus tantum. Et cum quereretur ab eo coram rege et parliamento quid dixisset si fuisset cum Christo in cena quando Christus dixit 'Hoc est corpus meum',[371] respondit: 'Dixissem quod Ipse dicit falsum.' Et cum insipienter uerba ad sui defensionem multiplicaret, uisa est quadam aranea horribilis repere super labia sua; quam, cum quidam amouere uoluisset, dixit archiepiscopus Cantuariensis: 'Sine! Nunc uidebimus quis eum docet loqui.' Qui, cum comburi cepisset, clamauit,

g-g underlined

[368] Robert Hallum returned to England in Oct. 1409, following which Henry IV announced his decision to recognize Alexander and ordered processions to be held (Harvey, *Solutions to the Schism*, pp. 181–3).

[369] This is Baldassare Cossa, who became the 'antipope' John XXIII. He was one of the cardinals who had deserted Gregory in May 1408. Cossa was not elected until 25 May 1410, after Alexander's death. Louis II and Cossa allied against Ladislas of Durazzo in 1409.

In this year blood could be seen bubbling up from springs in various parts of England, following which many people died of dysentery. The pope remitted all the arrears owed to the Roman Curia since the inception of the Curia until the time of his election. A certain friar minor went to the pope to ask him for a bishopric in Ireland; the pope told him: 'Go to that church and serve it, so that the people there ask for you as their bishop, and when you have been elected we shall confirm your election.' On his return from the council, the bishop of Salisbury told the king about the acts of the council [and] the circumstances of the election, praising the person elected, and describing how the king of France and towns overseas had held solemn processions giving praise to the Lord for unity in the Church. Whereupon, on the king's order, the archbishop of Canterbury organized a great procession in London on the following Friday, and a sermon was given at St Paul's Cross where all the aforesaid matters were recounted, and after the sermon they entered St Paul's church and solemnly sang the hymn *Te Deum laudamus*. Here too the archbishop granted to all those present forty days of indulgence, and the bishops who were there likewise granted an equivalent number. The archbishop also sent to all his suffragans to do likewise in their churches; whereupon word of these events was spread, as noted above.[368] The duke of Provence and Balthasar, antipope and cardinal of Bologna, campaigned against the king of Naples with a great army.[369]

At this time, after the feast of St Hilary [13 January], a parliament was held in London, in which the king declared that his coffers were empty and he owed great sums, and he asked for one and a half tenths from the clergy and one and a half fifteenths from the laity; and the parliament lasted until Easter, and nothing was achieved there.[370] In this parliament a lay heretic who said that it was not the body of Christ that was present on the altar, but only bread that had been blessed, was burned. And when he was asked in the presence of the king and parliament what he would have said if he had been there with Christ at the Lord's Supper, when Christ said 'This is my body',[371] he replied: 'I would have said that He spoke falsely.' And after he had said many other foolish things in his defence, a revolting spider was seen crawling across his lips; and when someone tried to remove it, the archbishop of Canterbury said: 'Leave it! Now we shall see who is teaching him to

---

[370] Parliament met on 27 January 1410 at Westminster, was prorogued on 15 March, reconvened on 7 April and was dissolved on 9 May (*PROME*, viii. 449–510). A subsidy was granted at the end of the second session (below, p. 152).
[371] Matt. 26: 26; Mark 14: 22; Luke 22: 19.

dicens 'Miseremini mei', et, quam cito potuerunt, absoluerunt eum, extrahentes eum de igne. Et uenerunt ad ipsum episcopi cum sollemnitate decenti portantes corpus Christi, et querebant si crederet ibi esse corpus Christi. Respondit quod non, et iterum composuerunt ignem et ipsum intromiserunt. Clamauitque sicut prius, tamen noluit fateri ibi esse corpus Christi. Tunc totaliter combustus fuit, et ad ignem sempiternum transiit.[372] In hoc parliamento statutum fuit quod fratres quattuor ordinum libere predicarent contra hereses Lollardorum per totum regnum, sine prohibitione episcoporum, non obstante statuto quocunque edito in contrarium in conuocatione cleri uel parliamento.[373]

1410. Anno Domini millesimo quadringentesimo decimo et regni Henrici quarti decimo, statim post Annunciationem uenit in Angliam magister Hospitalariorum generalis cum turba militum et familia copiosa, missus a papa ad reges Anglie et Francie;[374] per quem hortatur eos papa ut tractent de pace, et promittit se cum omnibus cardinalibus tractatui interesse. Et resumptum fuit parliamentum, in quo rex exegit decimam et dimidiam decime a clero et quintamdecimam cum dimidia laicorum.[375] Item statutum fuit quod omnes curati manerent in ecclesiis suis hospitalitatem tenentes; quare multi recesserunt de curia regis, domibus episcoporum et aliorum dominorum et de mansionibus suis apud Londoniam. Eodem anno, dux Burgundie fecerat quoddam castellum ligneum ualde magnum, cum multis gunnis et pulueribus pertinentibus, cogitans hoc anno obsidere Calesiam cum magno apparatu, in Sancto Audomaro. Sed, unus de eadem uilla accepto auro a Calesianis, apposuerunt ignem per noctem, et dictum castellum combustum fuit totaliter; et sic propositum ducis impeditum fuit. Unus incendiariorum captus fuit et amara morte occisus; et dixit moriens quod hoc fecit ne sanguis humanus effunderetur. Item dicebatur quod abbatia Sancti Bertini de igne ipsius Castelli combusta[h] fuit.[376]

---

[h] combustum *MS*

[372] The heretic was John Badby, a tailor from Evesham (Worcestershire), the second and last heretic to be burned during Henry IV's reign; for his trial, see McNiven, *Heresy and Politics*, pp. 199–219. The devil was sometimes compared to a spider in the way he set traps for the unwitting.

[373] This is not recorded on the official roll of the parliament.

[374] Philibert de Naillac, grand master of the Hospitallers 1396–1421, arrived in England in late Mar. or early Apr. 1410 (Harvey, *Solutions to the Schism*, pp. 185–6).

[375] For the grant of the subsidy in parliament, on 8 May, see *PROME*, viii. 482–3. Collection of the one and a half fifteenths was to be spread over two years from Nov. 1410.

speak.' And when he began to burn, he cried out: 'Have pity on me', and, as soon as they could, they set him free and pulled him out of the fire. Then the bishops approached him, carrying the body of Christ with proper decorum, and asked him if he believed that the body of Christ was present there. He replied that he did not, so they rekindled the fire and placed him in it. Whereupon he cried out as before, but he would not acknowledge that the body of Christ was present there. Thus was he completely incinerated, and passed over into eternal fire.[372] In this parliament it was decreed that the friars of the four orders might preach freely throughout the realm against the heresies of the Lollards, without any episcopal prohibition, notwithstanding any statute whatsoever issued to the contrary in either clerical convocation or parliament.[373]

1410. In the year of the Lord 1410 and the tenth year of Henry IV, the grand master of the Hospitallers arrived in England immediately after the Annunciation [25 March] with a large number of knights and a substantial household, having been sent by the pope to the kings of England and France;[374] through him, the pope exhorted them to treat for peace, and he promised that he and all the cardinals would attend the talks. And the parliament was continued, in which the king extracted one and a half tenths from the clergy and one and a half fifteenths from the laity.[375] Also, it was decreed that all curates should remain in their churches offering hospitality; whereupon many of them withdrew from the royal court, the houses of bishops and other lords, and their mansions in London. In the same year, the duke of Burgundy made a certain very large castle of wood, containing numerous guns and cannons, in Saint-Omer, planning to besiege Calais that year with a great deal of equipment. However, after someone from that town had been bribed by the men of Calais, they set fire to it by night, and the aforesaid castle was completely destroyed; thus was the duke's plan foiled. One of the arsonists was captured and put to a bitter death; and he said, as he was dying, that he had done it in order to avoid the shedding of human blood. It was also said that the abbey of Saint-Bertin was burned by the fire from this castle.[376]

Canterbury convocation granted one and a half tenths, and York convocation one tenth (Given-Wilson, *Henry IV*, p. 471).

[376] Duke John of Burgundy was certainly planning to attack Calais in the spring of 1410. For a more vivid account of his 'great machine', see *SAC* II, p. 592. Saint-Bertin was an ancient Benedictine abbey in Saint-Omer.

Antipapa Gregorius latenter fugiit in regnum Neapoli per mare Adriaticum, ibidem uocans se papam cum assistentia regis Karoli.[377] Tunc certi domini de Anglia transierunt mare ad tractandum de pace inter reges Anglie at Francie secundum monitionem pape.[378] Alexander papa quintus, cum sedisset mensibus decem, moritur Bononie,[379] longo et efficaci sermone exhor | tans circumsedentem cetum cardinalium ad diligendum unitatem ecclesie. Quo mortuo, eligitur Balthasar cardinalis Bononie, qui Iohannes uiginti tertius uocatus est; hic uir strenuus et auro abundans dicit se uelle Karolum et Gregorium omnino extinguere.[380] Alexander emiserat uiuens citationes prelatis ut conuenirent ad concilium generale post duos annos futurum, proponens in eo multa utilia statuisse; et si uixisset, pacem inter Christianos pro posse uoluit procurasse. Sepultus uero fuit apud fratres minores in Bononie.

1411. Anno Domini millesimo quadringentesimo undecimo regisque Henrici quarti undecimo, post festum Sancti Michaelis, Thamisia Londoniis fluxit et refluxit ter in die naturali, et capti fuerunt pisces in Thamisia magni et ignoti generis, qui uidebantur aliqua noua pronosticare. Hoc anno, dux Aurelianensis, adunatis sibi ducibus de Berry, de Burbon et Britannie, comite de Arminac et aliis magnatibus Francie australis, ducem Burgundie prosequitur in ultionem mortis patris sui cum magno exercitu, dicens quod rex Francie non facit sibi iustitiam. Dux autem, assistentia regis Francie et primogeniti sui, collegit nobiles multos et populum Francie borialis ac Flandrie et quosdam de Alemannia et Scotia,[381] misitque ad regem Anglie petens auxilium Anglicorum, promisitque dare filiam suam principi, primogenito suo, in uxorem. Missique sunt ad eum comites Arundellie et Kyme cum aliis nobilibus et exercitu decoro. Dux autem Aurelianensis uenit cum exercitu magno ad uillam uocatam Seynclo iuxta Parisius, ut ciuitatem et regem caperet ac ducem Burgundie et eius exercitum destrueret. Sed exercitus Anglicorum obuiabat sibi in Seynclo citius quam dux credebat, et multi de suo exercitu occisi sunt, et ipse dux cum ceteris fugiit.

---

[377] From this point onwards the chronicler refers consistently to Ladislas of Durazzo as Charles (his father's name). Ladislas remained Gregory's chief supporter from July 1409 until the summer of 1412, when he switched his support to Pope John XXIII, and it was his ship that carried Gregory to Gaeta (between Rome and Naples) in Sept. 1409 (Smith, *The Great Schism*, pp. 177–80, 185).

[378] For the English embassy to France in the spring of 1410, led by Bishop Henry Beaufort, and the renewal of the truce in June, see *Foedera*, viii. 637, 641–8.

[379] Alexander V died on 3 May 1410 at Bologna.

[380] For Baldassare Cossa, elected as Pope John XXIII on 25 May 1410, see above, p. 150 n. 369.

Gregory, the antipope, fled secretly to the kingdom of Naples via the Adriatic Sea, where, with the help of King Charles [*recte* Ladislas], he styled himself pope.[377] Then a number of English lords crossed the sea to treat for peace between the kings of England and France, in accordance with the pope's advice.[378] When Pope Alexander had been on the throne for ten months, he died at Bologna,[379] enjoining the college of cardinals seated around him in a lengthy and powerful sermon to cherish the unity of the Church. After his death, Balthasar, cardinal of Bologna, called John XXIII, was elected. A vigorous and wealthy man, he declared that he wanted to destroy utterly Charles [*recte* Ladislas] and Gregory.[380] While alive, Alexander had sent out summonses to the prelates to gather for a general council two years hence, planning to ordain many things of value there; and had he lived he would have tried everything in his power to make peace between Christians. And he was buried with the friars minor in Bologna.

1411. In the year of the Lord 1411 and the eleventh year of King Henry IV, following the feast of Michaelmas [29 September], the Thames in London rose and fell three times within the space of a day, and large fish of unknown species were caught in the Thames, which seemed to foretell something new. This year, the duke of Orléans, joined by the dukes of Berry, Bourbon, and Brittany, the count of Armagnac and other magnates of southern France, raised a large army to seek revenge against the duke of Burgundy for the death of his father, saying that the king of France was not treating him with justice. However, the duke [of Burgundy], with the help of the king of France and his eldest son, collected many nobles and people from northern France and Flanders, as well as some from Germany and Scotland.[381] He also sent to the king of England asking for English help, and promised his daughter in marriage to the prince, his eldest son. Whereupon the earls of Arundel and Kyme were sent to him, along with other nobles and a fine army. Then the duke of Orléans came with a large force to a town near Paris called Saint-Cloud, hoping to seize the city and the king and to destroy the duke of Burgundy and his army. However, the English army came up with him in Saint-Cloud sooner than the duke expected, and many in his army were killed, while the duke [of Orléans] himself and others fled. Then the English returned

---

[381] The Armagnac (or Orléanist)–Burgundian civil war broke out openly in the spring of 1411. The Armagnac party was now led by Charles, duke of Orléans, eldest son of the murdered Duke Louis; the eldest surviving son of Charles VI at this time was the Dauphin Louis, duke of Guyenne (d. 1415).

Et Anglici repatriabant cum magnis donis et gratiarum actionibus eis factis a rege Francie, primogenito suo et duce Burgundie.[382] Hoc anno factum est parliamentum Londoniis in quo rex habuit, a quolibet ualente expendere per annum uiginti libras, sex solidos et octo denarios.[383]

1412. Anno Domini millesimo quadringentesimo duodecimo et anno regis Henrici quarti duodecimo, dux Aurelianensis et ceteri duces de parte sua miserunt ad regem Anglie petentes auxilium ad uindicandum mortem patris sui; ipse <promisit>que[j] reddere regi totam Aquitanniam et ipsum <inseruire ut> hereditatem suam ibidem possideat. Dicebatque se habere filias honestas quas filiis regis daret, et firmam pacem inter Angliam et Franciam pro uiribus procuraret, salua fidelitate corone Francie debita.[384] Fecitque rex filium suum Thomam ducem Clarencie, quem, cum duce Eborum et aliis magnatibus ac uiginti milibus hominum, misit ad eos ut Aquitanniam in manus regis Anglie seisiret. Qui apud Hamptoniam prospere transierunt. Sed antequam transirent dicebatur dominos esse concordatos.[385] Hoc anno papa Iohannes uicesimus tertius misit quendam fratrem minorem, generalem ordinis, in Angliam, petens a rege ut filium suum Thomam mitteret ad Romam, ut capitaneus fiat exercitus papalis contra regem Neapoli et Gregorium antipapam; et ut sineret nuntium suum predicare cruciatam et pecunias colligere in regno suo, promittens indulgentiam omnibus conferentibus et adiuuantibus;[386] et dispensauit tum prefato Thoma, filio regis, ut duceret in uxorem uxorem patrui sui.[387] Rex breuiter respondebat quod noluit depauperare regnum suum propter papam, et quod oportebat ipsum mittere exercitum in Aquitanniam ad recuperandum hereditatem suam. Generalis tamen mansit in Anglia in expensis fratrum minorum ab Annunciatione usque ad Augustum, distribuens gratias suas et colligens pecunias.

---

[j] *the MS is damaged; interventions in brackets are conjectural*

---

[382] Burgundy and Orléans both sent envoys to Henry IV seeking English help in the spring of 1411; the decision to send a force under Thomas, earl of Arundel, and Sir Gilbert de Umfraville (who was popularly styled, though never created, earl of Kyme), was taken by Henry, prince of Wales, probably against the wishes of Henry IV (Given-Wilson, *Henry IV*, pp. 493–5). The engagement at Saint-Cloud, just outside Paris, was fought on 9 Nov. 1411 and is said to have resulted in between 600 and 900 Armagnac knights and esquires being killed.

[383] Parliament met at Westminster from 3 Nov. to 19 Dec. 1411 (*PROME*, viii. 511–58; for the grant of the subsidy, pp. 517–19).

[384] The decision to help the Armagnac party in 1412 was taken by the king, who had recovered control from Prince Henry in the 1411 parliament. The Treaty of Bourges between Henry IV and the Armagnac lords was concluded in London on 18 May 1412 (Given-Wilson, *Henry IV*, pp. 497–500).

home, after receiving many gifts and expressions of gratitude from the king of France, his eldest son, and the duke of Burgundy.[382] In this year a parliament was held in London in which the king received 6 shillings and 8 pence from every person capable of spending 20 pounds a year.[383]

1412. In the year of the Lord 1412 and the twelfth year of King Henry IV, the duke of Orléans and the other dukes on his side sent to the king of England asking for help to avenge the death of his father; and he promised to restore the whole of Aquitaine to the king and assist him so that he could possess his inheritance there. He also said that he had reputable daughters whom he would give to the king's sons, and that he would do his best to ensure that there was a firm peace between England and France, saving the fealty which he owed to the crown of France.[384] Whereupon the king made his son Thomas duke of Clarence and sent him to them, along with the duke of York and twenty thousand men, so that he could seize Aquitaine into the king's hands. Yet even before they departed, it was said that the lords had reached an agreement.[385] In this year, Pope John XXIII sent a certain friar minor, the minister-general of the order, to England, to ask the king if he might send his son Thomas to Rome to be captain of the papal army against the king of Naples and the antipope Gregory; also that he might allow his nuncio to preach the crusade and collect money in his kingdom, promising an indulgence to all those who contributed or assisted.[386] He also granted to the aforesaid Thomas, the king's son, a dispensation to marry the wife of his uncle.[387] The king replied briefly that he did not wish to deprive his own kingdom for the sake of the pope, and that he needed to send an army to Aquitaine to recover his inheritance. Nevertheless, the minister-general remained in England, at the expense of the friars minor, from the Annunciation [25 March] until August, distributing his indulgences and collecting money.

---

[385] Henry IV's second son Thomas was made duke of Clarence on 9 July 1412 and landed in Normandy with a 4,000-strong English force on about 10 Aug. The Burgundian and Armagnac lords had patched up their differences nearly a month before this, although it is not clear whether Clarence had heard this before he sailed.

[386] The minister-general of the Franciscans from 1410 to 1415 was Antonio da Cascia. John XXIII's planned crusade, for which he hoped to raise money through indulgences, was against Ladislas and Gregory XII (Smith, *The Great Schism*, p. 179).

[387] Margaret Holand was the wealthy widow of John Beaufort (d. March 1410) and plans for her to marry Clarence had been mooted since the autumn of 1410, but Bishop Henry Beaufort strongly opposed this and not until Nov. or Dec. 1411 was the marriage solemnized (Given-Wilson, *Henry IV*, pp. 469–70, 506).

CONTINUATIO EULOGII

Interim rex Neapoli et papa Gregorius submiserunt se pape Iohanni sub hac forma, quod ipse rex Karolus regnaret pro tempore uite sue, et quia heredes non habebat, Ludouicus, rex Cisilie, post eum regnaret; et antipapa factus est cardinalis et legatus pape in regno Neapolitano.[388]

1413. Anno Domini millesimo quadringentesimo tertio decimo et anno regis Henrici quarti tertio decimo, dominus Thomas, secundogenitus regis Henrici quarti, factus est dux Clarencie; qui cum magno exercitu, ut supradictum est, intrauit Franciam in adiutorium ducis Aurelianensis, qui guerram habuit contra ducem Burgundie; et cum ibidem uenisset, audiuit quod concordati fuerunt.[389] Sed dux Clarencie per uiam cuncta uastauit uersus Aquitanniam transeundo, et Burdegaliis hiemauit. Et tandem post Pascha rediit in Angliam cum exercitu satis paruo, sine honore. Eodem autem anno[j] | <dominus Thomas>[k] Beauford, dux Exonie, capitaneus transiit.[390] Eodem autem anno, facta fuit conuentio inter principem Henricum, primogenitum regis, Henricum episcopum Wintoniensem et alios, quasi omnes dominos Anglie, [quod quidam] ipsorum alloquerentur regem ut cederet coronam[l] Anglie et permitteret primogenitum suum coronari, pro eo quod erat ita horribiliter aspersus lepra.[m] Quo allocuto, ad consilium quorundam dominorum cedere noluit, sed statim equitauit per magnam partem Anglie, non obstante lepra supradicta.[391] Et, rediens Londoniis, apud Westmonasterium in domo abbatis, in quadam bassa camera que Ierusalem appellatur, mortuus est circiter festum Sancti Cuthberti, cum regnasset tertiis decimis annis et dimidio.[n] Apud Cantuariam sepultus est. Et Henricus primogenitus, princeps Wallie, dux Cornubie, comes Cestrie, natus apud Monnemouth in Wallia, uicesimo die Martii, Dominica in passione Domini, apud Westmonasterium coronatur.[o] [392]

fo. 208ᵛ

---

[j] Lylly *written twice at top of folio*   [k] *the MS is damaged; interventions in brackets are conjectural*   [l] corone *MS*   [m] *marginal in later hand*: lepra infectus   [n] *marginal in later hand*: camera Hierusalem   [o] *marginal in later hand*: Quintus Henricus regnat

---

[388] Following Ladislas's decision to switch his allegiance to John XXIII, in Oct. 1412, Gregory fled from Gaeta to Rimini, where he was protected by Carlo Malatesta, lord of Rimini; he did not finally renounce the papacy until 1415, at the Council of Constance, whereupon he was made a cardinal and papal legate in Ancona.

[389] This repeats information given above (see n. 385).

[390] Clarence arrived at Bordeaux on 11 Dec. 1412, having reached an agreement with the French at Buzançais on 14 Nov.; he returned to England before June 1413 to attend his father's memorial service and was replaced by Thomas Beaufort, earl of Dorset, who was

Meanwhile, the king of Naples and Pope Gregory submitted to Pope John, under this condition, that King Charles [*recte* Ladislas] himself would rule for the term of his life, whereupon, because he had no heirs, Louis, king of Sicily, would succeed him as king; and the antipope was created a cardinal and papal legate in the kingdom of Naples.[388]

1413. In the year of the Lord 1413 and the thirteenth year of King Henry IV, Lord Thomas, the second-born son of King Henry IV, was made duke of Clarence; whereupon, as stated above, he entered France with a large army in order to help the duke of Orléans, who was at war with the duke of Burgundy; and when he arrived there, he heard that they had made peace.[389] Nevertheless, on his way towards Aquitaine, he laid waste everything along the way, then spent the winter in Bordeaux. At length, after Easter, he returned to England with a rather small army, without honour. In the same year, however, Lord Thomas Beaufort, duke of Exeter, went over as captain.[390] In the same year, moreover, an agreement was made between Prince Henry, the king's first-born son, Henry, bishop of Winchester, and others, indeed almost all the lords of England, that some of them would speak to the king to ask him to resign the crown of England and allow his first-born son to be crowned, because he was so terribly afflicted with leprosy. When he had been spoken to, on the advice of various lords he refused to resign, instead setting out on a journey through much of England, notwithstanding the aforesaid leprosy.[391] Then, returning to London, he died around the feast of St Cuthbert [20 March], in the abbot's house at Westminster, in a certain low chamber known as Jerusalem, having reigned for thirteen and a half years. He was buried at Canterbury. And Henry, his firstborn, prince of Wales, duke of Cornwall, earl of Chester, who was born at Monmouth in Wales, was crowned at Westminster on 20 March [*recte* 9 April], the Sunday of the Lord's Passion.[392]

---

created duke of Exeter in Nov. 1416. Other chroniclers took a more favourable view of Clarence's campaign of 1412–13 (Given-Wilson, *Henry IV*, pp. 509–12).

[391] It was probably during the parliament of Nov.–Dec. 1411 that Prince Henry and his uncle Henry Beaufort, bishop of Winchester, tried to persuade Henry IV to resign the crown. As noted above, the king's illness was almost certainly not leprosy, but he was very ill by this time and did not stray far from Canterbury or London in 1412–13 (Given-Wilson, *Henry IV*, pp. 495–6, 513–16).

[392] 20 Mar. 1413 (the feast of St Cuthbert) was the date of Henry IV's death, in the Jerusalem chamber at Westminster abbey. He was buried, in accordance with his wishes, close to the shrine of St Thomas Becket in the Trinity Chapel of Canterbury cathedral. Henry V was crowned on 9 Apr.

Eodem autem anno, in hebdomada Natalis Domini, in festo Sanctorum Innocentium, accidit Winchelseie subitum tonitruum, et coruscatio campanile Sancti Egidii cum tota ecclesia et campanis in cineres uertit, nec potuit humano adiutorio releuari.[393] Eodem anno, in festo Natiuitatis Beate Virginis, apud Sclusam ecclesia eiusdem Virginis percussa est; et uilla de Ponte Roberti combusta est.

Miraculum Sancti Ricardi archiepiscopi Eborum. Et iuxta Eboracum, circa festum Sancte Katerine, campanile quoddam consimiliter combustum est usque ad medium; sed, emisso uoto a circumstantibus ad[p] Sanctum Ricardum archiepiscopum Eborum, subito ignis cessauit, et sic medietas campanilis incombusta remansit, cunctis ibidem hominibus Deum et Sanctum Ricardum glorificantibus.

---

[p] *interlined above* a

[393] The church of St Giles at Winchelsea appears to have been abandoned soon after this, and no remains survive.

Also in this year, on the feast of the Holy Innocents in Christmas week [28 December], there was a sudden thunderstorm at Winchelsea [East Sussex], and the lightning reduced the belfry of St Giles to ashes, along with the whole church and the bells, and there was nothing any man could do to restore it.[393] In the same year, on the feast of the Nativity of the Blessed Virgin [8 September], the church of the said Virgin at Sluys [Flanders] was struck; also, the town of Robertsbridge [East Sussex] was burned.

A miracle of St Richard archbishop of York. Also, near York, around the feast of St Katherine [25 November], a certain belfry was burned to its midway point in a similar fashion; however, once a prayer had been said by people standing around St Richard, archbishop of York, the fire suddenly ceased, and thus half of the bell tower was saved from the flames, and all the people there gave praise to God and St Richard.

BIBLIOGRAPHY

MANUSCRIPTS CONSULTED

The British Library, London

Additional MS 11714   The 'Southern Chronicle'
Cotton MS Galba E VII   *Eulogium Historiarum* and *Continuatio Eulogii*
Cotton MS Galba E XI   Grey Friars Canterbury, book of histories

Canterbury Cathedral Archives, Canterbury

CC/Supp. MS 11   Deeds of purchase of Grey friars Canterbury
DCC Ch Cant C1031   Grey Friars Canterbury, seal

The National Archives, Kew

C 49/96   Schedule of oath-takers in Sussex, 1388
E 101/397/5   Wardrobe of household account book, 1371–3

PRIMARY SOURCES

The Anonimalle Chronicle 1333 to 1381, ed. V. Galbraith (Manchester, 1927).
Calendar of the Close Rolls in the Public Record Office (London, 1892–1963).
Calendar of Papal Registers relating to Great Britain and Ireland: Letters, ed. W. H. Bliss (London, 1893–1998).
Calendar of Papal Registers relating to Great Britain and Ireland: Petitions, ed. W. H. Bliss (London, 1893–1998).
Calendar of the Patent Rolls in the Public Record Office (London, 1901–).
Calendar of Signet Letters of Henry IV and Henry V, 1399–1422, ed. J. L. Kirby (London, 1978).
The Chronicle of Adam Usk 1377–1421, ed. C. Given-Wilson (OMT, 1997).
Chronicles of the Revolution 1397–1400, ed. C. Given-Wilson (Manchester, 1993).
Chronique des quatre premiers Valois, ed. S. Luce (SHF; Paris, 1862).
Concilia Magnae Brittaniae et Hiberniae, ed. D. Wilkins (London, 1737).
An English Chronicle 1377–1461, ed. W. Marx (Woodbridge, 2003).
An English Chronicle of the Reigns of Richard II, Henry IV, Henry V and Henry VI, ed. J. S. Davies (Camden Society First Series, lxiv; London, 1855–6).
Eulogium Historiarum sive Temporis, ed. F. S. Haydon (3 vols., RS; London, 1858–63).
Fasciculi Zizaniorum Magistri Johannis Wyclif cum tritico, ed. W. Shirley (RS; London, 1858).
Flete, John, *History of Westminster Abbey*, ed. J. A. Robinson (Cambridge, 1909).
Foedera, Conventiones, Litterae, etc, ed. T. Rymer (20 vols., London, 1727–35).
Historia Vitae et Regni Ricardi Secundi, ed. G. B. Stow (Philadelphia, 1977).

Knighton's Chronicle 1337–1396, ed. G. Martin (OMT, 1995).
Leland, John, *Johannis Lelandi Antiquarii de Rebus Britannicis Collectanea*, ed. T. Hearne (6 vols., Oxford, 1715).
Monumenta Franciscana, ed. J. S. Brewer (2 vols., RS; London, 1858).
Parliament Rolls of Medieval England 1275–1504, ed. P. Brand, A. Curry, C. Given-Wilson, R. Horrox, G. Martin, M. Ormrod, S. Phillips (16 vols., Woodbridge, 2005).
The Peasants' Revolt of 1381, ed. R. B. Dobson (London, 1970).
The Reign of Richard II: From Minority to Tyranny 1377–1397. Selected Sources, trans. A. McHardy (Manchester, 2012).
Royal and Historical Letters of Henry IV, ed. F. C. Hingeston (2 vols., RS; London, repr. 1965).
St Albans Chronicle: The Chronica Maiora of Thomas Walsingham, ed. J. Taylor, W. Childs, and L. Watkiss (2 vols.: vol. 1, 1376–1394, OMT, 2003; vol. 2, 1394–1422, OMT, 2011).
Select Documents of English Constitutional History 1307–1485, ed. S. Chrimes and A. Brown (Edinburgh, 1961).
Sudbury's Register 1362–75, ed. R. Fowler and C. Jenkins (2 vols., Canterbury and York Society; Oxford, 1938).
The Westminster Chronicle 1381–1394, ed. L. Hector and B. Harvey (OMT, 1982).

SECONDARY SOURCES

Aston, M., 'The impeachment of Bishop Despenser', *BIHR* xxxviii (1965), 127–48.
Aston, M., *Thomas Arundel* (Oxford, 1967).
Barron, C., 'The quarrel of Richard II with London, 1392–7', in F. Du Boulay and C. Barron, eds., *The Reign of Richard II* (London, 1970), pp. 173–201.
Barron, C., 'The tyranny of Richard II', *BIHR* xli (1968), 1–18.
Bean, J., 'Henry IV and the Percies', *History*, xliv (1959), 212–17.
Britnell, R. 'Rochester Bridge, 1381–1530', in N. Yates and J. Gibson, eds., *Traffic and Politics: The Construction and Management of Rochester Bridge, AD 43–1993* (Woodbridge, 1994), pp. 43–60.
Brown, A., 'The Latin letters in MS All Souls 182', *EHR* lxxxvii (1972), 565–73.
Catto, J., 'An alleged Great Council of 1374', *EHR* lxxxii (1967), 764–71.
Clifford, S., 'An Edition of the Continuation of the *Eulogium Historiarum*, 1361–1413' (M.Phil. thesis, University of Leeds, 1975).
Cotton, C., *The Grey Friars of Canterbury, 1224 to 1538* (Manchester, 1924).
Cotton, C., 'Notes on the documents in the Cathedral library at Canterbury relating to the Grey Friars', *Collectanea Franciscana* 2, ed. C. L. Kingsford (Manchester, 1922), pp. 1–9.
Curry, A., Bell, A., King, A., and Simpkin, D., 'New regime, new army? Henry IV's Scottish expedition of 1400', *EHR* cxxv (2010), 1382–1413.
Davies, R. R., *The Revolt of Owain Glyndwr* (Oxford, 1995).
Deanesly, M., *The Lollard Bible* (Cambridge, 1920).

Dobson, R. B., 'The monks of Canterbury in the later Middle Ages', in P. Collinson, N. Ramsay, and M. Sparks, eds., *A History of Canterbury Cathedral* (Oxford, 1995), pp. 69–153.
Dohrn-van Rossum, H., *History of the Hour*, trans T. Dunlap (Chicago, 1996).
Duls, L., *Richard II in the Early Chronicles* (Paris, 1975).
Dunn, A., *The Politics of Magnate Power: England and Wales 1389–1413* (Oxford, 2003).
Edbury, P., *The Kingdom of Cyprus and the Crusades* (Cambridge, 1991).
Edwards, J., 'The parliamentary vommittee of 1398', *EHR* xl (1925), 321–33.
Emden, A. B., *A Biographical Register of the University of Oxford to A. D. 1500* (3 vols., Oxford, 1957–9).
'Friaries: The Franciscan friars of Canterbury', in *A History of the County of Kent*, ii, ed. W. Page (VCH; London, 1926), pp. 190–4.
The Friars' Libraries, ed. K. W. Humphreys (Corpus of British Medieval Library Catalogues; London, 1990).
Given-Wilson, C., *Chronicles: The Writing of History in Medieval England* (London, 2004).
Given-Wilson, C., *Henry IV* (New Haven and London, 2016).
Given-Wilson, C., 'The quarrels of old women: Henry IV, Louis of Orléans, and Anglo-French chivalric challenges in the early fifteenth century', in G. Dodd and D. Biggs, eds., *The Reign of Henry IV: Rebellion and Survival, 1403–1413* (York, 2008), pp. 28–47.
Given-Wilson, C., 'Richard II and the higher nobility', in A. Goodman and J. Gillespie, eds., *Richard II: The Art of Kingship* (Oxford, 1999), pp. 107–28.
Given-Wilson, C., 'Richard II, Edward II and the Lancastrian inheritance', *EHR* cix (1994), 553–71.
Given-Wilson, C., *The Royal Household and the King's Affinity, 1360–1413* (New Haven and London, 1986).
Goodman, A., *John of Gaunt* (London, 1992).
Gransden, A., *Historical Writing in England II: c. 1307 to the Early Sixteenth Century* (London, 1982).
Grummitt, D., 'The financial administration of Calais during the reign of Henry IV, 1399–1413', *EHR* cxiii (1998), 277–99.
Gwynn, A., *The English Austin Friars in the Time of Wyclif* (Oxford, 1940).
Harvey, M., *Solutions to the Schism* (St Ottilien, 1983).
The History of the King's Works 1–2: The Middle Ages, ed. H. M. Colvin, R. A. Brown, and A. J. Taylor (London, 1963).
The History of the University of Oxford, ii: *Late Medieval Oxford*, ed. J. Catto and R. Evans (Oxford, 1992).
Holmes, G., *The Good Parliament* (Oxford, 1975).
Housley, N., 'The Bishop of Norwich's crusade', *History Today*, xxxiii (1983), 15–20.
Hudson, A., *The Premature Reformation: Wycliffite Texts and Lollard History* (Oxford, 1988).

Jacob, E. F., *The Fifteenth Century* (Oxford, 1961).
Jones, E. J., 'The authorship of the Continuation of the *Eulogium Historiarum*: A suggestion', *Speculum*, xii (1937), 196–202.
Jones, M., *Ducal Brittany 1364–1399* (Oxford, 1970).
Kenny, A., *Wyclif* (Oxford, 1985).
Ker, N., *Medieval Libraries of Great Britain* (Royal Historical Society Guides, 3; 2nd edn., London, 1964).
Ker, N., *Medieval Manuscripts in British Libraries*, vol. 2 (Oxford, 1977).
Kingsford, C. L., *English Historical Literature in the Fifteenth Century* (Oxford, 1913).
Kingsford, C. L., *The Grey Friars of London* (London, 1915).
Knowles, D., 'The censured opinions of Uthred of Boldon', in *The Historian and Character and Other Essays* (Cambridge, 1964), pp. 129–70.
Lehoux, F., *Jean de France, duc de Berri: Sa vie, son action politique* (3 vols., Paris, 1966–8).
Little, A. G., *Franciscan Papers, Lists and Documents* (Manchester, 1943).
Little, A. G., *The Grey Friars in Oxford* (Oxford, 1892).
McFarlane, K. B., *John Wycliffe and the Beginnings of English Non-Conformity* (London, 1952).
McKenna, J., 'Popular canonization as political propaganda: The cult of Archbishop Scrope', *Speculum*, xlv (1970), 608–23.
McNiven, P., *Heresy and Politics in the Reign of Henry IV* (Woodbridge, 1987).
McNiven, P., 'The problem of Henry IV's health', *EHR* c (1985), 747–72.
Moorman, J., *The Franciscans in England* (London, 1974).
Morgan, P., *War and Society in Medieval Cheshire 1277–1403* (Chetham Society, 3rd ser., 34; Manchester, 1987).
Mortimer, I., 'Richard II and the succession to the Crown', *History*, xci (2006), 320–36.
Najemy, J., *A History of Florence, 1200–1575* (Oxford, 2006).
Nicol, D., 'A Byzantine emperor in England: Manuel II's visit to London in 1400–1401', *University of Birmingham Historical Journal*, xii (1969–70), 204–25.
Nuttall, J., *The Creation of Lancastrian Kingship* (Cambridge, 2007).
Ormrod, W. M., *Edward III* (New Haven and London, 2011).
Palmer, J., *England, France and Christendom 1377–99* (London, 1972).
Partner, P., *The Lands of St Peter: The Papal State in the Middle Ages and the Early Renaissance* (London, 1972).
Pepin, G., 'The French offensives of 1404–1407 against Anglo-Gascon Aquitaine', in A. Curry and A. Bell, eds., *Soldiers, Weapons and Armies in the Fifteenth Century* (Woodbridge, 2011), pp. 1–40.
Prestwich, M., *Edward I* (Berkeley, 1988).
Priestley, E., *The Battle of Shrewsbury 1403* (Shrewsbury, 1979).

Ramsay, N., 'The Cathedral archives and library', in P. Collinson, N. Ramsay, and M. Sparks, eds., *A History of Canterbury Cathedral* (Oxford, 1995), pp. 341–407.
Roskell, J., *The Impeachment of Michael de la Pole Earl of Suffolk in 1386* (Manchester, 1984).
Ross, J., 'Seditious activities: The conspiracy of Maud de Vere, Countess of Oxford, 1403–4', in L. Clark, ed., *Fifteenth-Century England III: Authority and Submission* (Woodbridge, 2003), pp. 25–41.
Saul, N., *Richard II* (New Haven and London, 1997).
Smith, J. H., *The Great Schism* (London, 1970).
Steel, A., *Receipt of the Exchequer 1377–1485* (Cambridge, 1954).
Storey, R. L., 'Clergy and common law in the reign of Henry IV', in R. F. Hunnisett and J. B. Post, eds., *Medieval Legal Records in Memory of C. A. F. Meekings* (London, 1978), pp. 341–61.
Stow, G., 'The continuation of the *Eulogium Historiarum*: Some revisionist perspectives', *EHR* cxix (2004), 667–81.
Stow, G., 'Richard II in the *Continuatio Eulogii*: Yet another alleged historical incident?', in N. Saul, ed., *Fourteenth-Century England V* (Woodbridge, 2008), pp. 116–29.
Strickland, M., and Hardy, R., *The Great Warbow* (London, 2005).
Sumption, J., *Cursed Kings: The Hundred Years War*, iv (London, 2015).
Sumption, J., *Divided Houses: The Hundred Years War*, iii (London, 2009).
Tatton-Brown, T., *Canterbury: History and Guide* (Stroud, 1994).
Taylor, J., *English Historical Literature in the Fourteenth Century* (Oxford, 1987).
Thornley, I. D., 'Treason by words in the fifteenth century', *EHR* xxxii (1957), 556–61.
Ullmann, W., *The Origins of the Great Schism* (London, 1948).
Vaughan, R., *John the Fearless* (London, 1966).
Whitfield, D. W., 'Conflicts of personality and principle: The political and religious crisis in the English Franciscan Province, 1400–1409', *Franciscan Studies*, xvii (1957), 321–62.
Workman, H. B., *John Wyclif: A Study of the English Medieval Church* (2 vols., Oxford, 1926).
Wylie, J. H., *History of England under Henry the Fourth* (4 vols., London, 1884–98).

INDEX

Members of the titled nobility are indexed under title rather than family name (e.g. 'Warwick', not 'Beauchamp'). Bishops are indexed under family name rather than see (e.g. 'Wykeham', not 'Winchester').

Abbeville (France), 4
Abingdon (Oxfordshire), abbey, xxiv
Albany, Robert duke of, 124
Albertus Magnus, xxii, xxvi
Albret, Arnaud lord of, 4
Alexander V, pope, xvii, xxi, xxx, xxxvi, xxxix, 32, 148, 150, 152, 154
Alexandria (Egypt), 2
Alfieri, Enrico, Franciscan minister-general, 130
Amiens (France), 68
Anagni (Italy), 18
Anglesey, Isle of, 102
Anjou, Louis I, duke of Anjou and Provence, 28
    Louis II, duke of Anjou and Provence, 148–50, 158
Annaghdown (Ireland), bishopric of, xxvi
Anne of Bohemia, queen of England, xlvi, 44, 62, 68, 72
Anselm, St, xxii
Anthony of Vienne, St, 52
Appellant, Lords, xxxi, xli, 60–5
Aquinas, Thomas, St, 12
Aquitaine (Gascony), 2, 4, 12, 28, 70, 72, 120, 156–8
    Eleanor of, 72
Aragon, 142
Ardres (France), 72
Aristotle, xxvi, 30
Armagnac, Bernard count of, 154
    John count of, 4
Armenia, Leo king of, 48
Arundel, John de, 28
Arundel, Richard earl of (d. 1397), xvi, xxxiii, xxxviii, xli, 50–4, 58–64, 70–80, 90, 100
    Thomas earl of (d. 1415), xlv, 88, 96, 154
Arundel, Thomas, bishop of Ely, archbishop of York, archbishop of Canterbury, xvi–xvii, xxxviii, xl, xli, xlii, l, 72–4, 100, 104, 106, 130, 142, 144, 150, 152
    appointed chancellor, 52

exiled, 80–2, 86–8
influence on chronicler, xxxix
offered cardinalate, xvi, 66–8
pleads for Archbishop Scrope, 132–6
regains archbishopric, 90, 96
under Henry IV, 94, 96, 100, 140
Ashbourne, Thomas, friar, 10–12
Augustine, St, 42
Augustinian friars, 14–16
Avignon (France), 4, 8, 12, 14, 18
Aylesbury (Buckinghamshire), Franciscans of, xxv, 104

Babylon, 88
Badby, John, heretic, xx, xxxiii, xxxvii, xxxix, 150–2
Baker, Thomas, of Fobbing, rebel, 38
Bardolf, Thomas, 136, 140
Barnet, John, bishop of Ely, xiii
Barton, William, chancellor of Oxford university, 36
Bayonne (France), Treaty of, 50
Bealknap, Robert, chief justice, 38, 55, 59
Beauchamp, John, executed, 62
Beaufort, Henry, bishop of Winchester, cardinal, xxxiv, xlviii, 126, 154, 157, 158
Becket, Thomas, St, xv, xxi, 50, 86–8, 159
Bede, St, xi, xiii, 20
Benedict, St, 42
Benedict XI, pope, 4
Benedict XIII, antipope, 142–6
Benedictine chroniclers, xxi
Berengar of Tours, xx, 34
Berkeley, Thomas, 114
Berners, James, executed, 62
Berry, John duke of, 8, 154
Berwick-on-Tweed (Berwickshire), xxxix, 136
Biscay, Bay of, 6
Black Death, plague, xxiii, 14, 68–9, 140
Blackheath, 38
Blake, John, executed, 55, 64
Blount, Walter, 116
Bologna (Italy), 154

INDEX

Boniface VIII, pope, 12
Boniface IX, pope, xvi, xlvii, 66, 68, 86, 90, 96, 124
Bordeaux (France), 72, 120, 144, 158
Bourbon, John duke of, 154
Bourges, Treaty of, 156
Bradmore, John, 118
Bramham Moor, battle of, 142
Brantingham, Thomas, bishop of Exeter, 6, 53
Bréhat (Brittany), island, 144
Brembre, Nicholas, mayor of London, 60–2
Brentwood (Essex), 38
Bridlington (Yorkshire), 88
  prophecies of, 106
Brinton, Thomas, bishop of Rochester, 38
Bristol, xlii, 90, 98
  Franciscan convent at, xvii, 110
Brittany, the Bretons, xxxii, 36, 114, 124, 126, 144
  John IV, duke of, 4, 6, 34, 36, 46
  John V, duke of, 112, 154
Brocas, Bernard, executed, 98
Bruges (Flanders), 8
Brut chronicle, xlix–li
Brutus, king of Britain, xlix
Bruyl, John, Franciscan, xxvi
Bryn Glas (Pilleth), battle of, 112
Burgh, William, justice, 55
Burgundy, duke of, *see* John the Fearless; Philip the Bold
Burley, Simon, xli, 16, 50, 62, 74, 78
Bury St Edmunds (Suffolk), abbey of, xix, 28–9
  prior of, 42
Bussy, John, 80, 90–2
Butler, William, provincial minister of the Franciscans, xxiv–xxvi, xxxiii, 130
Buzançais (France), Treaty of, 158

Cadzand (Flanders), 55, 124
Calais (France), 8, 68, 72, 74, 76, 100, 120, 124, 152
  garrison of, xxxix, 140
Calf, John, executed, 108
Calveley, Hugh, 3
Cambridge, Franciscans of, 104, 128
Camden, William, xiv
Canterbury (Kent), xv–xvii, xxxix, xli, 14, 36, 42, 81, 84, 86, 90
  cathedral priory, xxi–xxii, 8, 14, 26–30, 50, 72, 158
  Franciscans of, xxi–xxvii, 42

Carbonarius, Franciscus, cardinal-protector of the Franciscans, 129
Cardiff, Franciscans of, xxxix, 122–4
Carlisle (Cumbria), 48
Carmarthen (Carmarthenshire), 90, 118
Carmelite friars, xviii, 32, 140
Cary, John, justice, 55
Cascia, Antonio da, Franciscan minister-general, 156
Cassiodorus, xxii
Castile, civil war in, xlv, 2–4
  Enrique king of, xxxii, 2–4
  Juan king of, 50, 66
Cavendish, John, chief justice, 42
Charles IV, Holy Roman Emperor (d. 1378), 44
Charles V, king of France (d. 1380), 4, 18
Charles VI, king of France (d. 1422), 46, 68, 72, 100, 112, 114, 138, 140, 146, 148, 152, 154–6
  plans to invade England, 48–50
Charles 'of the Peace', king of Naples and Sicily, 28
Chastel, Guillaume de, 114, 128
Cheltenham (Gloucestershire), 126
Chester, Cheshiremen, 114–16
  supporters of Richard II, xli, 62, 86
Cheyne, John, 80
Chichele, Henry, bishop of St David's, archbishop of Canterbury, xxx, 146
Chillenden, Thomas, prior of Canterbury, 146
Cirencester (Gloucestershire), 96–8
Clarence, Lionel duke of, xliii, 2, 70, 126
  Margaret, duchess of, 157
  Thomas duke of, son of Henry IV, xxxv, xxxviii, xlv, xlvii, 124, 156–8
Clarendon (Wiltshire), 14, 32
Clarendon, Roger of, 104, 108
Clement VII, antipope, 18, 28, 46
Clifford, Richard, bishop of London, xxxiv, 126
Clifford, William, 118
Clisson, Olivier de, 4
clocks, invention of, 8
Cobham, John de, 52, 80, 96
Coety (Glamorgan), castle, 136
Colchester (Essex), 130
Colchester, William, abbot of Westminster, 98, 124
Cologne (Germany), 126
Commission of Government (1386), xxxiii, 52–8, 76, 78

INDEX

Constance, Council of, xxiv, xxx, xxxv, 65, 146, 158
Constantine, emperor, 12
Constantinople, 102
Constanza of Castile, duchess of Lancaster, 4, 48, 50
Continuatio Eulogii
　authorship of, xiv–xxi, xxvi–xxvii, xxxiv
　Canterbury provenance of, xv–xvi, xxi–xxvii
　chronology, structure and sources of, xxvii–xxxvii
　Church and State in, xix
　Latin orthography of, li–liii
　legal knowledge in, xviii–xix, xliv
　manuscript of, xii–xvi, xxxv, xlvi
　style and tone of, xxxv–xxxviii, li
　texts related to, xlvi–li
　theological learning in, xx
　value of, xxxvii–xlvi
Conwy (Gwynedd), castle, xlix, 90, 98, 102
Corfe (Dorset), castle, 52
Corringham (Essex), 38
Cosyn, John, 96–8
Cotton, Robert, xiv
Courtenay, William, bishop of London, archbishop of Canterbury, xvi, xvii, xx, 6, 28–30, 52, 60, 64–5, 72
Coventry (Warwickshire), 84–6
　parliament at, 124
'Crouchback Legend', 70

Dallingridge, Edward, 66
Daniel, Book of, xxiii
Dartmouth (Devon), 128
Dee, John, xii
Denia, Alfonso count of, 18
Despenser, Constance, 126
　and see Gloucester
Despenser, Henry, bishop of Norwich, xix, 44–6, 98
　and see 'Flemish Crusade'
Devereux, John, 53
Digge, John, xxi
Dominican friars, xviii, 14, 70–2, 112, 144
Dorset, John marquis of, earl of Somerset, 74, 82, 96, 126, 157
Douglas, Archibald earl of, 112, 118
Dover (Kent), 50, 66, 82
du Guesclin, Bertrand, 2–4
Dunbar, George, Scottish earl of March, 100, 146

Dunkirk (Flanders), 46
Dyckenson, Mr, of Poplar, xii

Eastry, Henry, prior of Canterbury, xxii
Eccleston, Thomas de, chronicler, xxi
Edinburgh, 48
Edward the Confessor, St, king (d. 1066), 20, 94
　shrine of, 38, 82
Edward I, king of England (d. 1307), 24, 32, 70, 120
Edward II, king of England (d. 1327), 52, 58
Edward III, king of England (d. 1377), xxxiv, xxxviii, xxxix, xlvi, 2–14, 32, 68, 70, 132
　death of, 14
Edward, the 'Black Prince', prince of Wales, xxxvii, xxxix, xlvi, 104
　at Westminster council (1373), 10–12
　death of, 14
　in Aquitaine, 2–4
Eltham (Kent), 52
English Chronicle (*Davies' Chronicle*), xlix–liii, 76
Epiphany rising (1400), xvi, xxxiii, xxxvii, xxxviii, xxxix, xlii, xlvii, 96–8
Erik VII, king of Denmark (d. 1459), 138
Erith (Kent), 36
Ethelbert, king of Kent (d. 616), 20
Eulogium Historiarum, xi–xiv, xxiii, xxxiv
　manuscripts of, xi–xv
Exeter, John duke of, earl of Huntingdon (d. 1400), xlvii, 54, 74, 82, 86, 96–8
　Thomas duke of, earl of Dorset, xxx, xlviii, 158
Exodus, Book of, xxiii
Exton, Nicholas, mayor of London, 60–2

Fakenham, Nicholas, Franciscan, 130
Falkland (Fife), 124
Ferrers, Robert, xlix
Ferriby, William, executed, xlvii, 98
Flanders, the Flemings, 38–9, 44, 124, 140, 154
　'Flemish Crusade', xix, xxx, xxxiii, xxxvi, xlviii, 44–6
　Louis count of, xxx, 44, 46
　Margaret of, xxx, 44
　rebellions in, xlv, 44
Flint (Flintshire), castle, xvi, xlix, 90
Florence, the Florentines, xix, xxxi–xxxii, xxxviii, 6, 10, 11
Fobbing (Essex), 38

INDEX

Folkestone (Kent), 16
Fondi (Italy), Onorato count of, 16–18
Fordham, John, treasurer, bishop of
    Durham, 52, 58
Forster, Henry, Franciscan, 106
France, the French, 74
    civil war in, xxxi, xlv, 138–40, 146,
        154–8
    war with England, xxxiii, xxxv, xlv, li,
        4–8, 12–14, 34–6, 46, 48–54, 100,
        120, 124, 154
Francis, St, xxii, xxiv, 42
Franciscan friars, xxi–xxvii, xxxiv, 24, 42–4,
        102–12, 128–32, 134, 138, 148,
        152, 156
    Conventuals and Observants, xxi,
        xxiv–xxv
    dispute within English province, xvii,
        xix, xxiii–xxvi, xxxi, xxxiii, xxxviii,
        128–30, 139
    knowledge of in *Continuatio*, xv–xx
    trial and execution of (1402), xvii,
        xxxi–xxxii, xxxiii, xxxvii, xxxviii,
        xlii, l, 104–12
Frisby, Richard, Franciscan, 106
Frisby, Roger, Franciscan, trial and
    execution of, xvii, xxi, xliii,
    106–12
Fulthorpe, Roger, justice, 55

Gaeta (Italy), 154
Gascony, *see* Aquitaine
Genesis, Book of, xxiii
Genoa (Italy), 124, 138
Germany, the Germans, 138, 140, 154
Ghent (Flanders), xix, xlvi, 44
Gilbert, John, bishop of Bangor, 12
Gloucester, parliament at, 24
Gloucester, Humphrey duke of (d. 1447), xlix
    Thomas duke of, earl of Buckingham
        (d. 1397), xviii, xxxii, xxxiv, xxxviii,
        xxxix, 34, 36, 48, 50–4, 58–64, 70,
        74–6, 80, 84, 86, 96, 126
    Thomas earl of, 74, 82, 96–8
Glyndwr, Owain, prince of Wales, 100, 102,
    112, 114, 122, 126
    Catherine daughter of, 118
    favours friars, xvii, xxxix, 108, 122
    Gruffudd son of, 125
Gournay, Matthew, 3
Gower, John, poet and chronicler, xvi
Gravesend (Kent), 16
Green, Henry, executed, 90
Gregory the Great, pope, 20

Gregory XI, pope, 6–16, 30
Gregory XII, pope, xix, xxiv, xxxiii, xliv,
    137–46, 150, 154–8
Grey, Reginald, of Ruthin, 100, 102, 112

Hadley, John, 122
Hailes (Gloucestershire), abbot of, 140
Halley's comet, 104
Hallum, Robert, bishop of Salisbury, xvi,
    xxxiii, 146, 150
Harding, Robert, Franciscan, xxiv
Harringay Park, 58–60
Hartlepool, Hugh of, Franciscan, xxii
Hastings (Sussex), 16
Hauley, Robert, murder of, xxxiii, xxxviii,
    xlix, 18–20, 24
Hende, John, mayor of London, 66, 128
Henry II, king of England (d. 1189), 28, 72
    Eleanor, daughter of, 28
Henry III, king of England (d. 1272), 70,
    94, 120
Henry IV, king of England (d. 1413), xvi,
    xxiii, xxxii, xxxiii, xxxvi, xxxix,
    xlvi, xlviii, xlix, l–li, 126, 130, 144
    and execution of Archbishop Scrope, xix,
        xxviii, xxxiv, xlii, 132–4
    and Percy rebellion, 114–16
    as duke of Hereford, xviii, xxxiii, xxxviii,
        xxxix, 82–6
    as duke of Lancaster, 92, 106, 110, 126
    as earl of Derby, 54, 58–62, 70, 78
    campaigns in Scotland, 100
    campaigns in Wales, 102, 112,
        118, 136
    chronicler's opinion of, xxxviii–xliii
    coronation of, 94
    daughter of (Blanche), 126
    daughter of (Philippa), 138
    death of, xxviii, xxxv, xlvii, 130, 158
    Franciscans tried and executed by
        (1401–2), xvii, xxv, xliii, 102–10
    Mary de Bohun, first wife of, 112
    mother of (Blanche of Lancaster), 70
    relations with France, 100, 112–14,
        140, 154–8
    usurpation of, 88–90
Henry V, king of England (d. 1422), xii,
    xlvi, xlvii, xlviii, 158
    as prince of Wales, li, 96, 110, 118,
        154–8
Henry VI, king of England (d. 1471), xlvii
Henry VII, king of England (d. 1509), xxi
Hereford, Humphrey earl of, xxxiv, 6–8
    Joan countess of, xlvii, 98

INDEX

Higden, Ranulf, chronicler, xi
Highgate, 110
Holborn, 110
Holt, John, justice, 55
Holy Land, 44, 86–8
Hospitallers, master of (Robert Hales), 40
   grand master of (Phillibert de
     Naillac), 152
Houghton, Adam, bishop of St David's,
   chancellor of England, 6, 30
Hugh of St Victor, xx, 34
Humbleton Hill, battle of, 112
Huntingdon (Huntingdonshire), 60

Imworth, Richard, murdered, 38
Innocent III, pope, xix, 11
Innocent VII, pope, 124, 132–6, 138
Ireland, the Irish, xviii, xxxix, 28, 54, 70,
   72, 86–90, 144, 150
Ireland, Robert duke of, earl of Oxford,
   marquis of Dublin, 50, 54,
   58–64, 78
Isabeau, queen of France, 140, 146
Isabella of Castile, duchess of York, 4
Isabella of France, queen of England, xl,
   72, 100
Isaiah, Book of, xxii, xxiii
Isidore of Seville, xi
Islington, 110

Jeremiah, Book of, xxiii
Jerome, St, xi
Joan of Navarre, queen of England, xxxii,
   112, 122, 126
Johanna, queen of Naples, 28
John the Baptist, St, lii
John XXII, pope, xxiv, 24
John XXIII, antipope, 150, 156–8
John, king of England (d. 1216), xix,
   10–12, 94
John, king of France (d. 1364), xii, 2, 8, 28,
   68–70
John the Fearless, duke of Burgundy
   (d. 1419), xxxix, 138–40, 146, 152,
   156–8

Kent, Edmund earl of, 124, 140, 144
Kings, Books of, xl, 94
Kings Langley (Hertfordshire), 8, 100
Kingston (Surrey), 96–8
Knighton, Henry, chronicler, xxxvii
Knolles, Robert, 14, 40, 64, 140
Knolles, Thomas, mayor of London, 122
Knyvet, John, chancellor, 6, 11

Ladislas, king of Naples and Sicily, 140,
   142, 148, 150, 154–8
Lakenheath, John, Franciscan, 104
Lambeth, 74
Lancaster (Lancashire), 111
Lancaster, Edmund earl of (d. 1296), 70
   Henry duke of (d. 1361), 2
   John 'of Gaunt', duke of (d. 1399), xviii,
     xxxii, xxxviii, xlv, 2–8, 14, 18, 24,
     32, 35, 38, 40, 46, 50, 68, 70, 72,
     78, 80
   campaigns in Iberia, 46–50, 66
   Catherine, daughter of, 50
   death of, 88
   Philippa, daughter of, xxxii, 50
   and see Henry IV
Langham, Simon, archbishop of
   Canterbury, cardinal, xvi, xxxviii, 4,
   8, 14
Langley, Thomas, bishop of Durham,
   xvi, 146
La Rochelle (France), 12, 54
Latimer, William, xlix
Launde (Leicestershire), prior of, 104, 108
Leicester, Franciscans of, xxv, 102, 106–10
Leland, John, xii, xv, xxxv
Leulingham (France), 70
Lewes (Sussex), 16, 82, 86
Lichfield (Staffordshire), 110, 114
Limoges (France), 4
Llanfaes (Anglesey), Franciscans of,
   xxxix, 102
Lockton, John, sergeant-at-law, 55, 64
Lollards, views of, xx, xxxvi, li, 24, 36, 152
London, the Londoners, xvii, xix, xxiii,
   xxiii, xxxiii, xxxvi, xxxviii, xl, l, 6,
   16, 20, 36, 38–40, 58, 60, 66, 76, 84,
   86, 88, 96–8, 100, 106, 110, 120,
   126, 132, 140, 142, 150, 152, 154
   Franciscans of, xxiv–xxv, xxvi, 128
   Tower of, 18, 40, 60–2, 72, 86–92, 106,
     110, 124
Louis, duke of Guyenne, Dauphin of
   France, 155–6
Lucca (Italy), 142, 144
Lucia Visconti, countess of Kent, 140
Lucius, king of Britain, 20
Lumley, Ralph, 98
Lutterworth (Leicestershire), xxxii, 42, 64

MacMurrough, Art, king of Leinster, 72
Maidstone (Kent), 36
Malatesta, Carlo, lord of Rimini, 158
Malet, John, Franciscan, 130

INDEX

Malmesbury (Wiltshire), abbey, xi–xiv
Malmesbury, William of, chronicler, xi, xiii, xxii
Man, Isle of, 80
'Manner of King Richard's Renunciation', xxxiv, xlii–xliii, 92–4
Manuel II, emperor of Byzantium (d. 1425), xxxv, 102, 126
March, Edmund earl of (d. 1381), 3
  Edmund earl of (d. 1425), xliii, 126
  Roger earl of (d. 1360), 2
  Roger earl of (d. 1398), xxviii, xxxii, xxxviii, xlii, 54, 70, 86
Marck (France), castle, 124
Mardisley, John, Franciscan, 10–12
Mark, Gospel of, xxii
Marshalsea prison (Southwark), 38–40
Martin V, pope, xxx
Martin, Richard, xxiii
Mascy, John, of Puddington, 116
Matthew, Gospel of, xxii
Maudeleyn, Richard, executed, xlvii, 98
Mellitus, bishop of London, 20–5
Melro, Thomas, rebel, 38
Merks, Thomas, bishop of Carlisle, 92, 98
Merlawe, Richard, 122
Michael, St, 46
Milan, Gian Galeazzo duke of, 2
  Violante, daughter of, 3
Milford Haven (Pembrokeshire), 90
Molyneux, Thomas, 62
Monmouth (Monmouthshire), 158
Monmouth, Geoffrey of, xxii
Montiel, battle of, 4
Mortimer, Edmund, xxxvi, xxxix, 112, 114, 118
  Elizabeth, 114
  Philippa, 3
  Roger, 126
  Thomas, 62
Mortmain, Statute of, 120
Mowbray, Thomas, earl marshal (d. 1405), xxxix, xlii, 130–4
  and see Norfolk
Mum and the Sothsegger, xliii

Nájera, battle of, 4
Navarre, Charles king of (d. 1387), 14, 112
Nevill, Alexander, archbishop of York, xvi, 52, 58, 62–4, 68, 78
Newcastle, Franciscans of, xxvi
Newgate prison (London), 38
Norfolk, Margaret Marshall, duchess of, 82
  Thomas Mowbray, duke of, earl of Nottingham, earl marshal (d. 1399), xviii, xxxiii, xxxviii, xxxix, 54, 58–62, 74–6, 78, 82, 84–6, 130
Norham, William, hermit, xxxix, 88, 116
Northumberland, Henry earl of (d. 1408), 88, 112, 114, 118, 122, 136, 140, 146
  and see Percy
Norwich (Norfolk), xxi, 148
Nottingham (Nottinghamshire), xxxiii, 54, 66, 74, 84

Ockham, William de, xxii
Orléans, Charles duke of, 154–8
  Louis duke of, xxxiii, xxxvi, xliii, 112–14, 120
  assassination of, xlv, 138–40
Orwell (Suffolk), 55
Ottoman Turks, 102
Oudeby, John, 122
Oxford, 60, 98, 130, 142
  Chronicler's knowledge of, xx–xxi
  university of, xvii, xix–xxi, xxii, xxiii, xxxi–xxxiv, 24, 28–36, 42, 148
  Franciscans at, xxiv, xxvi–xxvii, 4, 10, 106–12
Oxford, Maud countess of, 124

Padilla, Maria de, 2
Padua (Italy), 148
Palmer, Thomas of, Dominican, xxii
Paris, 138–40, 146, 148, 154
parliament, xix, xlii, xliv–xlv, 54–8, 76, 82, 132
  1377, 16, 24
  1378, xviii, xxxiii, 24–8
  1379, 24
  1380, 32
  1381, 36, 44
  1382, xxxiii, 44, 46
  1383, 46
  1384, xviii, 32
  1385, 54
  1386, xxxiii, 50–60
  1388, xxxiii, xli, 60–4, 66
  1390, 68
  1393, 68
  1394, xxxiii, xxxviii, 70
  1397, xviii, xxxi, xxxiii, xxxiv, 74–84, 94
  1399, xxxiii, 94, 96
  1401, xxxvii, 100–2
  1402, xxxix, 112
  1404, xviii, xxxii, xxxiii, xxxvii, xxxix, xlii, 120–2, 124

INDEX

1406, xxxiv, xxxvii, xxxix, 136–8
1407, xlv, 144
1410, 150–2
1411, 156
Paul, St, xx, xxii, xxiii, 12, 42
Peasants' Revolt (1381), xv, xxx, xxxvi, xxxviii, li, 36–40
Pembroke, John earl of, 12–14
Percy family, rebellion (1403), xxxi, xxxix, 114–16
    Henry (Hotspur), xxxvi, xxxvii, xliii, 88, 112–18, 146
    and see Northumberland; Worcester
Pereto, Antonio de, Franciscan minister-general, xxiii–xxv, 130, 138
Peter, St, 10–12, 20–3, 28
Peter IV, king of Aragon (d. 1387), 32
Peter (Pedro), king of Castile (d. 1369), 2–4, 48
Peter, king of Cyprus (d. 1369), xiii, xxviii, 2
Peter Lombard, xxii
Pevensey (Sussex), castle, 124
Philip the Bold, duke of Burgundy (d. 1404), xxx, 8, 44
Philip the Chancellor, xxii
Philippa of Hainault, queen of England, 2
Pisa (Italy), 142,
    Council of (1409), xix, xxiv, xxviii, xxx, xxxiii, xxxv, 32, 143, 146–50
Pleshey (Essex), 74, 98
Plumpton, William, executed, 132–4
Plymouth (Devon), 29, 114
Poitiers (France), battle of, 70
Polychronicon, xi
Pontefract (Yorkshire), 94, 100, 122, 126, 134
Ponthieu (France), 4
Portugal, João king of (d. 1433), 18, 50, 66
Prittlewell (Essex), 98
prophecies, xxxiv
    of the eagle, xxxiii
    of John Thweng, prior of Bridlington, 106–7
Provisors, Statutes of, xix, xlvii, 29, 31, 68
Purvey, John, heretic, 100
Pwll Melyn (Monmouthshire), battle of, 124

Queenborough (Kent), castle, xv, 2, 8
Questions to the Judges (1387), xxxii, xlv, l, 54–8, 64

Radcot Bridge (Oxfordshire), battle of, xxxiii, xxxviii, 62
Ravenspur (Humberside), 88

'Record and Process' (1399), xxxiv, xliii, 92, 94
Reigate (Surrey), 59, 86, 96, 98
Rennes (France), 34
Repingdon, Philip, bishop of Lincoln, xvi, xxx
Revelation, Book of, xx, 34
Richard II, king of England (d. 1400), xv–xvi, xviii, xxv, xxviii, xxx, xxxiv, xlvi, xlix, li, 10, 30, 48, 114, 120, 132
    and crisis of 1386–8, 58–64
    and London, 66, 84
    and Peasants' Revolt, 38–42
    accession of, 14
    arrests and tries Appellants, 74–82
    'blank charters' of, xxxiii, 84, 96
    campaign in Scotland (1385), 48
    campaigns in Ireland (1394, 1399), 70–2, 86–8
    chronicler's opinion of, xxxvi, xxxviii–xlii, 94
    deposition and death of, xxxi, l, 92–100, 126
    in parliament of 1378, 26
    marriages of, 44, 72
    negotiations with France, 68–72
    posthumous rumours of, 102–18, 122, 124
    Questions to the Judges, 54–8
    statutes of, xxxiii, 90, 94
    'tyranny' of, 76–90
    will of, 88, 92
Richmond, earldom of, 100, 146
Rickhill, William, justice, xxxviii, 76
Rimini (Italy), 146
Ripon, John, 58
Robert III, king of Scotland (d. 1406), 112
Robertsbridge (Sussex), 160
Roccasecca (Italy), battle of, 148
Rochester (Kent), bridge, xv, xxx, 36, 64
Rokeby, Thomas, 142
Rolf, Thomas, xxi
Rome, the Romans, xviii, xxxviii, xliv, 4, 16–18, 32, 68, 84, 130, 140, 156
Rothesay, David duke of, 124
Rottingdean (Kent), 16
Roughton, Richard, 62
Roughton, Thomas, 62
Rupert of Bavaria, Holy Roman Emperor (d. 1410), 126
    Louis son of, 126
Rushook, Thomas, bishop of Chichester, 10, 58, 64, 68
Rye (Sussex), 16

INDEX

St Albans (Hertfordshire), abbey, 80
  chroniclers of, xxi, xlvi, 88
Saint-Cloud (France), 154–6
St John's Field (London), 40, 60
Saint-Malo (France), 14
Saint-Omer (France), 152
  abbey of Saint-Bertin in, 152
St Osyth (Essex), abbot of, 124
St Paul's (London), cathedral, 10, 20, 88, 98, 150
  council at (1408), xix, xxiv
  Cross, xxxvi, 6, 82, 100, 150
Saint-Pol, Waleran count of, 120, 124
Salisbury, John, executed, 64
Salisbury (Wiltshire), 68
  Franciscans of, xl, 68
  parliament at, xviii, 32
Salisbury, John earl of, 6, 14, 74, 82, 96–8
Sandwich (Kent), 12, 14
Saracens, 2
Savage, Arnold, 122
Savona (Italy), 138
Savoy palace, 38
Sawtre, William, heretic, xx, xlviii, 100
Schism, Great (1378–1417), xviii, xxx, xxxi, xxxv, xliv, xlv, xlvii, l, 16–18, 124, 138–48, 154
Scotland, the Scots, 18, 40, 48, 100, 104, 108, 112, 114, 118, 124, 126, 136, 140, 144, 146, 154
Scrope, Richard, archbishop of York, xxx, xxxiv, xliv, xlviii, 94, 160
  rising, capture and execution of, xvi, xviii, xix, xxviii, xxxi, xxxix, xlii, xlv, l–li, 130–4
  Richard, chancellor, 29, 53
  and see Wiltshire
Sebert, king of the East Saxons, 20
Septvans, William, 42
Serle, William, xxxix, 105, 122, 126
Shakell, John, 18
Shareshull, William, chief justice, xvii, 4
Sheen (Surrey), 72
Shelley, Thomas, executed, 98
Sheppey, John de, 12
Sheppey, Isle of (Kent), 2, 62
Shrewsbury (Shropshire), 55
  battle of, xxxi, xxxiii, xxxvi, xxxvii, xxxix, xliii, 114–18
  parliament at, 82
Shropshire, 122
Siena (Italy), 144
Sluys (Flanders), 48, 124, 160
Smithfield, 40–1, 100

Solomon, king of Israel, xl, 94
Southampton (Hampshire), 28
Southern Chronicle, xlvi–li
Spain, the Spaniards, xxxii, xlv, 12, 18, 48–50, 66
  'brother of the king of' (Petrus Infans), xvii, xxx, xxxv, 16, 32
Spilman, Thomas, xxi
Spofforth, Thomas, abbot of York, 146
Stable, Adam, mayor of London, 6
Stafford, Edmund earl of, 116
Standish, Ralph, 40
Stanford-le-Hope (Essex), 38
Stonor (Sussex), 16
Stony Stratford (Northamptonshire), 142
Stow, John, chronicler, xii
Straw, Jack, rebel, 38–40
Sudbury, Simon, archbishop of Canterbury, chancellor of England, xv–xvi, xix, xxvi, 14, 20, 26–30, 34–40
Suffolk, Michael earl of, xxxiii, 50–8, 62–4
Sulcard, chronicler, 20
Surrey, Thomas duke of, earl of Kent, xxxvii, 42, 74, 82, 96–8
Swaffham, John, bishop of Bangor, 58
Swynford, Thomas, 122

Tadcaster (Yorkshire), 142
Thanet (Kent), Isle of, xv, 50
Thoresby, John, archbishop of York, 68
Tintagel (Cornwall), 74
Tissington, John, Franciscan, 36
Tonworth, Adam, chancellor of Oxford university, 30
Tower Hill, xli, 78
Tresilian, Robert, chief justice, 55, 62
Trevor, John, bishop of St Asaph, xxvii, xxxix, 100
Troppau, Martin of (Martinus Polonius), xxii
Tudor, Rhys and Gwilym, 102
Tyburn, 106, 110
Tyler, Wat, xxxvi, xxxviii, 38–40

Ugguccione, Francesco, cardinal-archbishop of Bordeaux, xxxiii, xxxix, 142–4
Umfraville, Gilbert de, titular earl of Kyme, 154–6
Urban V, pope, xlv, 4–6
Urban VI, pope, xxxiii, xliv, 16–18, 26–8, 44, 66
Usk, Adam, chronicler, xxxviii, 102
Usk (Monmouthshire), castle, 124

INDEX

Ussher, James, archbishop of Armagh, xi
Uthred (John) of Boldon, monk of
   Durham, 10–12

Venice (Italy), 86
Vienne, Jean de, admiral of France, 16, 48
Vitry, Jacques de, xxii

Walden, Roger, bishop of London,
   archbishop of Canterbury, xv–xvi,
   xxxviii, xxxix, xli, 82–6, 90, 96, 98
Wales, 90
   rebellion in (1400–9), xvii, xxxvii, xxxix,
      100–2, 112–16, 122, 132, 136
   and see Glyndwr
Walsingham, Thomas, chronicler, xxxvii,
   28, 128
Waltham (Essex), abbot of, 52
Waltham (Hampshire), 126
Walton, Walter, Franciscan, 106
Walworth, William, mayor of London, 40
Ward, Thomas, of Trumpington, 112
Ware (Hertfordshire), 146
Warwick, Thomas earl of (d. 1369), 8
   Thomas earl of (d. 1401), xxxviii, 50–2,
      58–64, 70, 74–80, 96
Waterton, Robert, 122
Wenzel, Holy Roman Emperor (d. 1419),
   xliv, 44
Westminster, 8, 58–60, 76, 92–4, 106,
   108, 112
   abbey, xxxviii, 18–20, 64, 72, 100, 158
   chroniclers of, xxi, xxxvii, 44
   foundation of, xxxii, 20–4
   sanctuary in, 18–20, 24–6, 38
   council at (1373), xix, xxxi–xxxiii,
      xxxviii, 10–12
   council at (1408), 142–4
Westmorland, Ralph earl of, 82, 100, 132–6
Whittington, Richard, mayor of
   London, xxvi
Whittlesey, William, archbishop of
   Canterbury, xxxvii, 10–14

Wicheford, Hugh, xxvi
Wicheford, Robert, Franciscan,
   xxvi–xxviii
Wight, Isle of (Hampshire), 16, 74, 120
Wikeford, Robert, archbishop of Dublin, 58
Wilford, William, 114
Willesford, Edith de, 104
William, St, 134
Wiltshire, William earl of, 75, 82, 88–90
Winchelsea (Sussex), 14, 16, 54, 160
Winchester, cathedral, xxxii, 112, 126
   parliament at (1393), 68
Windsor (Berkshire), 8, 52, 66, 96, 126
   Treaty of, 3
Woodstock (Oxfordshire), 30, 66, 74
Worcester, Thomas earl of, 76, 82, 90,
   112–16
Wrawe, John, rebel, 38
Wyclif, John, xlvii, l
   heterodox views of, xvi, xvii, xix–xx,
      xxxi–xxxii, xxxiii, 24, 28–36, 42–4
   death of, xxx, 64
   posthumous condemnation of, xx,
      xxx, xxxv
Wydheye, Ralph de, xxii
Wykeham, William, bishop of Winchester,
   xxxiv, 52, 78, 126

Yevele, Henry, 29
York (Yorkshire), 116, 118, 142, 160
   rising at (1405), 130–6
York, Edmund duke of, earl of Cambridge
   (d. 1402), xxx, xxxii, 2, 44, 48,
   52–4, 78, 88
   Edward, duke of, earl of Rutland, duke of
      Aumale (d. 1415), 54, 74, 82, 96,
      126, 140, 144, 156
Ypres (Flanders), 46

Zouche, John de la, provincial minister of
   the Franciscans, xxiii–xxvi, 102,
   128–30
   bishop of Llandaff, xxiii, xxv, 130